Enhancing Global Competitiveness
Advantage India

Enhancing Global Competitiveness
Advantage India

A.N. SARKAR

I.K. International Publishing House Pvt. Ltd.
NEW DELHI • BANGALORE

Published by

I.K. International Publishing House Pvt. Ltd.
S-25, Green Park Extension
Uphaar Cinema Market
New Delhi - 110 016 (India)
E-mail : info@ikinternational.com

ISBN: 978-93-80026-46-6

Published by Krishan Makhijani for I.K. International Publishing House Pvt. Ltd., S-25, Green Park Extension, Uphaar Cinema Market, New Delhi – 110 016 and Printed by Rekha Printers Pvt. Ltd., Okhla Industrial Area, Phase II, New Delhi – 110 020.

Preface

With the phenomenal growth in Indian economy- particularly in past one decade, following the processes of globalization and economic liberalization, India is now better poised to integrate the National economy with the Asian economy in one hand- the global economy on the other. India is currently placed 48th in the ranking out of 131 economies covered under the Global Competitiveness Index (GCI). In recent years, both the Western and the Asian economies are emerging as major trading partners with India. The World Economic Forum (WEF, 2008) evaluates India as a member of the BRIC Nations 'poised to become global economic superpower'. The latest Goldman Sachs Report predicts that India's GDP will surpass USA before 2050. Indian economy is the twelfth largest with a GDP in excess of $1 trillion at a growth rate circa 9.0%, making it the second fastest emerging economy after China in the world. Whereas, the Global Competitiveness Index of the World Economic Forum points towards a huge potential for Indian all-round economic growth along with other BRIC's and Asian Nations in the next decade, India has still to go a long way to catch-up with the developed economies; especially in terms of creation of industrial and social infrastructure, alternate energy, R&D, HRD etc.

The foundation of India's competitive advantage -both in Asian and Global context, lies in abundant natural resources, second highest technical manpower; highest IT knowledgebase; highest English-knowing educated youth population; huge domestic market with a large middle-class (over 500 million) client-base, conducive investment climate, supportive domestic and foreign policy with liberalized and flexible regulatory regime.

Measured by global competitive standards and recent performances, India has demonstrated global leadership in Telecom and ITeS, Textiles, Gems and Jewllery, Automotive Engineering, Manufacturing, Pharma, Biotechnology, Agribusiness, Retails, Oil and Natural Gas, Energy and Power, Infrastructure, Banking and Insurance, Medico-Tourism, Hospitality, Entertainment and Media, Technical and Management Education etc. as evident from the fact that, of late, many lead Indian companies are transforming into MNCs to go global. In the given scenario, India has little choice but to enhance Global competitiveness to dominate the global market scene. The key areas that merit focused attention and proactive intervention to enhance global competitiveness are also seemingly those potential areas with considerable investment opportunities for long-term and sustained economic growth.

A holistic review of the various emerging sectors of the Indian economy reveals that there indeed exists a high potential for Indian industries to compete globally on the strength of possessing a huge technology and technological manpower as well as global client-base, coupled with and supported by abundant endowment of natural resources that need to be explored and fully exploited. On this premise, India needs to strategize on both comparative and competitive advantage in potential sectors which can then be leveraged to acquire the global competitive edge over its competitors across the economic regional boundaries and globally. The grey areas that would need focused attention should include a priori: industrial and social infrastructure, benchmarking global standards through innovative technologies, developing global brands, intensive global and regional negotiations for joint-ventures into FDI projects, expanding the scope of ITeS/ KPO and financial services to a wider domains both locally and globally. India should also participate more aggressively in off-shore ventures where global leadership is well established; viz. aerospace, nuclear sciences, biotechnology, nanotechnology, pharmaceuticals, renewable energy as a 'Blue-ocean Strategy' to compete globally. Total Quality Management, Competitive Intelligence, Six-Sigma approach, good corporate governance principle, backed up by sound corporate policy and business strategy will go a long way to enhance the Global competitiveness of India in future.

Looking into these emerging business opportunities for India- both in Asian and global context, a necessity was consciously felt to attempt a Book on 'Enhancing Global Competitiveness: Advantage India'. The Book, among other things, covers the following aspects which need to be addressed in order to India becoming globally competitive in the emerging and potential sectors of the global economy: (i) Global economy and global competitiveness,(ii) Global competitiveness in Regional and National context, (iii) Global competitiveness-Advantage India, (iv) Indian economic, industrial and foreign trade policies to foster Global competitiveness, (v) Sectoral investment opportunities in India for achieving Global competitiveness.

The author feels that the book will be useful to the planners, scholars, academia, and research workers in the field of Micro-economics, International Business, International Trade/Marketing, and Sustainable development.

A.N. Sarkar

Contents

1

Introduction

Globalization and Global Economy

Since the 1990s, globalization has become a major concept for fostering sustained economic growth. Keohane and Nye are among the pioneering research workers who advanced a broad understanding of the core concept of globalization that encompassed four different processes of globalization viz. Economic Globalization, Social and Cultural Globalization, Military Globalization and Environmental Globalization. Since the establishment of the first Corporations (e.g., the East and West India Companies) by European powers during the seventeenth century, there were major debates about the creation of Power Transnational Corporations (TNCs) that can hold the global economy and build the international trade regime, directing their future economic power. Many decades later, the International Forum on Globalization (IFG) has advocated and promoted a set of policy changes that generally fall into four categories: new measurements of economic development, stabilization of economies, local ownership, and democratic control. Put together, they stimulate and accelerate the ongoing pace of Globalization process and integrate it harmoniously with the Global economy. IFG also promotes the implementation of new measurements to evaluate economic development in the context of long-term ecological and economical sustainability.

Modern economy, in past two decades, has its roots deeply embedded into the globalization, backed-up and followed through by a series of reforms processes undertaken by several countries; thus constituting an integral part of the global economy. The Global economy has given business the ability to market products and services all over the globe. It has also allowed the corporate world at large to develop partnerships and alliances throughout the world, which has become essential for success in today's business. There are numerous advantages to a global economy, including the possibility to increase benefits from economies of scale, innovative brand developments aligned to consumer behaviour and changing lifestyle. The rapid changes in the context of the process of economic reform, globalization and liberalization have created greater compulsions for us to be productive and competitive than ever before. With rapid advancement in technology as well as management practices, the concept and techniques of productivity have undergone a sea change over time.

Global Competitiveness and Competitiveness Index

Competitiveness analyses how nations and enterprises manage the totality of their competencies to achieve prosperity or profit. Competitiveness of Nations is essentially a field of Economic theory, which analyses the facts and policies that shape the ability of a nation to create and maintain an environment that sustains more value creation for its enterprises and more prosperity for its people. World Competitiveness, in a broader perspective, provides a frame of reference to assess how nations manage their economic future. It does not only measure Economic Performance, Wealth or Power, it is the result of a long history of thoughts and of a vast array of research.

The Global Competitiveness Report (GCR), focusing on measuring concurrent Global competitiveness, was initially published by the World Economic Forum (WEF), based in Geneva, Switzerland, way back in 1979. The Global Competitiveness Report ranks the world's nations according to the *Global Competitiveness Index*. The Growth measure of competitiveness (GCI) covers 131 countries, including 66 of the 89 countries in which USAID currently works. Global Competitiveness Index measures the set of institutions, policies, and factors that set the sustainable current and medium-term levels of economic prosperity. India is placed 48th in the list of 131 economies covered under the Global Competitiveness Index (GCI) which tracks twelve parameters to come out with the rankings. Among the top emerging markets, India is however second this year (2008) behind China.

Asia is home to some of the most, as well as some of the least, competitive economies in the Global rankings. Singapore leads the pack, ranked 5th overall, followed by Japan in 7th place, Hong Kong in 11th and Taiwan in 13th place overall. These economies — all have high-quality infrastructure, flexible and efficient markets and healthy, well-educated/skilled workforces. They are also operating on the outer boundaries of the technology frontier, both at the firm and consumer level.

Asia's Role in the Global Economy

Asia has become a key player of the global economy, credited by three of the ten largest economies (China, Japan, and India) and accounting for more than 35 per cent of world GDP (IMF-F&D, 2006). Since the 1970's, the East Asian tiger economies of Singapore, South Korea, Hong Kong and Taiwan, along with Japan, have been maintaining highly impressive economic growth rates along with the rapid industrializing of their economies. With the introduction of the massive giants of China and India into the fold, along with the emergence of increasing competition from Korea, Thailand, Indonesia and Malaysia, the countries in Asia are fast catching up with the developed economy of the Western world. Asia's growing role in the global economy has also attracted the region's desire for a massive investment mainly into industrial/ manufacturing infrastructure and energy sector by the international financial institutions (viz. The World Bank, IMF, ADB, etc.). In the years to come, economic policy decisions in Asia will, hopefully, have profound impact on the global economy.

Indian Economy in the Global Context

India, a country of sub-continental dimension, has a share of total world trade of less than 1%. This amazingly small share of world trade is a reflection of India's inward looking mindset of the late 20th century. However, it is equally a measure of the vast opportunities that lie ahead as we move forward in the 21st century.

The point to be noted from this forward-looking perspective is that, though small, India's manufacturing export base is already remarkably diversified, ranging from traditional exports like textiles, garments, leather products, gems and jewellery, through to chemicals and pharmaceuticals to metals, metal products, plants and machinery. Estimates of 'Revealed Comparative Advantage' show that India's manufacturing exports across this entire range are globally competitive. For some of these products, the country already has a significant share of the global market; while in other products the share is rapidly rising. Of special interest in this context is the rapid growth in exports of automotive parts and components, and the future export potential of refinery, pharma, textiles, gems and jewllery, telecom and biotechnology products. The other exciting aspect of India's recent export performance is the dramatic growth in export of services. The share of services has risen from about 1/5th to 1/3rd of India's total exports in the past 10 years, thanks to the IT revolution and the dramatic growth in exports of IT-enabled services (e.g. BPO, KPO). Services already account for over 50% of India's GDP and it is quite conceivable that services could also account for over half of India's total exports in the next 5-10 years, or somewhere in the region of $ 80-$ 100 billion, according to some estimates.

Indian Competitiveness in Asian Context

In the recent years, the Asian economies are emerging as major trading partners with India. India's trade performance has grown faster with these countries than its overall trade growth per se. Emerging Asian economies accounted for a significant share of 22.4 per cent in India's total exports in 2004-05 and 20.1 per cent of total Indian imports. In 2004-05, China has emerged as the second major export destination for India after the US and it has now become the largest source of imports for India, surpassing the US. Exports to China surged by 81 per cent in 2004-05, while imports from China increased by 67 per cent reflecting growing trade relations between the two countries. A similar trend was noticeable *vis-à-vis* the ASEAN-5 (Singapore, Thailand, Malaysia, Indonesia and the Philippines), but tracking it forward — there is a vast scope and untapped potential for further expansion of trade opportunities with these countries. In a way, the increasing openness of the Indian economy to the external sectoral domains in recent years reflects its expanding economic relationships with the rest of Asia.

The BRIC Power in the Context of Regional Economic Growth

Time and again, the World Economic Forum evaluates India's candidacy as a member of the BRIC nations that are supposedly 'poised to become global economic superpowers'. The relevance of such evaluation stems from the fact that countries like China and Brazil are leaving no stone unturned to fortify their positions and it is pertinent for the Forum to take cognizance and reconfirm faith in India from a long-term development and growth perspective. The recent report on BRIC nations by Goldman Sachs positions India fifth amongst the fastest growing nations in the world by 2025, based on the countries' real GDP.

Over the next fifty years Brazil, Russia, India and China – the BRICs economies – could become a much larger force in the economy. When we map out GDP growth, income per capita and currency movements in the BRICs economies until 2050, the results are startling. If things go right, in less than 40 years, the BRICs economies together could be larger than the G6 in US dollar terms. By 2025 they could account for over half the size of the G6. Of the current G6, only Japan and US may be among the six largest economies in US dollar terms in 2050.

The 2003 Goldman Sachs - BRIC report projected China's GDP in 2050 at $ 44.45 trillion while India's GDP was projected at $ 27.8 trillion and that of US was projected at $ 35.17 trillion. BRIC II (a sectoral analysis in 2004) underscored Chinidia's importance. The latest Goldman Sachs Report (January, 2007) says India's GDP will surpass that of the USA before 2050 (http://www.usindiafriendship.net/viewpoints1/Indias_Rising_Growth_Potential.pdf).

The Foundations of India's Competitive Advantage

The foundation of India's competitive advantage both in Asian and Global context can be best explained in terms of her major strengths in (a) abundant natural, mineral resources and vast stretch of coastlines; (b) second highest technical manpower; (c) highest IT knowledgebase; (d) highest educated youth population; (e) India's huge domestic market, with a large middle-class (over 500 million) population and its rapidly growing buying power (this allows our enterprises to reap economies of scale and reduce costs within the domestic market, thereby positioning them to penetrate global markets) and (f) conducive investment climate with supportive reforms processes.

Indian Economy—An Overview

The Economy of India, measured in US $ exchange-rate terms, is the twelfth largest in the world, with a GDP in excess of $ 1 trillion (2008). It recorded a GDP growth rate of 9.0% for the fiscal year 2007–2008 which makes it the second fastest big emerging economy, after China, in the world. At this rate of sustained growth, many economists forecast that India would, over the coming decades, have a more pronounced economic effect on the global economy.

Global Competitiveness: Advantage India

The India Advantage: Automotive Industries

India has the potential to become one of the top 5 automotive economies by 2025 based on its present growth potential. Steered here by the country's high engineering skills, established production lines, a thriving domestic automobile industry and competitive costs, global auto majors are rapidly ramping up the value of components they source from India. The industry is poised to jump from exports of US $ 1.8 billion in 2004-05 to US $ 5.9 billion in 2008-09. According to the Automotive Component Manufacturers Association of India, more than a third (36 per cent) of Indian auto component exports head for Europe, with North America a close second at 26 per cent. In 2006, components worth US $ 2 billion were exported by Indian companies, 75 per cent of which were bought directly by car companies. The original equipment manufacturers (OEMs) include firms like General Motors, Ford Motor Company, Cummins International, Bosch, Volkswagen, BMW, MAN (trucks) and JCB (earthmoving equipment) amongst others. Over 20 OEMs have set up their International Purchase Offices (IPO's) in India to the components. This number is expected to double by the year 2010. India enjoys a cost advantage with regard to castings and forgings. The manufacturing costs in India are 25 to 30 per cent lower than its western counterparts. India's competitive advantage does not come from costs alone, but from its full service supply capability.

Some Highlights of Automotive Industry

1. From 2001-02 to 2005-06, the Indian automobile sector has grown at an average annual rate of over 18 per cent in terms of value of output at constant 1993-94 prices and the auto-component sector has grown at about 26 per cent (http://www.icrier.org/pdf/Executive%20Summary%20201.pdf).
2. During the same period, in terms of domestic sales in numbers, two-wheelers have grown at over 13 per cent per annum, three-wheelers at more than 15 per cent, commercial vehicles at about 25 per cent per annum and the number of passenger vehicles by 17 per cent per annum.
3. Vehicle exports at constant 1993-94 prices have grown at an average

annual rate of more than 55 per cent from 2001-02 to 2005-06, while auto-component exports have grown at 21 per cent. Two-wheeler exports have seen an annual average growth rate of 27 per cent, passenger car exports have grown at 80 per cent, and commercial vehicles at about 55 per cent.

4. The effective rate of protection on automobiles is much higher than on components. For example, during 2006-07, while nominal custom duties were 60 per cent for automobiles (other than commercial vehicles), 12.5 per cent for commercial vehicles and 12.5 per cent for auto-components, effective rates of protection were 183.5 per cent, 12.5 per cent and 10.1 per cent, respectively.
5. With the higher countervailing duty and other cesses/levies, the effective rate of protection for automobile sector would be even higher.
6. This differential rate of effective protection distorts resource allocation and investment pattern in the industry.
7. The auto-component sector has much higher employment-generation potential and export-intensity than the auto assembly segment of the sector. The component manufacturers are now globally competitive and are also maintaining reasonable profitability levels despite a tariff protection of only 7.5 per cent.
8. The import tariff for the assembled vehicles is 60 per cent. Given the low level of protection both for the auto components and CKD/SKD kits, this clearly reflects a policy bias in favour of auto assemblers.
9. The reduction in import duties on assembled units may be undertaken in a phased manner and after ensuring that Indian automobile companies get comparable access to ASEAN and Chinese markets.
10. The anti-dumping mechanism should be strengthened to prevent the dumping of vehicles in the Indian market.
11. The government must also ensure that the large infrastructure deficit faced by this important sector is addressed urgently so that any adverse impact of macroeconomic policies is avoided. These are important steps if import duty structure is to be rationalized.
12. Materials cost is the major component in production cost and its share is increasing. Policy measures to reduce domestic indirect taxes on all inputs for the auto industry would be a welcome step to enhance competitiveness. The Chinese auto industry faces a flat 17 per cent indirect tax incidence, so our aim should be to reach that level.
13. Significant scaling up is required at all levels in the Indian auto-component sector so that economies of scale are gained and cost of production reduced.
14. One of the major constraints for the smaller auto-component manufacturers in increasing their scales of production is lack of credit availability at interest rates comparable to other countries. This is also confirmed by our econometric analysis.

15. R&D expenditure as a share of turnover is low in the Indian auto-component sector ranging between 0 and 1.5 per cent while it is 0.5-3 per cent for the automobile sector. In fact, most of the smaller auto-component firms and a few of the bigger ones do not have an R&D facility. Policy intervention is urgently needed to improve the R&D activities in the Indian auto industry. Since fiscal incentives are not working, a scheme of special credit for R&D would be useful to induce the R&D activities.
16. India's current levels of tariff on capital goods are higher than those in the ASEAN and China. Thus, these tariffs should be brought down further to enhance competitiveness.
17. The Indian auto industry does not possess good design facilities. The Government needs to significantly strengthen non-proprietary R&D and design capacity that has strong connections with research institutes like IITs. This could be used by all the players in the industry to develop new models, reduce material costs and become more competitive.
18. Skill shortages and skill mismatches have emerged as a major constraint. To address this critical concern, the proposed National Auto Institute should be quickly established with active participation of private industry players.
19. There is a significant and increasing use to contract workers in the industry. Labour reforms, aimed at more flexibility, are widely considered among the industrialists as an essential step. This will encourage firms to employ and retain more permanent workers and improve learning and raise productivity levels.

Competing in Global Manufacturing and Service Networks

Despite its modest 17 per cent share of domestic GDP, Indian manufacturing has the potential to become a world power. To fully exploit its potential, the Indian government has created the National Manufacturing Competitiveness Council (NMCC). The NMCC has begun to develop a national strategy with regard to technology and academic leadership. Similarly, companies have so far been unable to tap the full potential of emerging markets, such as India, with only 29 per cent of executives in a global survey indicating their companies have actually achieved higher margins in these markets. Talent management has emerged as a crucial factor, as has the ability to move beyond successful developed-economy strategies that may not be optimal in the context of a multinational strategy. For Indian manufacturing, growth strategies can be viewed through the lens of the Four Forces framework of enablers, which encompasses modularity of products and supply chains, connecting technologies, economic integration, and resource management. National competitiveness—a prerequisite for corporate and industry competitiveness—tends to emerge from savvy decisions by governments and the private sector in these four areas.

Indian Outreach for Global Retailers

India is estimated to have around 15 million retail outlets, making it the country with the highest retail outlet density in the world. It also tops AT Kearney's list of emerging markets for global retailers. Currently the value of the retail market is estimated at around $ 270 billion with a growth rate of 5.7 per cent per annum according to the India Retail Report-2007. Indian merchandise exports grew from US $ 22.2 billion in 1993-94 to US $ 101 billion in 2005-06. They are expected to reach US $ 150 billion in 2008-09. This impressive growth can be attributed to the liberalization of the investment policy, export subsidies and the devaluation of the rupee. Also, global retailers' increased interest in India's unique product mix, available at low costs, fuelled this growth.

Way Forward for Small and Medium Enterprises (SME's)

The importance and contribution of the SME sector to the economic growth and prosperity is well established. Their role in terms of employment creation, upholding the entrepreneurial spirit and innovation has been crucial in fostering competitiveness in the economy. Towards meeting the National developmental objective of a growth rate of over 8% on a sustained basis, it is imperative for the industrial sector to grow at a faster pace supported by a vibrant SME sector. Towards this, Government's policy initiatives like enactment of the new Micro, Small and Medium Enterprises Development Act, 2006, pruning of reserved SSI list, advising FIs to increase their flow of credit to the SME sector, are all initiatives towards boosting entrepreneurship, investment and growth.

There is an urgent need to enlarge flow of credit to the SSI sector from institutional sources. The creation of a facilitating environment for SSIs will centre on access to credit. The Ninth Five Year Plan (1997-2002) estimated additional working capital funds at Rs. 1420 to 1460 billion for the small sector.

In order to improve the performance of Small and Medium Enterprises and to enable them to compete globally, Government has set up SMEs Renewal Fund for Technology Upgradation, Creation of Quality Consciousness, and Promotion of Branding for Improved Marketing, Adoption of Improved Management Practices and Capacity Building. State Governments have also initiated action to set up Centre for Competitiveness to assist the small and medium scale industry to reap benefits of new technology, providing technology information services, consultancy and advisory services in agri-food processing and bio-technology sector. The Centre would undertake sectoral studies with the help of specialized organizations so that the industry in the region can regain its competitive edge. The centre will be funded from SME Renewal Fund. State Government will encourage the existing Small Scale Industrial units to undertake modernization and/or technology upgradation to meet the challenges of WTO regime.

Indian IT and ITES Sector on the Boom

The information technology and information technology enabled services (IT/ITES) industry has impacted the Indian economy and its social fabric immensely. The irreversible initiatives taken by both government and organizations are a case in point. ITES sector has matured considerably with its expansion into varied verticals, well differentiated service offerings and increasing geographic penetration. India's importance among emerging economies, both as a supply and demand centre is fuelling further growth of the sector. The IT/ITES industry continues to be one of the fastest growing industries in India, while India maintains its position as a strategic off-shoring destination for MNC's worldwide. The ITES-BPO employee base has grown to 553,000 in FY 07 from 415,000 in FY 06. Over the past decade, the Indian BPO segment has witnessed significant transformation. Starting with basic data entry tasks, the industry graduated to a high proportion of voice-based services and a range of back-office processing activities.

Future Outlook of the Indian IT Industry

With a moderate degree of competitive advantage working to their favour, the top Indian IT companies can make inroads against the weaker competition. Put differently, though there may be new entrants it is certainly impossible for them to create another TCS, Infosys or Wipro. However, the competition from global players such as IBM and Accenture is accelerating at a great pace. The *comparative advantage* of low cost (highly skilled) labour that the Indian IT industry had been enjoying over other countries is now getting eroded with global MNCs setting up their shops in India.

Highlights of Domestic BPO Industry

BPO demand in the domestic market has witnessed noticeable growth over the past few years. The annual revenue aggregate of the domestic market for ITES-BPO grew to US $ 1.2 billion in FY 2006-07 from US $ 0.9 billion in FY 2005-06, illustrating a significant increase in demand. While the high growth rate may be attributed to a small-base effect, the rapid adoption of BPO in the domestic market is receiving well-deserved attention. The Indian economy is increasingly being integrated globally, businesses in India are beginning to face increasing levels of global competition and being pushed to deliver world class levels of product and service quality. ITES-BPO has emerged as an effective means of entrusting specialists with the task of consistently delivering the desired high-levels of quality – leaving the client organizations to focus on their core businesses.

Focus on Services Exports

Over the years, India, by virtue of exploitation of core competencies in IT/

ITE sector, amply backed up by conducive National Policy— such as IT Act, has gained global recognition as the Global leader in the sector— more prominently so in other inter-related Service Sector just as well. Most of the developing economies are in rapid transit towards becoming 'service economies" and therefore 'competitiveness of service sector' is emerging as a crucial factor influencing the overall competitiveness of a country, and India is no exception to this, where the share of services is increasingly getting higher in the total GDP, and also the growth rate of India's 'service exports' is higher than the world average. Services include all the 161 tradable services covered under the General Agreement on Trade in Services. All provisions of this Policy shall apply *mutatis mutandis* to export of services as they apply to goods, unless otherwise specified. 58% of Indian GDP now comes from Services sector and large FDI has started flowing into this sector in India. IT/ITES appears to be largest and fastest growing services sector with estimated revenue of US $ 34 billion this year.

Indian Gems and Jewellery

The Gems and Jewellery (G&J) market essentially comprises sourcing, processing, manufacturing and selling of precious metals and gemstones, such as, Gold, Platinum, Silver, Diamond, Ruby, and Sapphire etc. The G&J market is a significant contributor to the Indian economy, based on the size of the domestic market and through its contribution to the country's exports. India is the largest consumer of gold (around 20 per cent of global consumption) and also the largest diamond processor (around 90 per cent by pieces and 55 per cent by value of the global market). India's G&J industry is highly unorganized and fragmented with 96 per cent of the total players being family owned businesses. The gold processing industry has around 15,000 players, with only 80 having revenues over US $ 5 million. India is also home to around 450,000 goldsmiths, 100,000 gold jewellers along with 6,000 diamond processing players and 8,000 diamond jewellers.

The value-chain of the industry starts from sourcing and mining of the metals and extends to jewellery retail. While India is not a major miner of precious metals and stones, the country's inexpensive and well-skilled workforce makes it a world leader in processing of diamonds. The country's jewellery retail sector is also expected to evolve with a shift among consumers towards branded jewellery, driven by greater quality consciousness. The bulk of the Indian G&J exports comprise import of rough diamonds, cutting and polishing in India, and re-export. As per data released by the Gems and Jewellery Export Promotion Council (GJEPC), cut and polished diamonds (CPDs) accounted for 71.1% of India's G&J exports of Rs. 733 billion during FY 2006, followed by gold jewellery (23.2%), rough diamonds (3.4%), and others (2.3%). Thus, two items, namely CPDs and gold jewellery account for around 95% of India's G&J exports.

Potentials of Food-Processing Industries

The food processing industry is coming of age. It is ranked fifth among industries of India. Nearly one third of the entire Indian food market share comprises of processed food. With policy measures from the government, the food processing industry accounts for 13% of the country's exports. The industry's size is estimated at US $ 70 billion; including US $ 22 billion of value added products. Indians spend half of their household expenditure on food items at present. The industry would create 9 million employment opportunities from the current 1.6 million and investment of Rs. 1,50,000 crore in the coming 10 years.

Indian Leadership in Pharma Industry

Although India currently represents just US $ 6 billion of the $ 550 billion global pharmaceutical industry, its share is increasing at 10% a year. The organized sector of India's pharmaceutical industry consists of 250 to 300 companies, which accounts for 70% of the market, with the top ten companies representing 30%. The Indian pharmaceutical industry has developed a wide-ranging capabilities in the complex field of drug process development and production technology. It is well ahead of other developing countries in process R&D capabilities and the range of technologically complex medicines manufactured. The value of the Indian pharmaceutical industry's overseas acquisition has grown from just US $ 8 million in 1997 to $ 116 million in 2004. Indian firms have acquired over US $ 1 billion worth of pharmaceutical companies overseas in 2005. Over the last seven years, about US $ 1.5 billion have been spent in the country on building up one of the best pharmaceutical manufacturing infrastructures in the world. India has more than 85 plants that are approved by the USFDA—the highest number outside the United States. World-class research institutes are beginning to thrive. The industry has moved from manufacturing bulk drugs to formulations and from generics to the branded sector. Key international players are setting up shops in India either for manufacturing or R&D. The industry is now ready for the next step of getting into the basic research around discovery.

There are three developments which are pushing expansion of the Indian pharmaceutical industry into overseas markets: (a) opportunities opened in the US generic market due to the Hatch-Waxman Act, (b) increasing outsourcing by MNC pharmaceutical firms, and (c) strengthening of patent laws in the domestic market. These three developments are creating new challenges and opportunities for Indian industry and internationalization is one of the viable routes adopted by India to succeed in this new environment.

The contract research and manufacturing services (CRAM) market has emerged as huge opportunity for the Indian pharmaceutical industry (http://www.mindbranch.com/listing/product/R3438-14.html). The global outsourcing market is worth $ 37 billion and growing at almost 11%; 50% of the contract manufacturing market is in North America, 40% in Europe and just 10% in Asia and the rest of the world. Indian firms possess requisite capabilities to cater for the requirements of outsourcing markets; still India accounting for barely 1.5% of the global CRAM industry. Due to untested patent protection law and lack of data protection, MNC firms are reluctant to outsource early stage R&D work to Indian firms. Therefore, Indian firms are trying to increase their share in the outsourcing market by moving closer to the market. The following, however, appear to be some of the recognized competitive advantages for the Indian Pharma Industries:

Competent workforce: India has a pool of personnel with high managerial and technical competence as also skilled workforce. It has an educated work force and English is commonly used. Professional services are easily available.

Cost-effective chemical synthesis: Its track record of development, particularly in the area of improved cost-beneficial chemical synthesis for various drug molecules is excellent. It provides a wide variety of bulk drugs and exports sophisticated bulk drugs.

Legal and Financial Framework: India has 60-year-old democracy and hence has a solid legal framework and strong financial markets. There is already an established international industry and business community.

Information and Technology: It has a good network of world-class educational institutions and established strengths in Information Technology.

Globalization: The country is committed to a free market economy and globalization. Above all, it has a 70 million middle-class market, which is continuously growing.

Consolidation: For the first time in many years, the international pharmaceutical industry is finding great opportunities in India. The process of consolidation, which has become a generalized phenomenon in the world pharmaceutical industry, has started taking place in India.

Indian Oil and Gas Industry for Energy Security

The Indian Oil and Gas Sector report, developed by specialists after extensive research and due diligence, traces the trends that are most likely to emerge in this industry in the beginning of this new decade. With the Government gradually giving up control on the oil and gas sector in favour of market forces, Indian oil companies—both upstream and downstream players—are getting exposed to international price fluctuations. This is changing the ground realities for this vital sector of the Indian economy. Unlike their global counterparts, Indian oil and gas companies have so far been operating in specific segments of the value-chain. Oil and gas exploration, crude oil refining, distribution and marketing of petroleum products, and natural gas distribution are the key sub-sectors of the Indian oil and gas sector. The Indian oil and gas sector has historically been a regulated sector, dominated by Government undertakings. The regulation took the form of the Administered Pricing Mechanism (APM) under which the returns on investment were guaranteed. But now, with the APM being dismantled in phases and private players gaining a presence in the Indian oil and gas sector, the existing public sector oil companies are getting exposed to market forces and competition.

The share of natural gas in India's energy mix has increased more than three times since the early 1980s. Energy efficiency, multiplicity of applications, and environment neutrality are the key factors that are likely to propel further rise in demand for gas in India. The increase in demand could come both from the existing uses of natural gas and from newer applications. A rising demand for gas has implications on the supply level. An increased thrust on liquefied natural gas imports would signal positive developments on the supply front. The Gas Authority of India Limited (GAIL), with a monopoly in natural gas distribution, is likely to benefit from the expected rise in natural gas supplies. Besides, its exposure to price risks would be minimal because of the fixed nature of natural gas transportation tariffs.

Indian Entertainment and Media Industry

The Indian entertainment and media (E&M) industry has out-performed the Indian economy and is one of the fastest growing sectors in India. The E&M industry generally tends to grow faster when the economy is expanding. The Indian economy has been growing at a fast clip over the last few years, and the income levels too have been experiencing a high growth rate. Above that, consumer spending is also on the rise, due to a sustained increase in disposable incomes, brought about by reduction in personal income tax over the last decade. All these factors have given an impetus to the E&M industry and are likely to contribute to the growth of this industry in the future.

India's Trade Policy

India's trade policy consists of three levels: (i) its multilateral negotiating position at the international level; (ii) the framing and operation of import-export policy at home ('traditional' trade agenda) and (iii) sectoral policy affected by trade agreements ('new' trade agenda). The first level deals mainly with trade agreements, WTO, Free Trade Agreements (FTAs), etc. The second one focuses on changes in the tariff level, duty drawback, subsidies, incentives for exporters and the concession for importers, etc, and in a sense is a support mechanism for its exporters to deal with uncertainties of the exposure to globalisation. The last level deals with emerging sectoral trade agreements such as General Agreements on Trade in Services (GATS).

Comprehensive Foreign Trade Policy

To take an integrated view of the overall development of India's foreign trade a comprehensive Foreign Trade Policy (FTP) for 2004-2009 was announced on 31st August 2004 and its Annual Supplement was released for the year 2005-06 on 8th April 2005. The basic objective of this policy is to double

India's share in world trade and to make exports an effective instrument of economic growth by giving thrust to employment generation through a number of policy initiatives. These include: simplification of procedures, reduction in transaction cost, neutralization of incidence of levies and duties on inputs used for exports and development of global hubs for manufacturing, trading and services.

Foreign Direct Investment Policy and Business Opportunity in India

The strong macro-economic fundamentals, growing size of the economy and improving investment climate has attracted global corporations to invest in India. A major outcome of the economic reforms process aimed at opening up the economy and embracing globalization has led to tremendous increase in Foreign Direct Investment (FDI) inflows into India. According to AT Kearney Report, India ranks second in the world, in terms of attractiveness for FDI. At Kearney's 2007 Global Services Location Index ranks India as the most preferred destination in terms of financial attractiveness, people and skills availability and business environment. Similarly, UNCTAD's World Investment Report, 2005 considers India the 2nd most-attractive investment destination among the Transnational Corporations (TNCs). The positive perception as a result of strong economic fundamentals driven by 16 years of reforms has helped FDI inflows grow at about 20 times till the time of the opening up of the economy to foreign investment since August 1991. The major sources of FDI in India are mainly through the equity route, which accounted for 82% of the total FDI inflows in India. Reinvested earnings of FDI companies accounted for 15% of the total Direct Investment. Acquisitions accounted for 32% of total FDI.

The potential sectors that opened up enormous opportunities for investment in India through FDI route are: Oil and Natural gas, energy and power, Port and shipping, Airport, Rapid Mass Transport Systems (Metro-Rail), Roads and Bridges, Realty Estates, Tourism (Eco- and Medico) and Hospitality, Entertainment (Cinema and TV), Banking and Insurance etc. The role of International Financial Institutions, Capital and Derivative Market is truly enormous; especially based on equity participation and long-term Production Sharing Contract arrangement through effective collateral and multi-lateral negotiations and creating more of a win-win situation.

Increasing competitiveness of Indian industry due to globalization of Indian Economy has led to emergence and growth of Indian multinationals. This is evident from the FDI overseas from India, which increased by 13.5 times during the last 7 years. The year 2006-07 witnessed large overseas acquisition deals by Indian corporate to gain market shares and reap economies of scale, supported by progressive liberalization of the external payments regime. Overseas investment that started off initially with the acquisition of foreign companies in the IT and related services sector has now spread to other areas such as manufacturing including auto components.

FDI in Indian Infrastructure

Infrastructure in India includes transportation, agriculture, water management, telecommunications, industrial and commercial development, power, petroleum and natural gas, housing and other segments such as mining, disaster management services, technology-related infrastructure.

Within the Infrastructure of India, the transportation sector is the most important, including the aviation, ports, roads, rail system and logistics. The agriculture sector comprises infrastructure-related storage facilities, construction relating to agro-processing projects and reservation and storage of perishable goods. Among other essential sectors, real-estate development, including industrial parks, special economic zones, tourism and entertainment centers, educational institutions and hospitals and solid waste management systems, also play significant role in Indian economy.

Capital Needs for Investment

According to the India infrastructure Report (IIR), currently 5.5 per cent of the GDP is invested in the infrastructure sector. This needs to be increased to 7 per cent within the next three years and 8 per cent by 2005-06, by which time the annual level of investment in infrastructural facilities is projected to treble or rise even more, from the current level of Rs. 6000 billion (US $ 52 billion) by 2005-2006. The total infrastructure investment requirements for the next five years again have been estimated in the report at about Rs. 4000-4500 billion (US $ 115-130 billion).

In 2002, India invested just US $ 18 billion in its power and transport infrastructure, an amount equal to about 6 per cent of its GDP (by comparison, China invested US $ 128 billion in the same year, or about 20 per cent of GDP). The Indian government recognizes that much more needs to be done— it estimates that US $ 320 billion needs to be invested in roads, ports, and other infrastructure if India's current economic growth is to be sustained. The challenge, though, is to find the necessary funding. For example, of the US $ 4.3 billion capital investment required to upgrade India's railway network, just one-quarter will come from government. The remainder is to be attracted from the private sector. One of the easiest ways to boost infrastructure development may simply be to simplify India's regulatory environment. According to the International Monetary Fund (IMF), India's current tough regulatory regime is an important reason why the country is unable to generate adequate infrastructure spending.

Infrastructure in Power Sector

The 1991 Power Policy seeks to attract significant private sector investment in the Indian power sector. The key initiatives include: (i) Private sector permitted to set up coal, gas or liquid-based thermal projects, hydel projects and wind or solar projects of any size; (ii) Foreign equity participation brought under automatic approval of generation, transmission and distribution of power generated in hydroelectric, oil-based and coal/lignite-based power projects; (iii) Role of the Central Government curtailed and the State Governments and State Electricity Boards (SEBs) empowered to negotiate directly with developers, facilitating speedy clearances for the investor; (iv) Ancillary sector such as coal significantly deregulated; (v) 100% foreign equity permitted.

Opportunities: Demand is expected to grow to 570 billion kWh by 2001-02 and to 782 billion kWh by 2006-07. Over the 10 year period from 1997-2007, a total capacity addition of 98,000 MW is envisaged, entailing an investment of Rs. 5,750 billion in power generation, transmission and distribution.

Non-Conventional Energy Sources

Foreign investors can enter into a joint venture with an Indian partner for financial and/or technical collaboration and also for setting up of renewable energy-based power generation projects. The liberalized foreign investment approval regime is aimed at facilitating foreign investment and transfer of technology through joint ventures. 100% foreign investment as equity is permissible. Government of India is presently encouraging foreign investors to set up renewable energy-based power generation project on Build-Own-Operate basis.

Opportunities: In India, investment opportunities are available for the following types of investors and users: Investment by foreign investors for manufacturing of renewable energy systems and devices based on wind, solar photovoltaic, solar thermal, small hydro, biomass, co-generation, geothermal, tidal and urban and industrial wastes for their utilization in India and also for exports to developing and Third World countries.

FDI Policy in Oil and Natural Gas Sector

The Government has announced significant new policy initiatives to attract foreign investment:

In exploration and production, oil and gas fields are open to the private sector as well as for foreign participation under production sharing contracts. Foreign investment is to be permitted up to: (i) 100% in small-sized oil fields; (ii) 60% for unincorporated joint ventures; (iii) 51% for incorporated joint ventures; and (iv) 100% for exploration and production of blocks identified under the New Exploration Licensing Policy (NELP). In the case of private Indian companies, FDI in refining is permitted up to 49%. For the petroleum products and pipeline sector, FDI is permitted up to 51%; Similarly, FDI is permitted up to 74% in infrastructure related to marketing and marketing of petroleum products; 100% wholly-owned subsidiary (WOS) is permitted for purpose of market study and formulation; 100% wholly owned subsidiary is permitted for investment/financing. For actual trading and marketing, minimum 26% Indian equity is required over 5 years.

Telecommunication

In Basic, cellular Mobile, Paging and Value Added Service, and Global mobile communications by satellite, FDI is limited to 49% subject to grant of licence from the Department of Telecommunications and adherence by the companies (who are investing and the companies in which investment is being made) to the licence condition for foreign equity cap and lock-in-period for transfer and addition of equity and other licence provisions. FDI up to 100% is allowed for the following activities in the telecom sector: Infrastructure Providers providing dark fibre (IP category); Electronic Mail; and Voice Mail.

Opportunities: There exists an enormous demand-supply gap for basic services, with the average waiting period for telephone connections exceeding one year.

Chemicals

The chemical industry in India is well established and has recorded a steady growth in the overall Indian industrial scenario. The chemical and allied industries have been amongst the faster growing segments of the Indian industry. The chemical industry is highly heterogeneous encompassing many sectors like organic and inorganic chemicals, dyestuffs, paints, pesticides, and specialty chemicals, some of the prominent individual chemical industries are caustic soda, soda ash, carbon black, phenol, acetic acid, methanol and azo dyes. Currently, there is tremendous scope for growth in chemical sector. The per capita consumption of chemicals in India is well below the prevailing world level. For instance, in sulphuric acid, which is considered the barometer of growth in the chemical industry, the per capita consumption is only about 5 kg per annum in India as compared to 40 kg in industrially developed countries.

Biotechnology

The setting up of a separate Department of Biotechnology (DBT) under the Ministry of Science and Technology in 1986 gave a new impetus to the development of modern biology and biotechnology in India. In more than a decade of its existence, the department has promoted and accelerated the pace of development of biotechnology in the country. In India, concerted efforts for over a decade in R&D in the identified areas of modern biology and biotechnology have paid rich dividends. The proven technologies at the laboratory level have been scaled up and demonstrated in field. Patenting of innovations, technology transfer to industries and close interaction with them have given a new direction to biotechnology research. Necessary guidelines for transgenic plants, recombinant vaccines and drugs have also been evolved. A strong base of indigenous capabilities has been created.

Opportunities: Biotechnology industry serves as a research arm to Agritech and Pharma industry with increased Potential for strategic alliances. Global trends show that all large pharmaceutical players are putting their money in healthcare for long-term benefits. It is expected that nearly half the drugs in the next decade would be biotech Products. Tremendous potential exists in agri-business in an agrarian economy like India. Potential therefore exists for transgenic seeds, bio-fertilizers etc. Number of small firms is high, knowledge based, research intensive industry, with low capital Requirements.

Roads

FDI up to 100% under automatic route is permitted in projects for construction and maintenance of roads, highways, vehicular bridges, toll roads, vehicular tunnels, ports and harbours.

Opportunities: Investment worth an estimated US $ 34 billion needed, till 2005-06, for the development of National and State Highways. Of this figure, the requirement of private sector investment is US $ 8.3 billion.

Opportunities:(i) Highway construction; (ii) Four-Lining of over 35,000 km of National Highways; (iii) Highway related *en route* activities like restaurants, motels, and rest/parking areas as may be decided by the implementing agency. The *Select project opportunities include:* (i) Chennai-Nellor (US $ 350 million); (ii) Bangalore-Chennai (US $ 305 million); (iii) Surat-Manor (US $ 180 million); and (iv) Jaipur-Ajmer (US $ 147 million).

Ports

Importance of Port Infrastructure: The port sector has been identified as the prime catalyst to accelerate the process of industrialization, international trade and economic progress. Port development and economic development are mutually related. On one hand economic development necessitates port development as a part of infrastructure development and on other hand, port development itself facilitates import-export and attracts industries to its hinterland, which in turn create forward and backward linkage with the rest of the economy. The development of port sector as associated with maritime trade is an axiom that no maritime nation can afford to ignore in today's global world. With the thrust towards economic reforms in India and the capacity limitations of major ports, the State Governments have to pay attention to the development of their minor ports often combining industrial sites development projects with port development. India, with the port reforms has to prove that any globalization that is to take place has to take place through the ports of international class only.

Investment Policy: The principal legislations governing Indian ports are The Indian Ports Act, 1908, and the Major Ports Trust Act, 1963, the Indian Government recently announced a series of following measures to promote foreign investment in the port sector: (i) No approval required for foreign equity up to 51% in projects providing supporting services to water transport, such as operation and maintenance of piers, loading and discharging of vehicles; (ii) Automatic approval for foreign equity up to 100% in construction and maintenance of ports and harbours, however, if the total foreign equity investment exceeds Rs. 15 billion, the proposal will be referred to the FIPB; and (iii) Open tenders are to be invited for private sector participation on a Build-Operate-Transfer (BOT) basis. Evaluation of bids will be based on the maximum licence period which will not exceed 30 years and at the end of the BOT period all assets will revert to the port in accordance with the conditions of the agreement.

The Government has announced guidelines for private/foreign participation that permit formation of joint venture between major ports and foreign ports, between major ports and minor ports, and between major ports and companies. The measures are aimed at attracting new technology, fostering strategic alliances with minor ports to create on optimal port infrastructure and enhancing private sector confidence in the funding of ports.

Civil Aviation

Investment Policy: The monopoly of public sector air carriers ended with the repealing of Air Corporation Act, 1953 on March 1, 1994. Automatic approval for foreign equity participation in airport infrastructure is upto 100 per cent foreign equity upto 40 per cent; investment by Non-Resident Indians upto 100 per cent permitted in domestic air-transport services. Equity from foreign airlines not allowed in domestic air-transport services either, directly or indirectly. Foreign Financial Institutions allowed to hold equity in the domestic air-transport sector provided they do not have foreign airlines as their shareholders. Foreign Investors are allowed to have representation on Board of Directors of the domestic airline company. Government considers private sector participation in construction and operation, new airports on a BOT basis. Minimum fleet size for a scheduled operator raised from the existing 3 aircraft to 5. Management contract with a foreign airline is not permitted.

Opportunities: Construction of world class international airports in five cities, permitting upto 100% foreign equity investment announced. Important private sector aided projects: New airport near Kochi (US $ 85.7 million). Projects for development of new airports at Bangalore and Mumbai with private sector participation are under consideration. Other private sector aided airports planned: Ahmedabad airport, Amritsar airport upgradation, Chennai cargo complex, new international terminal and a second runway for Delhi airport, runway extension and international block for Jaipur airport, Hyderabad and Bangalore airports.

Airport infrastructure: In India, airports were totally owned and managed by central government or the armed forces. The Airport Authority of India (AAI), a body functioning under the Ministry of Civil Aviation was responsible for managing the airports in India. It owns 122 airports, 61 of which are operational. The breakdown is as follows: (i) 11 international; (ii) 94 civil; and (iii) 27 civil enclaves at defence airfields. The AAI operates most aspects of the airport (including air traffic control) and procures most of their equipment directly (via global/local tenders). India's airports handle 42 million passengers, of which the four Metro gateway airports (Delhi, Mumbai, Kolkata and Chennai) account for 47% of revenue and 66% of the passengers. Until 2000, there were five major international airports — Mumbai, Kolkata, Delhi, Chennai and Trivandrum. But the Government of India announced a further six airports including Amritsar, Bangalore, Hyderabad, Cochin during the course of 2002. According to projections, Indian air passenger traffic was estimated to grow to 100 million passengers by 2012 from 36.98 million in 1998-99. Growth projections in the cargo front were also promising. Airport infrastructure is linked to development of India's international competitiveness and her ability to attract foreign investments. The policy opened the doors of private investment in this sector, including investments from foreign airport authorities.

Hotel Industry in India

Hotel industry in India has witnessed tremendous boom in recent years. Hotel industry is inextricably linked to the tourism industry and the growth in the Indian tourism industry has fuelled the growth of Indian hotel industry. The thriving economy and increased business opportunities in India have acted as a boon for Indian hotel industry. The arrival of low-cost airlines and the associated price wars have given domestic tourists a host of options. In recent years, government has taken several steps to boost travel and tourism which have benefited hotel industry in India. The opening up of the aviation industry in India has exciting opportunities for hotel industry as it relies on airlines to transport 80% of international arrivals. The government's decision to substantially upgrade 28 regional airports in smaller towns and privatization and expansion of Delhi, Mumbai, Hyderabad, Bangalore airports will improve the business prospects of hotel industry in India. Substantial investments in tourism infrastructure are essential for Indian hotel industry to achieve its potential. The upgrading of national highways connecting various parts of India has opened new avenues for the development of budget hotels in India. With the US $ 23 billion software services sector pushing the Indian economy skywards, more and more IT professionals are flocking to Indian metro cities. 'Hotel Industry in India' is set to grow at 15% a year. This figure will skyrocket in 2010, when Delhi hosts the Commonwealth Games. Already, more than 50 international budget hotel chains are moving into India to stake their turf. Therefore, with opportunities galore the future 'Scenario of Indian Hotel Industry' looks rosy.

India is expected to see an influx of 10 million international tourists by 2010, up from just 5 million in 2007. Andhra Pradesh, Uttar Pradesh, Tamil Nadu, Karnataka and Rajasthan are the leading tourism destinations in India in terms of total tourist arrivals. India has been promoting its healthcare tourism by providing the visitors with private healthcare facilities. It is expected that the total market for medical tourism will reach US $ 2 billion by 2012, representing a CAGR of 60.69%. Personal disposable income during 2002-2007 grew at a CAGR of 14.16%, thereby driving domestic as well as outbound tourism. Indian outbound tourist flow is expected to increase at a CAGR of 13.30% over the five-year period spanning from 2008 to 2012. India's share in the global tourism is expected to reach 1.5% by 2010. The growth in India's tourism market is expected to serve as a boon, driving the growth of several associated industries, including hotel industry, medical tourism industry and aviation industry.

Tourism

With tourism accounting for 5.83 per cent of the GDP and 8.27 per cent of employment in the country, it calls for special attention. It has been estimated that the shortfall in tourist accommodation in the country will be 1.50 lakh rooms by 2010, of which more than one lakh will be in the budget category. India's tourism sector has the potential to generate significant additional income and employment. In 2005, international tourist arrivals were just under 4 million, though the average stay per visitor was over 20 days. India's domestic tourism increased from 67 million in 1991 to 366 million in 2004, and is also growing rapidly.

Medical Tourism – Healthcare in the Competitive Global Marketplace

'Medical tourism' or 'Medico-tourism' is a marketplace phenomenon that works outside the organized medical community and usual medical referral systems. Patients pursue offshore healthcare options because this enables them to maximize value. Medical tourism is a clear signal that patients greatly value the opportunity to receive the care they need promptly while conserving personal resources and avoiding financial distress.

Four Types of Healthcare Services: In India, Healthcare services have evolved into four varieties. The classification of a specific service into one of these four varieties is essential to understanding and selecting the most appropriate response to the challenge medical tourism poses in India today.

- *Big Healthcare Events:* This is the primary target for medical tourism – inpatient surgeries, for the most part. For the patient, these are both clinically and financially big events, such as heart surgeries, hip replacements, neurosurgery, cancer surgeries, etc. Some of the surgeries are actually outpatient (e.g., major dental surgery, etc.).
- *Small Healthcare Events:* Today, outpatient surgeries are not the primary target for medical tours. For instance, one of my sons broke his arm skiing a couple of weeks ago. Other "small" healthcare events include immunizations, many dental procedures, etc.

- *Big Healthcare Relationships:* Think chronic disease management, which sadly involves what are often long, protracted, expensive relationships with one's healthcare providers. While there is a seminal event (e.g., initial diagnosis), the time, clinical intervention and the cost do not come in one or a few discrete chunks.
- *Small Healthcare Relationships:* Most people have a very good relationship with their primary care physician as well as with the professional staff (PAs, NPs, RNs, etc.) that they see frequently. Checkups, immunizations, routine and some focused visits make up a significant portion of healthcare providers' revenue streams and form the basis of a relationship with the person and the community.

Banking and Insurance Sector – Emerging Opportunities

Banking Sector: The economic reform undertaken in the last 15 years have brought about a considerable improvement in the health of banks and financial institutions in India. The banking sector is a very important sector of the Indian economy. The sector has made a marked improvement in the liberalization period. There has been extraordinary progress in the financial health of the commercial banks with respect to capital adequacy, profitability, asset quality and risk management. Deregulation has opened new doors for banks to increase revenues by entering into investment banking, insurance, credit cards, depository services, mortgage, securitization, etc. The limit for foreign direct investment in private banks has been increased from 49% to 74%. In addition, the limit for foreign institutional investment in private banks is 49%. Liberalization and globalization have created a more challenging environment in the banking sector as well as in the other segments of the financial sector such as mutual funds, non-banking finance companies, post offices, capital markets, venture capitalists, etc. Now the challenges faced by the sector would be gaining profitability, reinforcing technology, maintaining global standards, corporate governance, sharpening skills, risk management and, the most important of all, to establish 'Customer Intimacy'.

Emerging Insurance Sector: Indian insurance sector is likely to register unprecedented growth of 200% and attain a size of Rs. 2000 billion by 2009-10, in which a private sector insurance business will achieve a growth rate of 140% as a result of aggressive marketing technique being adopted by them against 35-40% growth rate of state owned insurance companies. Currently, the insurance sector size is estimated at Rs. 500 billion. On account of intense marketing strategies adopted by private insurance players, the market share of state owned insurance companies like GIC, LIC and others have come down to 70% in last 4-5 years from over 97%. The private insurance players despite the sector is still regulated has been offering rate of return (RoR) to its policy holders which is estimated at about 35% as against 20% of domestic insurance companies. This factor is mainly responsible for hike in private insurance market share which will grow further which is why the ASSOCHAM estimates that its growth rate could even exceed 140%.

The IRDA Act 1999 (Insurance Regulatory and Development Authority of India Act) has given new opportunities to private players to enter into the market on the fulfillment of certain prerequisites. The IRDA is the licensing authority in the sector; the current FDI cap/equity in the sector stands at 26 per cent. There is no doubt the challenges ahead will become tougher with more companies competing both in general and life insurance. Also mortgage insurance will soon be coming into the industry. New players have contributed to the launch of innovative products, services and value-added benefits. Major foreign players have entered the country and announced partnership for joint-venture operations—both in life and non-life areas. These include: New York Life, Aviva, Tokio Marine, Allianz, Standard Life, Lombard General, AIG, AMP and Sun Life among others.

Branding India for Global Competitiveness

There has been a lot of debate in the press lately on the idea of 'Brand India'. Fundamentally, three broad questions have emerged from this debate: First, should we brand India? Second, is this the right time to brand India? Third, how should we go about the task?

The idea of whether or not India should be branded induces reactions that range from mild discontent to violent disagreement. Clearly, Brand India's success lies in managing and leveraging this opportunity. The India Brand Equity Foundation (IBEF- earlier India Brand Equity Fund) was founded under the aegis of the Ministry of Commerce of the Government of India with the explicit purpose of developing a strong global identity for India, by leveraging these emergent opportunities. The IBEF aims to do this through a proactive effort to create a strong Nation Brand for the country based on positive and relevant associations. The entire effort is directed towards taking India beyond name recognition, by firmly establishing a relevant position for the country on the world map. The immediate goal: build positive economic perceptions of India in key global markets. The IBEF moved to the CII to manage, in October 2002. It was decided that a broad-based branding exercise would best be facilitated through a strong partnership between the government and industry. It is in this context that the CII provides for the executive management and the operational day-to-day functioning of the Foundation. Indian industry is becoming globally competitive in many sectors such as Pharmaceuticals, Auto Components, IT, Biotech, R&D and ITeS. Second, the abundant intellectual capital available in the country continues to provide further impetus to an emergent world-scale economy that is slated to be the 3rd largest by 2050. Third, the achievements of global Indians, and the contributions of the Indian Diaspora abroad, are a tremendous source of pride, and strongly reinforce the competitiveness of Indians across sectors.

It is in this context, that we should undertake the task of Nation Brand Building, which is firmly rooted in the positive, changing reality of the 21st century India. IBEF plans to include a series of coordinated marketing initiatives that will use conventional methods like advertising and developing a brand ambassador's network to make an impact in the short term. Innovative and proactive measures like bringing select groups from media houses and educational institutions for structured India Tours are also planned to support the development of the brand over the long term. On the domestic front, IBEF drives alignment across stakeholders to ensure that messages emanating from the country are coherent and consistent. With this view, the IBEF is developing a strong partner network that includes select Ministries, Sectoral Associations and Community Institutions to drive alignment and coherence in brand communication efforts. As a facilitator, IBEF services this network through workshops, a brand communication toolkit, and research reports that help track perceptions of brand India.

Summing-up

India has witnessed economic boom particularly in last one decade following a series of reforms and transient globalization processes initiated in 1991. Though initially the pace of growth for Indian economy has been rather slow to adapt in fast-changing business environment especially under WTO regime, but introduction of various conducive investment, trading and export policy, supported by prudent economic and banking reforms paved the way for India to be globally competitive so much so that India now boasts not only to be among the fastest growing developing economy as a BRIC Nation, it is attracting the global attention to be one of the most favoured trading and investment destinations in the world. Indian leadership is evidently vibrant and visible both in Asian and to a large extent in global context in emerging sectors beset with tough global competition such as Telecom and ITeS, Textiles, Gems and Jewellery, Automotive Engineering and Manufacturing, Pharma, Biotechnology, Agribusiness, Oil and Natural Gas, Energy and Power, Infrastructure, Banking and Insurance, Medico-Tourism and Hospitality, Technical and Management Education etc., as could be evident from the fact that many lead Indian companies have transformed into MNCs and gone global through overseas operations.

A critical review and trend analysis of India's past performance vis-à-vis perspective for future growth potential suggests that India has no choice but to enhance the Global competitiveness in many spheres as detailed in the Book appropriately titled as 'Enhancing Global Competitiveness: Advantage India.

Framework of the Book

In terms of overall orientation, the Book has been so conceived and structured that it has followed a certain natural corollary and logical framework in comparing Indian economy with the Asian and the Global economy in respect of the sectors wherein India is perceived to play a leadership role—both in the Regional and the Global context. Secondly, an attempt has also been made to identify areas, where, India, despite possessing a huge potential, could not so far convincingly demonstrate its competitive advantage to compete globally. Thirdly, Competitive advantage in certain chosen fields, where India can excel and outperform its competitors are elaborated and highlighted with broad indication of the future strategy. Last, but not the least, the Book has dealt in length the various Sectoral Investment Opportunities in India for achieving Global Competitiveness. Based on these core approaches, the Book is divided into 6 Chapters:

Chapter I: Introduction
Chapter II: Global Economy and Global Competitiveness
Chapter III: Global Competitiveness in Regional and National Context
Chapter IV: Global Competitiveness—Advantage India
Chapter V: Indian Economic, Industrial and Foreign Trade Policies Fostering Global Competitiveness
Chapter VI: Sectoral Investment Opportunities in India for Achieving Global Competitiveness

This is an exciting Book with innovative concepts for use on International and Global Strategy courses in Management Schools, and providing supplementary text for use by the students and scholars. The Book is also so designed and customized that this will prove to be useful to the planners, exporters, business houses, business executives, academia, and research workers in the field of Macro and Micro-economics, International Business, International Trade/Marketing, Foreign Trade Policy and Sustainable Economic Development.

2

Global Economy and Global Competitiveness

Processes of Globalization and Global Trading

In order to develop a clear understanding about the global economy and its interrelationship with global competitiveness—as a basic step, it would be useful to keep abreast with the concept of globalization as a process and its relevance with the global trading as a system.

Since the 1990s, globalization has become a major concept for fostering sustained economic growth, with different groups understanding it in so many different ways. Keohane and Nye are among the pioneering ones who advanced a broad understanding of globalization that encompassed four different processes of globalization (Robert O. Keohane, and Joseph S. Nye, Jr. 2000):

1. Economic Globalization
2. Social and Cultural Globalization
3. Military Globalization
4. Environmental Globalization

These various types of globalization continuously interact with each other in varying context and degrees. For example, economic globalization enhances and stimulates international trade. Shipping of traded goods can transport goods from one continent to another. Such interactions make the understanding of the process of globalization fairly complex and integrated. A deeper understanding of the above mentioned 4 elements, their interrelationship and impact on the overall business environment should serve, to a large extent, the relevance of Global competitiveness in the context of dynamic global economic environment. This chapter is devoted to help build that understanding.

Economic Globalization and Trade

Economic globalization is essentially characterized by intercontinental trading and management relationships effected through multi-national corporations

(MNCs). Almost one-quarter of all the goods and services currently being produced in the world are exported to another country for consumption (IMF, 2002). This type of globalization has created interdependent economic systems because most national economies are greatly reliant on increased trade relations; some could encounter economic depression, as it did in the 1930's, leading to the Great Depression in Europe (David Held, Anthony McGrew, David Goldblatt, and Jonathan Perraton, 1999).

Since the establishment of the first corporations by European powers during the seventeenth century, there have been major debates about the creation of Power Transnational Corporations (TNCs) that held in the global economy and the international trade regime, as it were, directing its economic power in the future. The problems often relate to the fact that the producers, consumers, and managers live in different communities and cross-cultures in different geographic locations, and have different sets of priorities, understandings, and worldviews so much so that many goods and services that are produced on one continent, consumed on another, and managed by a corporation located yet in another continent. During the Industrial Revolution (i.e. following Renaissance in France) of the eighteenth and nineteenth centuries, improvements in communications and transportation systems greatly increased the importation and exportation of goods and services in many parts of the world. The wave of economic globalization beginning in the late twentieth century is now being characterized by the global governance of the World Trade Organization (WTO) as well as innovative trade negotiations now happening in the new areas such as intellectual property rights, genetic engineering, nanotechnology, pharma sector and in biotechnology.

As the open access to Internet has allowed traders/exporters in many nations to communicate freely and more easily, sophisticated "anti-globalization" movements of workers, environmentalists, and indigenous peoples have also sprung-up side by side. Anti-globalization movements tend to oppose economic globalization and its effects on the environment, human rights, and cultural integrity. The names "anti-globalization movement" and, in India, "living democracy movement," have been utilized to describe the global network of organizations proposing environmentally sustainable alternatives to economic globalization.

These organizations highlight several negative aspects impacting economic globalization:

1. The World Bank, International Monetary Fund (IMF), and World Trade Organization (WTO) make decisions concerning trade and development outside of the United Nations system and with little accountability to the national governments that created them.
2. Corporations and international investors move from nation to nation to escape labor, environmental, and consumer standards. This mobility creates great financial instability and unemployment in poorer, "single-industry" regions. National and local governments must then pay

"corporate welfare" payments in an effort to entice corporations to relocate and remain within their jurisdictions (David C. Korten, 1999).
3. Corporations fund political parties and campaigns, often leading elected officials to make unpopular decisions that favor corporate profits over citizen safety, rights, and needs.
4. Governments are increasingly converting various "commons"— properties historically held in common by communities of people (e.g., land, seed varieties, and water)—into private properties held by corporations.
5. Economic planning fails to consider the effects of growth and industrialization on the ecological capital upon which human wealth relies.

In order to help reverse many of the negative effects of globalization, different sectors of the anti-globalization movement have proposed various policies. As a leading group of theorists, the International Forum on Globalization (IFG) has promoted a set of policy changes that generally fall into four categories: new measurements of economic development, stabilization of economies, local ownership, and democratic control. The International Forum on Globalization (IFG) also promotes equitable, democratic, and ecologically sustainable economies. IFG were formed in response to widespread concerns over economic globalization, a process dominated by international institutions and agreements unaccountable to democratic processes or national governments (http://www.wiserearth.org/organization/view4de132d4eab1997ef627220ab83b94de).

1. **New Measurements of Economic Development**
   IFG promotes the implementation of new measurements to evaluate economic development in the context of ecological sustainability. Utilizing new theories in the field of ecological economics, IFG assists economists with their examination of how economic decisions impact the Earth's life-support systems. This ideal is accomplished when measurements of economic growth reflect the manner in which economic activities are expanding or damaging opportunities for future generations (Rajaram Krishnan, Jonathan M. Harris, and Neva R. Goodwin, 1995).
2. **Stabilization of Economies**
   IFG promotes the stabilization of global economic conditions by curbing international financial speculation (Fritjof Capra, 2002). Short-term investments in foreign currency markets can create havoc in the global economy by reducing the ability of national governments to maintain stable currency rates and, by extension, to keep their national economies stable.
3. **Local Ownership**
   IFG promotes the increase of local business ownership in order to reduce pollution and create stable employment situations. Increasing local business ownership may help raise environmental and labor standards for two main reasons:

a) Local stakeholders would more than likely choose cleaner production methods because they would have a personal stake in the local release of the pollution created by the enterprise.

b) Local stakeholders would more than likely choose better labor policies because business employees would include people (e.g., family, friends, and neighbors) from their own geographic region. Local owners would also be much less likely to relocate their factory out of their home region and therefore would help preserve local jobs, stabilize local job markets, and reduce unemployment levels (Michael Shuman, 1998).

4. **Democratic Control**

IFG promotes the assertion of democratic control over national governments and the global economy. Proposals for increasing democracy vary from nation to nation, depending upon what type of governmental system is currently being utilized in that country. In the United States, for example, the anti-globalization movement calls for the public financing of election campaigns, in order to reduce the influence of corporations on government decisions. At the global level, the movement has debated whether to reform or abolish the World Bank, International Monetary Fund (IMF), and World Trade Organization (WTO). The anti-globalization movement is also concerned with the effects of economic globalization on various cultures throughout the world. Indigenous cultures are particularly impacted because increases in economic globalization lead to rapid social changes that can easily eliminate much of their cultural heritage. This phenomenon is called 'social and cultural globalization'.

Social and Cultural Globalization

Economic globalization has been supported by new technologies in the communications and transportation industries. These technologies have also led to an unprecedented mixing of world cultures, which has resulted in the second type of globalization, social and cultural globalization. Although cultural inventions have been exchanged throughout history, technology is making the global exchange of ideas and inventions possible on a much larger scale than has previously occurred. The earliest globalization of technology was the spread of Chinese inventions such as paper to Africa, Europe, and the rest of Asia. More recently, new communication technology has made entertainment imports relatively inexpensive and this has increased the amount of information that is transferred among various countries. Most of the world now watches imported movies and television programs that are primarily produced in the United States. These entertainment venues have brought American cultural conventions to the rest of the world and have had the effect of influencing, if not changing traditional cultures.

Although cultural globalization may enrich the various cultures involved in these interactions, it may also function to marginalize these cultures by replacing the distinguishing characteristics of the culture with imported traditions, entertainment, and religious beliefs. Globally, this process produces a trend toward the creation of a monoculture, because a variety of different cultural expressions are now being replaced by the expression of one single culture. These cultural losses may also be exacerbated by person-to-person cross-cultural changes made available through the possibility of rapid intercontinental travel. Airline technology has greatly increased tourism, and this has led to an unprecedented level of interaction among individuals from different continents.

Social and cultural globalization potentially brings various types of innovations that are beneficial to the environment, but it can also lead to new environmental challenges. On the negative side, social and cultural globalization, spread through various forms of global communication technology, tends to deliver messages that support higher levels of consumption. People in other countries are readily adopting these ideas, which often result in negative environmental effects. For example, many environmental problems (e.g., global climate change) will be exacerbated if low-income nations develop their economies in a manner that leads to the same rate of consumption and pollution as is found in high-income nations. On the positive side, increased communication among nations through the direct transfer of ideas and technology, or "technology transfer," is making international environmental efforts to globalize sustainable technologies a reality for many nations. Technology transfers encourage a new path of sustainable development that has the potential to help reduce poverty in developing nations while at the same time, decreasing or severely limiting the destruction of the environment (Oxford University Press, 1987). Governance also may be transformed by social and cultural aspects of globalization. British economist Susan Strange proposed that economic, social, and cultural globalization is leading to the decline of national governmental structures (Susan Strange, 1996). These changes in governance are interacting with recent trends in the globalization of military activity.

Military Globalization

Historically, organized military conquests have served as a form of globalization. This is perhaps the oldest form of globalization, dating back to at least the seventh and eighth centuries, when Arabs from West Asia conquered peoples in Europe and Africa. Expansive examples of intercontinental military conflict include the European conquest of both North America and Latin America (1492 through the late nineteenth century) and World War I, World War II, and the "Cold War" conflicts of the twentieth century. Though the former instigated vast intercontinental change, the latter were in fact the most globalized military conflicts in history, involving large groups of allies comprised of nations from every inhabited continent. War became less globalized during the 1990s, as many conflicts were regionally, rather than globally, focused (Eduardo Viola, 1999).

Environmental Globalization

Globalization in economic, social, and military affairs contributes to the fourth process, environmental globalization—the increase of movement between continents of pollutants and species. Of the many environmental challenges found around the world, two in particular are driven by environmental interactions between continents: the loss of biological diversity and the increase of global atmospheric pollution.

Erosion of Biodiversity and Global Environmental Pollution

One key aspect of environmental globalization is the decrease in biological diversity. In the past, species distribution has been influenced by three main factors: temperature, geological history, and the structure of the Earth's surface. Natural barriers have isolated certain terrestrial species in specific areas and terrestrial barriers have kept different types of marine species in specific aquatic locations. American biologist Edward O. Wilson described this type of "geographic speciation" as the process in which populations of plants and animals located in separated regions "diverge from each other in evolution because of the inevitable differences of the environments in which they find themselves" (Edward O. Wilson, 1988).

The effort to protect the ozone layer has been the most successful global environmental project in history. It has involved the cooperation of many international organizations and nearly every national government. Industrialized countries have stopped producing nearly all of the worst ozone-depleting chemicals after signing the Montreal Protocol on Substances that Deplete the Ozone Layer (UNDP, 2002).

The successful cooperation on the Montreal Protocol gave the United Nations Environmental Programme (UNEP) hope that there could be some agreement on the issue of global climate change. Global climate change has been the subject of intense negotiations since the creation in 1992 of the United Nations Framework Convention on Climate Change (UNFCCC). The 1997 Kyoto Protocol has been ratified by many developed and developing nations in Europe and Asia, but the United States and Australia have shown reluctance in complying with the various recommendations of the Protocol (viz. Kyoto Protoco). The lack of international progress and cooperation in slowing global climate change illustrates the difficulty of organizing global responses to globally initiated environmental degradation, caused primarily by the polluting 'Green-House gases'.

As a concept, globalization is broad-based and comprehensive to be useful and effective. However from the angle of operational effectiveness, it is broken down into at least four interconnected trends—economic globalization, social and cultural globalization, military globalization, and environmental globalization as outlined above. These trends are interrelated. Economic globalization has increased the specialization of workers, as their employers compete in global markets. Social and cultural globalization has changed cultures through the increased dissemination of communication, information, and technology. Military globalization has consisted of intercontinental blocs of allied nations engaging in military conflict with terrorists and with each other. Economic, social, cultural, and military globalization has often had negative impacts upon the environment, requiring that all nations of the world cooperate in an effort to slow the process of environmental globalization. Four environmental issues in particular—biodiversity, global climate change, ozone-layer depletion, acid rains, and nitrogen loading—are either caused by globalization or have serious consequences warranting global cooperation and intervention.

Global Economy

The technology advancement in all conceivable fields of significance to overall economic growth has allowed our environment to be characterized as a global one. "The global economy" has given business the ability to market products and services all over the globe. It has also allowed them to develop partnerships and alliances throughout the world, which has become essential for success in today's business. It is obvious how global economy helps in promoting international cooperation and peace for the nations involved in the international trade by increasing mutual-dependence (http://en.wikipedia.org/wiki/Global_economy).

With the ever-increasing Global Economy and widespread use of the internet, people and businesses are realizing that they are often competing with people around the world for contracts and business deals. The global economy has created an environment in which many large corporations are becoming transnational firms. Trade barriers (both technical and non-technical) more often hamper economic development in the Global South, as compared to the North. New technologies like the internet, along with extended regional cooperation, innovative technologies, trade negotiations etc., to a large extent, may speed up the reduction of such trade barriers.

The *World Economic Outlook* presents the IMF staff's analysis and projections of economic developments at the global level, in major country groups (classified by region, stage of development, etc.), and in many individual countries. It focuses on major economic policy issues as well as on the analysis of economic developments and prospects. It is usually prepared twice a year, as documentation for meetings of the International Monetary and Financial Committee, and forms the main instrument of the IMF's global surveillance activities (IMFC, 2007).

Rationale for Organizations Entering the Global Environment

The benefits of international expansion are known and include additional growth and expansion; the opportunity to increase revenues, profits and return on investment. Global companies have special requirements that are significant organizational challenges. The structures that the managers of global companies adopt must assist them in their efforts to exploit opportunities to achieve economies of scale by centralizing their marketing and production activities—whenever possible. At the same time, the structures of international companies must also accommodate differences in national cultures and variations in business practices. As in any organization, the structures of international companies must serve to coordinate business activities and to move information quickly and accurately across borders and around the world (Bourgeois *et al.*,1999). Developments introduced by foreign firms can seriously affect local communities and local businesses. The international arena entails some significant challenges and risks. Language, cultural and business practices, and political and legal environments can differ greatly across national borders. Practices that are perfectly acceptable in one country can be taboo in another country. McDonald's decision to enter India meant that its menu had to change drastically in order to accommodate the culture of a country in which cattle are revered (Bourgeois *et al.*, 1999). Clark and Arbel (1993) cite several challenges, such as communication difficulties, little control over regulatory, legal and political decisions, political instabilities, different labour patterns, costs, product supplies, religions, customs, work ethics, languages, lack of codes and standards. Globalization is primarily about negative effects on the environment, culture, social values, with the imitation of the western culture in the first place, and standardization, which leads to a uniform product in tourism and disappearance of local standards (Klanènik, 2003).

Global Economic Trends

The term global economic trends means the way most of the world economy is behaving in a recent period of time within a set of well-defined parameters. Global economy or the world economy is largely centred on a few large or developed economies of the world, namely, the USA, UK, France, Germany and Japan, some newly emerging economies of the world such as India, China and some South East Asian economies and certain pockets of Latin America like Brazil, Mexico and Argentina (UNCTAD, 2001: http://www.unctad.org/en/docs/pogdsm21.en.pdf).

The economic recession in the US economy in 2001 was downplayed and a surge in inventories has not proven sufficient to lead the economy on a sustained path of investment recovery. More so, growth in the US economy seems to be driven by increased consumer spending on consumer goods such as cars and electronic appliances. Although tax cuts and other measures have provided a temporary stimulus for higher disposable incomes, employment levels have actually been falling and with decline in equity rates and a general rise in international oil prices, the USA is perceived by many to be heading to a second plunge for recession in the new millennium.

As with the case of Europe, Germany's private consumption and demand are failing to take-off and, with the appreciation of the Euro, their exports have also been hit hard. Labour market inflexibility and lack of sound demand management policies have created growth in domestic demand of only 3.9% in UK, 1.5% in Germany and 2.3% in France between 1996 and 2000. Japan, the only developed economy of Asia, has experienced a rapid growth in its industrial production and that has also been reflected in the positive growth of its exports. But domestic demand being low remains its problem growing only at 1.2% in the period between 1996 and 2000. Japan suffers from a problem of deflation and although there has been no real fall in real income levels, consumers live in uncertainty and postpone purchases which bring about further deflation. In terms of investment flows and movement of capital, Asian exporters have benefited from the stability in US markets whereas restrictive fiscal policies for the Latin American economies have resulted in reduced investment flows to the country as also a decline in earnings from the countries' exports. African economies have by and large been uninfluenced by world capital markets. But the net private capital inflows are said to have reduced for the developing economies as a whole, falling by 11.3% between 2001 and 2002. Latin American countries as described above are going through a recession with prices of the country's exports falling by 10 to 30 per cent. Coupled with reduced investment flows, South America is at present reeling under severe depression. Argentina and Brazil remain the only bright spots with procyclical fiscal policies like increase in interest rates being adopted to restore investment flows into the region.

By grouping the world into the developed and the developing nations it was observed by a study group of UNCTAD, that (UNCTAD, 2001): The share of agriculture as a part of the economic activity fell to about 2% in developed countries compared to 11% in the developing nations from 1970 to 2001. But the per cent of labour engaged in agriculture in the developed countries was the highest at about 55% in 2001. But the problems of low agricultural productivity and surplus labour persist which explain the minimal contribution of agriculture to the total output. China has 45% of its population working in the agricultural sector producing only 12% of the GDP. Poverty still remains the most difficult to tackle with 14.5% of the population of East Asia and the Pacific living on less than $ 1 a day. The corresponding figure for Europe and Central Asia is 4.2% and that for Sub-Saharan Africa is at a staggering 49%. The World Politics and Economics or the Global Political Economy should address the associated burning issues of Global Economic Trends like poverty, inflation and under-nutrition, illiteracy unemployment etc. as they tend to fall in the arena of Human Development Index and Sustainable Development.

GLOBAL ECONOMIC TRENDS AND PROSPECTS

After attaining the highest growth rate in 2000 for more than a decade, the world economy experienced a sharp downturn over the last quarter of 2000 and into the New Year. The principal factors behind this reversal and near-term economic prospects were examined in *Trade and Development Report, 2001* (http://www.unctad.org/en/docs//tdr2001_en.pdf), issued in April, on the basis of preliminary data available for the first quarter of 2001. Based on an analysis of underlying imbalances and fragilities in the world economy, the UNCTAD secretariat argued that without a coordinated global policy response, the slowdown in the United States would produce a synchronous cyclical downturn in the world economy. Rather than a rapid rebound, the United States economy could experience a prolonged period of sluggish growth which even quick conventional policy actions might be unable to remedy.

The *Report* also suggested that even Europe could be much more vulnerable to the slowdown in the United States than was generally expected by policy makers in the region, and without a determined change in economic policy, European growth would fall substantially below the 3 per cent experienced in the previous year. Similarly, without more aggressive measures designed to reverse persistent deflation, Japan's recovery remained highly fragile. If all these risks became reality, there would be a sharp deterioration in the external trading environment of developing countries, many of which were struggling to re-establish conditions for rapid and sustained growth after recent bouts of financial crisis.

While some emerging markets were expecting to improve their performance as a result of lower United States interest rates and a weaker dollar, these benefits could be easily wiped out by reassessment of risks, rising risk spreads and falling capital inflows brought about by slowdown in global growth and a further round of uncertainty. Already on the eve of events of 11 September, global economic conditions had been deteriorating over a year. The decline in the pace of demand in the first half of 2001 had been sharper than expected and for the first time since the late 1970s much of the world economy was simultaneously experiencing slower growth. The slowdown in the major industrial countries had begun to affect the rest of the world through trade and financial linkages, and many economies in Asia and Latin America were confronting recessionary pressures. Until the events of September 11, however, policy makers in most major industrial countries were reluctant to adopt a coordinated approach to stabilizing and reviving the world economy. But the recent events that have made possible such a coordinated macroeconomic policy response have also made the world economy more fragile and unpredictable and vulnerable, especially in the wake of rampant trade distortions and some negative impacts of emerging disruptive technologies that are taking place in the hyper-competitive environment.

Shifting Paradigm in the Rapid Pace of Globalization

Management and organization studies dealing with the phenomenon of globalization have in recent years been dominated by an instrumental, rational, economic and functionalist paradigm, which can be collectively referred to as instrumentalism. The foundation of instrumental reasoning or instrumentalism is the focus on the development of means-ends chains. Argument for instrumentalism in explaining globalization is often legitimized with reference to the efficiency needs of multinational corporations to make profits by extending their productive facilities and goods or services to new territories or markets. Globalization or the global economy is thus viewed in terms of the existence of resources or opportunities available to organizations, and serves means for achieving corporate ends (Goliath, 2002).

As global competition escalates, learning and earning are becoming more closely aligned. "Knowledge workers," social philosopher Peter F. Drucker observes, are becoming central to our economy and our society. They possess critical thinking skills and, importantly, an ability to continue expanding their knowledge and adapting to change. Their earnings power is increasing, and they may eventually possess rising political power and status (http://www.kltprc.net/books/leadershipchallenge/Chpt_2.htm).

The embrace of instrumental doctrine in contemporary discussion of globalization is also manifested in terms of its conceptualization as a process of internationalization of production, availability of economic opportunities and resources such as raw materials, labor, capital, markets, etc. Similarly, globalization is synonymous to economic performance through the internationalization of the means of production and access to the conventional "factors of production" long identified by economists as "factor conditions" that can impinge on competitive advantage: physical resources, human resources, infrastructure, knowledge resources, and capital resources (Porter, 1990).

Thus, in standard international management books, globalization is presented as "the tendency of firms to extend their sales or manufacturing to new markets abroad", "characterized by networks that bind countries, institutions, and people in an interdependent global economy", "a worldwide integration of economic systems driven by multinational corporations" (Berry, Conkling and Ray, 1997), "the production and distribution of products and services of a homogenous type on a worldwide basis" or else in Darwinian terms, as companies which are under pressure to globalize or face extinction. From the efficiency perspective, economics defines everything else and the multinational or global corporation is upheld as the driver of the global economy. In order to survive, firms must "globalize" through various forms of internationalization strategies such as export, global franchising, joint ventures, strategic alliances, etc.

By conceptualizing globalization as "the global search for bigger markets" arising from competitive pressures at MNCs' home markets and pressures for cost reductions, instrumental rationalism becomes the pervading doctrine in the globalization discourse. In order to achieve this economic aim, it is imperative that different people and cultures of the world adopt a monolithic culture with uniform consumption patterns. Hence, different cultures and global diversity must be managed in order to produce a global mindset. Similarly, the instrumental doctrine upholds a vision of unity, characterized by unanimity of values among the global populace. As a functionalist paradigm, the doctrine of the "survival of the fittest" is explicitly embedded in the future perspective to emphasize the types of strategies multinational enterprises must adopt to survive in a fiercely competitive global environment. To the extent that instrumental reasoning dominates the globalization discourse, it lays claim to the concept of rationality while alternative forms of interpreting the phenomenon of globalization appear irrational: a firm is either an active participant in the global economy or faces extinction. Global imperative is seen as "an absolute necessity that forces companies to embrace globalization or face extinction" (Goliath, 2001).

Related to this view is the justification of globalization as the panacea for the world's socio-economic problems. Globalization is also seen as the gift of capitalism, "progress", "industrialization", and/or "modernization" from developed societies to the underdeveloped nations of the world through the mechanisms of a global economy defined within the context of a free market system. Thus, the functionalist approach also focuses on Western economic and socio-political advancement as a premise for action. Thus, within the context of the globalization discourse, the idea behind this perspective is also rooted in the convergence thesis (Francesco and Gold, 1998; Clegg and Gray, 1996), which states that for all societies there is only one direction of significant change, culminating in the essentials of modern Western society, driven by technological imperatives, capitalist ethos, and increasingly, the imperatives of a market system. As communication technologies advance and countries become more closely linked through trade, more information about other cultures becomes available and as products are sold worldwide and marketed in the same way everywhere, the world is increasingly becoming one "global village". Thus, globalization is seen as a natural phenomenon catapulting the world into a pristine state of progress along the direction of Western cultural values.

Globalization and the "Modern Economy"

Modern economy has its roots deeply embedded into the globalization—backed up by the series of reforms processes undertaken by several countries, constituting an integral part of the global economy in past two decades. Let us therefore try and examine the characteristics as well as interrelationship between Globalization and the 'Modern Economy'.

The "Modern economy" is a global phenomenon characterized by:

- increasing economic integration across national boundaries;
- increasing pace of technological and social change;
- increasing pace of flow and transformation of information and knowledge;
- productivity growth linked to the rising influence of information and communication technologies (ICT); and
- Entrepreneurship in creating and growing firms.

The term "*modern economy*" is often used interchangeably with the term "knowledge economy" or "*Knowledge-based economy*": A distinction should be drawn between these terms and "new economy" and "information economy". These latter "economies" are subsets of the broader knowledge-based economy.

A knowledge-based economy **(KBE)** is an economy in which the production, distribution, and use of knowledge is the main driver of growth, wealth creation and employment across all industries. In this context, being a KBE means more than simply having a thriving "new economy" or "information economy" somehow separate from a stagnant "old economy". In a truly knowledge-based economy, all sectors have become knowledge-intensive, not just those usually called "high technology". In other words, it is not merely an "information technology issue" but very much a 'Knowledge-based issue in totality'.

Global Economic Growth Driving Higher Emissions

Global economic growth, by choice or by default, is highly energy-intensive, and predominantly dependent on fossil fuels, that cause a substantial proportion of environmental pollution and degradation. The major polluting countries in the world are those that are members of G-8 Nations. Growth in carbon dioxide (CO_2) emissions from fossil fuel burning and industrial processes has gone up markedly in the early twenty-first century. These emissions grew at only 1.1 per cent a year on average from 1990 to 1999. They increased at 3.1 per cent per year from 2000 to 2006. This increase occurred despite the dampening effect of extraordinarily large increases in petroleum prices, and through short-term cross-substitution, prices of other fossil fuels. Global emissions from combustion of fossil fuels accelerated sharply from around 2000.

CO_2 emissions from fossil-fuel burning and industrial processes (i.e. greenhouse gases) have been accelerating at a global scale, with their growth rate increasing from 1.1% y^{-1} for 1990–1999 to >3% y^{-1} for 2000–2004. The emissions growth rate since 2000 was greater than for the most fossil-fuel intensive of the Intergovernmental Panel on Climate Change emissions scenarios developed in the late 1990s. Global emissions growth since 2000 was driven by a cessation or reversal of earlier declining trends in the energy intensity of gross domestic product (GDP) (energy/GDP) and the carbon intensity of energy (emissions/energy), coupled with continuing increases in population and per capita GDP. Nearly constant or slightly increasing trends in the carbon intensity of energy have been recently observed in both developed and developing regions. No region is decarbonizing its energy supply and planning to go Carbon-neutral. The growth rate in emissions is strongest in rapidly developing economies, particularly in BRIC countries viz. Brazil, Russia, India and China. Together, the developing and least-developed economies (forming 80% of the world's population) accounted for 73% of global emissions growth in 2004 but only 41% of global emissions and only 23% of global cumulative emissions since the mid-18th century. The results have implications for global equity (Clerk, 2007).

The Global Competitiveness Report

The Global Competitiveness Report (GCR) was initially published by the World Economic Forum (WEF), based in Geneva, Switzerland, way back in 1979. The latest edition, dated 2007-2008, was edited by Michael Porter of the Harvard Business School, Xavier Sala-i-Martin of Columbia University, and Klaus Schwab, Executive Chairman of the WEF. Its Global Competitiveness Index—the Growth measure of competitiveness (GCI)—covers 131 countries, including 66 of the 89 countries in which USAID currently works.

Each edition of the recently published Global Competitiveness Report (http://www.weforum.org/en/initiatives/gcp/Global%20Competitiveness%20Report/index.htm) contains a genuine wealth of information on the countries covered. The report's cornerstone is the GCI, the construction of which is inspired by Michael Porter's analysis of national competitiveness. The index scores countries on a total of 131 variables grouped under twelve "pillars." The pillars are institutions (public and private), infrastructure, macroeconomic stability, health and primary education, higher education and training, goods market efficiency, labor market efficiency, financial market sophistication, technological readiness, market size, market share, business sophistication and innovation etc. (http://www.businessgrowthinitiative.org/KeyPracticeAreas/Pages/GlobalCompetitivenessIndex.aspx).

Global Competitiveness Index—Definition and Criteria

The Global Competitiveness Index is the accepted tool for evaluating a country's potential for growth. By comparing most of the world's countries, it provides insight into the comparative advantages of each of the competing countries in the global scene (http://reut-institute.org/Publication.aspx?PublicationId=1312).

World Economic Forum's Global Competitiveness Index supplies information regarding an economy's competitiveness for a large set of countries (125 in 2006). The rankings are drawn from a combination of publicly available hard data and the results of the Executive Opinion Survey. The latter is a comprehensive survey conducted on an annual basis by the World Economic Forum, together with its network of partner institutes (leading research institutes and business organizations) in the countries covered by the report. There are four variables in the IPRI Ranking for which data had been obtained from the 2006 WEF Global Competitiveness Index: "Judicial Independence", "Physical Property Rights Protection", "Intellectual Property Rights Protection", and "Access to Loans". The respective questions that survey participants were asked to answer are displayed in Appendix II. For more detailed information on the Global Competitiveness Index (www.weforum.org/en/initiatives/gcp/Global%20Competitiveness%20Report/index.htm).

Composition of the Global Competitiveness Index

This appendix of the Global Competitive Index provides details on how the

Global Competitiveness Index is constructed. All of the Survey and hard data variables used in this index can be found in the data tables section of this *Report* with more detailed descriptions: (http://www.kfuriconsulting.com/GlobalCompetitive.pdf).

1st Pillar: Institutions

A. Public institutions

1. Property rights
6.03 Property rights

2. Ethics and corruption
6.24 Diversion of public funds
6.26 Public trust of politicians

3. Undue influence
6.01 Judicial independence
6.08 Favoritism in decisions of government officials

4. Government inefficiency (red tape, bureaucracy and waste)
6.06 Wastefulness of government spending
6.07 Burden of government regulation

5. Security
2.02 Business costs of terrorism
6.14 Reliability of police services
6.15 Business costs of crime and violence
6.16 Organized crime

B. Private institutions

1. Corporate ethics
8.04 Ethical behavior of firms
2. Corporate accountability
8.16 Efficacy of corporate boards
8.21 Protection of minority shareholders' interests
8.23 Strength of auditing and reporting standards

2nd Pillar: Infrastructure

5.01 Overall infrastructure quality
5.02 Railroad infrastructure development
5.03 Port infrastructure quality
5.04 Air transport infrastructure quality
5.05 Quality of electricity supply
5.08 Telephone lines (hard data)

3rd Pillar: Macro economy

2.13 Government surplus/deficit (hard data)
2.14 National savings rate (hard data)
2.16 Inflation (hard data)
2.17 Interest rate spread (hard data)
2.20 Government debt/GDP ratio (hard data)
2.15 Real effective exchange rate (hard data)

4th Pillar: Health and primary education

A. Health

4.04 Medium-term business impact of malaria
4.05 Medium-term business impact of tuberculosis
4.06 Medium-term business impact of HIV/AIDS
4.10 Infant mortality (hard data)
4.11 Life expectancy at birth (hard data)
4.12 Tuberculosis prevalence (hard data)
4.13 Malaria prevalence (hard data)
4.14 HIV/AIDS prevalence (hard data)

B. Primary education

4.15 Gross primary enrollment (hard data)

5th Pillar: Higher education and training

A. Quantity of education

4.16 Gross secondary enrollment (hard data)
4.17 Gross tertiary enrollment (hard data)

B. Quality of education system

4.01 Quality of the educational system
4.03 Quality of math and science education
8.15 Quality of management schools

C. On-the-job training

7.09 Local availability of specialized research and training services
8.11 Extent of staff training

6th Pillar: Market efficiency

A. Goods markets: distortions, competition and size

1. Distortions

2.12 Agricultural policy costs
6.02 Efficiency of legal framework
6.11 Extent and effect of taxation
7.10 Number of procedures to start business (hard data)
7.11 Time required starting a business (hard data)

2. Competition

Domestic competition

7.01 Intensity of local competition
7.02 Effectiveness of anti-trust policy

Foreign competition

2.19 Imports (hard data)
2.09 Prevalence of trade barriers
8.22 Foreign ownership restrictions

3. Size

Local markets

GDP – exports + imports (hard data)

Foreign markets (exports)

2.18 Exports (hard data)

B. Labor markets: flexibility and efficiency

1. Flexibility

8.17 Hiring and firing practices
8.18 Flexibility of wage determination
8.19 Cooperation in labor/employer relations

2. Efficiency

8.14 Reliance on professional management
8.20 Pay and productivity
4.08 Brain drain
4.09 Private sector employment of women

C. Financial markets: sophistication and openness

2.03 Financial market sophistication

2.05 Ease of access to loans
2.06 Venture capital availability
2.04 Soundness of banks
2.08 Local equity market access

7th Pillar: Technological readiness

3.01 Technological readiness
3.02 Firm-level technology absorption
3.15 Laws relating to ICT
3.04 FDI and technology transfer
3.18 Cellular telephones (hard data)
3.19 Internet users (hard data)
3.21 Personal computers (hard data)

8th Pillar: Business sophistication

A. Networks and supporting industries

7.05 Local supplier quantity
7.06 Local supplier quality

B. Sophistication of firms operations and strategy

8.05 Production process sophistication
8.06 Extent of marketing
8.08 Control of international distribution
8.12 Willingness to delegate authority
8.01 Nature of competitive advantage
8.02 Value chain presence

9th Pillar: Innovation

3.05 Quality of scientific research institutions
3.06 Company spending on research and development
3.07 University/industry research collaboration
3.08 Government procurement of advanced technology products
3.09 Availability of scientists and engineers
3.17 Utility patents (hard data)
6.04 Intellectual property protection
8.03 Capacity for innovation

Measuring Global Competitiveness through Index

The rapid changes in the context of the process of economic reform, globalization and liberalization have created greater compulsions for us to be productive and competitive than ever before. With rapid advancement in technology as well as management theory and practice, the concept and techniques of productivity have undergone a change over time, thereby creating a need for devising fresh approaches, coining new message and adopting a new idiom to spread the message to the stakeholders. Since 2001, the World Economic Forum has been using the Growth Competitiveness Index (Growth CI) developed by Jeffery Sachs and John McArthur to assess the competitiveness of nations. Although it was cutting-edge at the time it was developed, more recent advances in economic research and the rising importance of the international dimension, as well as the increasing diversity of countries covered by the report, call for adjustment of methodology. The new Global Competitiveness Index (GCI) and a full description of its main methodological underpinnings were presented in the Global Competitiveness Report 2004-2005. A set of scores and rankings was again published in the Global Competitiveness Report 2005-06. With this year's (2007-2008) Global Competitiveness Index Report it has been considered as the main indicator to be used by the forum. The Global Competitiveness Index provides holistic overview of factors that are critical to driving productivity and competitiveness and group them into nine pillars (Nayak, 2008):

1. Institutions
2. Infrastructure
3. Macro economy
4. Health and Primary Education
5. Higher Education and Training
6. Market Efficiency
7. Technological Readiness
8. Business Sophistication
9. Innovation

It is important to note that none of these factors alone can ensure competitiveness. Therefore, the most competitive economies in the world will typically be those where concerted efforts have been made to frame policies in a comprehensive way, that is, those which recognize the importance of a broad array of factors, their interconnections and need to address the underlying weakness they reveal in a proactive way. By institution they mean the system of rules that shapes incentives and defines the way economic agents interact in an economy. The concept of competitiveness developed by the Forum explicitly incorporates notions of public sector accountability, efficiency, transparency and, more generally, the various ways in which the government interacts with economic agents in the domestic economy, particularly the business sector. The justifications for doing so are varied, sometimes reflecting reasonably well-established findings in empirical research. There are strong indications that differences in institutions explain much of the growth differential between countries, and therefore have an influence upon countries' growth performance well beyond simply getting inflation right or addressing other macroeconomic weaknesses. More specifically, to assess the effectiveness of public institutions, the GCI uses five criteria:

1. Respect for property rights
2. Ethics of government behaviour and the prevalence of corruption
3. Independence of the judiciary and the extent to which the government gives the private sector freedom to operate or engages in interventionist discretionary practices (concepts captured under the heading "undue influence")
4. Government inefficiency reflected in the waste of public resources and a heavy regulatory burden
5. The ability to provide an environment for economic activity characterized by adequate levels of public safety.

The Global Competitiveness Report ranks the world's nations according to the *Global Competitiveness Index*. The report states that it is based on the latest theoretical and empirical research. It is made up of over 90 variables, of which two thirds come from the Executive Opinion Survey, and one third comes from publicly available sources such as the United Nations. The variables are organized into nine pillars, with each pillar representing an area considered as an important determinant of competitiveness.

The report notes that as a nation develops, wages tend to increase, and that in order to sustain this higher income, labor productivity must improve in order for the nation to be competitive. In addition, what creates productivity in Sweden is necessarily different from what drives it in Ghana. Thus, the GCI separates countries into three specific stages: factor-driven, efficiency-driven, and innovation-driven, each implying a growing degree of complexity in the operation of the economy.

In the factor-driven stage countries compete based on their factor endowments, primarily unskilled labor and natural resources. Companies compete on the basis of prices and sell basic products or commodities, with their low productivity reflected in low wages. To maintain competitiveness at this stage of development, competitiveness hinges mainly on well-functioning public and private institutions (pillar 1), appropriate infrastructure (pillar 2), a stable macroeconomic framework (pillar 3), and good health and primary education (pillar 4).

As wages rise with advancing development, countries move into the efficiency-driven stage of development, when they must begin to develop more efficient production processes and increase product quality. At this point, competitiveness becomes increasingly driven by higher education and training (pillar 5), efficient markets (pillar 6), and the ability to harness the benefits of existing technologies (pillar 7).

Finally, as countries move into the innovation-driven stage, they are only able to sustain higher wages and the associated standard of living if their businesses are able to compete with new and unique products. At this stage, companies must compete by producing new and different goods using the most sophisticated production processes (pillar 8) and through innovation (pillar 9).

Thus, the impact of each pillar on competitiveness varies across countries, in function of their stages of economic development. Therefore, in the calculation of the GCI, pillars are given different weights depending on the per capita income of the nation. The weights used are the values that best explain growth in recent years. For example, the sophistication and innovation factors contribute 10% to the final score in factor and efficiency-driven economies, but 30% in innovation-driven economies. Intermediate values are used for economies in transition between stages.

The 2007-2008 Global Competitiveness Report contains:

- Detailed country competitiveness profiles of 131 economies
- Data tables for survey and hard data variables ranking profiled economies
- Global rankings: the Global Competitiveness Index and the Business Competitiveness Index, measuring growth and productivity, respectively
- Exclusive data from the Executive Opinion Survey, with over 11,000 responses from business leaders worldwide.

The United States tops the overall ranking in The Global Competitiveness Report 2007-2008. Switzerland is in second position followed by Denmark, Sweden, Germany, Finland and Singapore, respectively.

The rankings are calculated from both publicly available data and the Executive Opinion Survey, a comprehensive annual survey conducted by the World Economic Forum together with its network of Partner Institutes (leading research institutes and business organizations) in the countries covered by the Report. This year, over 11,000 business leaders were polled in a record 131 countries. The top ten countries figuring in the Global Competitiveness Survey are as given in Table 1.

Table 1: Ranking of the Top 10 Countries

Rank	Country	Score
1	US	5.67
2	Switzerland	5.62
3	Denmark	5.55
4	Sweden	5.54
5	Germany	5.51
6	Finland	5.49
7	Singapore	5.45
8	Japan	5.43
9	UK	5.41
10	Netherlands	5.40

India is becoming more competitive and ranking better than Brazil, Russian Federation, China and the neighbouring countries. The World Economic Forum has released the Global Competitiveness Report 2006-2007 based on nine factors.

Here is the list of competitive countries based on global competitiveness index (GCI):

Table 2: Ranking of countries based on Global Competitiveness Index (GCI)

No.	Country	Rank (out of 125 countries)
1.	Switzerland	1
2.	Sweden	3
3.	United States	6
4.	India	43
5.	China	54
6.	Russian Federation	62
7.	Brazil	66
8.	Sri Lanka	79
9.	Pakistan	91
10.	Bangladesh	99
11.	Nepal	110
12.	Angola	121
13.	Burundi	122
14.	Chad	123
15.	Timor-East	124
16.	Mozambique	125

India is at good place in **Innovation factor** (26) and in **Business Sophistication category** (25). However, in the Basic Requirements category, India is ranked at 60. However, China is at 44th place and the US is at 27th place. Here is the list of **Factors responsible for driving productivity and competitiveness.** It describes India's performance on different categories on which the final list has come out.

Table 3: India's ranking according to different factors

No.	Factors	Ranking
1.	Market efficiency	21
2.	Business sophistication category	25
3.	Innovation factor	26
4.	Institutions factors	34
5.	Efficiency enhancers	41
6.	Higher education and training	49
7.	Technological readiness	55
8.	Infrastructure category	60
9.	Macro-economy	88
10.	Health and primary education	93

Produced in collaboration with a distinguished group of international scholars and a global network of over 130 leading national research institutes and business organizations, the Report also showcases the latest thinking and research on issues of immediate relevance for business leaders and policy-makers (http://www.weforum.org/en/initiatives/gcp/Global%20Competitiveness%20Report/index.htm). The Country-wise ranking position reflected in the Global Competitiveness Index of 2007-08 vis-à-vis 2006-07 is shown below in Table 4.

Table 4: Global Competitiveness Index rankings and 2006-2007 comparisons

Country/Economy	GCI 2007-2008 Rank	GCI 2007-2008 Score	GCI 2007-2008 rank (among 2006 countries)*	GCI 2006-2007 rank
United State	1	5.67	1	1
Switzerland	2	5.62	2	4
Denmark	3	5.55	3	3
Sweden	4	5.54	4	9
Germany	5	5.51	5	7
Finland	6	5.48	6	6
Singapore	7	5.45	7	8
Japan	8	5.43	8	5
United Kingdom	9	5.41	9	2
Netherlands	10	5.40	10	11
Korea	11	5.40	11	23
Hong Kong SAR	12	5.37	12	10
Canada	13	5.34	13	12
Taiwan China	14	5.25	14	13
Austria	15	5.23	15	18
Norway	16	5.20	16	17
Israel	17	5.20	17	14
France	18	5.18	18	15
Australia	19	5.17	19	16
Belgium	20	5.10	20	24
Malaysia	21	5.10	21	19
Ireland	22	5.03	22	22
Iceland	23	5.02	23	20
New Zealand	24	4.98	24	21
Luxembourg	25	4.88	25	25
Chile	26	4.77	26	27
Estonia	27	4.74	27	26
Thailand	28	4.70	28	28
Spain	29	4.66	29	29
Kuwait	30	4.66	30	30
Qatar	31	4.63	31	32
Tunisia	32	4.59	32	33
Czech Republic	33	4.58	33	31
China	34	4.57	34	35
Saudi Arabia	35	4.55	n/a	n/a
Puorto Rico	36	4.50	n/a	n/a
United Arab Emirates	37	4.50	35	34
Lithuania	38	4.49	36	39
Slovenia	39	4.48	37	40
Portugal	40	4.48	38	43
Slovak Republic	41	4.45	39	37
Oman	42	4.43	n/a	n/a
Bahrain	43	4.42	40	48
South Africa	44	4.42	41	36
Latvia	45	4.41	42	44
Italy	46	4.36	43	47
Hungary	47	4.35	44	38
India	48	4.33	45	42
Jordan	49	4.32	46	46
Barbados	50	4.32	47	41
Poland	51	4.28	48	45
Mexico	52	4.26	49	52

Table 4: Continued

Country/Economy	GCI 2007-2008 Rank	GCI 2007-2008 Score	GCI 2007-2008 rank (among 2006 countries)*	GCI 2006-2007 rank
Turkey	53	4.25	50	58
Indonesia	54	4.24	51	54
Cyprus	55	4.23	52	49
Malta	56	4.21	53	51
Croatia	57	4.20	54	56
Russia	58	4.19	55	59
Panama	59	4.18	56	60
Mauritius	60	4.16	57	55
Kazakhstan	61	4.14	58	50
Uzebekistan	62	4.13	n/a	n/a
Costa Rica	63	4.11	59	68
Morocco	64	4.08	60	65
Greece	65	4.08	61	61
Azerbaijan	66	4.07	62	62
El Salvador	67	4.05	63	53
Vietnam	68	4.04	64	64
Colombia	69	4.04	65	63
Sri Lanka	70	3.99	66	81
Philippines	71	3.99	67	75
Brazil	72	3.99	68	66
Ukraine	73	3.98	69	69
Romania	74	3.97	70	73
Uruguay	75	3.97	71	79
Botswana	76	3.96	72	57
Egypt	77	3.96	73	71
Jamaica	78	3.95	75	67
Bulgaria	79	3.93	75	74
Syria	80	3.91	n/a	n/a
Algeria	81	3.91	76	77
Montenegro	82	3.91	n/a	n/a
Honduras	83	3.89	77	90
Trinidad and Tobago	84	3.88	78	76
Argentina	85	3.87	79	70
Peru	86	3.87	80	78
Guatemala	87	3.86	81	91
Libya	88	3.85	n/a	n/a
Namibia	89	3.85	82	72
Georgia	90	3.83	83	87
Serbia	91	3.78	n/a	n/a
Pakistan	92	3.77	84	83
Armenia	93	3.76	85	90
Macedonia, FYR	94	3.73	86	84
Nigeria	95	3.69	87	95
Dominican Republic	96	3.65	88	93
Moldova	97	3.64	89	96
Venezuela	98	3.63	90	95
Kenya	99	3.61	91	98
Senegal	100	3.61	n/a	n/a
Mongolia	101	3.60	92	89
Gambia, The	102	3.59	93	103
Ecuador	103	3.57	94	94

Table 4: Continued

Country/Economy	GCI 2007-2008 Rank	GCI 2007-2008 Score	GCI 2007-2008 rank (among 2006 countries)*	GCI 2006-2007 rank
Tanzania	104	3.56	95	97
Bolivia	105	3.55	96	100
Bosina and Herzegovina	106	3.55	97	82
Bangladesh	107	3.55	98	82
Benin	108	3.49	99	107
Albania	109	3.48	100	98
Cambodia	110	3.48	101	106
Nicaragua	111	3.45	102	101
Burkina Faso	112	3.43	103	114
Surinam	113	3.40	104	104
Nepal	114	3.38	105	105
Mali	115	3.37	106	115
Cameroon	116	3.37	107	99
Tajikistan	117	3.37	108	96
Madagascar	118	3.36	109	111
Kyrgyz Republic	119	3.34	110	109
Uganda	120	3.33	111	110
Paraguay	121	3.30	112	108
Zambia	122	3.29	113	118
Ethiopia	123	3.28	114	116
Lesothe	124	3.27	115	102
Mauritania	125	3.26	116	117
Guyana	126	3.25	117	113
Timor-East	127	3.20	118	120
Mozambique	128	3.02	119	119
Zimbabwe	129	2.88	120	112
Burundi	130	2.84	121	122
Chad	131	2.78	122	121

* To countries that were covered in last year's Report but are not included in the present Report for lack of Survey data are excluded from the comparison (Angola and Malawi). Serbia and Montenegro, treated as one country last year, are now treated as two individual countries. We therefore do not show data for Serbia and Montenegro for last year.

Asia's Position in Global Competitive Index

Asia is home to some of the most, as well as some of the least, competitive economies in our rankings. Singapore leads the pack, ranked 5th overall, followed by Japan in 7th place, Hong Kong in 11th and Taiwan in 13th place overall. These economies all have high-quality infrastructure, flexible and efficient markets and healthy, well-educated workforces. They are also operating on the outer boundaries of the technology frontier, both at the firm and consumer level.

In Japan, economic recovery has begun with deflation on the wane, yet a number of challenges, mainly in management of the public finances and market efficient remain. Nevertheless, private sector commitment to R&D, sophisticated production process and a highly educated labour force contribute to deliver one of the most innovative economies in the world.

Another strong performer this year is Malaysia, ranked 26th overall, just behind the Republic of Korea which was ranked 24th. Malaysia exhibits one of the most efficient economies in the region; flexible labour market, relatively undistorted goods markets, and public institutions which in many areas. India ranked 43rd overall and, as the leading country in the GCI's first stage of development, scores remarkably high in capacity for innovation and sophistication of firm operations. This is especially true of the quality of scientific research and the number of scientists and engineers, which are increasingly supplying highly skilled profession to the private sector. Indian enterprises tend to utilize sophisticated production processes and use numerous high-quality local suppliers, thus lowering input costs.

Additionally, successive Indian governments have proven to be remarkably ineffective in reducing the public sector deficit, one of the highest in the world. China's ranking has fallen from 48 to 54. Its performance is highly uneven and this raises a number of concerns consistent with the cautious macro-economic management of its authorities and extremely high GDP growth rates, the macroeconomy pillar of the GCI shows a very high rank, 6th overall in the world. This reflects China's low inflation, one of the highest savings rates in the world, and manageable levels of public debt. Perhaps more than any other country in the world, China's large and rapidly growing market has attracted large volumes of FDI in recent years.

The banking sector is largely state-controlled and the capacity to price risk is limited. Levels of financial intermediation are low and the state has had to intervene from time to time to mitigate the adverse effects of a large nonperforming loan portfolio. Like India, China has low penetration rates for the latest technologies (mobile telephones, internet, and personal computers) and because these are expanding more quickly in other countries, China's ranks in these indicators are actually falling behind. Secondary and tertiary school enrollment rates are better than they are in India, but still low by international standards.

India's Position in Global Competitive Index

India has fallen five notches in the latest annual rankings of the Global Competitiveness Report released by the World Economic Forum. India was placed 48 in the list of 131 economies covered under the Global Competitiveness Index (GCI) which tracks twelve parameters to come out with the rankings. Among the top emerging markets, India is second this year behind China. Last year India ranked 43 and was ahead of other BRIC markets. This year China, at 34, is the top ranked BRIC market. Russia at 58 and Brazil at 72 are behind India. Among the three sub-indices under GCI, India improved its ranking from 41 to 31 in 'efficiency enhancers' but dropped from 60 to 74 in 'basic requirements'. Its ranking on 'innovation factors' remained unchanged this year at 26.

The United States tops the overall ranking followed by Switzerland, Denmark, Sweden and Germany in that order. Last year Switzerland topped the charts followed by Finland, Sweden, Denmark and Singapore.

Chile is the highest ranked country from Latin America this year, followed by Mexico and Costa Rica. Several countries from the Middle East and the North Africa region are in the upper half of the rankings, led by Israel, Kuwait, Qatar, Tunisia, Saudi Arabia and the UAE. In sub-Saharan Africa, only South Africa and Mauritius feature in the top half of the rankings. Nine Asia-Pacific countries are among the top 30 in the GCI rankings, led by Singapore, Japan, Korea and Hong Kong SAR.

"The quality of the business environment in India has improved tangibly in recent years, with increased efficiency of goods, labour and financial markets and greater innovation and sophistication of firm operations. However, a number of weaknesses persist that need to be addressed especially in the area of infrastructure quality. Moreover, dealing with shortcomings in the provision of health services and education will ensure that the benefits of economic growth are more broadly distributed," said World Economic Forum's head of strategic insight teams, Fiona Papua. The rankings are based on publicly available data and the executive opinion survey, which is a business leader's poll, conducted by the World Economic Forum. The survey is designed to capture a broad range of factors affecting the economy's business climate.

India in a Global and Regional Context

India Poised to Become a Global Player

India, a country of sub-continental dimensions, has a share of total world trade of less than 1%. This amazingly small share of world trade is a reflection of India's inward looking mindset of the late 20th century. However, it is equally a measure of the vast opportunities that lie ahead as we move forward in the 21st century. This issue needs to be addressed.

The first point to note from this forward looking perspective is that, though small, India's manufacturing export base is already remarkably diversified, ranging from traditional exports like textiles, garments, leather products, gems and jewellery, through chemicals and pharmaceuticals to metals, metal products and machinery. Estimates of Revealed Comparative Advantage show that India's manufacturing exports across this entire range are globally competitive. In some of these products, the country already has a significant share of the global market, while in other products the share is rapidly rising. Especially interesting in this context is the rapid growth in exports of automotive parts and components, and the future export potential of biotechnology products.

The other exciting aspect of India's recent export performance is the dramatic growth in export of services. The share of services has risen from about 1/5th to 1/3rd of India's total exports in the past 10 years, especially thanks to the IT revolution and the dramatic growth in exports of IT-enabled services. Services already account for over 50% of India's GDP and it is quite conceivable that services could also account for over half of India's total exports in the next 5-10 years, or somewhere in the region of $ 80-$ 100 billion according to some estimates (http://www.adb.org/Documents/Speeches/2004/sp2004005.pdf).

Growth and Responsibility in the Global Economy

G-8 Agenda for Global Growth and Stability

The G8 is an unofficial forum which brings together the heads of the richest industrialized countries: France, Germany, Italy, Japan, the United Kingdom, the United States, Canada (since 1976), Russia (since 1998), the President of the European Commission (since 1981).

The Prospective Agenda flagged for discussion in the Global Heiligendamm Summit, held on June 6-8, 2007 were as follows: (G-8 Summit, 2007: http://www.g-8.de/Webs/G8/EN/G8Summit/Agenda/agenda.html):

Heiligendamm Summit, June 6-8, 2007

Investment, Innovation, Sustainability

- World Economy
- Free Trade
- Protectionism
- Employment
- Global Imbalances
- Systematic Stability and Transparency of Financial Markets and Hedge Funds
- Freedom of Investment and Global Investment Conditions
- Innovation and Trademark Piracy
- Nuclear Energy
- Sustainable Resource Use and Climate Change

Africa: Good Governance, Sustainable Investment, Peace and Security

- Partnership for Reform
- Health and HIV/AIDS
- Official Development Assistance
- African Economic Development and Democratic Development
- African Outreach

Cooperation with Emerging Countries

Regional Issues

- Sudan
- North Korea
- Iran
- Middle East

Social Dimensions of Globalization

Russian Participation

Other Attendance
Physical Preparations
Notes
Earlier Versions

The following is the Text of G-8 Summit held at Heligendamm on 7 June, 2007 (http://www.g-8.de/Content/EN/Artikel/__g8-summit/anlagen/2007-06-07-gipfeldokument-wirtschaft-eng, property=publicationFile.pdf):

1. We have agreed on a policy agenda to promote a smooth adjustment of global imbalances which should take place in the context of sustained robust global economic growth. We have taken stock of the progress made to date and discussed further challenges lying ahead. Our agenda builds on discussions at the IMF and other international fora. Open markets and competition are crucial elements, as are our efforts to promote freedom of investment and the dynamics of innovation described hereafter.
2. We note that the world economy is in good condition and economic developments are now more conducive to an adjustment than in the past, not least because we have made progress in implementing our joint strategy. However, further efforts will be required to better rebalance global demand. Global imbalances took a long time to build. Likewise, their unwinding is likely to be a gradual process, entailing a medium-term rebalancing of demand growth across countries.
3. The economic environment has developed in a direction which favours the adjustment of global imbalances. Growth is now more balanced across regions, as it has moderated to a more sustainable pace in the US, while domestic demand has strengthened in Europe and remains supported by robust investment in Japan. We have made progress in implementing our joint policy strategy:
   - The United States has lent support to national savings by quickly and substantially reducing the federal budget deficit.
   - In Canada, domestic demand has been strong, supported by robust employment growth. Governments have significant ongoing budget surpluses.
   - In Europe, domestic demand has strengthened and the recent growth performance reflects prudent macroeconomic policies and a pay-off from structural reforms, including an improved labour market.
   - In Japan, as strenuous structural reform efforts continue, the upswing has proceeded and is becoming broader based. Fiscal consolidation is progressing, which is indispensable to reinforce confidence in the economy and to ensure sustainable, solid growth.
   - Russia has been enjoying seven consecutive years of robust economic

growth based on strong domestic consumption, a take-off in investment and a disciplined macroeconomic and financial management.

4. Outside of our group, a number of countries in emerging Asia have taken first steps on the road towards a more flexible exchange rate regime and a strengthening of the financial sector, a move which would support this adjustment. Oil producing countries have increased investment in oil production capacity and many have made prudent use of their additional export revenues to promote the diversification of their economies and employment. Their import growth has accelerated substantially.
5. Global imbalances have been showing some signs of stabilization more recently and deficits have been relatively easily financed. An orderly adjustment, which is in the interest of the world economy, will take time. We are committed to implementing domestic policies to promote this. They are first and foremost in each of our own best interests:
   - The United States is targeting the elimination of its federal budget deficit by 2012. Policies also have been proposed to strengthen long-term fiscal sustainability through entitlement and health care reform, tax incentives to promote private saving, and proposals have been made to boost the use of alternative fuels and enhance energy efficiency. The United States will continue to follow pro-growth economic policies.
   - Europe will continue its structural reform efforts guided by the Lisbon strategy to promote growth and employment.
   - Japan will continue its effort to enhance growth potential by implementing the comprehensive program for boosting productivity growth announced in this April. Fiscal reform will be steadily implemented to meet the targets committed by the government, namely achieving surplus in the primary balance of the combined central and local governments by 2011 as a first step for reducing the debt-to-GDP ratio in a stable manner by the mid-2010s.
   - Russia is committed to pursue a sound macroeconomic policy framework and prudent financial policies along with a range of structural reforms facilitating its transition to self-sustaining, investment- and innovation-led growth.
   - Canada is committed to continuing to reduce government debt and has set an objective of eliminating total government net debt in a generation. Canada is also committed to continuing to lower taxes on persons and business and to reducing regulatory burdens, as well as promoting knowledge creation and investing in infrastructure.
6. We encourage a contribution from the emerging market countries towards reducing imbalances. Continued reforms to rebalance growth

towards domestic demand, thus enhancing its sustainability, are a key to reducing imbalances while sustaining the robust global expansion. In emerging economies with large and growing current account surpluses, it is crucial that their effective exchange rates move so that necessary adjustments will occur. Oil-producing countries should continue accelerating investment in capacity and economic diversification.

Systematic Stability and Transparency of Financial Markets/Hedge Funds

7. We discussed recent developments in global financial markets, including hedge funds, which, along with the emergence of advanced financial techniques and products, such as credit derivatives, have contributed significantly to the efficiency of the financial system. Nevertheless, the assessment of potential systemic and operational risks associated with these activities has become more complex and challenging. Given the strong growth of the hedge fund industry and the increasing complexity of the instruments they trade, we reaffirm the need to be vigilant.
8. In this context, we welcome the Financial Stability Forum's (FSF) update of its 2000 Report on Highly Leveraged Institutions and support its recommendations. The global hedge fund industry should review and enhance existing sound practices benchmarks for hedge fund managers; in particular in the areas of risk management, valuations and disclosure to investors and counterparties in the light of expectations for improved practices set out by the official and private sectors. Counterparties and investors should act to strengthen the effectiveness of market discipline, including, by obtaining accurate and timely portfolio valuation and risk information. Supervisors should act so that core intermediaries continue to strengthen their counterparty risk management practices. In the exercise of their supervision of hedge funds counterparties, relevant authorities should monitor developments and cooperate among themselves. We welcome that the Financial Stability Forum (FSF) will report to finance ministers as from October of this year on the progress and actions taken in respect of these recommendations.

Freedom of Investment, Investment Environment and Social Responsibility

9. We recognize that the increase of cross-border direct investment is a major factor shaping the world's economy. Provided appropriate framework conditions are in place, such inflows make a major positive contribution to economic growth, social and environmental development. We note four areas for action in order to maximize the benefits from cross-border investment:
   - reinforcing our G8 commitment to the freedom of investment,

- promoting an open investment environment in industrialized countries and emerging economies,
- enabling greater benefits from and sustainability of foreign direct investments (FDI) for developing countries,
- promoting and strengthening corporate and other forms of social responsibility.

Freedom of Investment

10. We will work together to strengthen open and transparent investment regimes and to fight against tendencies to restrict them. Erecting barriers and supporting protectionism would result in a loss of prosperity. We therefore agree on the central role of free and open markets for the world economy, respecting sustainability concerns, and the need to maintain open markets to facilitate global capital movements. We reaffirm that freedom of investment is a crucial pillar of economic growth, prosperity and employment.

    We call on all developed countries, major emerging economies and others to critically assess their investment policies, the potential costs incurred from unnecessarily restrictive or arbitrary policies and the economic benefits of open investment regimes.
11. Against this background we remain committed to minimize any national restrictions on foreign investment. Such restrictions should apply to very limited cases which primarily concern national security. The general principles to be followed in such cases are non-discrimination, transparency and predictability. In any case, restrictive measures should not exceed the necessary scope, intensity and duration. Applicable treaties relating to investment remain unaffected. We encourage the OECD to continue its work on these issues, especially by identifying best practices and by further developing general principles. We will work with the OECD and other fora to develop further our common understanding of transparency principles for market-driven cross border investment of both private and state-owned enterprises.

The Global Investment Environment

12. Emerging economies benefit considerably from inward FDI while acting increasingly as countries of origin of FDI. We see the need and the opportunity to work towards a level playing field for all investors. Companies from G8 countries investing in emerging economies expect to find the same open investment environment as companies from such countries investing in G8 countries. Openness to investment is beneficial for all parties involved.
13. We underscore that market-driven technology transfer is an important globalization catalyst. Governments have a role in establishing and

maintaining the appropriate institutions and legal regulatory policy frameworks necessary to enable technology flows on a commercial basis and assuring the respect of intellectual property rights.

14. Open and transparent procurement markets are an important precondition for cross-border investments. We invite all our partners, in particular the major emerging economies, to create a level playing field for national and foreign tenderness. This may include considerations to join the WTO's Government Procurement Agreement (GPA).
15. We call on the emerging economies to adopt the OECD Declaration on International Investment and Multinational Enterprises. We invite the major emerging economies to participate in a structured High Level Dialogue on investment conditions in industrialized countries and emerging economies as part of the Heiligendamm Process. A stocktaking exercise, an examination of best practices and the implementation of peer review mechanisms to promote an open, efficient investment environment that aims to remove remaining barriers to investment should be a good start. We ask the OECD to provide a platform for such a dialogue.

Investment in Developing Countries

16. Unlike industrialized and emerging economies, many less advanced developing countries often reap only inadequate benefits from FDI. In shared responsibility with our developing country partners we want to enable quality FDI inflows to grow, inflows that help local infrastructure facilitate the operations of national and foreign investors that improve the skills of the local labour force and the advantages of transfers of management skills and technology that accrue from FDI increase, and that support the ability of domestic firms to supply inputs to foreign-invested companies or strengthen international value chains. Economic, social and environmental aspects of sustainability are crucial in order to maximize the FDI benefits for all developing countries, including least developed countries.
17. We support the regional and multilateral development banks (MDBs), including the International Finance Corporation (IFC) and the Multilateral Investment Guarantee Agency (MIGA), in addressing the problem of poor business environments in their borrowing members and urge them to integrate efforts to address these impediments to investment in their country strategies and budgets.
18. We support the initiative of G8 Finance Ministers to foster the development of deeper, more liquid local bond markets in emerging economies. This can make an important contribution to reducing the vulnerability of individual countries to crises and to enhancing the financial stability of emerging countries as a whole.
19. We support the OECD Policy Framework for Investment and UNCTAD Investment Policy Reviews as valuable mechanisms in defining a shared

understanding of healthy investment climates in emerging economies and developing countries. The OECD Policy Framework for Investment could be translated into national practices and development strategies, especially for countries under the New Partnership for African Development (NEPAD) and Asia-Pacific Economic Cooperation (APEC) framework. We invite the OECD, UNCTAD and other organizations such as the World Bank to consider providing the necessary support for this purpose.

20. We invite UNCTAD and the OECD to jointly engage industrialized countries, emerging economies and developing countries in the development of best practices for creating an institutional environment conducive to increased foreign investment and sustainable development. Such a comprehensive process should be closely connected with the twelfth UN Conference on Trade and Development (UNCTAD XII) planned for 20th to 25th April 2008 in Accra (Ghana).

Investment and Responsibility — The Social Dimension of Globalization

21. Globalization and technological progress have resulted in rapid structural change in many regions and economic sectors. We acknowledge that structural change is the inevitable result of progress and that it brings dislocations along with opportunities. Open markets rest on political acceptance, social inclusion, gender equality and the integration of traditionally under-represented groups such as older workers, youth, immigrants and persons with disabilities. In order to address the social dimension of the globalization process, we identify the four following areas of action.
22. Promoting and further developing social standards: We are convinced that a globalization that is complemented with social progress will bring sustainable benefits to both industrial and developing countries. We recognize our responsibility for an active contribution towards this objective. Therefore, we support the International Labour Organization's (ILO) Decent Work Agenda with its four pillars of equal importance: the effective implementation of labour standards, especially the ILO core labour standards, the creation of more productive employment, further development of inclusive social protection systems and the support of social dialogue between the different stakeholders.
23. While stressing that labour standards should not be used for protectionist purposes, we invite the WTO members and interested international organizations, in close collaboration with the ILO, to promote the observance of internationally recognized core labour standards as reflected in the ILO declaration on Fundamental Principles and Rights and its follow-up. We also commit to promoting decent work and respect for the fundamental principles in the ILO Declaration in bilateral trade agreements and multilateral fora.

24. Strengthening the principles of Corporate Social Responsibility: In this respect, we commit ourselves to promote actively internationally agreed corporate social responsibility and labour standards (such as the OECD Guidelines for Multinational Enterprises and the ILO Tripartite Declaration), high environmental standards and better governance through OECD Guidelines' National Contact Points. We call on private corporations and business organizations to adhere to the principles in the OECD Guidelines for Multinational Enterprises. We encourage the emerging economies as well as developing countries to associate themselves with the values and standards contained in these guidelines and we will invite major emerging economies to a High Level Dialogue on corporate social responsibility issues using the OECD as a platform.
25. We stress in particular the UN Global Compact as an important CSR initiative; we invite corporations from the G8 countries, emerging nations and developing countries to participate actively in the Global Compact and to support the worldwide dissemination of this initiative.
26. In order to strengthen the voluntary approach of CSR, we encourage the improvement of the transparency of private companies' performances with respect to CSR, and clarification of the numerous standards and principles issued in this area by many different public and private actors. We invite the companies listed on our Stock Markets to assess, in their annual reports, the way they comply with CSR standards and principles. We ask the OECD, in cooperation with the Global Compact and the ILO, to compile the most relevant CSR standards in order to give more visibility and more clarity to the various standards and principles.
27. Reinforcing Corporate Governance: Corporate governance is a key element in improving economic efficiency and growth as well as enhancing investor confidence. Good corporate governance provides proper incentives for the board and management to pursue objectives that are in the interests of the company and its shareholders and facilitates effective monitoring and surveillance. While corporate governance challenges are present everywhere, they are particularly acute in emerging economies. We encourage the widest adherence to the OECD Corporate Governance Principles and support the continuation of the work of the OECD/World Bank Regional Corporate Governance Roundtables.
28. Investing in social protection systems: Social protection is an investment in a country's economic future and a cost-effective way of fighting poverty. It includes appropriate protection against life's major risks and appropriate coverage for everyone, aiming at improved education and health. Social protection has the capacity to contribute to individual employability and to ensure that those who can work obtain adequate support to find employment and to obtain skills demanded by the labour market.

29. Social protection systems contain some universal elements and should be based on values such as social equity, fairness, and justice in order to promote equal opportunities and participation. We believe that social security systems require further development and extension of coverage taking into account nations' abilities to provide such coverage given their varying states of economic growth and recognizing the fact that there can be no one size fits all model of social protection. We agree to keep this issue on our development policy agenda, encouraging relevant international organizations to work in close cooperation on this issue. We recognize that in conjunction with economic growth and active labour market policies, social security is an instrument for sustainable social and economic development.

PROMOTING INNOVATION – PROTECTING INNOVATION

Promoting and Protecting Innovations

30. Science, research and innovation today more than ever form the basis of economic growth and prosperity. Political and economic strategies to foster innovation are therefore key elements for the future development of industrialized countries, emerging economies and developing countries alike. We will undertake to bring forward an international economic and political environment that promotes and protects innovation.

Innovation for Sustainable Growth

31. Forward looking innovation policy is geared towards promoting the research community and towards translating ideas, the product of the research process, into innovative products and services. Whereas the promotion of research involves education and higher-education policy, economic policy can play a crucial role in promoting the translation of research into innovative products and in fostering an innovation-friendly business environment. Both tasks benefit from the engagement of national governments. International cooperation and exchanges can supply a substantial impetus in the shaping of national policy. Cooperation between advanced and developing countries in research activities in the field of science and technology should also be strengthened.
32. Because we strive to provide scientific and technical leadership we also recognize our responsibility for a long-term oriented research initiative that will focus on concentration of scientific research and improved technological capacity in order to be able to react most effectively to future global challenges. We recognize the increasing significance of many emerging economies in science and research and invite them to actively participate in this process by reinforcing already existing cooperative efforts in the OECD building also on the results of ongoing work promoted inter alia by the relevant UN bodies.

33. In this respect we support the engagement of the OECD to work on proposals for topical international collaborative efforts. Based on the work of the Global Science Forum (GSF), we recognize the value that the GSF will bring as the moderator of this process. We also support the sharing of information among the G8 and emerging economies on national research endeavours in order to identify priorities that could be enhanced by collaborative research efforts, joint initiatives and programmes on areas of common interest. Possible areas of cooperation could be sustainable use of water and land and research in the field of energy efficiency as well as the promotion of environmentally-related innovations both in the public and in the business sector. We will work together to achieve more effective coordination and cooperation in our research efforts in these fields.

Intellectual Property Protection as the Backbone of Innovation

34. A fully functioning intellectual property system is an essential factor for the sustainable development of the global economy through promoting innovation. We recognize the importance of streamlining and harmonizing the international patent system in order to improve the acquisition and protection of patent rights worldwide.
35. The benefits of innovation for economic growth and development are increasingly threatened by infringements of intellectual property rights worldwide. We therefore strongly reaffirm our commitment to combat piracy and counterfeiting. Trade in pirated and counterfeit goods threatens health, safety and security of consumers worldwide, particularly in poorer countries. In this regard we welcome work on the WHO initiative to implement the International Medicinal Products Anti-Counterfeit Taskforce (IMPACT). Our common efforts in this combat are therefore in the interest of all countries at all levels of development.
36. We commit to strengthen cooperation in this critical area among the G8 and other countries, particularly the major emerging economies, as well as competent international organizations, notably the World Intellectual Property Organization (WIPO), WTO, the World Customs Organization (WCO), Interpol, the World Health Organization (WHO), the OECD, APEC, and the Council of Europe. We invite these organizations to reinforce their action in this field.
37. We welcome the joint Declaration of the business communities of all G8 countries on "Strategies of G8 Industry and Business to Promote Intellectual Property Protection and to Prevent Counterfeiting and Piracy" which highlights actions companies are taking to secure their intellectual property rights at home and abroad and to keep their global supply chains free of pirated and counterfeit goods – from producers and distributors, retailers and merchandisers. Industry and business have an

essential role to play in protecting innovation, and we will engage our respective private sectors on effective solutions with regard to both the supply and the demand side of piracy and counterfeiting. We also welcome educational campaigns with the help of business communities in our countries directed at raising awareness of consumers with regards to the negative effects of counterfeiting and piracy.

38. In light of the urgency to implement concrete measures which will improve and deepen cooperation among G8 partners and deliver real enforcement results, we decide to undertake the following:
    (a) We endorse the Guidelines for Customs and Border Enforcement Cooperation designed to strengthen cooperation and coordination among our national customs and law enforcement administrations. In this context we especially welcome the development of an effective information exchange system – where appropriate - in close association with the WCO which will lead to improved cooperation among the relevant enforcement authorities worldwide.
    (b) We endorse new Guidelines for Technical Assistance on intellectual property rights protection to interested developing countries, as well as a mechanism to better coordinate and leverage existing G8 assistance to such countries with a view to building the capacity necessary to combat trade in counterfeited and pirated goods to strengthen intellectual property enforcement. In partnership with certain developing countries we agree to launch technical assistance pilot plans with a view to building the capacity necessary to combat trade in counterfeited and pirated goods to strengthen intellectual property enforcement. The progress on these pilot plans will be reviewed by the G8 in 2008.
    (c) We endorse the recommendations aimed at improving G8 member countries cooperative actions to combat serious and organized intellectual property rights crimes and the further work on their basis to facilitate structured international cooperation regarding the investigation and prosecution of those crimes.
    (d) While appreciating the information contained in the OECD report estimating the economic impacts of counterfeiting and piracy on national economies and right holders, as well as public health and safety, we will encourage the OECD to work with member states to further identify and target in its report specific areas for concrete actions.
    (e) We recognize the need for continued study by national experts of the possibilities of strengthening the international legal framework pertaining to IPR enforcement.
    (f) We consider the establishment of an IPR Task Force focusing on anti-counterfeiting and piracy to look together at how best to improve the working of the international IPR protection and

enforcement, and produce recommendations for action including improved peer review. The issue will also be considered in the Heiligendamm Process.

A New Dialogue on Innovation and Intellectual Property Protection

39. Lively interaction between science and business, strong protection and enforcement of intellectual property rights, and the combination of market-based entrepreneurship and science-based research are increasingly decisive factors in promoting economic growth and development around the world. We invite the major emerging economies to a follow up process using the OECD as a platform with the aim of establishing a new international dialogue on innovation and intellectual property protection as part of the Heiligendamm Process. Such a dialogue will provide a forum for the positive exchange on topics critical for growth of successful knowledge economies and the promotion of an innovation-friendly business environment also taking into account the needs of small and medium sized enterprises, including: (a) the crucial role and economic value of intellectual property protection and implementation as a central framework condition for the development of a future-oriented economy based on technological progress and innovation; (b) effective market incentives for innovation and the diffusion of knowledge at the national level taking into account recent developments in technology markets; and (c) the crucial importance of efficient innovation value chains that promote business commercialization of patented research results and exploit licensing as a major driver for the international transfer of technology. The dialogue could furthermore ascertain measures the industrialized countries and major emerging economies can take to achieve fully effective implementation and protection of intellectual property rights within their own territory. Fully respecting the mandate, function and role of the competent multilateral organizations, in particular the WTO and the WIPO, participants in the dialogue may also discuss initiatives aimed at strengthening intellectual property rights protection which should then be addressed in the appropriate international fora. The G8 Summit 2009 will take stock of the progress made by that date.

Climate Change, Energy Efficiency and Energy Security

40. Humanity today faces the key interlinked challenges of avoiding dangerous climate change and ensuring secure and stable supplies of energy. Since we met in Gleneagles, science has more clearly demonstrated that climate change is a long-term challenge that has the potential to seriously damage our natural environment and the global economy. We firmly agree that resolute and concerted international action is urgently needed in order

to reduce global greenhouse gas emissions and increase energy security. Tackling climate change is a shared responsibility of all, and can and must be undertaken in a way that supports growth in developing, emerging and industrialized economies, while avoiding economic distortions.

41. We recognize the important opportunities offered by effective action addressing climate change, in particular for innovation, technological development as well as poverty reduction. Strong economies together with a wide range of policy instruments such as market-based mechanisms, including emissions-trading, tax incentives, and regulatory measures as well as technology cooperation and a shared long-term vision, are key to guide investment decisions, to generate technology commercialization, to enhance energy security, to promote sustainable development and to slow, stabilize and then significantly cut global emissions of greenhouse gases.
42. We are committed to take strong leadership in combating climate change. We confirm our determination to work among ourselves and with the global community on global solutions that address climate change while supporting growth and economic development. We commit ourselves to implement approaches which optimally combine effective climate protection with energy security. To this end, we are committed to the further development of the international regime to combat climate change, especially in the run-up to the UN Climate Change Conference in Indonesia at the end of this year. Addressing climate change is a long-term issue that will require global participation and a diversity of approaches to take into account differing circumstances.
43. Energy is a fundamental driver of growth and development around the world, and the use of energy has been steadily expanding along with the world's populations and economies. Our ability to provide secure access to clean, affordable and safe sources of energy to maintain global economic growth complements our desire to protect our environment. Addressing the challenge of energy security will require unprecedented international cooperation in several areas, including market transparency, enhancing energy efficiency, diversifying energy supplies and developing and deploying new and transformational technologies.
44. Energy has been a major field of action for the G8, not least in recent years. We recall that after focusing on resource efficiency in a broader sense (in particular the 3R Initiative) following the Evian and Sea Island Summits, the Gleneagles G8-Action Plan dealt intensively with clean energy. At the St. Petersburg Summit we adopted groundbreaking decisions on energy security and committed ourselves to a set of agreed areas of cooperation, inter alia to increase transparency, predictability and stability of global energy markets, improving investment climate in the energy sector, enhance energy efficiency, diversify the energy mix,

ensure the security of critical energy infrastructure, reduce energy poverty and address climate change. To maintain the momentum of those achievements we herewith strongly reaffirm our commitment to Global Energy Security Principles, including our commitment to enhance dialogue on relevant shareholders' perspectives on growing interdependence, security of supply and demand issues, facilitate diversification of different types of contracts, including market-based long-term and spot contracts, promote investment in upstream and downstream assets internationally, support the principles of the Energy Charter and the efforts of the participating countries to improve international energy co-operation.

45. To maintain the momentum of that groundbreaking achievement, we invite China, Brazil, India, Mexico and South Africa and other major emerging economies to adopt these Global Energy Security Principles, will prepare national reports, with the assistance of the IEA, evaluating G8 member states' efforts to adhere to those principles, for delivery at the 2008 G8 summit, and note the importance of government-controlled strategic oil reserves, to lessen the impact of sudden and severe natural or man-made disruptions to oil supplies, and encourage the IEA to further assist major emerging oil consuming countries to adopt best practices with regard to building, maintaining and coordination the release of strategic oil reserves.
46. This year we have focused our discussions on energy efficiency in order to make an effective contribution towards meeting global climate and energy security challenges. Improving energy efficiency worldwide is the fastest, the most sustainable and the cheapest way to reduce greenhouse gas emissions and enhance energy security.
47. We welcome the progress made so far at the meetings of the Gleneagles Dialogue on Climate Change, Clean Energy and Sustainable Development, held in the United Kingdom in 2005 and Mexico in 2006. We also welcome the intentions of Germany and Japan to host the Dialogue meetings during their G8 Presidencies. We look forward to receiving a report of the Dialogue at the G8 Summit next year under the Japanese G8 Presidency.

Climate Change

48. We take note of and are concerned about the recent UN Intergovernmental Panel on Climate Change (IPCC) reports. The most recent report concluded both, that global temperatures are rising, that this is caused largely by human activities and, in addition, that for increases in global average temperature, there are projected to be major changes in ecosystem structure and function with predominantly negative consequences for biodiversity and ecosystems, e.g. water and food supply.

Fighting Climate Change

49. We are therefore committed to taking strong and early action to tackle climate change in order to stabilize greenhouse gas concentrations at a level that would prevent dangerous anthropogenic interference with the climate system. Taking into account the scientific knowledge as represented in the recent IPCC reports, global greenhouse gas emissions must stop rising, followed by substantial global emission reductions. In setting a global goal for emissions reductions in the process we have agreed today involving all major emitters; we will consider seriously the decisions made by the European Union, Canada and Japan which include at least a halving of global emissions by 2050. We commit to achieving these goals and invite the major emerging economies to join us in this endeavour.
50. As climate change is a global problem, the response to it needs to be international. We welcome the wide range of existing activities both in industrialized and developing countries. We share a long-term vision and agree on the need for frameworks that will accelerate action over the next decade. Complementary national, regional and global policy frameworks that co-ordinate rather than compete with each other will strengthen the effectiveness of the measures. Such frameworks must address not only climate change but also energy security, economic growth, and sustainable development objectives in an integrated approach. They will provide important orientation for the necessary future investment decisions.
51. We stress that further action should be based on the UNFCCC principle of common but differentiated responsibilities and respective capabilities. We reaffirm, as G8 leaders, our responsibility to act. We acknowledge the continuing leadership role that developed economies have to play in any future climate change efforts to reduce global emissions, so that all countries undertake effective climate commitments tailored to their particular situations. We recognize, however, that the efforts of developed economies will not be sufficient and that new approaches for contributions by other countries are needed. Against this background, we invite notably the emerging economies to address the increase in their emissions by reducing the carbon intensity of their economic development.

    Action of emerging economies could take several forms, such as sustainable development policies and measures, an improved and strengthened clean development mechanism, the setting up of plans for the sectors that generate most pollution so as to reduce their greenhouse gas emissions compared with a business as usual scenario.
52. We acknowledge that the UN climate process is the appropriate forum for negotiating future global action on climate change. We are committed

to moving forward in that forum and call on all parties to actively and constructively participate in the UN Climate Change Conference in Indonesia in December 2007 with a view to achieving a comprehensive post 2012-agreement (post Kyoto-agreement) that should include all major emitters.

53. To address the urgent challenge of climate change, it is vital that major economies that use the most energy and generate the majority of greenhouse gas emissions agree on a detailed contribution for a new global framework by the end of 2008 which would contribute to a global agreement under the UNFCCC by 2009. We therefore reiterate the need to engage major emitting economies on how best to address the challenge of climate change. We embrace efforts to work with these countries on long-term strategies. To this end, our representatives have already met with the representatives of Brazil, China, India, Mexico and South Africa in Berlin on 4 May 2007. We will continue to meet with high representatives of these and other major energy consuming and greenhouse gas emitting countries to consider the necessary components for successfully combating climate change. We welcome the offer of the United States to host such a meeting later this year. This major emitters' process should include, inter alia, national, regional and international policies, targets and plans, in line with national circumstances, an ambitious work program within the UNFCCC, and the development and deployment of climate-friendly technology. This dialogue will support the UN climate process and report back to the UNFCCC.

Technology

54. Technology is a key to mastering climate change as well as enhancing energy security. We have urgently to develop, deploy and foster the use of sustainable, less carbon intensive, clean energy and climate-friendly technologies in all areas of energy production and use. We have to develop and create supportive market conditions for accelerating commercialization of new less carbon intensive, clean-energy and climate-friendly technologies. Furthermore, to ensure sustainable investment decisions worldwide, we need an expanded approach to collaboratively accelerate the widespread adoption of clean-energy and climate-friendly technologies in emerging and developing economies.

    Therefore, we will:

    - stimulate global development, commercialization, deployment and access to technologies;
    - promote major emerging and developing economies' participation in international technology partnerships and collaborations;

- scale up national, regional and international research and innovation activities; and
- undertake strategic planning and develop technology roadmaps to strengthen the role of advanced technology in addressing climate change.

Market Mechanisms

55. Private sector investment is and will remain the primary means of technology deployment and diffusion. Strong economies and a wide range of policy instruments are required to develop, deploy and foster climate-friendly technologies. Market mechanisms, such as emissions-trading within and between countries, tax incentives, performance-based regulation, fees or taxes, and consumer labelling can provide pricing signals and have the potential to deliver economic incentives to the private sector. Fostering the use of clean technologies, setting up emissions-trading systems and, as many of us are doing, linking them are complementary and mutually reinforcing approaches.

    Therefore, we will share experience on the effectiveness of the different policy instruments in order to:

    - better provide the international business community with a predictable and long-term perspective, and
    - strengthen and extend market mechanisms by, inter alia, developing and extending existing programmes, taking into account the appropriate metrics for such systems.

Reducing Emissions by Curbing Deforestation

56. We are determined to assist in reducing emissions from deforestation, especially in developing countries. Reducing, and in the long term halting deforestation provides a significant and cost-effective contribution toward mitigating greenhouse gas emissions and toward conserving biological diversity, promoting sustainable forest management and enhancing security of livelihoods. To this end, we will:

    - encourage the establishment of a pilot project dedicated to building capacity, creating and testing performance-based instruments to reduce emissions from deforestation in developing countries, in support of and without prejudice to ongoing UN climate change discussions. We therefore encourage the World Bank, in close cooperation with the G8, developing countries, the private sector, NGOs and other partners, to develop and implement such a forest carbon partnership as soon as possible;
    - continue to support existing processes to combat illegal logging. Illegal logging is one of the most difficult obstacles to further progress in realizing sustainable forest management and thereof, in protecting forests worldwide;

- remain engaged in supporting developing countries to achieve their self commitments for halting forest loss and to implement sustainable forest management, as stated in various regional initiatives, i.e. the Congo Basin and the Asia Forest Partnerships. Good results and good practice in international cooperation have also been achieved through ITTO projects and the Brazilian Pilot Program to conserve the tropical rain forests.

57. At the St. Petersburg Summit, we agreed to enhance international co-operation in the area of sustainable forest management. We welcome the recent agreement at the UN Forum on Forests on a non-legally binding instrument on the sustainable management of all types of forests. We note that the effectiveness of this instrument will be reviewed by the UN Forum on Forests in 2015. Building on these initiatives, we are determined and urge the international community to strengthen co-operation and the sharing of best practices at all levels. Consideration of additional actions on sustainable forest management could be a possible next step for parties willing to expand on their commitments.

Adapting to Climate Change

58. We acknowledge that even implementing the ambitious mitigation steps described above will not avoid further climate impacts, especially in those developing countries and regions which are most vulnerable to climate change. We are committed to enhancing resiliency to climate variability and climate change in a way that fully supports our common goal of sustainable development. We welcome the adoption of the Nairobi work programme on impacts, vulnerability, and adaptation to climate change. We also note the importance of the UN adaptation funds in helping developing countries mainstream adaptation into policies and programming. We emphasize our willingness to continue and enhance cooperation with and support for developing countries in adapting to climate change and enhancing their resilience to climate variability, in particular those most vulnerable to the negative impacts of climate change. We also emphasize our willingness to work with developing countries on the costs and benefits of climate change adaptation measures to help integrating them in national development planning. We reaffirm our commitment to assist with climate research and risk assessments including through helping developing countries benefit from satellite observation systems.

59. We will also endeavour under the Montreal Protocol to ensure the recovery of the ozone layer by accelerating the phase-out of HCFCs in a way that supports energy efficiency and climate change objectives. In working together toward our shared goal of speeding ozone recovery, we recognize that the Clean Development Mechanism impacts emissions

of ozone-depleting substances. We will continue to exercise leadership in the development of the Global Earth Observation System of Systems (GEOSS).

60. We will report on the progress achieved in the areas mentioned above at the G8 Summit in 2008.

Biodiversity

61. We emphasize the crucial importance of the conservation and the sustainable use of biodiversity as an indispensable basis for the provision of vital ecosystem services and the long-term provision of natural resources for the global economy. We acknowledge the "Potsdam Initiative – Biological Diversity 2010" presented at the G8 Environmental Ministerial meeting in March 2007 and will increase our efforts for the protection and sustainable use of biological diversity to achieve our agreed goal of significantly reducing the rate of loss of biodiversity by 2010.

Energy Efficiency

62. The global potential for saving energy is huge. According to the International Energy Agency, successfully implemented energy efficiency policies could contribute to 80% of avoided greenhouse gases while substantially increasing security of supply.

63. We recognize that enhanced international cooperation offers enormous opportunities. Against this background we are committed to further strengthening and increasing our efforts of co-operation, both at inter-state level as well as within the framework of the respective international fora and organizations.
To this end, we will:
    - continue and further substantiate our energy-efficiency dialogue begun at Evian;
    - move forward with implementing the Gleneagles and St. Petersburg Action Plans, thereby retaining and supporting the IEA's close involvement;
    - take forward the concrete recommendations on energy efficiency presented by the IEA and consider drawing on these when preparing national energy efficiency plans;
    - encourage the World Bank and other IFIs to further broaden and improve their financial framework for energy efficiency and clean energy;
    - note the EU's proposal for an international agreement on energy efficiency and ask the Gleneagles Dialogue on Climate Change, Clean Energy and Sustainable Development and the IEA to explore the most effective means to promote energy efficiency internationally, including through the exchange of best practices, sharing

methodologies and further cooperation and by inviting other countries with significant energy needs to join;

- promote international research, encourage investment and development cooperation aimed at energy efficient technologies and other greenhouse gas mitigation options;
- report on progress in the policies and measures on energy efficiency outlined below at the G8 summit in 2008.

64. We note that, in view of their high energy needs, industrialized and emerging economies have a fundamental joint interest in taking measures to encourage the most effective use of their energy.
65. Against this background we commit ourselves to a model of efficient energy systems and call on other countries with high energy demand, including the major emerging economies, to join us in this endeavour. Our goal of building less energy intensive economies will also advance economic growth and competitiveness. To this end, we will promote the appropriate policy approaches and instruments, including inter alia economic incentives and sound fiscal policies, minimum standards for energy efficiency, sound and ambitious energy performance labelling, information campaigns aimed at consumers and industry that enhance national awareness, sector-based voluntary commitments agreed with industry, investment in research and development and guidelines for public procurement. We will develop and implement national energy efficiency programmes and advance international cooperation on energy efficiency, notably on efficiency standards. We ask the IEA to continue to support our national efforts by appropriate advice and make proposals for effective international co-operation.
66. We will furthermore work together with the major emerging economies towards a reduction in energy consumption in priority sectors. To this end we will invite the IEA, its members and their respective industries to increase the dialogue with the major emerging economies on more efficient energy policies and develop guidance mechanisms.

Sustainable Buildings Network

67. The opportunities for making buildings more efficient are enormous. Following the EU/G8 conference on energy efficiency, held in Berlin in April 2007, we will:
    - set up a "Sustainable Buildings Network", involving the G8 and open for participation of the major emerging economies. The network will develop practical instruments for assessing and advising on the implementation of energy efficiency in buildings and the use of renewable energies, especially for cooling and heating, taking into due consideration the different situations of new and existing buildings, and development and deployment of low and zero-carbon buildings.

- invite the IEA to take a central role in creating this network,
- work to increase energy efficiency in the building sector and to reach a considerable expansion of renewable energies in this area. To this end we will consider the role of nationally determined targets in sustainable buildings and their importance for energy efficiency in the medium to long term. We will actively support the energy efficient technologies and the use of renewable energies by employing market mechanisms, promotion instruments and framework legislation, as well as through public-private-partnership initiatives to move towards low or zero-energy buildings. Instruments to this end include consumer information such as energy performance certificates ("building passports") and individual energy standards — which also consider renewable energies — for new buildings, modernization or household equipment.

Transportation

68. Today there are 600 million motor vehicles around the globe, a figure which is projected to double by 2020. With this in mind, we will:
    - work to increase energy efficiency in the transport sector. To this end we will ask our governments to foster a large number of possible measures and various instruments that can clearly reduce energy demand and CO_2 emissions in the transport sector, including inter alia innovative engine concepts, alternative fuels, city planning measures, public transport, best possible inter-linkage of transport methods, increase the share of alternative fuels and energy carriers (biofuels, hydrogen, LPG/CNG, electricity, hybrid, etc.) in total fuel consumption; fuel diversification, for example synthetic and cellulosic biofuels and CO_2-free hydrogen, particularly in combination with the fuel cell, will be decisive in reducing transport CO_2 emissions, provided that second generation biofuel technologies become commercially available,
    - step up coordination on development of international biofuel quality standards from various feed stocks to achieve optimal interoperability and emission profiles, avoid possible negative side-effects in biofuel development, particularly in developing countries in order to prevent competition between different forms of land uses, and promote sustainability in biomass cultivation. We invite the Global Bioenergy Partnership (GBEP) to continue its work on biofuel best practices and take forward the successful and sustainable development of bio-energy,
    - monitor the implementation of the necessary measures and discuss progress at two-year intervals during the Environmentally Friendly Vehicles Conference the results of which shall be reported to G8-leaders,

- introduce energy efficiency labels for new cars along the lines of those already on some white goods.

Power Generation

69. Over the next 25 years, fossil fuels will remain the world's dominant source of energy. Making power generation more efficient, climate friendly and sustainable is therefore crucial.
70. Current innovations in power station design bear significant saving potential. Therefore, we will:
    - stimulate investments in high efficient power plants and grids and promote refurbishment of existing ones by an appropriate national policy framework. By this we aim to increase average power plant efficiencies in each of our countries,
    - continue and expand national and international research and development efforts to further advance modern power station technologies, with the aim of achieving higher efficiency levels,
    - adopt instruments and measures to significantly increase the share of combined heat and power (CHP) in the generation of electricity.
71. The centre of gravity of global energy demand is continuously shifting towards the emerging economies. We will:
    - enhance energy co-operation with those countries as a priority issue, including by actively supporting co-operative research, voluntary technology partnerships and private investment in clean technologies,
    - work in close partnership with industry, science and with governments of other industrialized countries and, in particular, of major emerging economies in order to foster the diffusion and adoption of best practices along the entire fossil fuel process chain with a focus on fuel treatment as well as new and existing power plants. We particularly underline the need to promote capacity building and technology transfer on plant renovation and modernization. To achieve these goals we will invite the IEA to take a central role in guiding our joint efforts.
72. In recognition of the increasingly urgent needs to achieve longer term greenhouse gas abatement, we will work on accelerating development and deployment of carbon capture and storage (CCS), including by
    - prioritizing national and international research and development efforts and encouraging international research and technology cooperation, to minimize efficiency losses of the different carbon capture technologies and to clarify geotechnical conditions for secure CO_2 storage,
    - encourage research, development and deployment of clean coal technologies in both developed and emerging economies with the highest energy needs,

- supporting national and international geo-scientific and political efforts in the field of CCS on ensuring security of storage and the provision of necessary legal frameworks to create a stable investment climate, thereby working in cooperation with industry as well as national and international research programmes,
- reinforcing our commitment made under the Gleneagles and St. Petersburg Plans of Action to support the initiatives taken by IEA and Carbon Sequestration Leadership Forum (CSLF), encouraging our governments to design mechanisms to stimulate the construction and operation of a growing number of large-scale demonstrations of sustainable fossil fuels technologies in commercial power generation,
- encouraging industry to consider the concept of capture ready when developing new fossil fuel power plant.

73. We reaffirm our support of the efforts of the Global Gas Flaring Reduction Partnership (GGFR) and we commit ourselves to reduce to minimal levels natural gas flaring, and to encourage all oil producing states and private sector stakeholders to do likewise.

Industry

74. Over the next 25 years, global energy consumption in the industrial sector is projected to increase significantly. There is a considerable potential for improving energy efficiency. Therefore, we will:
    - cooperate more closely with major emerging economies and leading industries on improving energy efficiency in energy intensive industries utilizing on-going work of the IEA for developing sector energy efficiency indicators and combining good practices,
    - encourage the introduction of cost-effective technology as well as promote research and development for further innovation for breakthrough of the technology in such areas as iron, steel and cement.

Energy Diversification

75. Diversification of energy sources, markets, transportation routes and means of transport and types of energy is essential to energy security and to a low-carbon energy path. Increasing and varying our sources of energy helps to defuse the risks of disruption from any one source. Increasing the use of alternative sources of energy can over time greatly relieve pressure on markets for conventional fossil fuels and reduce the adverse environmental impacts of energy use.
76. Underlining the importance of energy diversification, and recognizing that G8 members will choose different ways to achieve their energy diversity goals, we

- will continue to develop and implement the policy frameworks needed to support our intensive commitment to the global use of all clean fuels, including clean coal, renewable energy sources (wind, solar, geothermal, bio-energy, hydro power). We will make efforts to integrate renewable into the power grid,
- reaffirm our pledge at former summits regarding the peaceful use of nuclear energy. Those of us who have or are considering plans relating to the use and/or development of safe and secure nuclear energy believe that its development will contribute to global energy security, while simultaneously reducing harmful air pollution and addressing the climate change challenge,
- reaffirm our commitment to work towards the reduction or, where appropriate, the elimination of tariff and non-tariff barriers to environmental goods and services through the WTO Doha negotiations, which will also help us to address our shared energy security and climate goals,
- welcome concerted global action to promote renewable energy and the support of interested parties for initiatives and partnerships such as the Renewable Energy Policy Network for the 21st Century (REN21), the Renewable Energy and Energy Efficiency Program (REEEP), the Global Bio-Energy Partnership (GBEP) and the Mediterranean Renewable Energy Partnership (MEDREP),
- take note of national and international initiatives to go along with the further development of a peaceful use of nuclear energy including the Global Nuclear Energy Partnership (GNEP), the Russian initiative on multinational centres to provide nuclear fuel cycle services, the Six party proposal of a standing mechanism for reliable access to nuclear Fuel, the Japanese initiative on IAEA standby arrangements system for the assurance of nuclear fuel supply, and the German initiative for an enrichment centre under the exclusive control of the IAEA as well as ongoing debate on other multilateral approaches to a nuclear fuel cycle for a reliable fuel supply program, the work of the International Project on Innovative Nuclear Reactors and Fuel Cycles (INPRO), and advanced nuclear energy research under the Generation IV International Forum (GIF).

77. We are committed to the paramount importance of safety, security and non-proliferation in using nuclear power. We reiterate common interest to continuously improve nuclear safety, radiation protection, waste management, nuclear security and nuclear liability in our respective countries, and we call upon all other states to do the same. IAEA standards and recommendations form a good basis for the continuous improvement of nuclear safety and security, as well as national nuclear regulatory systems. We underline the need for effective national

regulatory infrastructures, in particular the importance for national regulatory body to have sufficient authority, independence, and competence.

We remain committed to a robust regime for assuring nuclear non-proliferation as well as a reliable safety and security system for nuclear materials, radioactive wastes and nuclear facilities. We ensure full implementation of the international conventions and treaties in force today which are a prerequisite for a high level of nuclear safety and security as well as a basis to achieve a peaceful and proliferation-resistant nuclear energy use. The responsibility of all nations to support the work of the IAEA and all measures to implement these conventions and treaties in these fields is emphasized.

78. Considering the above mentioned challenges, the G8 Nuclear Safety and Security Group (NSSG) will continue in its work to consider nuclear safety and security issues.

79. In recognition of the Chernobyl accident in 1986 we reaffirm our commitments – under former G7/G8 Summit declarations and memoranda of understanding and through Chernobyl Shelter Funds (CSF) and Nuclear Safety Account (NSA) programmes – to undertake joint efforts with Ukraine to convert the damaged reactor unit site into safe conditions.

Responsibility of Raw Materials for Sustained Growth

80. Raw materials produced by the extractive sector are a key factor for sustainable growth in industrialized, emerging and developing economies. They are a particularly valuable asset for sustaining growth and reducing poverty in many of the poorest countries in the world. It is in our common global interest that resource wealth be used responsibly so as to help reduce poverty, prevent conflicts and improve the sustainability of resource production and supply. We firmly agree that significant and lasting progress in this area can only be achieved on the basis of transparency and good governance. Against this background, we support increased transparency with regard both to the extractive sector and the subsequent trade and financial flows. In doing so, we will work closely together with resource rich economies as well as important raw-material consuming emerging economies.

81. Free, transparent and open markets are fundamental to global growth, stability and sustainable development. We, therefore,
   - reaffirm our strong commitment to the principles of free trade and to a further strengthening of the multilateral trading system,
   - will work to promote global applicability of and compliance with WTO rules, also with regard to trade in primary and secondary mineral raw materials,

- call on our trading partners to refrain from restraints on trade and distortion of competition in contravention of WTO rules and to observe market economy principles.

82. Mineral resources have a great potential to contribute to poverty alleviation and sustainable development. In some cases, nonetheless, extraction and processing of resources are associated with misuse of revenues, environmental destruction, armed conflict and state fragility. We firmly agree on the need to further enhancing the contribution of mineral resources to sustainable growth and will continue to support resource rich countries in their efforts to further expand their resource potential while promoting sustainable development and good governance. To this end we will build capacity for good governance of mineral resources consistent with social and environmental standards and sound commercial practices by reducing barriers to investment and trade, through the provision of financial, technical and capacity building support to developing countries for the mining, processing and trading of minerals. Based on sound life cycle analyses, we will also encourage conservation, recycling and substitution of raw materials, including rare metals, for sustainable growth.
83. Increased transparency in the extractive sector is of crucial importance for achieving accountability, good governance and sustainable economic growth worldwide. We welcome the proposal of the G8-Presidency to convene in 2007 a global conference on transparency in the extractive sector with the participation of governments, business, civil society and science from industrialized, emerging and developing economies.
84. The development of a consolidated set of principles and guidelines that apply to the international mining sector in developing countries would help ensure that the sector contributes to development while at the same time providing a clear and more predictable set of expectations for investors. It is important that all stakeholders be involved in a process to build consensus around a set of recognized principles and guidelines in the mining sector. In order to encourage such a consensus among key stakeholders we:
    - reaffirm our support of the OECD Guidelines for Multinational Enterprises as important international benchmark for corporate social responsibility, will promote wider understanding of and support for the following standards, tools and best practices for the mining sector: the OECD Risk Awareness Tool for Multinational Enterprises in Weak Governance Zones, the Voluntary Principles on Security and Human Rights and the International Finance Corporation (IFC) Performance Standards,
    - encourage active engagement of mining sector companies with the UN Global Compact, encourage mining sector companies to undertake regular reporting using inter alia the Global Reporting

Initiative (GRI) framework, and welcome the adaptation of this instrument for small and medium enterprises as well as to the specific needs of the mining sector,
- will support the work of the UN Special Representative of the Secretary General for Business and Human Rights.

85. Certification systems can be a suitable instrument in appropriate cases for increasing transparency and good governance in the extraction and processing of mineral raw materials and to reduce environmental impacts, support the compliance with minimum social standards and resolutely counter illegal resource extraction. Therefore, we reaffirm our support for existing initiatives such as the Kimberley Process, Green Lead, the Intergovernmental Forum on Mining, Minerals, Metals and Sustainable Development, the International Council on Mining and Metals or the International Cyanide Management Code, and encourage the adaptation of the respective principles of corporate social responsibility by those involved in the extraction and processing of mineral resources.

86. The artisan and small-scale mining sector provides important livelihoods to many people in developing countries, and also contributes to global production of minerals. We are concerned that these activities often are conducted in an informal manner and do not meet minimum social and environmental standards which apply to the extractive sector. In order to better support the development of sustainable livelihoods and positive developmental impacts associated with artisan and small-scale mineral production, we
    - encourage collaborative partnerships between public, civil society and private actors in the mining sector in order to develop systems for the transparent use of funds for local development from mining companies and donors, consistent with aid effectiveness principles,
    - support a pilot study, in co-operation with the World Bank and its initiatives, concerning the feasibility of a designed certification system for selected raw materials. In taking this initiative we will focus on the artisan and small-scale mining sector and work in close partnership with governments from mineral resource rich developing countries as well as industry on the basis of their voluntary commitments. The pilot study shall strive on the basis of the existing principles and guidelines, in order to comply with internationally recognized minimum standards by verifying the process of mineral resource extraction and trading. We invite major emerging economies to work with us on this issue,
    - encourage support for the Communities and Small-scale Mining (CASM) initiative, housed at the World Bank, and for the multi-stakeholder Diamond Development Initiative (DDI), which emerged from the Kimberley Process to strengthen the developmental impacts associated with artisan diamond mining in Africa,

- support efforts to develop techniques to limit pollution associated with artisan mining, such as education and training to encourage the use for example of safer retorts for gold extraction.

The Heiligendamm Process with Major Emerging Economies

87. At the Heiligendamm Summit we discussed with the leaders of Brazil, China, India, Mexico and South Africa the major challenges that have arisen in the world economy. Neither the G8 countries nor major emerging economies will be able to cope with these challenges individually. Against the background of our respective responsibilities, common solutions need to be developed. Both the G8 countries and the major emerging economies have the chance to define a new partnership responding to these world economic challenges.
88. Building on our discussions, we decided to launch a new form of specific cooperation with major emerging economies in order to discuss substantive topics in a comprehensive follow-up process with the aim of reaching tangible results in two years.
89. We will initiate a new form of a topic-driven Dialogue in a structured manner based on this new partnership. We agreed to address four issues:
    - Promoting and protecting innovation,
    - Enhancing freedom of investment through an open investment environment including strengthening corporate social responsibility principles,
    - Defining common responsibilities for development with special regard to Africa,
    - Sharing knowledge for improving energy efficiency and technology cooperation with the aim to contribute to reducing CO_2-emissions, consistent with the Gleneagles Dialogue on Climate Change, Clean Energy and Sustainable Development, and the St. Petersburg Plan of Action on Global Energy Security.
90. We ask the OECD to provide a platform for this new dialogue process, with the IEA being the relevant organization in the field of energy efficiency. The dialogue process will begin in the second half of 2007. The G8 Summit in Japan in 2008 will receive an interim report on the progress made and at the G8 Summit in Italy in 2009 a final report on the outcomes of the Dialogue Process will be presented.

Energy's Role in Economic Growth and Job Creation

The energy and power sector creates and sustains millions of jobs—and the potential for good-paying jobs in the future is great. According to the Bureau of Labor Statistics, the gross domestic product (GDP) of the energy industry itself (including electric and gas utilities, nuclear power generation, mining, and oil and gas extraction) was $ 352 billion in 2003, a 3.2% share of the national economy. Public utilities employed around 600,000 workers in 2002. The process involved in finding, producing, transporting, and marketing oil and natural gas employs more than 1,620,000 people in the United States (http://www.aceee.org/press/e084pr.htm).

Additionally, one reputable study has concluded that the construction of 40 new nuclear power plants would add more than 600,000 good-paying jobs to the economy. Indeed, expansion of our energy infrastructure could reemploy manufacturing and construction workers who have lost jobs due to restructuring in these sectors. The impact of energy on jobs, business, and the economy extends far beyond the energy sector itself. Increases in prices mean that consumers have less to spend on other goods and services. Higher energy costs result in lower returns on capital investment, making each worker less productive and adversely affecting wages. Corporate decisions on where to locate, expand, and create jobs depend significantly on the reliability and affordability of fuel and power. Energy imports also substantially expand the U.S. trade deficit. By one estimate, on average, every time oil prices go up 10%, 150,000 Americans lose their jobs. The impact of potential supply disruptions—as the result of terrorism, weather, global competition for resources, or bad policy decisions—would be even more devastating to our economy, mobility, and even our ability to defend the nation.

Growing Demand of Energy on a Global Scale

Securing our energy supply, and thus our economic competitiveness, is also under pressure from the demands of other nations. Worldwide demand for fuel and power will expand much faster than our own. The Energy Information Administration (EIA, 2003) predicts growth of more than 70% in global energy consumption between 2003 and 2030. Americans will feel the impact of this growing demand in prices, availability, geopolitics, and vulnerability to security threats, especially if we continue to heavily restrict energy development here at home. Burgeoning global energy consumption, most of which will come from fossil fuels, also means that efforts to address environmental and climate change concerns will have little or no effect without worldwide participation.

The rapidly expanding economies of China and India (along with Brazil and Russia) are becoming massive consumers of energy and will put serious pressure on global energy supplies, as well as on demand for energy-saving technologies. China and India are powering much of their industrial development with impressive coal reserves. By some estimates, China is building an average of one coal-fired plant every week to power its booming economy. The two countries are each planning to build 20 new nuclear reactors by 2020. Even so, by 2050 both nations could be importing 70% to 80% of their energy needs. By 2020, China will have 140 million private cars, more than the United States has at present. Competitive economies need affordable and reliable energy. Our global competitors are embracing this reality.

Firms and States in Global Competition

A tendency since the late 1980s and the early 1990s in international business and political economy has been the growing interdependence between the state and the transnational corporation (TNC). The relation between the state and the firm is no longer a one-way process. It has grown into triangular relationships and diplomacy along the state-TNC nexus: (1) state-state; (2) state-TNC; and (3) TNC-TNC. The increasingly complex relationships between the state and the TNC have prompted many host governments to reconsider their concerns when negotiating with TNCs. The concern of governments varies with the type of TNCs with which they are negotiating. In general, there are two trends that draw growing attention from government authorities. The first trend is *increasing global interdependence*: Governments are particularly concerned whether they will lose their competitiveness and power in the interdependent global economy. Their main concerns are, namely, (1) the equity and efficiency of adjustment processes in declining industries; (2) the development of new industries for strategic reasons; and (3) the specialization of national economies.

In today's interdependent global economy, the fate and prospect of industries in one country or region is often intertwined with industries in another country or region. Technological development in advanced industrialized economies, for example, has reduced the need for primary products in the production processes. This results in the decline of traditional industries such as mining and plantations in many Southeast Asian countries. Many of these Southeast Asian countries have since learnt to adjust to this process of global shift in production processes and consumption patterns. Their main concern is to remain competitive in the global economy and, yet, to capture value-added activities mainly through the local presence of foreign investments. Malaysia and Thailand are good examples as reform-minded governments have been consciously attracting foreign investors and TNCs, particularly those in electronics sector, to pull the economy out of declining industries. Another concern for many natural resources-poor countries is to develop new industries for strategic reasons.

To capture greater value-added activities and to share the success of the global economy, many countries begin to develop strategic plans for their industrialization processes. Singapore is well-known for its consistent drive towards high-tech and information-intensive industrialization. Today, the clustering of many leading world-class electronics, chemicals, and biomedical science manufacturers and their research and development facilities in the city-state testifies the success of such a strategy in attracting TNCs. A final concern of governments is related to specialization and hence trade. Countries in the Asia-Pacific region, in particular those newly industrialized economies (NIEs), have long realized that import-substitution is not an ultimate solution to economic underdevelopment. They instead have relied on export-oriented platform to economic growth and development.

To be a successful export-oriented economy, one must specialize in order to capture comparative advantages that maximize the skill and resource endowments of a particular country. Singapore, for instance, offers a strong comparative advantage in human resources, whereas natural resources sustain the comparative advantage of Indonesia. Both countries specialize in different industries to gain from international trade and, more recently, foreign direct investment. On the other hand, governments are also driven by the second structural trend – *growing global competition*. Their response varies according to the nature of TNCs. If they are concerned with global competition without. the presence of TNCs, the tendency is to regulate the extent and speed of exposing national producers and markets to international competition (e.g. Taiwan and South Korea). If multi-domestic TNCs are preferred and discrete subsidiaries are maintained by these TNCs, a minimum regulation is enforced (e.g. Singapore). Sometimes, host country governments are overpowered by global TNCs having worldwide operations. Integrated TNCs are likely to have substantial bargaining power so that there is a transition from regulation to negotiation in the attitude of government authorities (http://courses.nus.edu.sg/course/geoywc/teaching/GE4202%20Outline%2007-08.htm).

Value-Chain in Global Competitiveness

Global value chains are radically altering how goods and services are produced: parts made in one country, for instance, are increasingly assembled in another and sold in a third. The globalization of production has changed the industrial structure within OECD countries, and in some sectors blunted their competitiveness. Another major consequence has been fears of job losses, due to outsourcing and off-shoring—not only in manufacturing but also in services. The rapid integration of China and India, with their large pool of educated people, further reinforces these concerns. How should OECD countries respond?

To address this issue, the OECD Report (OECD, 2007: http://www.oecd.org/document/54/0, 3343, en_2649_34173_38726774_1_1_1_37461, 00.html) on 'Staying Competitive in the Global Economy: Moving up the Value Chain' brings together OECD data on the globalization of value chains, including the rise of outsourcing/off-shoring. It first examines how OECD countries are affected by the globalization of production, on both the macroeconomic and sector-specific levels. The costs and benefits of globalization are then discussed, with an emphasis on employment and productivity. Finally, this report analyses how globalization impacts the competitiveness of OECD countries, highlighting the need for an effective innovation strategy. The report discusses not only the moving up the value chain that takes place in OECD countries but also in China, as R&D is increasingly going to emerging countries.

Competitive Strategy in International Business

Any effort to formulate a competitive strategy has to be preceded by a clear understanding of competition. Competition in an industry is determined by customers, suppliers, potential entrants, existing competitors and substitute products. Once a firm understands the forces driving competition in the marketplace, it can understand its strengths and weaknesses in the context of the industry. After identification, it can concentrate on formulating strategies to take on the competitive forces. A firm can follow three approaches to design a competitive strategy. It can position the firm to defend itself against existing competitive forces, change the balance of forces to the firm's advantage through strategic moves, so that the firm's relative position improves, or respond to changes in the factors that underlie competitive forces, before competitors do so.

Firms operating in international markets operate in a highly competitive marketplace. To succeed, they need a strategy that sets them apart from competitors. These strategies include transfer of core competencies. Multinational strategy concentrates on customization of products, which increases the cost of production. The system for transferring core competencies from headquarters to subsidiaries, and the system for sharing skills, technology and know-how among subsidiaries are not yet well developed or utilized.

This frequently creates problems for MNCs. Companies that increased overseas expansion after World War II adopted this strategy. The top management of the parent company takes full control of the subsidiary with the help of sophisticated management information systems and corporate staff, who are often specialists in the area. The top management maintains a continuous flow of information to guide subsidiaries. Global strategy was adopted by companies that expanded worldwide after World War II. The diminishing trade and tariff barriers and converging global markets encouraged these companies to implement this strategy (http://www.icmrindia.org/courseware/International%20 Business%20&%20International%20Marketing/IBIM-DS5.htm).

Competitive Strategy: Porter's Three Axes of Competition

A decisive advance in understanding competition took place in 1980 with the publication of Michael Porter's *Competitive Strategy.* Porter's model of how companies compete had three dimensions:

- Price
- Differentiation of the product or service from its competitors
- Customer focus-concentrating upon meeting the needs of specific groups of customers.

Companies are naturally not restricted to employing only one of these modes of competing, shown in diagrammatic form in Figure 1. They may mix a couple or even all three of them and firms with a wide range of products often use a different competitive mode for various parts of their portfolio.

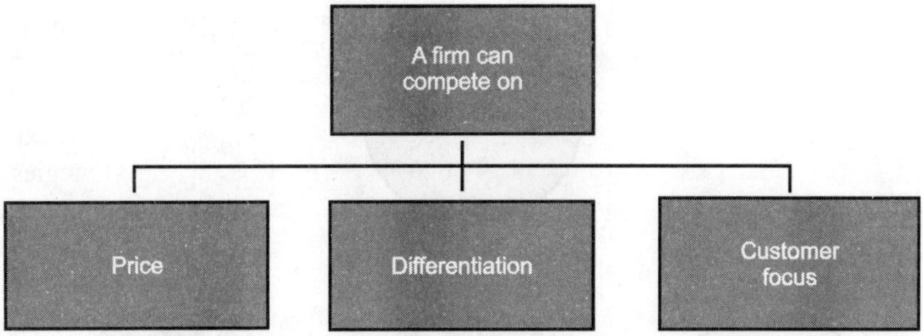

Fig. 1: Porter's three axes of competition

Porter's scheme met with initial resistance from some sections of academia on the grounds that it was too simplistic and failed to cover the full range of ways of competing. This is undoubtedly true, but the Porter model won favour from the business community exactly because it made sense to them in terms how their firms competed. His framework organized the complex numerous elements of competing into an easily grasped summary that nonetheless had considerable explanatory power of how the real world worked. This also accounts for its popularity with Competitive Intelligence analysts.

Porter's 'Five Forces' Model

Professor Porter further enriched the literature of competition by devising his 'five forces' approach to analyzing an industry and the players operating in it. He looked at the balance of bargaining power between a company and, on the one side, its suppliers and, on the other, its customers. Porter also examines the competitive threat posed by new entrants to the market and by substitute products which its customers can use to replace the company's offering. The fifth force (shown as the central box in Figure 2) is the intensity of competition within the industry itself.

Increased Global Competition from New Competitors: Cruising into 'Blue Ocean'

For the first time in history, we are experiencing a global economy. Companies no longer think in terms of political borders when it comes to running their businesses or selling their products. This trend is growing as world and regional trade agreements such as GATT (General Agreement on Tariffs and Trade) and the European Union, and NAFTA (North American Free Trade Agreement) become institutionalized. Countries such as Korea, China, Indonesia, and Brazil that were never world economic players in the past are now part of the global economy. Industrialized countries are building facilities all over the world, even in other industrialized countries—so it's not just a matter of finding cheap labour as in the past. Japanese and German automakers now have plants in North America. Kodak Films have 3 Strategic Business Units located in the Republic

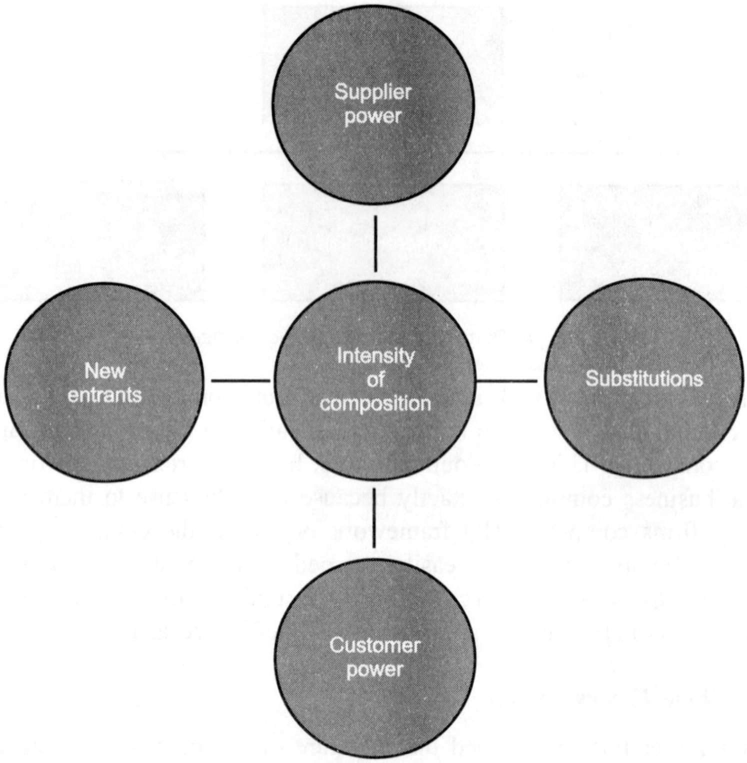

Fig. 2: Porter's 'Five forces' model

of China. Because of better telecommunications, financial firms can be located anywhere and global banking is commonplace. For your business, it means that competition can come from any country. Competitive intelligence can help identify new and emerging competitors. In Asia, most of the large Japanese companies have been actively conducting research on their domestic, regional and international markets, and thorough competitive landscape reviews are undertaken before any major corporate decisions are made. Although the commercial intelligence community in Japan remains small and closed to most foreigners, the Japanese have developed the most advanced competitive intelligence processes in Asia (http://www.fastcompany.com/blog/damien-duhamel/marketing-strategy-asia/competitive-intelligence-asia-strategic-edge-corporate-a).

Kim and Mauborgne's 'Blue ocean strategy' metaphor elegantly summarizes their vision of the kind of expanding, competitor-free markets that innovative companies can navigate. As W. Chan Kim puts it 'Blue ocean strategy' is all about "How to create an uncontested market space and market competition irrelevant". Unlike "red oceans," which are well explored and crowded with competitors, "blue oceans" represent "untapped market space" and the "opportunity for highly profitable growth." The only reason more big companies don't set sail for them, they suggest, is that "the dominant focus of strategy work over the past twenty-five years has been on competition-based red ocean strategies" i.e., finding new ways to cut costs and grow revenue by taking away market share from the competition. With this groundbreaking book, Kim and Mauborgne—both professors at France's INSEAD, the second largest business school in the world—aim to repair that bias. Using dozens of examples—from Southwest Airlines and the Cirque du Soleil to Curves and Starbucks—they present the tools and frameworks they've developed specifically for the task of analyzing blue oceans. They urge companies to "value innovation" that focuses on "utility, price, and cost positions," to "create and capture new demand" and to "focus on the big picture, not the numbers" (http://www.amazon.com/gp/product/product-description/1591396190/ref=dp_proddesc_0? i.e. =UTF8&n=283155&s=books).

Case on Competitive Intelligence Strategy

Southwest Airlines created a unique and exceptional value curve to unlock a blue ocean. As shown in the strategy canvas, Southwest Airlines' value curve has *focus;* the company does not diffuse its efforts across all key factors of competition. The shape of its value curve *diverges* from the other players', a result of not benchmarking competitors but instead looking across alternatives. The *tagline* of Southwest Airlines' strategic profile is clear: a fun and simple wine to be enjoyed every day.

When expressed through a value curve, then, an effective blue ocean strategy like Southwest Airlines has three complementary qualities: focus, divergence, and a compelling tagline. Without these qualities, a company's strategy will likely be muddled, undifferentiated, and hard to communicate with a high cost structure. The four actions of creating a new value curve should be well-guided toward building a company's strategic profile with these characteristics. These three characteristics serve as an initial litmus test of the commercial viability of blue ocean ideas (Kim and Renée Mauborgne, 2005).

Six Principles of Blue Ocean Strategy

Formulation Principles attenuates	**Risk factor each principle**
Reconstruct market boundaries	↓ Search risk
Focus on the big picture, not the numbers	↓ Planning risk
Reach beyond existing demand	↓ Scale risk
Get the strategic sequence right	↓ Business model risk
Execution principles attenuates	**Risk factor each principle**
Overcome key organizational hurdles	↓ Organisational risk
Build execution into strategy	↓ Management risk

A look at Southwest Airlines' strategic profile illustrates how these three qualities underlie the company's effective strategy in reinventing the short-haul airline industry via value innovation (Fig. 3).

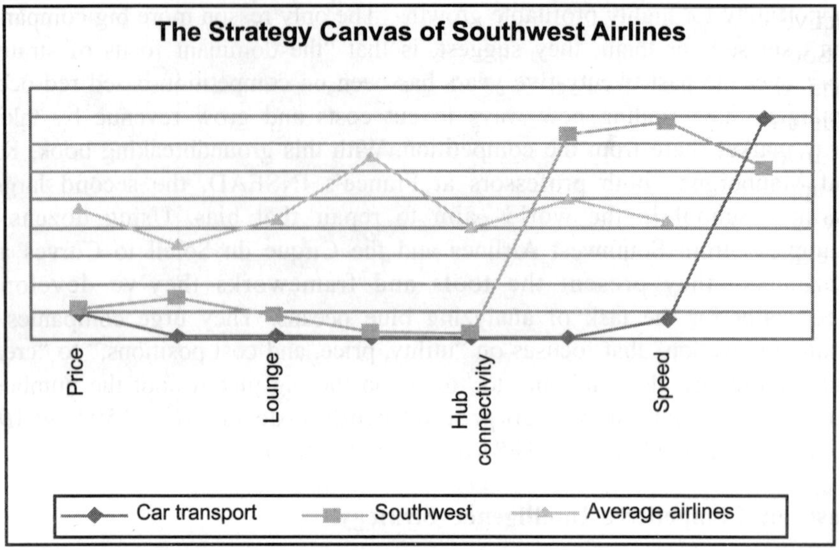

Fig. 3: The Strategy Canvas of Southwest Airlines

Southwest Airlines created a blue ocean by breaking the trade-offs customers had to make between the speed of airplanes and the economy and flexibility of car transport. To achieve this, Southwest offered high-speed transport with frequent and flexible departures at prices attractive to the mass of buyers. By eliminating and reducing certain factors of competition and raising others in the traditional airline industry, as well as by creating new factors drawn from the alternative industry of car transport, Southwest Airlines was able to offer unprecedented utility for air travellers and achieve a leap in value with a low-cost business model. The value curve of Southwest Airlines differs distinctively from those of its competitors in the strategy canvas. Its strategic profile is a typical example of a compelling blue ocean strategy.

Every great strategy has focus, and a company's strategic profile, or value curve, should clearly show it. Looking at Southwest's profile, we can see at once that the company emphasizes only three factors: friendly service, speed, and frequent point-to-point departures. By focusing in this way, Southwest has been able to price against car transportation; it doesn't make extra investments in meals, lounges, and seating choices. By contrast, Southwest's traditional competitors invest in all the airline industry's competitive factors, making it much more difficult for them to match Southwest's prices. Investing across the board, these companies let their competitors' moves set their own agendas. Costly business models result.

When a company's strategy is formed reactively as it tries to keep up with the competition, it loses its uniqueness. Consider the similarities in most airlines' meals and business-class lounges. On the strategy canvas, therefore, reactive strategists tend to share the same strategic profile. Indeed, in the case of Southwest, the value curves of the company's competitors are virtually identical and therefore can be summarized on the strategy canvas with a single value curve.

In contrast, the value curves of blue ocean strategists always stand apart. By applying the four actions of eliminating, reducing, raising, and creating, they differentiate their profiles from the industry's average profile. Southwest, for example, pioneered point to point travel between midsize cities; previously, the industry operated through hub-and-spoke systems.

A good strategy has a clear-cut and compelling tagline: "The speed of a plane at the price of a car - whenever you need it." That's the tagline of Southwest Airlines, or at least it could be. What could Southwest's competitors say? Even the most proficient ad agency would have difficulty reducing the conventional offering of lunches, seat choices, lounges, and hub links, with standard service, slower speeds, and higher prices into a memorable tagline. A good tagline not only delivers a clear message but also advertise an offering truthfully to reinforce and win over customers' sustained interests, trust and loyalty. In fact, a good way to test the effectiveness and strength of a strategy is to look at whether it contains a strong and authentic tagline to complement its strong Branding strategy.

Six-Sigma for Global Competitiveness

Sigma is defined as "a statistical unit of measurement that describes the distribution about the mean of any process or procedure" (Motorola, 1998). As the sigma value is raised, the variation around the mean value decreases eventually approaches zero variation, mythically known as "zero defects". Theoretically, Six-Sigma equates to a variation about the mean of no more than .002 dpmo (defects per million opportunities) outside allowable standards. However, in industry terms, achieving Six-Sigma Quality means that the defects in a given process or procedure do not exceed 3.4 dpmo. Most of today's successful businesses, including GE, operate at a 3.5 sigma level. This produces approximately 33,000 dpmo.

The Six-Sigma process was introduced by Motorola on their way to winning the 1988 Malcolm Baldridge National Quality Award. The process is more than a quality definition applied to statistical tools — it is an identifiable and achievable means to reach the allusive goal of continuous improvement in all business areas. Six-Sigma quality is important to world-class organizations such as GE and Motorola because quality and customer satisfaction are assumed to be proportionate.

Six-Sigma is a fundamental approach to delivering very high levels of customer satisfaction through disciplined use of data and statistical analysis for maximizing and sustaining business success. It will energize your organization and will bring about a strategic shift in thinking and participation by all employees. It is an absolute must for your organization, regardless of what products you make or what services you offer. Thus, six-sigma is appropriate to all work processes under the purview of your company (Pande and Holpp, 2002).

Only those companies and organizations will survive and thrive in the fiercely competitive global marketplace, which can provide highest quality products and services at competitive prices. The negative consequences of not adopting Six-Sigma are equally profound. Six-Sigma programs are implemented in five phases: scope, measure, analyze, improve, and control (http://jobfunctions.bnet.com/abstract.aspx?docid=59951). Globalization has intensified competition, worldwide. Rising cultures in the East, with a population base of over 2 billion, are in the process of opening up their economies to international competition creating tremendous opportunities. To take due advantage of the opportunities and to meet the challenges, a large number of enterprises in the United States have embarked on a program of quality improvement through a concept first deployed at Motorola called Six-Sigma. Six-Sigma processes can produce virtually defect-free products and services, with the concomitant outcome of achieving the highest level of customer satisfaction. The net result is best possible bottom-line performance. An interesting feature of six sigma is that it applies equally well across the board to all endeavors, manufacturing and transactional, and to all organizations, Universities included. Among notable successes is General Electric which embarked on an ambitious six sigma initiative in 1995 in all its divisions ranging from GE Capital, Consumer Services, and NBC to Aircraft Engines, Appliances, Plastics, and Medical Systems. The benefits from Six-Sigma efforts at GE exceeded $ 1 billion in 1998 and $ 2 billion in 1999. Du Pont and Dow Chemical claim annual benefits of $ 1 billion from their recently embarked six sigma initiatives (Deshpande, 2008). For the benefit of readers some of the illustrative case studies highlighting the significance and impact of Six-Sigma approach on corporate excellence are presented below.

Six-Sigma at General Electric

Jack Welch, Chief Executive Officer of GE, has set a company-wide goal to have all processes reach Six-Sigma Quality by the year 2000. Welch and GE realize that attaining Six-Sigma Quality will require retraining their entire workforce to think and act like engineers — an enormous feat with remarkable benefits. To understand the needs of customers, GE stresses five "CTQ's" — Critical to Quality measures: get the customers what they want, when they want it, on time, undamaged, and working (Trotter, 1997).

The GE Six-Sigma program has identified and defined the phases used to optimize processes to ensure a resultant product or service is defect free. These phases, known by the acronym DMAIC, are explicitly followed, and with that, successful results are noticed. The DMAIC process steps include: Define, Measure, Analyze, Improve, and Control. In order to optimize any and all processes within GE, a thorough and rigorous analysis of the applicable data is processed using Minitab, an extremely powerful statistical data analysis program (http://www.theleibys.com/susandocs/sixsigma.html).

Lessons Learnt: Experiences gained by General Electric

At the General Electric, implementation of Six-Sigma Programme resulted in the following pattern of return on investment over the years:

- In 1996, costs of $ 200 million and returns of $ 150 million
- In 1997, costs of $ 400 million and return of $ 600 million
- In 1998, cost of $ 400 million and return of more than $ 1 billion

GE's former CEO, Jack Welch, wrote in the annual report that in just 3 years, Six-Sigma had saved the company more than $ 2 billion. His following statement summarizes the lesson learnt by embracing Six-Sigma principles for GE:

"We did not invent Six-Sigma – we learnt it. The cumulative impact on the company's numbers is not an anecdotal, nor a product of charts. It is the product of 276000 people executing and delivering the result of Six-Sigma to our bottom line." — Jack Welch, 1997

Vince Fayad, Director of value–based sigma for ITT industries, Inc. attributes the success of the programme primarily to observance of the following code of Six Best Practices, which are value-based and result-oriented:

- Link projects to the strategic plan. Decide where you want a part of the organization to be in the future and then pick projects that will help it get there,
- Go for quick wins. Select projects that can succeed in little time. Quick success generates enthusiasm for the initiative and energizes people,
- Match projects and resources. Don't yield to the natural tendency to try to do a lot of projects at one time,
- Secure support from management. Senior managers must be committed to the DFSS initiative and to facilitating work on projects,
- Provide training for top managers. When executives understand what the DFSS players are doing, they're likely to take their own responsibilities for the initiative more seriously,
- Recognize, reward, and share successes.

Sustaining Design for Six-Sigma

Six-Sigma is basically a methodology that needs to continue indefinitely and in an uninterrupted manner since there is always a room for improvement in designs, approaches and processes involved.

The first and the most effective means of sustaining gains achieved through Six-Sigma is use it diligently to improve the processes designed through DFSS; that is to say maintaining the capability of the design. Second sustaining factor is to continue to focus on customers in specific context of customer demand, complaints, feed-back information, focus group, one-to-one interview, contextual enquiry etc. Third crucial aspect relates to efficient knowledge management involving maintaining a database of the 'lesson learned', followed by continuous knowledge transfer.

A good communication system enabling knowledge sharing with Six-Sigma Group, combined with good leadership quality of the CEO/Champion, can ensure sustenance. Combined with this, a high quality of infrastructure, reinforcement and control can considerably help the organization to promote and sustain DFSS. Last, but not the least, Organizational culture can influence and stimulate the process of designing and redesigning of Six-Sigma to see through not only its successful conclusion but also its long-term sustainability perspective.

Non-Manufacturing Six-Sigma Solutions

Transactional Six-Sigma, Six-Sigma for Soft Processes, Six-Sigma for Services Call it what you will, Six-Sigma is a methodology for success in all processes. Only two per cent of all processes in the United States are manufacturing processes. Numerous corporations have benefited from the increased efficiency, higher quality, and improved customer relationships delivered by Six-Sigma. Most of these corporations have reaped these benefits through implementation of Six-Sigma in the manufacturing environment. As consumers, we see the results of Six-Sigma in products that meet our needs, last longer, are priced affordably, and are available where and when we want them. Most people enjoy the benefits of Six-Sigma when using pagers, cars, cell phones, and printers and never even realize it.

Today, the world class corporations that implemented Six-Sigma for manufacturing processes are implementing Six-Sigma in the non-manufacturing environment on soft processes such as Order to Cash, Customer Acquisition, After Sales Service and Support, etc. They are doing this because they realize that no matter how good your manufacturing processes are, if soft processes are of poor quality, the company and its customers will suffer.

Why is Six-Sigma Important for Soft Processes?

- Soft processes are the ones that touch customers and suppliers,
- Soft processes initiate manufacturing and distribute the products of manufacturing,
- Soft processes often have fewer transactions and these transactions are of greater value,
- Soft processes are human centric and are full of variation and special cases, science must be applied to reduce and manage this variation,
- In non-manufacturing industries, there are only soft processes,
- Soft processes manage your money.

In most corporations, the quality of soft processes is critical to success. Yet implementation of Six-Sigma in such environments is no easy task and you typically only get one shot at it. This is why organizations should focus on the implementation of Six-Sigma in soft processes, and the automation of such processes.

Leverage the Best of Six-Sigma Tailored for Application on Non-Manufacturing Processes

First, a process is a process and every process can benefit from Six-Sigma. Second, non-manufacturing/soft processes and manufacturing processes present very unique challenges when implementing Six-Sigma. Third, all modern Six-Sigma or process engineering projects must leverage well designed information technology to be successful and fourth, nearly all information system projects involve process automation which should be engineered properly (http://www.streetdirectory.com/travel_guide/21777/corporate_matters/six_sigma_for_the_non_manufacturing_sector.html).

Experience shows that soft processes can be substantially more difficult to get into a Six-Sigma project. The challenges lie in the difficulty to clearly identify process variables, the difficulty to find process variables that can be measured without undue burden, and cultural resistance to changing white collar processes. The Six-Sigma program should eliminate concerns by moving to the improvement of key processes, integration of horizontal process centric application design, and reducing the training and analysis traditionally associated with Six-Sigma. Traditional DMAIC Six-Sigma, some of the fundamental differences between traditional Six-Sigma as found in manufacturing, and the Six-Sigma for transactional processes are described below.

- Places more emphasis on the big picture – whole process optimization,
- Emphasizes use of information systems for process automation,
- Emphasizes greater use of technological and procedural benchmarking,
- Specifically addresses evolution as a phase and places emphasis on continuous improvement, seeking to deal with the greater degree of random variation and special case situations inherent to human driven processes.

However, Six-Sigma has proven significantly more difficult to implement off the shop floor. The reasons are many, but lie within a few root causes. Two of these root causes are: (1) data and (2) human behaviour.

The use of the Six-Sigma techniques for obtaining data, applying quantitative measures to seemingly un-quantifiable information, identifying significant measures, data collection techniques, and meaningful reports has seen resistance. For example, Six-Sigma should use a key decision point approach for collecting data on human behaviour and integrates techniques that identify process variables differentiating control variables from others and building relationships between process and output variables. Working with Six-Sigma in this area has proven to drive cost savings, increased effectiveness, and increases customer satisfaction.

Further, the use of information technology such as BPM enables businesses to collect and analyze process data with accuracy and ease. By using a process excellence centric approach to "system" engineering processes traditionally considered an un-manageable art are engineered to efficient and effective science. By system, it means all elements of the system including, people, processes, and technology.

Some of the techniques in this area include:

- Collection, segmentation, analysis, and reporting of existing data volumes,
- Identification of process variables both X and Y,
- Integration of X and Y (cost, time, performance) variable data collection in automated processes,
- Implementation of Special Cause detection and alert systems,
- Identification and data collection of key decision variables.

Ultimately, Six-Sigma's unique abilities in the area of collecting data and building statistical models on transactional processes means that companies are able to easily realize the benefits of transactional Six-Sigma.

Six-Sigma: A Case Study in Motorola

When a Japanese firm took over a Motorola factory that manufactured Quasar television sets in the United States in the 1970s, they promptly set about making drastic changes in the way the factory operated. Under Japanese management, the factory was soon producing TV sets with 1/20th the number of defects they had produced under Motorola management. They did this using the same workforce, technology, and designs, making it clear that the problem was Motorola's management. Eventually, even Motorola's own executives had to admit "our quality stinks" (Motorola, 1988; Motorola University, 2006).

Finally, in the mid 1980s, Motorola decided to take quality seriously. Motorola's CEO at the time, Bob Galvin, started the company on the quality path known as Six-Sigma and became a business icon largely as a result of what he accomplished in quality at Motorola. Today, Motorola is known worldwide as a quality leader and a profit leader. After Motorola won the Malcolm Baldrige National Quality Award in 1988 the secret of their success became public knowledge and the Six-Sigma revolution was on. Today it's hotter than ever (Mikel, 1988).

It would be a mistake to think that Six-Sigma is about quality in the traditional sense. Quality, defined traditionally as conformance to internal requirements, has little to do with Six-Sigma. Six-Sigma is about helping the organization make more money. To link this objective of Six-Sigma with quality requires a new definition of quality. For Six-Sigma purposes I define quality as the value added by a productive endeavor. Quality comes in two flavors: potential quality and actual quality. Potential quality is the known maximum possible value added per unit of input. Actual quality is the current value added per unit of input. The difference between potential and actual quality is waste. Six-Sigma focuses on improving quality (i.e., reducing waste) by helping organizations produce products and services better, faster and cheaper. In more traditional terms, Six-Sigma focuses on defect prevention, cycle time reduction, and cost savings. Unlike mindless cost-cutting programs which reduce value and quality, Six-Sigma identifies and eliminates costs which provide no value to customers: waste costs.

For non-Six-Sigma companies, these costs are often extremely high. Companies operating at three or four sigma typically spend between 25 and 40 per cent of their revenues fixing problems. This is known as the cost of quality, or more accurately the cost of poor quality. Companies operating at Six-Sigma typically spend less than 5 per cent of their revenues fixing problems. The dollar cost of this gap can be huge. General Electric estimates that the gap between three or four sigma and Six-Sigma was costing them between $ 8 billion and $ 12 billion per year.

Six-Sigma is a rigorous, focused and highly effective implementation of proven quality principles and techniques. Incorporating elements from the work of many quality pioneers, Six-Sigma aims for virtually error-free business performance. Sigma, is a letter in the Greek alphabet used by statisticians to measure the variability in any process. A company's performance is measured by the sigma level of their business processes. Traditionally companies accepted three or four sigma performance levels as the norm, despite the fact that these processes created between 6,200 and 67,000 problems per million opportunities! The Six-Sigma standard of 3.4 problems per million opportunities is a response to the increasing expectations of customers and the increased complexity of modern products and processes.

If you're looking for new techniques, don't bother. Six-Sigma's magic isn't in statistical or high-tech razzle-dazzle. Six-Sigma relies on tried and true methods that have been around for decades. In fact, Six-Sigma discards a great deal of the complexity that characterized Total Quality Management (TQM). By one expert's count, there were over 400 TQM tools and techniques. Six-Sigma takes a handful of proven methods and trains a small cadre of in-house technical leaders, known as Six-Sigma Black Belts, to a high level of proficiency in the application of these techniques. To be sure, some of the methods used by Black Belts are highly advanced, including the use of up-to-date computer technology. But the tools are applied within a simple performance improvement model known as DMAIC, or Define-Measure-Analyze-Improve-Control. DMAIC can be described as follows:

Define the goals of the improvement activity. At the top level the goals will be the strategic objectives of the organization, such as a higher ROI or market share. At the operations level, a goal might be to increase the throughput of a production department. At the project level goals might be to reduce the defect level and increase throughput. Apply data mining methods to identify potential improvement opportunities.

Measure the existing system. Establish valid and reliable metrics to help monitor progress towards the goal(s) defined at the previous step. Begin by determining the current baseline. Use exploratory and descriptive data analysis to help you understand the data. Analyze the system to identify ways to eliminate the gap between the current performance of the system or process and the desired goal. Apply statistical tools to guide the analysis.

Improve the system. Be creative in finding new ways to do things better, cheaper, or faster. Use project management and other planning and management tools to implement the new approach. Use statistical methods to validate the improvement. Control the new system. Institutionalize the improved system by modifying compensation and incentive systems, policies, procedures, MRP, budgets, operating instructions and other management systems. You may wish to utilize systems such as ISO-9000 to assure that documentation is correct.

Infrastructure: A very powerful feature of Six-Sigma is the creation of an infrastructure to ensure that performance improvement activities have the necessary resources. In this author's opinion, failure to provide this infrastructure is the #1 reason why 80% of all TQM implementations failed in the past. Six-Sigma makes improvement and change the full-time job of a small but critical per centage of the organization's personnel. These full time change agents are the catalyst that institutionalizes change.

Six-Sigma involves changing major business value streams that cut across organizational barriers. It is the means by which the organization's strategic goals are to be achieved. This effort cannot be led by anyone other than the CEO, who is responsible for the performance of the organization as a whole. Six-Sigma must be implemented from the top-down.

Champions and Sponsors: Six-Sigma champions are high-level individuals who understand Six-Sigma and are committed to its success. In larger organizations Six-Sigma will be led by a full-time, high level champion, such as an Executive Vice-President. In all organizations, champions also include informal leaders who use Six-Sigma in their day-to-day work and communicate the Six-Sigma message at every opportunity. Sponsors are owners of processes and systems that help initiate and coordinate Six-Sigma improvement activities in their areas of responsibilities.

Master Black Belt: This is the highest level of technical and organizational proficiency. Master Black Belts provide technical leadership of the Six-Sigma program. Thus, they must know everything the Black Belts know, as well as understand the mathematical theory on which the statistical methods are based. Master Black Belts must be able to assist Black Belts in applying the methods correctly in unusual situations. Whenever possible, statistical training should be conducted only by Master Black Belts. Otherwise the familiar "propagation of error" phenomenon will occur, i.e., Black Belts pass on errors to green belts, who pass on greater errors to team members. If it becomes necessary for Black Belts and Green Belts to provide training, they should do only so under the guidance of Master Black Belts. For example, Black Belts may be asked to provide assistance to the Master during class discussions and exercises. Because of the nature of the Master's duties, communications and teaching skills are as important as technical competence.

Black Belt: Candidates for Black Belt status are technically oriented individuals held in high regard by their peers. They should be actively involved in the process of organizational change and development. Candidates may come from a wide range of disciplines and need not be formally trained statisticians or engineers. However, because they are expected to master a wide variety of technical tools in a relatively short period of time, Black Belt candidates will probably possess a background including college-level mathematics and the basic tool of quantitative analysis. Coursework in statistical methods may be considered a strong plus or even a prerequisite. As part of their training, Black Belts receive 160 hours of classroom instruction, plus one-on-one project coaching from Master Black Belts or consultants.

Successful candidates will be comfortable with computers. At a minimum, they should understand one or more operating systems, spreadsheets, database managers, presentation programs, and word processors. As part of their training they will be required to become proficient in the use of one or more advanced statistical analysis software packages. Six-Sigma Black Belts work to extract actionable knowledge from an organization's information warehouse. To ensure access to the needed information, Six-Sigma activities should be closely integrated with the information systems (IS) of the organization. Obviously, the skills and training of Six-Sigma Black Belts must be enabled by an investment in software and hardware. It makes no sense to hamstring these experts by saving a few dollars on computers or software.

Green Belt: Green Belts are Six-Sigma project leaders capable of forming and facilitating Six-Sigma teams and managing Six-Sigma projects from concept to completion. Green Belt training consists of five days of classroom training and is conducted in conjunction with Six-Sigma projects. Training covers project management, quality management tools, quality control tools, problem solving, and descriptive data analysis. Six-Sigma champions should attend Green Belt training. Usually, Six-Sigma Black Belts help Green Belts define their projects prior to the training, attend training with their Green Belts, and assist them with their projects after the training.

Staffing Levels and Expected Returns: As stated earlier in this article, the number of full time personnel devoted to Six-Sigma is not large. Mature Six-Sigma programs, such as those of Motorola, General Electric, Johnson and Johnson, AlliedSignal, and others average about one per cent of their workforce as Black Belts. There is usually about one Master Black Belt for every ten Black Belts, or about 1 Master Black Belt per 1,000 employees. A Black Belt will typically complete 5 to 7 projects per year. Project teams are led by Green Belts, who, unlike Black Belts and Master Black Belts, are not employed full time in the Six-Sigma program. Black Belts are highly prized employees and are often recruited for key management positions elsewhere in the company.

After Six-Sigma has been in place for three or more years, the number of former Black Belts tends to be about the same as the number of active Black Belts.

Estimated savings per project varies from organization to organization. Reported results work out an average savings of about US $ 150,000 to US $ 243,000. It could be noted here that these are not the huge mega-projects pursued by Re-engineering. Yet, by completing 5 to 7 projects per year per Black Belt, the company will add in excess of US $ 1 million per year per Black Belt to its bottom line. For a company with 1,000 employees the numbers would look something like this:

Master Black Belts: 1 Black Belts: 10
Projects: = 50 to 70 (5 to 7 per Black Belt)
Estimated saving: US $ 9 million to US $ 14.6 million
(US $ 14,580 per employee)

Do the math for your organization and see what Six-Sigma could do for you. Because Six-Sigma savings impact only non-value added costs, they flow directly to your company's bottom line.

Implementation of Six-Sigma: After over two decades of experience with quality improvement, there is now a solid body of scientific research regarding the experience of thousands of companies implementing major programs such as Six-Sigma. Researchers have found that successful deployment of Six-Sigma involves focusing on a small number of high-leverage items. The steps required to successfully implement Six-Sigma are well-documented.

1. Successful performance improvement must begin with senior leadership. Start by providing senior leadership with training in the principles and tools they need to prepare their organization for success. Using their newly acquired knowledge, senior leaders direct the development of a management infrastructure to support Six-Sigma. Simultaneously, steps are taken to "soft-wire" the organization and to cultivate an environment for innovation and creativity. This involves reducing levels of organizational hierarchy, removing procedural barriers to experimentation and change, and a variety of other changes designed to make it easier to try new things without fear of reprisal.
2. Systems are developed for establishing close communication with customers, employees, and suppliers. This includes developing rigorous methods of obtaining and evaluating customer, employee and supplier input. Base line studies are conducted to determine the starting point and to identify cultural, policy, and procedural obstacles to success.
3. Training needs are rigorously assessed. Remedial skills education is provided to assure that adequate levels of literacy and numeracy are possessed by all employees. Top-to-bottom training is conducted in systems improvement tools, techniques, and philosophies.

4. A framework for continuous process improvement is developed, along with a system of indicators for monitoring progress and success. Six-Sigma metrics focus on the organization's strategic goals, drivers, and key business processes.
5. Business processes to be improved are chosen by management, and by people with intimate process knowledge at all levels of the organization. Six-Sigma projects are conducted to improve business performance linked to measurable financial results. This requires knowledge of the organization's constraints.
6. Six-Sigma projects are conducted by individual employees and teams led by Green Belts and assisted by Black Belts. Although the approach is simple, it is by no means easy. But the results justify the effort expended. Research has shown that firms that successfully implement Six-Sigma perform better in virtually every business category, including return on sales, return on investment, employment growth, and share price increase.

Case of Crystal Ball

In a paper and accompanying model, Crystal Ball showed how the future opportunity is formulated as a Six-Sigma project and showcase how Crystal Ball Professional Edition is used within each of the DMAIC (Define, Measure, Analyze, Improve, and Control) process phases to deliver responsiveness to the customer and financial results to the business (http://www.decisioneering.com/articles/download/cb-and-jmp.pdf).

As with most business situations of this nature, Crystal Ball is seeking the best (or most profitable) tradeoff between conflicting actions or strategies. This example specifically balances responsiveness to customer needs (higher levels of inventory given uncertain demand) against efficiency for the business (lower cost of goods sold). Of particular interest in seeking this optimal balance is how we can improve the solution and account for the effects of uncertainty in the key process input variables (KPIV's). This method (stochastic optimization) enables us to specify objective functions (Y's) and requirements (constraints on X's) in terms of likelihood of occurrence (i.e., maximize profit and provide at least 90% certainty that the total inventory costs would not exceed $ 169,000).

Fortune 1000 organizations have realized immense success by implementing the Define, Measure, Analyze, Improve, and Control (DMAIC) methods made famous by Six-Sigma practitioners. These practitioners can maximize their project results (e.g., cost savings and defect reduction) by incorporating real variability and uncertainty in their processes and into their process models or spreadsheets.

Simulation, optimization, and forecasting can be used throughout the DMAIC process. In this case study, a company that sold perishable inventory used

Crystal Ball Professional Edition software within the Six-Sigma process to create and maintain an optimal balance between lost sales and wasted inventory. In the recent past, these companies all too often turned away customers due to unanticipated demand and a lack of inventory. This problem was identified and handed off to a Six-Sigma project team for resolution.

The Importance of Using Stochastic Methods: If the company was not using Crystal Ball Professional Edition, they still could have completed this project to reduce lost sales and minimize our total inventory costs. By excluding the variability in demand and lead delivery time and using the average values of 149 units and 2 weeks, Crystal Ball would have come up with an optimal solution of order quantity 300, reorder point 400, and initial inventory 500.

However, when the company included the actual, known variability in the model, and the results of the two methods are compared, it was found that 99.6% of the time the stochastic solution results in lower costs than the deterministic solution. The value in using the stochastic method is, on average, over $ 85,000 per year for this project.

Case Study: Siemens Westinghouse Power Corp

Designing for Quality and Excellence

The task of the Quality Systems Group at Siemens Westinghouse Power Corp. was challenging. It endeavored to systematically implement a supplier—facing standardized product—and process qualification process for gas turbine blades. The new process would help reduce PPQ cycle time, eliminate or minimize product failure points downstream, reduce scrap and improve first-time yield. In the highly complex and demanding power-generation industry, business success depends on effective collaboration with suppliers to ensure superior, reliable and efficient designs; rapid planning to production cycle time; and containment of development and manufacturing costs. For SWPC, the main business objective was to improve economic performance while achieving customer satisfaction and strategic supplier relationships through standardized processes and consistent methodologies (Tonny Soars, 2008).

Headquartered in Orlando, Florida, SWPC is the regional business entity in the Americas for Siemens Power Generation's global fossil power generation business, which has an installed fleet of more than 600,000 megawatts worldwide. Siemens Power Generation offers a full spectrum of products and services, throughout the entire power plant life-cycle, including gas and steam turbines, electric generators, process control and power management systems, and fuel cells for the distributed generation market. With about 250 multi-tier suppliers across the globe providing components for gas turbines, the supplier quality management function plays a vital role in the sourcing process. Gas turbine blades have one of the most complex sourcing processes involving up to five unique sourcing steps:

1. Investment casting
2. Root machining
3. Cooling hole drilling (electrical discharge machining and electro-chemical machining)
4. Diffusion and ceramic coatings
5. Airflow testing and moment weight

The process of designing a turbine blade is inherently complex, involving precise and unique product characteristics, such as high-strength and high-temperature alloys, thermal barrier coating, and complex cooling to withstand extreme turbine operating temperatures and tight dimensional tolerances. Meeting the stringent requirements of the design intent and close to zero tolerance for failures requires the skills of many design, manufacturing and quality professionals across various organizations. This makes the design and qualification process for gas turbine blades highly collaborative and complex.

In Pursuit of Continuous Process Improvement

With the suspicion that variation in the PPQ process was affecting optimization of first-time yield, SWPC conducted a Six-Sigma study of the turbine blade PPQ process and its effect on the costs of poor quality, such as scrap and rework. Given the complexity of the turbine blade, the study hypothesized that an ability to define and solve problems collaboratively with suppliers through standardized processes at the early stages of the supplier manufacturing process development cycle can significantly improve downstream reaction times and costs. The Six-Sigma study was completed in October 2001. The findings confirmed the Group's suspicions.

After reviewing the data collected during the measurement phase of the study and comparing them with the goals of a closed-loop PPQ process, it was apparent that the existing PPQ process failed to map these goals. The Six-Sigma study also identified a direct link between the up-front effort put into process development and qualification as well as the nonconformance costs.

Among other improvements, the study demonstrated that a standardized, closed-loop PPQ process with consistent methodologies would improve first-time yield, thereby reducing or eliminating rework cycles and scrap.

A standardized closed-loop PPQ process must:

- Minimize supplier product nonconformance
- Minimize PPQ cycle time with suppliers
- Ensure ongoing process control
- Predict future quality
- Provide visibility across PPQs
- Document the qualification process
- Provide complete documentation of qualification
- Effectively balance workload and resources

Furthermore, the Six-Sigma study concluded that a system leveraging the Internet would drive the PPQ process in a way that steers suppliers to focus on up-front process development as opposed to the current practice of creating a basic process and modifying it after full production has begun.

Applying Six-Sigma Methodology to Energy-Saving Projects: A Case of Dow Chemical Company

The Dow Chemical Company is a leading science and technology company that provides innovative chemical, plastic, and agricultural products and services to many essential consumer markets. With annual sales of $ 27 billion, Dow serves customers in more than 170 countries and a wide range of markets that are vital to human progress, including food, transportation, health and medicine, personal and home care, and building and construction, among others. Committed to the principles of Sustainable Development, Dow and its approximately 50,000 employees seek to balance economic, environmental, and social responsibilities. In 1998 Dow chose to implement Six-Sigma methodology to accelerate the company's rate of improvement in quality and productivity (http://portal.acm.org/citation.cfm?id=1181965).

A trial of Six-Sigma in two of Dow's global businesses convinced management that the value proposition was well worth the effort, and in September 1999 the company launched a corporate-wide program to incorporate the Six-Sigma methodology into all of its businesses and functions. The company's 1999 annual report stated that by the end of 2003, Dow expected its Six-Sigma implementation to deliver revenue growth, cost reductions, and asset utilization totaling $ 1.5 billion in earnings before interest and taxes (EBIT). At the close of 2002, Dow achieved its $ 1.5 billion cumulative financial goal—a full year ahead of schedule. This case study presents four examples of Six-Sigma implementation for projects at Dow facilities in Texas and Louisiana:

- Steam Trap Improvement
- Polycarbonate Unit Energy Reduction
- Styrene Unit Energy Envelope
- Angus Site Energy Reduction

Dow employs Six-Sigma MAIC methodology to upgrade performance. **MAIC** is defined as follows:

Measure – Gather the right data to accurately assess a problem.

Analyze – Use statistical tools to correctly identify the root causes of a problem.

Improve – Correct the problem (not the symptom).

Control – Put a plan in place to make sure problems stay fixed and sustain the gains.

Key Roles and Responsibilities

When implementing Six-Sigma, Dow assigns each project a unique organizational structure starting with top-level support from Dow's CEO. The key roles in all Six-Sigma efforts at Dow are as follows:

- Sponsor – Business executive leading the organization.
- Champion – Responsible for Six-Sigma strategy, deployment, and vision.
- Process Owner – Owner of the process, product, or service being improved—responsible for long-term sustainable gains.
- Master Black Belts – Coach Black belts—expert in all statistical tools.
- Black Belts – Work on 3 to 5 $ 250,000-per-year projects; create $ 1 million per year in value.
- Green Belts – Work with black belt on projects.

The Advanced Defense Technology Company Mind Manager to Facilitate Lean Six-Sigma Process-Improvement Events

This Fortune 500 defense technology company is a world leader in building extremely complex defense systems — everything from missiles to fighter aircraft. But when the company needs to improve the mission-critical business processes behind its products, it finds there's no substitute for visually mapping information. The company's Lean Six Sigma facilitators use Mindjet® MindManager® to map information collected during Lean Six Sigma process-improvement events. "Lean Six-Sigma initiates structured change into the environment," says one of the company's leading Lean Six Sigma event facilitators. "Change is very frightening to most people, and inevitably generates resistance. Mapping helps address the challenges of changing an environment, because employees are able to focus better with the visual representation of that change."
(http://books.google.co.in/books?hl=en&lr=&id=UZhEciGE3wIC&oi=fnd&pg=PR13&dq=Six- Sigma+applications+by+MindManager&OTS=FH36oLzFyW&sig=v0Y2vtnzqzwZOlQtX0GPQNq9Hi8).

Capturing the way things are the facilitator uses MindManager to facilitate week-long Lean Six-Sigma events that bring together up to ten people from across many functional areas involved in a business process. The events have addressed hardware design, software development, networking and telecommunications, and horizontal integration. (Because the company's products are classified, we are not able in this case study to go into more detail on these processes.) Event participants most often have not worked together in a team environment. As such, it is important to level-set the team thinking as quickly as possible. The facilitator starts by capturing the group's brainstorming ideas on flip charts that are retained during the course of the event. The flip charts serve as references throughout the event, enabling team members to recall what they initially articulated regarding the current, ideal and future states of the process requiring the improvements. The facilitator then has the team start to explore the identification of waste and inefficiency in the processes. An associate at the meeting captures this information into a PowerPoint template that is used to out-brief at the end of the event.

Bringing the process into focus Midway through the event, the facilitator exports to MindManager the information captured in Power-Point. She begins arranging the ideas presented by the team into categories, such as the execution of work, the decision-making process, leadership and governance, communication processes, people's behaviors and attitudes, and reactions from customers and stakeholders.

When she reveals the categorized ideas to the team, she finds that it is easier for the participants to discuss ways to improve the process to meet the needs of customers.

"I have found that the mind map stimulates their thinking, which helps them come to conclusions faster," she says. "When they look at the map, they say, 'Now we "see" what our current environment looks like,' because it's all categorized into nice neat groups. The initial brainstorming process is effective in generating new ideas.

But it is hard to organize ideas written on multiple flip charts. The map adds structure to the ideas so the team members can easily view their environment as they have perceived and articulated it." The facilitator uses the map through the remainder of the event. "The map changes dynamically from the time it is first created through to the end of the event," she says. "It becomes the team's holistic view of the process under assessment, categorized and on one page, which is always included in the event outbrief. This leading defense technology company uses MindManager to create visual representations of current, ideal and future state characteristics.

Product Mindjet MindManager Result

Team members are able to quickly grasp the current and future state characteristics, issues and process improvements related to those characteristics, and to work together to devise ways to improve mission-critical business processes.

Conclusion

According to Greg Brue (2003), Six-Sigma is today's most honoured and effective quality initiative. Yet to achieve optimal results from such an initiative, companies must fast master the building blocks of Six-Sigma. Design for Six-Sigma (DFSS) shows decision makers at all levels how to implement and improve the DFSS tools and techniques from earliest design through final production of virtually any product, service or process. Six-Sigma principles and methodologies also show us how to join today's quality leaders by incorporating DFSS to each step of new product or service development programme for maximum impact and return on Six-Sigma Investment.

The Future of Six-Sigma

In terms of its future directions, three trends have clearly emerged and a fourth is a logical conclusion. The three emerging trends, which should be a surprise to no one, are:

1. Continuing evolution of Six-Sigma, both in terms of tools and deployment strategies.
2. Growth in new application areas, particularly financial services and healthcare.
3. Further development and standardization of design for Six-Sigma (DFSS).

The fourth, less obvious, future direction for Six-Sigma is that it will become integrated within organizations' overall quality management systems (QMS), rather than being a standalone initiative. Six-Sigma has also been integrated with other improvement approaches, including Baldrige, ISO 9000 and lean manufacturing. Many organizations integrate these approaches with their Six-Sigma approach because of Six-Sigma's brand recognition. The improvement approach used by AlliedSignal, now part of Honeywell, evolved from a focus on operational excellence to Six-Sigma to Six-Sigma Plus. This evolution and integration is natural when we note all the other improvement approaches and Six-Sigma focus on process improvement. Hence the process view of work becomes the integrating concept.

As an organization uses Six-Sigma in every way possible, Six-Sigma becomes part of its corporate signature, just as the Packer Sweep was the signature of the Green Bay Packers in the early 1960s. When all the players did what they were supposed to do and followed the process, the Packer Sweep was unstoppable. The team used its signature play whenever it wanted. The sweep defined the football team just as Six-Sigma can define a corporate culture and become its signature (http://sqp.asq.org/pub/sixsigma/past/vol3_issue4/ssfmv3i4youropinion.pdf).

Six-sigma is likely to remain as one of the key initiatives to improve the management process than just being remembered as one of the fads. The primary focus should be on improving overall management performance, not just pinpointing and counting defects. Researchers and practitioners are trying to integrate Six-Sigma with other existing innovative management practices that have been around to make Six-Sigma methods even more attractive to different organizations that might have not started or fully implemented the Six-Sigma method. Integrating and comparing principles and characteristics of Six-Sigma with Total Quality Management, Human Resource Functions, Lean Production, ISO 9000, ISO 9001, and the capability maturity model are all part of the quality community's effort to maximize the positive effect of the Six-Sigma method (Kawaka and Anbari, 2004).

3

Global Competitiveness in Regional and National Context

Regionalism and Globalization

Globalism can be defined as programmatic globalization, the vision of a borderless world. Globalization can be seen as a qualitatively new phenomenon. If globalization implies a tendency towards a global social system, its origins may be traced far back in history, but one could also argue that the process reached a new stage in the post-Second World War era. The subjective sense of geographical distance is dramatically changed; some even speak of "the end of geography". Also in ecological terms the world is experienced as one. Economic interdependence was made possible by the political stability of the American world order, which lasted from the end of the Second World War until the late '60s or early '70s. Basically, globalization indicates a qualitative deepening of the internationalization process, strengthening the functional and weakening the territorial dimension of development.

Globalism thus implies the growth of a world market, increasingly penetrating and dominating the "national" economies, which in the process are bound to lose some of their "nationness". This means dominance of the world market over structures of local production, as well as the increasing prevalence of Western-type consumerism. From this, there may emerge a political will to halt or to reverse the process of globalization, in order to safeguard some degree of territorial control and cultural diversity. One way of achieving such a change could be through the New Regionalism.

The two processes of globalization and regionalization are articulated within the same larger process of global structural transformation, the outcome of which depends on a dialectical rather than linear development. It can therefore not be readily extrapolated or easily foreseen. But rather it expresses the relative strength of contending social forces involved in the two processes. They deeply affect the stability of the Westphalian state system; and therefore they at the same time contribute to both disorder and, possibly, a future world order. There is an intricate relationship between regionalization and globalization. Compared to "regionalism", with an impressive theoretical tradition behind it, "globalism" is a more recent concept in social science (http://www.unu.edu/unupress/globalism.html#Global).

To consider the relative advantages of regional versus global organizations one must begin with clarity about why it is that particular international organizations are created. Some organizations are essentially single purpose, others have multiple purposes. Among the purposes, or functions, for which international organizations are designed are (1) to secure peace among their members; (2) to provide for external security vis-à-vis other states; (3) to carry out a variety of economic-related tasks, such as development, managing or promoting interdependence; (4) to address problems of environmental protection; or (5) securing human rights. These purposes are of course carried out by a wide range of international organizations, including international non-governmental organizations (INGOs) as well as intergovernmental organizations (http://www.unu.edu/unupress/globalism.html#Global).

That the term 'regionalism' – inextricably linked with 'globalization' in the first place, might be *prima facie* unclear to many. How the basic question that needs to address is 'Does Regionalism, in its several manifestations, advances the processes and pace of globalization when it reinforces the very geographical boundaries that globalization seeks to eliminate?' In what way does the apparent definition of Asia and for that matter the other regions of the world, not conflict with its integration? Consequently, the world community, unsettled by these rhetorical questions, is diametrically opposed to any attempts by Asian countries to regionalize. Yet in doing so the world community is instead destroying the link between Asia and the world. The concept of regionalism has long been associated with protectionism, where countries in the region form trading blocs, accorded preferential treatment only to one another and closed their doors to the global economy.

The lack of regionalism might, on the other hand, may worsen the anti-globalization stance already adopted by certain Asian countries. It is precisely regionalization, or the lack of it, that saw China and India not opening their doors to foreign trade in the earlier decades—especially during their pre-reforms era. In contrast, Singapore, having reaped the benefits of regionalization, later moved on to become one of the freest economies in the world. Thus, regionalization today should instead be viewed as a stepping stone which provides conservative states with an option to open up their economies on a regional basis. It might also help the participating countries in a region to achieve strategic advantages, tax and tariff concessions, reduction of entry barriers etc. and thus help build synergy over a period of time. The other key advantage of Regionalism is to minimize the economic disparity across the countries in a Region and attain strategic advantage, competitive advantage and building synergy over a fairly longer period of time. Given the risk that globalization itself carries when it forces the economic door open, for example when in the wake of the 1997 Asian Financial Crisis, it was pertinent that states cooperate with one another, with regionalism to tide over the impending Financial crises. Having recognized the inherent benefits of regionalism, states should be encouraged to open up to a larger economic platform of common economic interest, and ultimately be the part of the global economy. This is also precisely one of the objectives how and why WTO was created after a series of international, multilateral and regional trade negotiations.

If the regionalism of Asia were to take place, however, we should see it differently from the conventional paradigm which we viewed from the regionalism of entities such as the European Union (EU). The economies of Asia are intertwined naturally in the first place; without the "teamwork" in place the Asian development would never have been that impressive. The establishment of ASEAN-plus Three (APT), a dialogue between Asian countries, can be viewed as the catalyst for the Regional progress—particularly in East Asia. ASEAN, already an established grouping, can serve to bridge the divide between Sino-Japan relations, insofar the limiting reagent to the growth of Asia's economy. Economic heavyweights Japan and China can work towards developing a financial mechanism, helping developing economies in the process. Moreover, the transfers of trade, investments and technologies have already been a parcel of the workings of the ASEAN economy and APT can serve to provide an institutional framework to it, thereby enhancing the process (Lahiri, 2001).

To sum-up it may be stated that the global economy needs Asia, as much as Asia needs the global economy. Being mutually dependant, it serves Asia to contribute to her best of the abilities so that both parties can benefit as much as possible. Given the spirited growth associated with Asia, so should her contributions. In terms of trade, Asia can expand her role via a gradual shift of emphasis from production to consumption. The international financial system is also a direct platform whereby Asia can play her role as an emerging power, instead of the silent participant that she usually is. Yet in order to work with the world, Asian countries must first be able work with each other. Both Asia and the world community are concerned about the global economy, but when taking their different approaches towards their concerns, there is bound to be friction and implicit conflict in interests among them. In the face of this, both parties should bear in mind that the improvement of the global economy is not a strictly competitive game, whereby Asia's gain is equated with the world's loss but the whole idea should evolve around working for a win-win situation to all across economic regions and try and transcend beyond the narrow confines of regionalism.

Asia's Role in the Global Economy

Asia is currently one of the world's most economically vibrant and emerging regions. In the past decade, Asia's importance in the global economy has been growing phenomenally, taking full advantage of demography and the related factors. Since the 1970s, the East Asian tiger economies of Singapore, South Korea, Hong Kong and Taiwan, along with Japan, have been maintaining highly impressive economic growth rates along with the rapid industrializing of their economies. With the introduction of the massive giants of China and India into the fold, along with the emergence of increasing competition from Thailand and Malaysia, the countries in Asia are fast catching up with the developed economy of the Western world. Asia's growing role in the global economy has also attracted the region's desire for investment mainly into industrial infrastructure and energy sector by the international financial community. In the years to come, economic policy decisions in Asia will have profound effects on the global economy (http://www.mas.gov.sg/resource/eco_research/eco_education/ess2005/2005_2nd_PU64essay.pdf). The rapid growth of emerging market economies in Asia has been a notable feature of the global economy in recent years. This growth has been led most visibly by China and, increasingly, India, but several other Asian countries play an important and vibrant role as well. The strong performance of these economies, combined with the continued dynamism of the U.S., has helped sustain the current worldwide expansion, offsetting ongoing sluggishness in Europe and also in Japan, where growth has remained sporadic despite progress in bank and corporate sector restructuring. This positive performance has spurred new confidence about the future. Asia's growing role in the global economy has also naturally increased the region's desire to assume a higher profile in the international financial community, including the World Bank, IMF, ADB etc (http://www.indonesia-ottawa.org/information/details.php?type=news_copy&id=959).

An Analysis into Economic Development in Asia

Clearly, Asia's growth over the last half century has been dramatic. Japan leapt past the post first, soon to be followed by the Newly Industrialized Economies of Hong Kong, China, the Republic of Korea, Singapore and Taipei, China. Then came the rapid development of countries now joined together in the Association of South East Asian Nations, or ASEAN.

Particularly impressive these days are the economic rise of the People's Republic of China and India. Over the last 10 years, China grew at an average annual rate of 9.1% and India at a rate of 6.3% of GDP. And most forecasters see continued rapid growth in these countries in the years ahead - likely 8% to 9% in China and 7% to 8% for India. But more importantly, growth is widely shared. Our latest figures show an estimated average GDP growth of 6.6% across the developing economies of Asia and the Pacific last year, and we expect to see continued growth in the coming years (ADB, 2005).

The ascent of Asia's economy in the last quarter of a century is highly remarkable. From Asian Tigers and ASEAN to Japan, the world has seen economies recording unprecedented, nearing double digit growth rates over the years. However, these economies, impressive their developments were, can only be viewed in lesser light when comparing with global heavyweights.

While Japan undeniably remains as the region's powerhouse geographically, not many will view her so when defining the Asia in political and economical context due to her alignment with Western economies. Moreover, having peaked by the 1990s, Japan has established herself as a global leader who contributes massively to the world finance system.

Approximately two decades after the drastic pro-market reforms swept their economies, China and India were no longer that of the yesteryear. The massive influx of Foreign Direct Investments (FDI) and production of exports propels these economies forward at such breakneck speed that even conservatives keen to make their point on trade restrictions will attribute, to a certain degree, China and India's economic growth to their participation in the global economy. Today, China and India are the fourth and tenth largest economies in the world, and are still growing. Populous Asia is often linked with the economics of scale she enjoys and comparative advantage as a low wage labour market. Demographically, Asians are in their prime years and investors are hence more likely to view them as being consumption-orientated. Geographically, the mobility of factors of production and the proximity of Asian cities those factors encourages the agglomeration of production.

Asia's Position in the World Trade

Asia's integration into the world trading system has been a win-win situation for both Asian and the global economy. By blending large quantity of capital, which originated from massive FDI and entrepreneurs, with low wage market, Asia's economy is able to generate an upward spiral in production. Japan is a leader in many international finance institutions, most significantly being a co-founder of the Group of Seven (G7). It has consistently ranked top in the Official Donor Assistance (ODA) scheme. This export led strategy has so far been able to propel Asia's economy to high growth, and allowed international economies, especially developing ones, to enjoy cheaper prices for economic goods.

Traditionally, much of Asia's resources have been directed towards creating means of production to satisfy world demand. However, as the growth of Asia's economy outpaces the growth in international demand, producers should now cater for domestic consumption instead. From the viewpoint of the global economy, Asia has outgrown her role a production base and it is now timely for her to play the global consumer instead. The reasons that can be ascribed for this are: Firstly, producers should note that Asia accounts for over half the world population and is henceforth a massive untapped market. With Asia's economic growth, the spending power of consumers rises, and so should production catering to domestic demand. Producers should also realize that marginal consumption decreases with increased consumption, making it more viable to direct more resources to locals' consumption, rather than investment and eventually to developed world citizens whose appetites are largely satisfied.

Secondly, viewing from national interest, many Asian countries, especially China, have accumulated large reserves and US securities from trading surpluses over the years. The value of these securities is based entirely on confidence towards the US economy and with accumulation, is low-yielding. It hence serves better to utilize these securities now than in the future.

Thirdly, the government needs to take into account the casual relation between economic growth and economic welfare. For Asia, rising opportunity costs of economic growth has been brought about by overinvestment, the consequence being the lack of production of consumption goods, which is a better measure of economic welfare. To the global economy, Asia's shift to the global consumer not only provides an alternative to US preponderance but also allows developing countries to set up their own production bases.

Over the last 25 (1980-2007) years, the contribution of Asia to global trade has increased substantially, notably its exports. From about 16% of global exports in 1980, this share climbed to about 27% in 2005. This trend can partially be explained by substantial investments that went into new export-oriented manufacturing facilities using the advantages of low production costs, notably in terms of labor. The gap between exports and imports has also substantially increased after 1997 when currency devaluations made the region more competitive. Yet, as development takes place, Asian economies are consuming increasing amounts of resources (http://people.hofstra.edu/geotrans/eng/ch2en/conc2en/shareworldtrc.html).

International Financial System and Global Issues

The global financial system (GFS) is a financial system consisting of institutions and regulations that act on the international level, as opposed to those that act on a national or regional level. The main players are the global institutions, such as International Monetary Fund and Bank for International Settlements, national agencies and government departments, e.g., central banks and finance ministries, and private institutions acting on the global scale, e.g., banks and hedge funds (http://en.wikipedia.org/wiki/Global_financial_system).

Following the meteoric rise of Asian economies such as Japan, and more recently, China and India, and the near saturation of the US and EU economies, there is a distinct distribution and depolarization of regional economic power base. Having established the might of ASEAN economy earlier it will be inevitable that international financial institutions confer a greater role to Asia reflecting on its economic power. However, to gain approval in the international community, the Asian economy, especially China, must show a greater commitment to global issues. Japan, China and India, with the second, fourth and tenth largest economies in the world, are clearly Asian countries which have reached a point whereby they can influence the global economy. Yet these countries, in particular China and India, hold little influence in affecting or changing financial regulations, partly because their interactions with the global economy only started during the 1990s. India, wanting to achieve self-reliance, closed her door to the international finance system until recently. Similarly, China began participating in international economic groupings only recently, having joined the International Monetary Fund (IMF) in 1980 and World Trade Organization (WTO) in 2001.

While Asia has maintained a good track record of cooperating with these organizations, establishing her position in these organizations takes time. Political insecurities may also account for the reluctance of the international community to accept Asia's place in the international financial system. The collapse of the Soviet Union might have taken place long ago, but the policy of containment still remained deeply rooted in Western democracies, explaining for the lukewarm reactions to the rise of countries affiliated with communism, examples being Vietnam, China and Myanmar. For example, the tying up of trade with human rights resulted in widespread resentment in China, in what was perceived to be a hidden political agenda to impose Western values on non-Western countries. To rectify such problems, Asia must continue to prove herself in the world stage. China's participation in organizations such as the G-20 is no doubt laudable, but Asia cannot afford to limit herself to mere participation, but should advocate issues to the benefit of the international community, and respond to their concerns. One issue which concerns the world community will be the impact of economic growth in Asia to the environment.

Asia Leading the World Economy

Asia has become a key player of the global economy, boasting three of the ten largest economies (China, Japan, and India) and accounting for more than 35 per cent of world GDP (IMF-F&D, 2006). This could be evident from the relative contribution of Asia's share of GDP versus those of EU and the US.

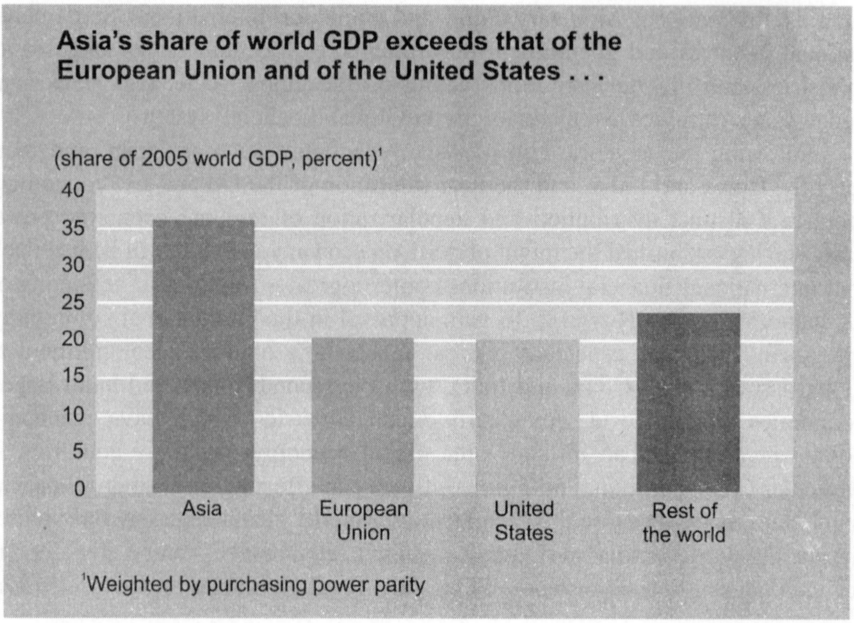

Asia's share of world GDP is rising: thanks to its economic dynamism. Indeed, the region's economy, having fully recovered from the 1997–98 financial crises, is now the fastest growing in the world, contributing close to 50 per cent of world growth, as would be evident from the following illustration (Finance and Development, 2006).

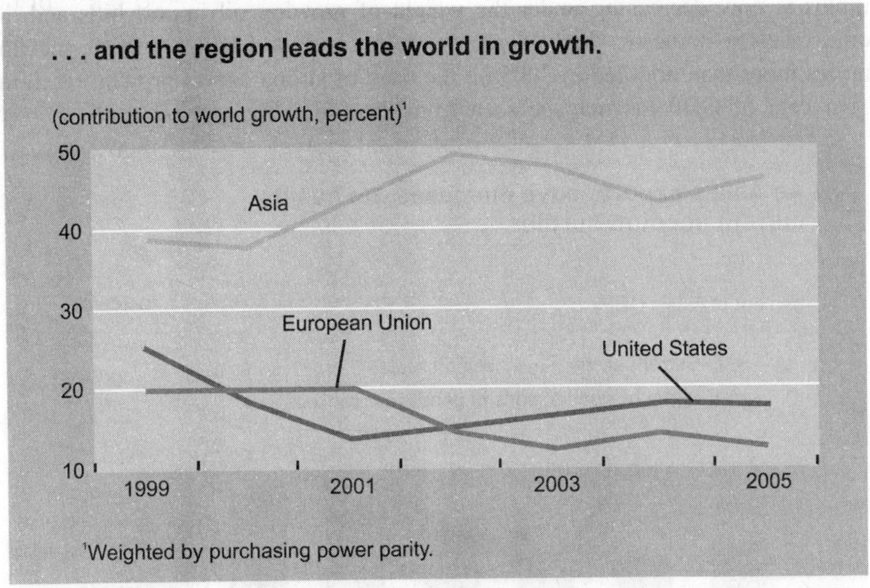

Asia's economic viability and growth trends in the recent years (1997-2005) largely reflect its ability to successfully integrate its economy with the world economy. Apart from a brief dip after the collapse of the 2001 information technology boom, its share of world exports has increased steadily and now stands at 27 per cent. Intraregional trade is also growing as countries position themselves at different stages of a regional supply chain.

India's growth story is set to contribute significantly to global GDP from now until 2020, according to a mid-August report of the International Labour Organization (ILO). The report, which was discussed at the Asian Employment Forum at Beijing earlier this month, says if Asia continues to grow at 4.6-4.7%, it would account for a growing share of global GDP — up from 24.7% to around 30-31% in 2020. Within the region, India and China would be the big drivers of growth as in the run-up to 2006. India's share of Asia's GDP is expected to rise from 7.2% to 8.7-10% by 2020.

India's short-run share of the world GDP in 2020 has been estimated at 3% and the long-run share is pegged at 2.7%, at a projected annual growth rate of 7.5% (short-run) and 6.3% (long-run), respectively. China's share of world GDP in 2020, both short and long-run, has been estimated at 9.7% at an annual growth rate of 8.5% (short-run) and 8% (long-run). "As Asia's two giants grow and comprise an even larger share of regional output, other regional countries will see an increase in potential benefits...," says the report 'Visions for Asia's Decent Work Decade: Sustainable Growth and Jobs to 2015' (http://economictimes.indiatimes.com/Indicators/India__China_to_help_Asia_make_up_30_of_world_GDP_by_20/articleshow/2316152.cms).

The rise in exports, coupled with generally sluggish domestic demand, has translated into sizable current account surpluses. But if China is excluded, Asia's surplus is now decreasing under the weight of growing oil import bills and, in some cases, a domestic demand recovery. In contrast, China's current account surplus more than doubled in 2005 on the back of strong export growth, reaching 7 per cent of GDP (as may be seen from the following graphs).

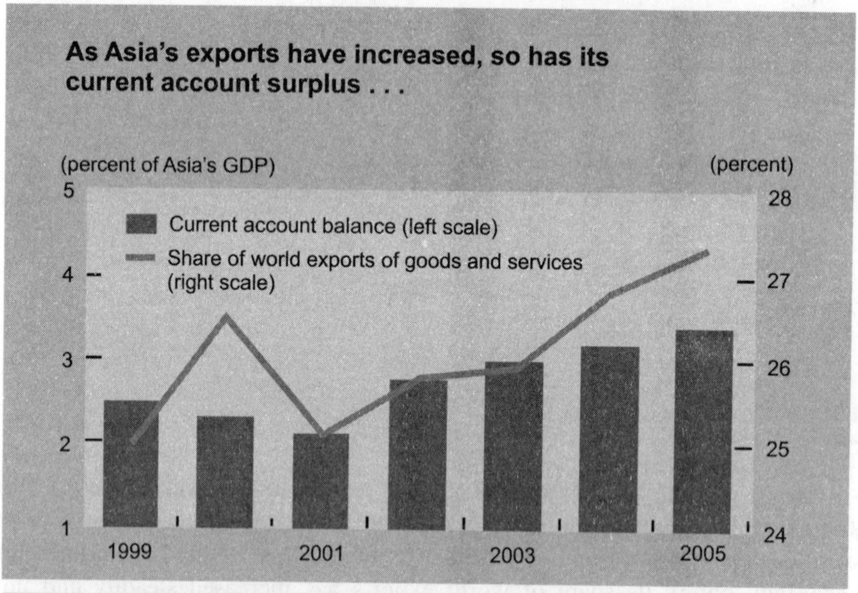

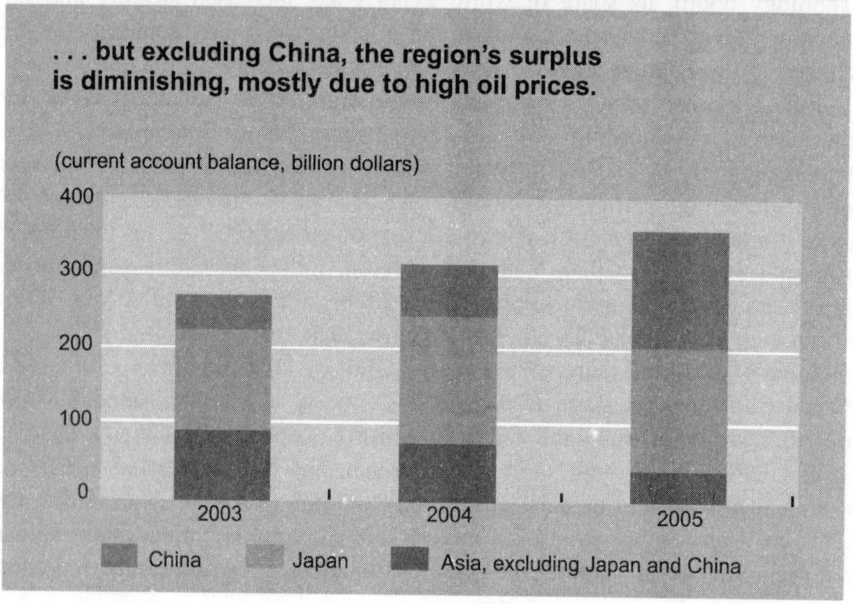

Asia has also integrated into global capital markets, capturing about 40 per cent of net private capital flows going to emerging markets. Two-thirds of private equity flowing into the region is in the form of direct investment. These capital inflows, combined with the region's current account surplus, have led to a large accumulation of foreign exchange reserves.

Over the past few years, foreign exchange reserves have risen sharply . . .

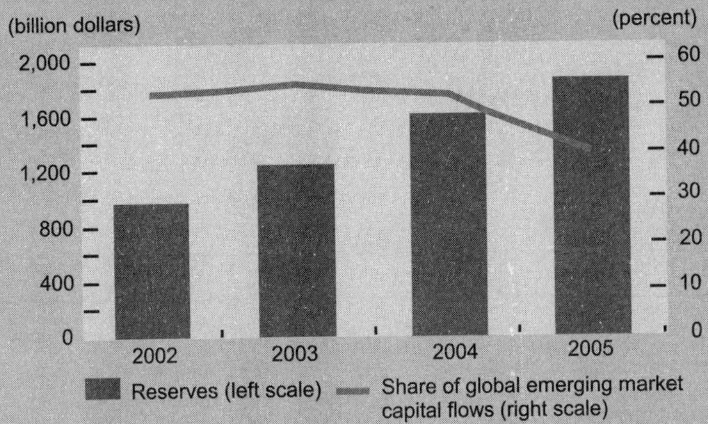

[1]China, Hong Kong SAR, India, Indonesai, Korea, Malaysia, Philippines, Singapore, Taiwan Province of China, and Thailand.

Sources: IMF, *World Economic Outlook*, and staff estimates; and CEIC Data Company Ltd.

Exchange rate flexibility has increased significantly in most of the region (outside China, Hong Kong SAR, and Malaysia). While the strong wave of capital inflows in 2003 led to a large accumulation of reserves, more recent waves have led to less reserve accumulation and greater exchange rate movement.

In the years ahead, the region is expected to account for a rising share of the world economy, thanks in large part to fast-growing India and China. The challenge will be to strengthen domestic demand by reviving investment in emerging Asia and consumption in China.

In Asia, the proportion of old people is expected to increase, as it is in other regions. This is particularly true in Japan, where the overall population is already shrinking. Aging populations will reduce potential GDP growth and strain fiscal positions, as pension and healthcare expenditures increase.

. . . but outside China, the reserve buildup has slowed since 2004, as exchange rates have become more flexible.

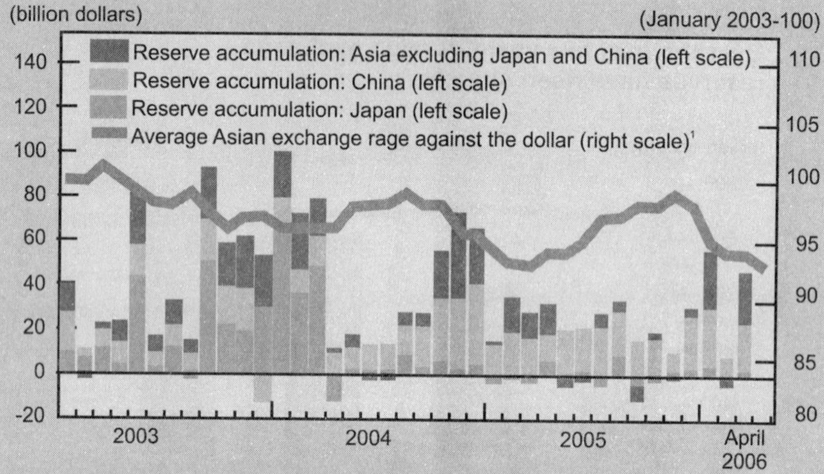

[1]Comprises India, Indonesia, Japan, Korea, Philippines, Singapore, Taiwan Province of China and Thailand; a decline in the exchange rate signifies an appreciation.

Sources: CEIC Data Company Ltd.; and IMF staff estimates.

Asia needs to put its surpluses to work at home . . .

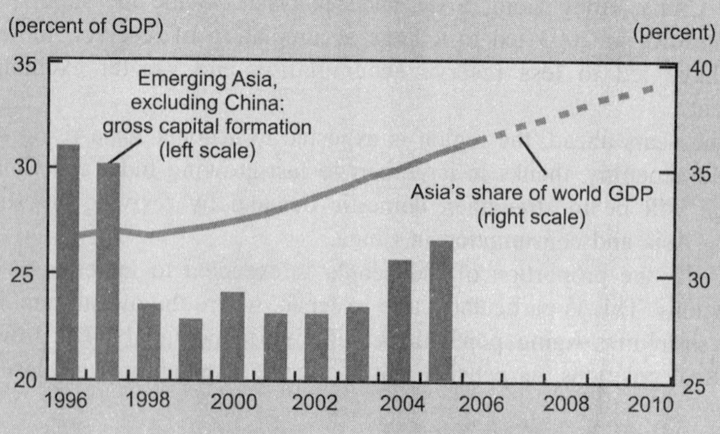

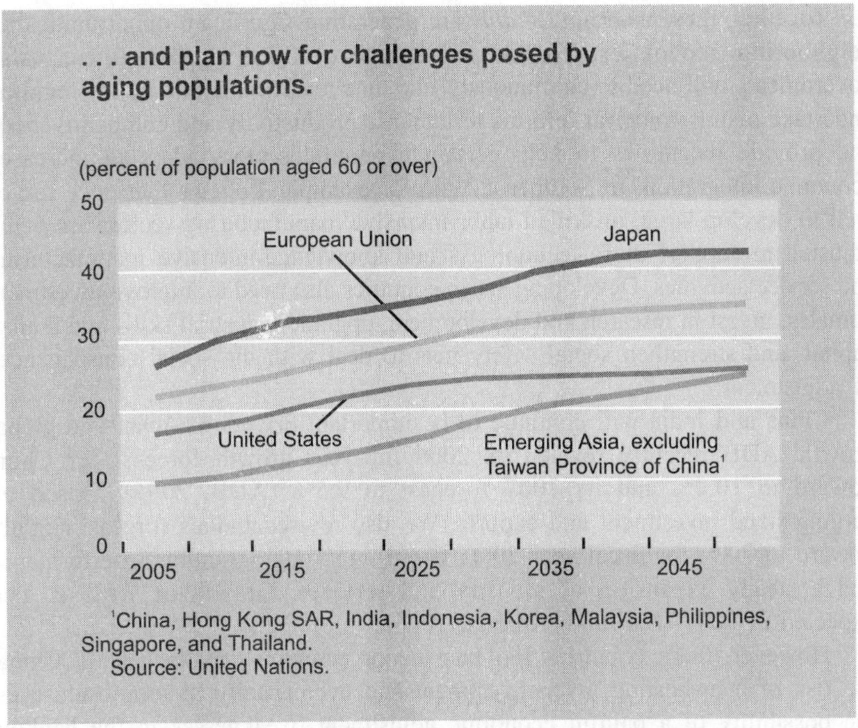

Source for all the above graphs: IMF, 'World Economic Outlook database'

Emerging Asia and the Global Economy

Opportunities and Challenges for Asia

China's spectacular growth has had a profound impact on economic relationships among the deeply integrated trading economies of East Asia. China is now a key link in the regional production network, absorbing a large volume of *foreign direct investment*, importing materials and components from East Asian neighbors, and exporting finished products to the region, the United States and Europe. It is the largest market for all the Newly Industrialized Economies, and an important and growing market for Japan, Malaysia, Philippines, Singapore and Thailand, as well as global exporters and foreign services providers (Kuroda, 2006).

Similarly, India's ties with neighboring South Asian economies have strengthened in recent years with the spread of Indian exports and investment. Its trade and investment linkages with East Asian economies are expanding rapidly as a result of its large and dynamic market, English-speaking workforce, and international reputation in information technology services and pharmaceuticals.

Together, these *emerging giants* are generating significant opportunities for neighboring economies. To take advantage of these opportunities, Asian governments will need to continuously fine tune macroeconomic policy regimes; undertake major structural reforms to increase productivity and competitiveness; and provide incentives to help certain economic sectors adapt to increased economic integration. In Southeast Asia, for example, policies that once served well to develop large, unskilled labor-intensive manufacturing sectors are being adjusted to support more technology- and knowledge-intensive manufacturing and service activities. Developing Asian countries also need to improve investment climates, invest in research and development, upgrade industrial skills and human capital, and strengthen social safety nets to deal with the social consequences of adjustment.

China and India will continue to be important drivers of Asian and global growth. ADB recently revised its 2006 full-year growth forecast for China upward to 10.4% and its 2007 forecast to 9.5% (ADB, 2006) based on surging fixed investment and exports. We also revised India's forecast slightly upward to 7.8% for fiscal year 2006, based on strong agricultural performance and a steady expansion of industry and services. Growth of 7.8% is also expected in 2007 (Haruhiko Kuroda, 2006).

However, these countries too face major economic challenges. In China, the risk of over-heating, over-investment and overcapacity in some industries, the possibility of a painful economic adjustment, weaknesses in the banking sector, energy inefficiency and environmental degradation are of ongoing concern. India has a huge need for infrastructure investment. India also needs to accelerate domestic market integration, as well as economic integration with its Asian neighbors.

Above all, China, India and their neignbors must find ways to bring the poor into the mainstream economy. Despite remarkable success in reducing poverty, the Asia and Pacific region is home to a huge proportion of the world's poor, with nearly 1.9 billion people living on less than $ 2 a day in 2003 (ADB, 2005). Inequality is growing – in India as well as China – and there are wide income gaps among Asian countries. Narrowing these development gaps is crucial to sustain regional growth and stability.

Regional Economic Integration – Progress and Prospects

Regional cooperation and economic integration, while not a panacea, holds an important key to meeting these challenges. By working together, Asian countries can ensure that they and their citizens have greater opportunities to connect to the global economy, participate in growth and pull themselves out of poverty. The Asian Development Bank is strongly committed to promoting such efforts with support for "cross-border infrastructure and logistics development", trade and investment integration; monetary and financial integration, and cooperation in the provision of regional public goods (http://www.adb.org/Documents/Speeches/2006/ms2006008.asp).

Asia has historically been a very open and integrated region. Trade and investment liberalization, the emergence of global value chains, improved physical connectivity, reductions in transport and logistics costs, and technological progress have brought Asian economies ever closer. In East Asia, intraregional trade has risen from 43% of total trade in 1990 to 55% in 2005 – only modestly lower than the 62% figure for the 15 European Union countries.

With the phenomenal growth the region is experiencing today, there is enormous potential to build on this success and realize an unprecedented era of prosperity. However, like globalization, the process of regionalization needs to be managed effectively so that its potential is realized for the benefit of all. For example, bilateral and regional trade agreements (FTAs) are spreading in Asia, with some 81 such agreements in existence and over 100 more either proposed or under negotiation. Such arrangements can be beneficial, as long as they induce domestic structural reforms and create open, competitive market environments. But the danger is that they are not of similar scope, nor is participation consistent throughout the region. In the wake of the suspension of multilateral trade negotiations – the WTO Doha development round – there are growing concerns that disparate and overlapping trade agreements could further proliferate.

To effectively manage regional integration, Asia will need new and stronger regional institutions to exploit opportunities and meet a variety of challenges. In this respect, the Association of Southeast Asian Nations, or ASEAN, is emerging as a regional leader. Through ASEAN, Asian policymakers are engaging in policy dialogue, coordination, and cooperation to further liberalize trade and investment and strengthen monetary and financial integration. The Chiang Mai Initiative, for example, was a significant step toward reserve pooling among the ASEAN+3 countries in the post-crisis years. The *Asian Bond Markets Initiative* is also making some progress in strengthening the region's financial architecture and promoting economic integration. And ASEAN countries are working together to improve cross-border infrastructure, facilitate trade, and manage shared risks such as environmental degradation, communicable diseases, natural disasters, and trans-boundary crimes. Similar efforts are beginning in other sub-regions, through initiatives such as the South Asian Association for Regional Cooperation and the Central Asia Regional Economic Cooperation program. And, there are positive signs that a more inclusive, pan-Asian community may eventually emerge.

For instance, South Asia, inspired by India's "Look East" policy and spearheaded by increasing trade and investment links with its neighbors, is gradually forging closer ties with East Asia and Central Asia. In Central Asia, there is a growing awareness of the need for regional integration, particularly in the area of transport logistics and trade liberalization and facilitation. And ASEAN leaders have agreed to accelerate the establishment of an ASEAN Economic Community (AEC) to 2015. This ambitious initiative would help ASEAN countries maintain economic cohesion, deepen intraregional integration, and enhance their competitiveness, while turning ASEAN into a vibrant hub for pan-Asian integration.

Asia in the Global Community

Asia's rise presents significant economic opportunities for all players in the international economy. But it also holds challenges for global governance and global integration. Asia now accounts for nearly 30% of world GDP – double the figure for the 1960s. Global institutions and mechanisms need to evolve to reflect the growing importance of developing economies in Asia and elsewhere. The IMF, for one, recognizes this and will be voting on an important package of reforms in the next few days. Other forums, such as the G8, also need to take this important reality into account. G8 member states today account for only about half of the world's exports and industrial output. It is difficult to see how global challenges can be met without the participation of some of the world's largest and fastest growing economies.

The global community is at a crucial point in its trade negotiations. While an ambitious Doha trade deal with a comprehensive agricultural agenda would be ideal, even a limited Doha agreement would raise global income, encourage globalization and avoid protectionism. Moreover, a 'Doha-deal' would open markets further, hasten domestic reforms, accelerate cross-border direct investment, create new jobs and lay the foundation for future economic growth. Owing to its high trade openness, strong human capital and modern infrastructure, Asian developing countries would witness notable gains from a 'Doha-deal'. As APEC strongly urged following its conference last week, efforts to restart the stalled negotiations are critical to the economic progress of Asia and the world.

In the meantime, inter-regional ties, such as those between Asia and Europe, must continually be deepened and nourished. There are a number of mechanisms through which this can be achieved. The Asia-Europe Meeting, for example – ASEM, as it is called – has for ten years worked to bring these two important regions closer together through policy dialogue and joint projects and actions. With the conclusion of its 6th Summit earlier this week, ASEM is well positioned to further strengthen its role in promoting cross-regional and global stability and prosperity.

One of the most important developments of the past decade has been the emergence of Asia as the most dynamic region of the world with the rise of China and India as engines of growth, recovery of Japan from a decade old recession, and emergence of Asian middle-class as source of final demand. This new-found dynamism makes regionalism a viable trade and development strategy for Asia. Although functional integration in the region has increased as is evident from the high and growing proportion of intra-regional trade and investments, Asia has lagged behind other regions in exploitation of potential of *Regional Trading Arrangements* (RTAs). The lack of an effective broader regional arrangement has prevented Asia from exploiting some fruitful opportunities for regional cooperation and from exercising its influence in global economic governance commensurate with its rapidly growing economic weight.

Recognizing the potential of regional cooperation over the past decade ASEAN has not only deepened the sub-regional cooperation between its 10 member states, but has also facilitated the cause of broader cooperation by holding plus one Summit with major Asian countries. These countries are now building a complex web of free trade arrangements linking ASEAN and themselves. There is need for building on these sub-regional and bilateral attempts a broader regional framework to provide a seamless market facilitating exploitation of their synergies more effectively. An important initiative in the direction was the launch of the East Asia Summit (EAS) in December 2005 in Kuala Lumpur, Malaysia, as an annual forum bringing together ASEAN, Japan, China, India, South Korea, Australia and New Zealand (http://www.newasiaforum.org/ANRAGR.htm).

India, Emerging Asia and the Global Economy

The emerging Asia accounts for around 45 per cent of world population and around 11 per cent of world GDP, though in PPP terms the share of GDP is about 27 per cent. However, in recent years, given the strong growth, the emerging Asia has contributed almost one-half of the global growth in GDP. In emerging Asia, the annual growth in GDP of 8.4 per cent and 8.3 per cent during 2004 and 2005, respectively, was impressive considering that the growth in the world economy during the corresponding period was 5.3 per cent and 4.8 per cent, respectively. According to the IMF, this growth momentum in Emerging Asia is expected to continue in 2006 as well and real GDP in the region is projected to expand by 8.0 per cent, while the global growth is placed at 4.8 per cent for the year 2006 (Srinivasan, 2006).

Since the beginning of the new millennium, the strong performance of emerging Asia, combined with the continued dynamism of the US has helped to sustain the current worldwide expansion, offsetting sluggishness in Europe and also in Japan. Being the fastest growing economies of the world, over the past two years, China and India contributed 73 per cent to the Asian growth and 38 per cent to the world GDP growth (World Economic Outlook, IMF, September, 2005). If the recent recovery of economic activity in Japan gets strengthened, Japan is expected to be another engine of growth for the Asian as well as the global economy.

Some observers prefer to describe the emerging economies of Asia as re-emerging economies to clarify that shift of wealth to Asia that is taking place is not an unprecedented situation, looking back into economic history, of course, by about three centuries. As per an OECD publication, in 1700, India's share in world GDP was 24.4 per cent, while China's share was 22.3 per cent. Asia as a whole (including Japan) accounted for 61.7 per cent in 1700, which fell to 59.2 per cent in 1820, and to a low of 18.5 per cent in 1950, before climbing to 37.2 per cent by 1998 (Maddison Angus, "The World Economy: A Millennium Perspective", OECD, 2001). The re-emergence in the second half of the 20th century was led by resurgence of Japan, succeeded by the miracle of East Asian economies, followed by China's outstanding success, and currently strengthened by Indian economy's impressive performance in terms of both growth and stability. According to the data published in the World Development Indicators of the World Bank, India ranks fourth next only to the USA, China and Japan in terms of size of the economies measured on the basis of Purchasing Power Parity (PPP). It is interesting that in terms of PPP, three out of the four largest economies of the world are in Asia.

In the recent years, the Asian economies are emerging as major trading partners of India. India's trade has grown faster with these countries than its overall trade growth. Emerging Asian economies accounted for a significant share of 22.4 per cent in India's total exports in 2004-05 (16.0 per cent in 1999-2000) and 20.1 per cent of total Indian imports (16.2 per cent in 1999-2000). In 2004-05, China has emerged as the second major export destination for India after the US and it has now become the largest source of imports for India, surpassing the US. Exports to China surged by 81 per cent in 2004-05, while imports from China increased by 67 per cent reflecting growing trade relations between the two countries. A similar trend was noticeable *vis-à-vis* the ASEAN-5 (Singapore, Thailand, Malaysia, Indonesia and the Philippines), but going forward there is vast scope for further expansion in trade with these countries. In a way, the increasing openness of the Indian economy to the external sector in recent years reflects its expanding economic relationships with rest of Asia. In recognition of the growing importance of Asian countries in India's foreign trade, the series of nominal and real effective exchange rate indices released by the Reserve Bank have been revised to include Chinese Renminbi and Hong Kong dollar in the weighting scheme. Japan being already included, the representation of Asian economies has increased to three out of the total of six countries.

The BRIC Power in Regional Economic Growth

BRIC or **BRICs** are terms used in economics to refer to the combination of Brazil, Russia, India, and China. The acronym was first coined in 2001 and prominently used in a thesis of the Goldman Sachs investment bank. The main point of these papers was to argue that the economies of the BRICs are rapidly developing and by 2050 will eclipse most of the current richest countries of the world. The Goldman Sachs thesis proposed something like an economic bloc, or a formal trading association, like the European Union (http://en.wikipedia.org/wiki/BRIC).

Time and again, the World Economic Group evaluated India's candidacy as a member of the BRIC nations that are supposedly 'poised to become global economic superpowers'. The 'BRICs' story is not simply about growth successes of developing economies. What makes the BRICs special is that they have the scale and the trajectory to challenge the major economies. Looking across the developing world today, the BRIC nations clearly stand out on both their economic and demographic size. The BRICs' impact on the global economy has continued to grow over the last few years, through a wide range of dimensions. The recent report on BRIC nations released by Goldman Sachs also highlights certain interesting facts in this regard.

1. **Growth and Trade:** Between 2000 and 2005, the BRICs contributed roughly 28% of global growth in US dollar terms and 55% in purchasing power parity (PPP) terms. Their share of global trade continues to climb at a rapid rate. At close to 15% currently, it is now double its level in 2001. Trade amongst the BRIC nations has also accelerated, with intra-BRICs trade now nearly 8% of their total trade compared to 5% in 2000. Also, India (in intellectual property) and Brazil (in agriculture) have illustrated their policymaking leadership among developing countries through the WTO negotiation process. The BRICs' share of oil demand is moving steadily higher, with an estimated 18% share in the current year.
2. **Capital Flows:** The BRICs have played an important part in global financial developments. Latest estimates suggest that the BRICs now hold more than 30% of world reserves. While China is the dominant holder, Russia, India and Brazil have also accumulated sizeable proportions. Also, despite the reserve accumulation, real exchange rates in each country have appreciated over the last couple of years. BRICs' current accounts continue to be in surplus, reflecting the group's key role in the global savings supply. With China's surplus increasing sharply, the BRICs' current account is estimated at around US $ 240 bn in 2005 (close to 6% of BRICs' GDP). Further, the BRICs' share as a destination for global FDI also continues to rise (now 15% of the global total, nearly three times higher than in 2000).
3. **Markets:** BRICs' stock markets have got gradually re-rated since 2003, with Brazilian, Russian and Indian indices all up by around 150% over that period. China, however, has been the only exception in this regard. The BRICs' market capitalization is currently close to 4% of the global total.

India's Positioning with BRICs

The BRIC countries are characterized by high economic growth rates, large populations and expanding middle classes. China and India will re-emerge as major economic and political powers over the next fifty years or so and China is projected to replace the United States as the world's largest economy by 2040 (http://www.dbresearch.com/PROD/CIB_INTERNET_EN-PROD/

PROD000000000230537.pdf). In the light of the above facts, it may be interesting to note that the recent report on BRIC nations by Goldman Sachs positions India fifth amongst the fastest growing nations in the world by 2025, based on the countries' real GDP. The same is founded on extrapolations based on changing demographics, per capita income and contribution to world trade.

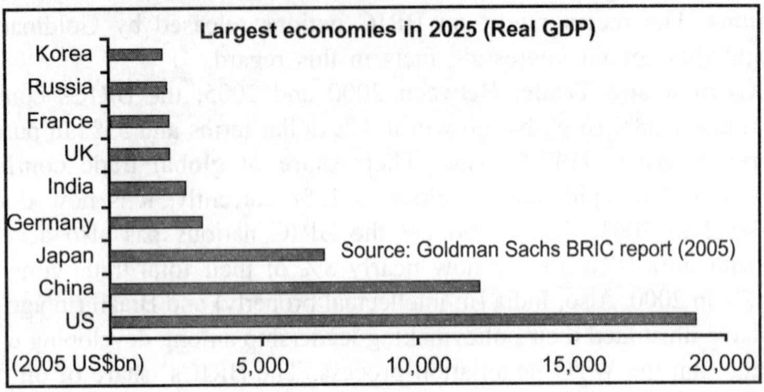

Also, 25 years hence i.e. by 2050, while China is expected to replace USA as the world's largest economy, India will not be lagging far behind in the third position. Nevertheless, it must also be noted that global economists have "identified" a new group of 'BRICs' that are expected to give the BRICs a run for their money. Christened as the 'Next Eleven (N-11)', this group shows broad representation by region and includes Bangladesh, Egypt, Indonesia, Iran, Korea, Mexico, Nigeria, Pakistan, Philippines, Turkey and Vietnam.

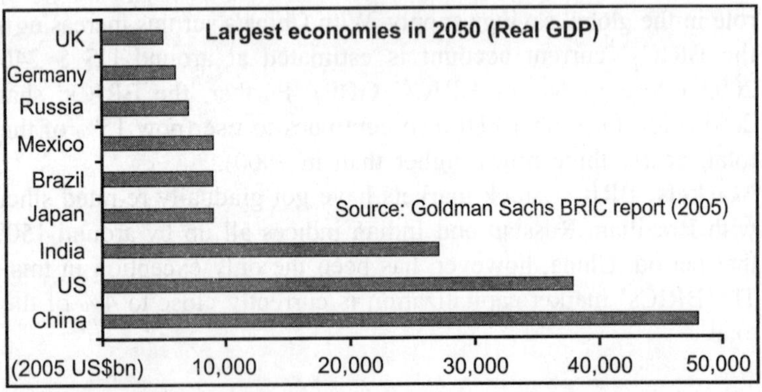

While the 'India story' has a sense of realism attached to it, what we are apprehensive about is the pace at which the 'India story' could unfold. Given the fact that coalition government is the name of the game going forward, there is a crying need for a ruling government with a 'backbone' to move the economy in its path to progress and development in the long term. Otherwise, like Mr. John Maynard Keynes put it rightly "In the long term, we are all dead".

Dreaming with BRICs: The Path to 2050

Over the next 50 years, Brazil, Russia, India and China—the BRICs economies—could become a much larger force in the world economy. Using the latest demographic projections and a model of capital accumulation and productivity growth, we map out GDP growth, income per capita and currency movements in the BRICs economies until 2050 (http://www.asiaing.com/dreaming-with-brics-the-path-to-2050.html).

- The results are startling. If things go right, in less than 40 years, the BRICs economies together could be larger than the G6 in US dollar terms. By 2025 they could account for over half the size of the G6. Currently they are worth less than 15%. Of the current G6, only the US and Japan may be among the six largest economies in US dollar terms in 2050.
- About two-thirds of the increase in US dollar GDP from the BRICs should come from higher real growth, with the balance through currency appreciation. The BRICs' real exchange rates could appreciate by up to 300% over the next 50 years (an average of 2.5% a year).
- The shift in GDP relative to the G6 takes place steadily over the period, but is most dramatic in the first 30 years. Growth for the BRICs is likely to slow significantly toward the end of the period, with only India seeing growth rates significantly above 3% by 2050. And individuals in the BRICs are still likely to be poorer on average than individuals in the G6 economies, with the exception of Russia. China's per capita income could be roughly what the developed economies are now (about US $ 30,000 per capita).
- As early as 2009, the annual increase in US dollar spending from the BRICs could be greater than that from the G6 and more than twice as much in dollar terms as it is now. By 2025 the annual increase in US dollar spending from the BRICs could be twice that of the G6, and four times higher by 2050.
- The key assumption underlying our projections is that the BRICs maintain policies and develop institutions that are supportive of growth. Each of the BRICs faces significant challenges in keeping development on track. This means that there is a good chance that our projections are not met, either through bad policy or bad luck. But if the BRICs come anywhere close to meeting the projections set out here, the implications for the pattern of growth and economic activity could be large.
- The relative importance of the BRICs as an engine of new demand growth and spending power may shift more dramatically and quickly than expected. Higher growth in these economies could offset the impact of graying populations and slower growth in the advanced economies.
- Higher growth may lead to higher returns and increased demand for capital. The weight of the BRICs in investment portfolios could rise

sharply. Capital flows might move further in their favour, prompting major currency realignments.

- Rising incomes may also see these economies move through the 'sweet spot' of growth for different kinds of products, as local spending patterns change. This could be an important determinant of demand and pricing patterns for a range of commodities.
- As today's advanced economies become a shrinking part of the world economy, the accompanying shifts in spending could provide significant opportunities for global companies. Being invested in and involved in the right markets—particularly the right emerging markets—may become an increasingly important strategic choice.
- The list of the world's ten largest economies may look quite different in 2050. The largest economies in the world (by GDP) may no longer be the richest (by income per capita), making strategic choices for firms.

Global Market Access Impacting Global Economy

The BRIC's study specifically focuses on large countries, not necessarily the wealthiest or the most productive and was never intended to be an investment thesis. If investors read the Goldman's research carefully, and agreed with the conclusions, then they would gain exposure to Asian debt and equity markets rather than to Latin America. According to estimates provided by the USDA, the wealthiest regions outside of the G-6 in 2015 will be Hong Kong, South Korea and Singapore. Combined with China and India, these five economies are likely to be the world's five most influential economies outside of the G-6. In terms of the List of countries by GDP (nominal) per capita in 2007, Brazil ranks 64th, Russia 54th, China 105th and India 131st. By comparison, South Korea currently ranks 34th, Singapore 21st, and Hong Kong 27th. BRICs' stock markets have got gradually re-rated since 2003, with Brazilian, Russian and Indian indices all up by around 150% over that period. China, however, has been the only exception in this regard. The BRICs' market capitalization is currently close to 4% of the global total.

The BRICs' share of world growth could rise from roughly 20 per cent in 2003 to more than 40 per cent in 2025. Their weight in the world economy could rise from less than 10 per cent now to more than 20 per cent in 20 years' time. The BRICs impact on global markets is likely to follow a sequence. Commodity markets are already the clearest pressure point for BRICs growth and their impact on those markets is likely to be at its peak in the next decade. The importance of the BRICs as consumer markets is likely to be the next phase and could be a major story in the next ten years. The importance of the BRICs to capital markets is likely to lag a little further behind that and to build gradually over the next twenty years.

Underlying global demand growth for energy and oil could remain very strong (well over two per cent annually) over the next 15 years or so as China's industrialization continues and India's follows behind, suggesting pricing pressure could persist for some time. After this period, the trend should decline gradually, as more economies move to a phase of lower demand growth. The BRICs could continue to increase their already substantial contribution to global oil demand growth. China's contribution should remain high but is likely to peak in 5-10 years time and should decline steadily thereafter. India's impact will become gradually more important. In less than 15 years, India's contribution to global demand growth could overtake China's. China's share of actual oil demand (as opposed to growth) may rise from 8-9 per cent currently to a peak of around 16.5 per cent in 25 years time, while India's share could nearly double and will gradually converge on China's.

As for the BRICs and the global autos markets, the report says that China is rapidly approaching the likely sweet spot for growth in autos ownership. Car ownership could increase nearly threefold in the next decade, though growth rates are likely to peak in the next few years. India's autos growth will also rapid, with the potential for a three-fold increase in car ownership over the next ten years. However, the best decade for India's growth is probably about ten years behind China's, beginning in around 2015. In fact, China and India may emerge as the world's No. 1 and 2 largest car markets. Within 20 years, China could overtake the US as the world's largest auto market, with India displacing the US perhaps as soon as 15 years later.

With regard to the BRICs and global capital markets, the report predicts that the BRICs' importance to global equity markets would rise from a paltry 3.5 per cent currently to around 10 per cent by 2020, depending on the extent of capital market development. If they choose a more market-based approach to corporate finance, their share could be as large as 16 per cent. Further, market capitalization in the BRICs economies could increase over the next decade by a factor of four times to $ 4 trillion, with a large increase in capital market activity. China and India alone could account for 60 per cent of that total. Despite this rapid growth, BRICs' capital markets are still likely to be dwarfed by the US market for decades — but could come to rival Europe as a group within 15-20 years and could increase the weight of emerging markets in global equity portfolios.

The forecast for 2007 is that the US economy will grow by about 2 per cent during 2007, and that both France and the UK are projected to grow slightly more than 2006, but that the overall Group of 7 (G-7) economies will grow by 2.1 per cent, compared with 2.8 per cent in 2006. By contrast, the projections for the BRIC economies are staggering — an average of 8.9 per cent for 2007 compared with 8.5 per cent in 2.6, but with wide BRIC growth variations. China leads the way at nearly 10 per cent, India at 8 per cent, Russia at around 7 per cent, and even Brazil at a respectable 3-4 per cent compared with the G-7 forecast.

Challenge of BRIC

One of the biggest challenges for marketeers and their agencies is the sheer scale of the 'BRIC' countries and the difficulty in reaching far-flung consumers with different cultures, languages and traditions. The marketing infrastructure in countries like China, India and Russia is still under development, and Western aspects of doing business that are taken for granted elsewhere - such as national retailers are still in the making. Companies like Unilever now derive over 40 per cent of their sales in developing and emerging markets, compared to 26 per cent in the '90s. To manage such dispersed operations, the packaged-goods giant had to centralize its brand-development efforts while tailoring its brand building locally.

Criticism

One of the major criticisms of 'BRIC Thesis' is the understatement of GDP growth in China over the next 45 years; which predicts growth to be falling far below normal development. This contradicts the rapid economic growth that has already taken place in the country and the experience of countries like South Korea catching up with western GDP per capita, which China has been growing faster than in a similar period of development. There are many uncertainties and assumptions in the BRIC thesis that could mean that any or all of these four countries will not live up to their promise. The preeminence of China and India as major manufacturing countries with unrealized potential has been widely recognized, but some commentators state that China's and Russia's disregard for human rights and democracy could be a problem in the future, as is the possibility of conflict over Taiwan in the case of China. Likewise, the population of Russia is steadily declining, and this may have implications for its future.

Flip-side of BRIC's Success Story: Lessons Learnt

A recent article in the 'Financial Times' highlights the growing investment trends and economic successes of the BRIC countries. Just six years ago, in late 2001, Jim O'Neill of Goldman Sachs school coined the term "BRIC" in predicting that Brazil, Russia, India, and China would account for more than 10 per cent of world GDP by 2010. Yet, even this bold prediction was short of the mark: Last year, for instance, the IMF calculated that the BRICs and other emerging markets already account for 30 per cent of the global economy and 47 per cent of global economic growth. Furthermore, during 2007, the BRIC nations accounted for about 12 per cent of the world's GDP, up from 8 per cent in 2000. If Goldman Sachs' forecasts are believed to be accurate, the BRIC economies could be half the size of the G-6 by 2025, and surpass them by 2045. Yet, this growing influence is not reflected in the leadership structure of the IMF or the World Bank, and while Russia is now part of the G-8, it is under constant pressure of being thrown out.

The BRICs boosted the share of global exports from emerging markets from 20 per cent in 1970 to 42 per cent in 2006. Their growth, furthermore, is not being driven solely by commodities exports and low-cost manufacturing. Instead, India and other emerging Asian economies are home to 26 per cent of the global information technology services market, and this share is growing quicker than IT services in developed countries.

Each of the BRIC nations has pushed for reforms on its own, with varying degrees of success. Brazil challenged U.S. cotton subsidies at the WTO and won its case, but Russia's political disputes have prevented it from being accepted into the WTO. Brazil, India, and China each saw an increase in their voting shares at the IMF in April, 2008 but the U.S. and European nations will still be able to use their combined vote to ensure the organization is headed by a European. Russia formally joined with the G-7 nations in 1997 to form the G-8, a privilege still denied to China, even though its economy may have already surpassed Germany to become the third largest in the world.

Napoleon is attributed to have once said that, "forethought we may have, undoubtedly, but not foresight." How true. If we have to go on by what happened in the past, countries like Saudi Arabia should not be creating new BRIC alliances. But foresight is rare, for who would have dreamt of China's economic growth taking place, if the Chinese had listened to "expert" advice in 1997 during the Asian currency crises that they must devalue their currency otherwise they too faced a meltdown? They did nothing and the results are evident today. China is now being pressed to revalue its currency or face dire consequences. The truth is that they will do what is best for them and sometimes it is better to ignore the best of advice. The BRIC economies are here to stay and shape the future of both the developing economies and the developed markets.

A Reasonable Perspective on China

In his article from the 'Globalize', Jianxiong Zhang argued that far from being a rising threat or an emerging global problem, China is a positive factor in the world economy. For example, the economic boost that China gives to the world economy may become especially important in the event of a US recession, as the Chinese economy can help pick up the slack and keep the world economic growth rate in the positive. Consequently, he added that, the Western countries should recognize the significant pressures and constraints weighing on Chinese leaders. With so much of American media's focus on China as the next great power and American job losses, it is easy to forget that on an individual level China is still a poor country. While its GDP now ranks 4th, behind the US, Japan, and Germany; per capita, its GDP is only 4.5% of America's. This means that there are still millions of poor people in China, including 135 million who live on under $ 1 per day.

Brazilian Lesson for China

With the growth-at-all-costs model that China has been employing over the last two decades has come rising inequality like that was seen in Brazil during the 60's and 70's, writes Geoff Dyer in the Financial Times. Several decades ago, Brazil followed the mantra "grow the cake now, divide it up later" to achieve tremendous economic growth, at the expense of social policy. The result: levels of inequality for which the country became notorious. Dyer draws similarities between that period in Brazil and present-day China, which has sacrificed state involvement in social service provision for unprecedented economic gains. Again, the result is growing inequality, not only between rural and urban areas, but within cities themselves. Meanwhile, over the past decade, the Brazilian government has spent twice as much of its GDP on health and education than China, and is seeing a steady reduction in its income inequality. While Brazil and China vary markedly in terms of economic history and colonial legacy, it seems as though Chinese leaders are well aware of the ramifications of high inequality for social and political stability.

China's Vast Expansion of International Trade

The People's Republic of China has the second largest economy in the world with a GDP of over 6.9 trillion (2007) when measured on a purchasing power parity (PPP) basis. In November 2007, it became the third largest in the world after the US and Japan with a nominal GDP of US $ 3.42 trillion (2007) when measured in exchange-rate terms. Since free market reforms in 1978, China's GDP has grown an average 9.9 per cent a year. China's per capita income has grown at an average annual rate of more than 8% over the last three decades, drastically reducing poverty, but this rapid growth has been accompanied by rising income inequalities. The country's per capita income is classified as low by world standards, at about $ 2,000 (nominal, 107th of 179 countries/economies), and $ 7,800 (PPP, 82nd of 179 countries/economies) in 2006, according to the International Monetary Fund.

Since the late 1970s and early 1980s, the economic reforms initially began with the shift of farming work to a system of household responsibility to start the phase out of collectivized agriculture, and later expanded to include the gradual liberalization of prices; fiscal decentralization; increased autonomy for state enterprises that increased the authority of local government officials and plant managers in industry thereby permitting a wide variety of private enterprise in services and light manufacturing; the foundation of a diversified banking system; the development of stock markets; the rapid growth of the non-state sector, and the opening of the economy to increased foreign trade and foreign investment.

China has generally implemented reforms in a gradualist fashion, including the sale of equity in China's largest state banks to foreign investors and refinements in foreign exchange and bond markets in mid-2000s. As its role in world trade has steadily grown, its importance to the international economy has also increased apace. China's foreign trade has grown faster than its GDP for the past 25 years. As of 2007, most of China's growth came from the private sector instead of exports. Particularly the smaller public sector, which was dominated by about 200 large state enterprises concentrated mostly in utilities, heavy industries, and energy resources (http://en.wikipedia.org/wiki/Economy_of_the_People's_Republic_of_China).

The expansion of its international trade has been a particularly noteworthy aspect of China's rising prominence in the world economy. China's exports and imports have grown at an average rate of 15 per cent each year since 1979, compared with a 7 per cent annual expansion of world trade over the same period. This process has been facilitated by trade reforms and the general opening of the economy that have led to a surge in foreign direct investment (FDI) and increased integration with the global trading system. Interestingly, as discussed in Section II, the rapid expansion of China's trade thus far is not unprecedented in either its scope or speed. Other Asian economies such as Japan, Korea, and the newly industrialized emerging economies of Asia were able to maintain even higher export growth rates, on average, for about a 30-year period. This international experience implies that China could maintain relatively strong export growth for a number of years. Given China's large population and still substantial development potential (as reflected by its current per capita income of only $ 1,060), China could have a bigger impact on the global economy than the other economies mentioned above.

China's trade expansion in part reflects greater specialization in production within the Asian region, with China now serving as the final processing and assembly platform for a large quantity of imports going from other Asian countries to Western countries through China (Prasad and Rumbaugh, 2003). These changes have resulted in a shift in China's bilateral trade balances, with its increasing trade surpluses with Western industrial countries being offset by rising trade deficits with many Asian countries. Reflecting its growing prominence and rising appetite for imports (including for meeting domestic demand), China has been an important source of growth for the world economy during the recent global slowdown. During 2001–03, China accounted for about 24 per cent of world growth (using purchasing-power-parity-based GDP).

China's imports are growing rapidly from all trading partners and it is now the third largest importer of developing countries' exports after the United States and the European Union. China has even contributed to the recent strength in world commodity prices; it is now the world's largest importer of copper and steel, and among the largest importers of other raw materials, including iron ore and aluminum. While China's integration into the global trading system is likely to benefit both the global and regional economies, there will no doubt be some short-run distributional effects across countries. The countries most likely to benefit from the expansion of China's trade include exporters of capital and resource-intensive products, while countries that specialize in labor-intensive exports similar to those of China will have to undergo significant adjustments to increased competition from China. Trade expansion will also pose some domestic challenges within China itself. Expanding trade could increase regional income disparities, while foreign competition could aggravate social pressures arising from job dislocation and rising unemployment (IMF, 2004).

The Outlook

China's economy has good potential for sustained robust growth over the medium term, based on its attractiveness as a destination for FDI, a high domestic saving rate, underlying improvements in productivity stemming from reduced barriers to both internal and external trade, and significant surplus labor. But fulfilling its potential for high growth and continued integration with the global economy will depend largely on successful management of the diverse set of financial and social risks that China faces. This, in turn, will depend crucially on the pace and effectiveness of core macroeconomic and structural reforms. Implementing a broad and concerted reform agenda and doing so in an expeditious manner, is indeed the crucial challenge facing Chinese policymakers.

India and China: Relative Strengths of Regional Economies

It is a measure of India's increasing external orientation that the trade-GDP ratio has doubled from around 15% in early 1980s to about 30% today. However, over the same period China's trade-GDP ratio rose from around the same level of 16% to over 50% of GDP. Statistics of this kind about comparative rates of growth, trade shares, FDI flows etc. between India and China frequently raise questions about who will win the India-China race. It seems to me that the question is based on a false premise, because it assumes that trade and development are zero-sum games, which they are not. Some firms in India will indeed compete with firms in China, but there will be other firms which will form strategic partnerships with Chinese firms to exploit their synergies for global competition.

It is quite likely that both China and India will win, feeding on each other's success through trade linkages, to emerge as leading players not only in Asia but globally, as recently forecast by the widely quoted BRICs study. Present trends in comparative advantage suggest that China is likely to emerge as a global manufacturing hub while India will become a global hub for services. This is quite a likely scenario since services already account for over half of India's GDP, whereas in China it is industry that accounts for over half of GDP. However, within these broad sectors, firms of both countries will be important players in many sub-sectors and products. Besides as a broad-based corporate strategy both the countries, sooner or later, will likely be venturing into a large number of joint-venture projects and strategic alliances with MNCs as global partners.

China and India—Basis for Different FDI Performance

On the basic economic determinants of inward FDI, China does better than India. China's total and per capita GDP are higher, making it more attractive for market seeking FDI. Its higher literacy and education rates suggest that its labour is more skilled, making it more attractive to efficiency-seeking investors (World Bank, 2003; UNDP, 2002). China also has large natural resource endowments. In addition, China's physical infrastructure is more competitive, particularly in the coastal areas (CUTS, 2003; Marubeni Corporation Economic Research Institute, 2002). But, India may have an advantage in technical manpower, particularly in information technology. It also has better English language skills.

Some of the differences in competitive advantages of the two countries are illustrated by the composition of their inward FDI flows. In information and communication technology, China has become a key centre for hardware design and manufacturing by such companies as Acer, Ericsson, General Electric, Hitachi Semiconductors, Hyundai Electronics, Intel, LG Electronics, Microsoft, Mitac International Corporation, Motorola, NEC, Nokia, Philips, Samsung Electronics, Sony, Taiwan Semiconductor Manufacturing, Toshiba and other major electronics TNCs. India specializes in IT services, call centers, business back-office operations and R&D.

Rapid growth in China has increased the local demand for consumer durables and nondurables, such as home appliances, electronics equipment, automobiles, housing and leisure. This rapid growth in local demand, as well as competitive business environment and infrastructure, has attracted many market-seeking investors. It has also encouraged the growth of many local indigenous firms that support manufacturing. Other determinants related to FDI attitudes, policies and procedures also explain why China does better in attracting FDI.

- China has "more business-oriented" and more FDI-friendly policies than India (AT Kearney, 2001).
- China's FDI procedures are easier, and decisions can be taken rapidly.
- China has more flexible labour laws, a better labour climate and better entry and exit procedures for business (CUTS, 2003).

A recent business environment survey indicated that China is more attractive than India in the macroeconomic environment, market opportunities and policy towards FDI. India scored better on the political environment, taxes and financing (EIU, 2003). A confidence tracking survey in 2002 indicated that China was the top FDI destination, displacing the United States for the first time in the investment plans of the TNCs surveyed; India came 15th (AT Kearney, 2002). A Federation of Indian Chambers of Commerce and Industry (FICCI) survey suggests that China has a better FDI policy framework, market growth, and consumers' purchasing power, rate of return, labour laws and tax regime than India (FICCI, 2003).

Regional Economic Integration in South Asia

Like many developing economies, the South Asian countries are opening-up their economies with a view to accelerating their economic growth through greater trade and investment. In this context, attempts have also been made to encourage regional trade under the aegis of the South Asian Association for Regional Cooperation (SAARC). In particular, the South Asian Preferential Trade Agreement (SAPTA) provides for reductions in tariffs and other restrictions on specific commodities on a reciprocal basis, and the eventual objective is to integrate the South Asian economies into a free trade area through South Asian Free Trade Area (SAFTA), which would come into force on January 1, 2006. However, despite greater attention on regional economic cooperation initiatives, there has been little progress in regional trade expansion: intra-regional trade continues to be minimal, not exceeding 5 per cent of the total trade of the South Asian economies (Musleh-Ud-Din and Shahbaz Nasir, 2004).

REGIONAL ECONOMIC INTEGRATION

In the last two decades, the trading system has given rise to the proliferation of the regional and bilateral trade agreements (RTAs). The number of such agreements more than quadrupled since 1990 to around 230 in 2004, and trade between these RTA partners now makes up almost 40 per cent of total trade (World Bank, 2005). A large body of theoretical and empirical literature has investigated the role of regional economic integration. The *Customs Union* theory, due to Viner (1950), predicts that regional economic integration schemes can promote new trade among members, but they can also divert trade from more efficient producers outside the integration scheme. More specifically, regional economic integration can result in trade creation by allowing the low-cost producers to have free access to the domestic market, reducing domestic prices, and displacing higher-cost domestic producers. However, a regional trading arrangement can also result in trade diversion by allowing less efficient producers that are members of the RTA to displace more efficient producers outside the RTA. Regional economic integration is likely to yield more economic benefit than harm when it leads to trade creation rather than trade diversion.

In as far as an RTA leads to trade creation, it is expected to spur competition in the domestic economies. Increased import competition results in lower prices for consumers, more product variety and quality, and increased incentives for innovation. By promoting a more efficient allocation of resources, import competition increases productivity, living standards, and long-run growth of the economy. Empirical research has shown that the welfare consequences of trade liberalization through regional trading arrangements generally tend to be positive.

The arguments for promoting regional economic integration in South Asia, as elsewhere, go beyond the traditional benefits of regional economic integration associated with trade creation. To begin with, RTAs are often viewed as a way for nations to lock in and institutionalize trade policy reforms. The improved policy credibility may also encourage both domestic and foreign investment by reassuring investors that policy will not be reversed in the future. Second, an RTA may act as a stepping stone to multilateral trade liberalization by providing an opportunity to experiment trade liberalization on a limited scale. Third, increased economic ties in the region may create stake-holding in the domestic economies, reduce the risk of conflict, and thus enhance regional security. Finally, it needs to be emphasized that South Asian countries can provide easier access to each other's markets because of geographical proximity, and shared economic, social and cultural characteristics; and this makes it all the more imperative for them to foster regional economic cooperation.

According to Fukase and Winters (1999), ASEAN membership is likely to strengthen the members' commitment to reform and thus enhance their external credibility. It must be pointed out here that regional economic integration initiatives are often subject to criticism mainly on two counts. First, critics focus on the welfare loss associated with trade diversion from more efficient producers outside the regional trading bloc to less efficient producers that are members of the RTA. However, whether or not trade diversion occurs depends on external trade regimes of member countries and its risk tends to fall with the level of external tariffs. Therefore, the likelihood of trade diversion can be minimized by keeping external tariffs low. Second, critics argue that RTAs may stall the process of multilateral trade liberalization, which is the first best policy. This question has been debated at length in the literature and most of the studies generally support the argument that RTAs tend to promote the process of multilateral trade liberalization rather than retard it.

Measures to Enhance Global Economic Cooperation

To move the process of regional economic integration forward, serious efforts are needed in several key areas including reduction in trade barriers, harmonization of customs procedures and tariff structures, improving transparency of trade and investment policies, collectivism, and effective implementation of SAFTA. These measures will contribute towards strengthening economic ties in the region thus helping to achieve the shared goal of economic development and prosperity.

Reducing Trade Barriers

Collective and concrete action to lower trade barriers and advance domestic reforms is important to facilitate regional trade. The regional countries need to reduce the high effective tariffs on the specific industries of each partner country which are applied to safeguard the interests of some of the local business communities at the cost of low competition and high domestic prices. In particular, high and specific duties on textiles and agricultural products should be reduced; incidentally a major reason for the failure of SAPTA to spur intra-regional trade was that most of the products of export interest to the regional countries were excluded from preferential treatment (Kemal, 2004) make available the cheaper goods in the domestic market, thereby improving consumer welfare. This will also lead to enhanced trade within the region.

Simplifying and Improving the Tariff Structure and Procedures

To reduce the complexity of the tariff structures, protective duties and exemptions provided to domestic producers need to be removed. Demand for such exemptions also goes down as effective tariffs are reduced. The improvement in the custom as well as tax administrations must complement tariff reduction policies. This process should be designed and implemented in close consultation with the stakeholders: business community, farmers, investors, traders and others. Some studies have pointed out a tendency to use anti-dumping duties as a tool for restricting imports in some South Asian countries. There should be mutual revision of anti-dumping policies on a regional basis. On the other hand, small countries including Nepal, Maldives and Bhutan need to build their capacity to deal with anti-dumping investigations on their exports on the one hand, and to improve their technical expertise for counter safeguard measures on the other.

Improving Trade Facilitation

Reduction in tariffs alone is not sufficient to promote economic ties in the region. What is needed is a regulatory environment that facilitates trade through reduction in the transaction costs associated with bringing goods and services across borders. Trade facilitation involves a wide range of initiatives, including, for instance, reforms in the regulation and harmonization of standards, promoting efficiency in customs, and improvement in regional transport infrastructure. The regional countries need to adopt a coherent strategy to harmonize their policies, focusing in particular on transport and transit systems, and customs procedures.

Domestic regulatory procedures and institutional structures based on international best practice models (e.g. ASEAN) can improve transparency and introduce professionalism in border clearance procedures. Streamlining regulations on technical barriers and liberalizing transport and telecommunications regimes can also facilitate trade. Collective action to raise capacity in trade facilitation in terms of upgrading ports, and introduction of information technology in border processing would lower transaction costs and expand trade across the region.

Promoting Collectivism

South Asian countries need to adopt a collective approach to safeguard the interests of the region. Collective forums help improve the bargaining position and South Asian countries can effectively deal in the multilateral negotiations on trade with other regions and at international forums like WTO. Member countries should also cooperate with each other in order to insulate the regional economy against external shocks.

Minimizing Trade Diversion

Due to preferential tariffs for the regional countries, it is apprehended that these reduced tariffs may result in trade diversion from the most competitive source to the lesser one in the region. To minimize trade diversion and the attendant welfare loss, the preferential removal of trade barriers in the region must be accompanied by a reduction in the level of external protection.

Confidence-building Measures

Confidence-building measures are needed to create the right atmosphere for greater economic ties in the region. First, the region is dominated by two large economies, India and Pakistan, and these countries must lead the way towards regional economic integration in South Asia. Actions of these economies have a strong influence on trade policies of other South Asian countries. Both the countries need to work together to ensure smaller regional countries that their interests will be safeguarded and their apprehensions about the domination of larger economies will be addressed in regional matters. Possibilities of trade expansion in South Asia would be rather limited unless the benefits of trade liberalization accrue to all the partners. Second, easing of travel and visa restrictions would promote contact between the business communities within the region, leading to ushering of new possibilities for economic cooperation. Third, opening up of bilateral trade beyond what is covered by SAPTA, though initially on a limited scale, would bring a new wave of relations and confidence, and may lead to a broader trade and economic ties within the region. Finally, there is a need to create awareness about the potential benefits of regional economic cooperation. This will make various regional economic cooperation initiatives more acceptable to general masses thus making it easier for governments to engage in such initiatives.

Making SAFTA Work

The SAARC member countries signed SAFTA agreement in January 2004, which promises to be influential in expanding intra-regional trade. Basic parameters of this agreement include tariff reductions, elimination of quantitative restrictions, rules of origin, safeguards, institutional structures, dispute settlement and various trade facilitation measures (harmonization of customs procedures and standards and mutual recognition of test results, and transport infrastructure cooperation). The agreement will come into force on January 1, 2006 and will be fully implemented by 2015. It envisages bringing down the import duties to 20 per cent by 2006 and in the range of 0-5 per cent by 2013. There is provision for the LDCs to reduce the rate of duties to 0-5 per cent by the year 2015 (http://en.wikipedia.org/wiki/South_Asia_Free_Trade_Agreement).

The SAFTA agreement provides a useful framework for strengthening trade ties in the region. However, the success of SAFTA depends on its effective implementation, which would require a conducive economic and political environment and a strong willingness for integration and liberalization of the SAARC members. This will reduce the chance of disruption of trade and derailment of the agreement. Also, there must be a strong acceptance of the members for the subsequent economic adjustments. Continuous dialogues and interaction along with sincere efforts towards understanding each other's point of view and the matters ahead are the essential ingredients for the success of SAFTA and any other integration efforts in the region.

SAFTA allows for sensitive list and if this list is large and is used to protect the interests of few industrialists, then SAFTA may not be helpful in increasing the intra-regional trade. Large negative lists and detailed product specific rules may blunt the potential benefits from the trade liberalization process. Therefore, there is a need for further deliberations in this matter in the future SAARC/SAFTA meetings. The countries should aim for broader tariff liberalization; it results in trade diversion towards more competitive sources and also creates competitiveness in the domestic market. Reduction in external protection will also result in trade creation. Transparent anti-dumping and countervailing duties in the region will be necessary for the confidence building between the SAARC members. Moreover, simplification in the SAFTA rules and measures is required for its speedy and effective implementation. The sector-wise reviews of the tariffs should not be allowed as these result in a more complex system and promote rent-seeking, ultimately making it difficult to implement the agreement. The capacity of the member countries should also be improved for effective implementation of the agreement. Monitoring and technical reviews are essential ingredients and may further help in this regard.

Exploring Potential in New Areas

For sustained economic cooperation in the region, there is a need to explore potential in new areas. For instance, Kemal *et al.* (2002) have highlighted the importance of developing 'vertical specialization' through regional production sharing arrangements. Vertical specialization would allow the regional trading partners to achieve economies of scale by concentrating on various segments of the value chain in a production process. In addition, it has been argued that intra-industry trade can play an important role in the process of regional economic integration, especially in view of the present lack of trade complementarities in the region. It must, however, be pointed out that intra-industry trade is more likely to emerge in a market structure characterized by product differentiation and increasing returns to scale. While larger markets as a result of economic integration would help firms realize economies of scale, they would have to develop technological capabilities to achieve product differentiation. In the latter context, evidence elsewhere has shown that regional trading arrangements have often led to the transfer of technology among the partner countries.

As a tool for achieving greater economic integration, regional trading arrangements intensifies competition in the domestic economies leading to lower prices, more product variety, better quality, and increased incentives for innovation. By promoting a more efficient allocation of resources, competition increases productivity, living standards, and long-run growth of the economy. In addition, regional trading arrangements may institutionalize trade policy reforms, act as a stepping stone towards multilateral trade liberalization, and help enhance regional security. Despite efforts to strengthen regional economic cooperation, intra-regional trade in SAARC region continues to be small and on average accounts for only 5 per cent of the total trade. Several factors are believed to be responsible for weak economic ties in the region including, for example, identical comparative advantage, lack of trade complementarities, restrictive trade policies, lack of regional transport network and transit system, and political problems. To move the process of regional economic integration forward, the paper recommends several measures including reduction in trade barriers, harmonization of customs procedures and tariff structures, improving transparency of trade and investment policies, collectivism, and effective implementation of SAFTA. These measures will contribute towards strengthening economic ties in the region thus helping to achieve the shared goal of economic development and prosperity.

India' Rising Role in Asia

Asia's Growth Prospects

Asia is projected to grow at 4.9 per cent during the 2006-20 period as compared to 3.5 per cent for the world as a whole (Table 1). In Asia, China, India, Pakistan, and Vietnam are projected to grow at the most rapid pace (Table 1). It should be noted that overall, the growth rates projected by the EIU are much lower than generally perceived. As an example, China is projected to grow at 6 per cent annually during the 2006-20 period as compared to 9 to 10 per cent growth rate routinely reported. India's GDP per head is expected to grow at an annual rate of 4-6 per cent during the 2006-20 period (Asher, 2007). This is exceeded by China (5.4 per cent) (Table 1).

EIU's projections for contribution to global growth for the 2006-20 period suggest that the largest contribution will be by China (26.7 per cent), followed by the United States (15.9 per cent), and India (12.2 per cent) (EIU, 2006). These countries are also projected to occupy the first three positions in GDP in PPP terms in 2020. The share of China in world's GDP is projected at 19.4

Table 1: Real GDP Growth of some Selected Asian Countries (Annual Average %)

Countries	GDP 2006-10	2011-20	2006-20	GDP/head 2006-10	2011-20	2006-20
World	4.0	3.3	3.5	2.7	2.4	2.5
Asia	5.5	4.5	4.9	4.5	3.6	3.9
China	7.8	5.1	6.0	7.2	4.5	5.4
India	6.6	5.5	5.9	5.2	4.3	4.6
Indonesia	5.6	5.0	5.2	4.2	3.9	4.0
Malaysia	5.3	4.8	5.0	3.4	3.1	3.2
Pakistan	5.9	5.3	5.5	4.0	3.6	3.7
Philippines	5.2	4.7	4.9	3.4	3.1	3.2
Singapore	4.5	4.0	4.1	3.6	3.4	3.5
South Korea	4.0	3.9	4.0	3.6	3.6	3.6
Taiwan	4.5	3.4	3.8	4.2	3.0	3.4
Thailand	4.5	4.7	4.7	3.8	4.2	4.1
Vietnam	7.0	4.6	5.4	5.7	3.4	4.2

Source: Economists Intelligence Group (2006)

per cent, of the U.S. 19.0 per cent, and of India 8.8 per cent (EIU, 2006). It should however be stressed that in spite of the above, both China and India in 2020 will continue to have relatively low per capita incomes (Asher, 2007).

Trade in Commercial Service Transactions

Table 2 provides data for 2004 concerning leading exporters and importers of commercial services in the world. India ranked 8th as a service exporter, and 7th as a global importer, when intra-EU trade is excluded. On the basis of these rankings, only 4 Asian countries, viz. Korea, Hong Kong, China and Japan were ranked ahead of India in commercial services exports in 2004. India ranked as the 4th largest importer of commercial services in Asia during the same year. There are reasons to suggest that India's ranking will improve further in the coming years. First, travel and transport accounted for about 10 per cent each of total exports of services by India, while four-fifths were other commercial services, including IT services (WTO, 2005).

The IT services industry is expected to amount to US $ 38 billion in 2006-07, with exports of about US $ 30 billion. NASSCOM-McKinsey study has projected US $ 60 billion in IT exports by 2009-10, with total direct and indirect employment of 4.3 million persons. Apart from these, India's potential in healthcare and education services trade is only beginning to be exploited. Traditionally, international organizations and individual countries have focused on merchandise trade statistics. The services trade transactions however are significant proportion of total world trade. Thus, in 2004, world trade in service transactions was US $ billion 4222 (22 per cent of the merchandise trade of US $ billion 18648) (WTO, 2005). On a value-added rather than gross flow basis, the share of service transactions is likely to be even higher as production fragmentation is much more advanced in merchandise than in services.

Table 2: Leading Exporters and Importers of the World Trade in Commercial Services in 2004 (In Billion $ & %)

Rank	Exporters	Value	Share in World (%)	Rank	Importers	Value	Share in World (%)
1	Extra-EU(25) Exports	427.1	27.8	1	Extra-EU (25) imports	381.7	25.1
2	United States	318.3	20.7	2	United States	260.0	17.1
3	Japan	94.9	6.2	3	Japan	134.0	8.8
4	China	62.1	4.0	4	China	71.6	4.7
5	HK, China	53.6	3.5	5	Canada	55.9	3.7
6	Canada	46.8	3.0	6	Korea Republic	49.6	3.3
7	Korea, Republic	40.0	2.6	7	India	40.9	2.7
8	India	39.6	2.6	8	Singapore	36.2	2.4
10	Singapore	36.5	2.4	10	Taipei, Chinese	29.9	2.0
12	Taipei, Chinese	25.5	1.7	11	HK, China	29.8	2.0
15	Russian Federation	20.2	1.3	12	Australia	25.6	1.7
16	Thailand	18.9	1.2	14	Thailand	23.0	1.5
26	Indonesia	6.7	0.4	15	Indonesia	21.3	1.4
				16	Malaysia	18.8	1.2
				34	Vietnam	4.5	0.3
	World (Excl. Intra-EU (25))	1540.0	100.0		World (excl. intra-EU))	1520.0	100.0

Source: (WTO, 2005)

India's advantage as an off-shoring is evident in all three areas, though the margin varies. Philippines and China are however close competitors. There are also indications that talent shortages may limit growth of off-shoring, which would adversely impact India, China and other countries. India's limited physical infrastructure and lower investments in health and education strongly suggest that there is no room for complacency by Indian policymakers and Indian industry. Chanda and Krishnan (2006) indicate that the focus on Indian companies are currently engaging increasing cross border collaborations such as joint ventures and training arrangements between Indian and other Asian IT services firms. Motivations of Indian companies vary from desire to be close to their MNC customers (e.g. China, Singapore), to expand human talent pool (e.g. China, Philippines, and Vietnam), and to more effectively tap certain markets (e.g. Japan and Korea). It is also worth noting that manpower for IT industries in many countries is being provided by the Indian diaspora. US companies are estimated to have saved over US $ 25 billion in 2005 through outsourcing (Chanda and Krishnan, 2006). The organizations in Asian countries, however do not appear to have taken sufficient advantage of the opportunities to realize cost savings from partnering India in off-shoring (Asher and Nandy, 2006). Countries such as Malaysia desiring to create IT industries have also not pursued policies which are sufficiently conducive for deeper engagement and cooperation with the Indian IT industry and manpower. Top 250 global technology firms are outsourcing part of their work to small specialist firms, some of whom are in India, China and Taiwan. As a result, the Asian region is being welded into the global technology supply chain (The Economist, October 7, 2006, pp. 73-74). This in turn benefits firms outside of Asia as well.

It is important to note that while East Asia's integration with the global economy is evident in the analysis of production networks in trade in manufactured goods, such integration of India with the global economy, which is undoubtedly more services, and technology oriented, is not captured by conventional merchandise trade data. As an example, Intel's India centre contributed complete design of the *Centrino mobile chip* called *Napa* (The Economic Times, November 2, 2006) which will be subsequently incorporated in the variety of electronic products. Such non-trivial design work should logically be regarded as part of the overall value chain in the process of production fragmentation. The merchandise trade flows are recorded by gross amounts rather than value-added. The design work's importance therefore may not be fully reflected in the conventional trade data. More than 250 of the Fortune 500 companies in India are undertaking research that may lead to future high technology products. While their actual contribution in trade value terms may be relatively small, India nevertheless constitutes a vital part of the electronics production, research, distribution, and customer servicing chain. India is currently drawing 25 per cent of fresh global investments in R&D centers (www.ibef.org). Saxenian (2006) has persuasively argued that dynamic new centers of technology entrepreneurship, extending Silicon Valley system to distant locations in India, China, Israel, and Taiwan are creating cross regional networks and communities which are an integral part of the global integration and competition.

The above analysis thus strongly suggests that contrary to what may emerge from conventional merchandise trade focused research, India's integration with the rest of Asia is far greater, deeper, and of high quality. There is therefore a strong case for broadening the scope of production network and fragmentation definitions, found in the current literature; and to mandate WTO to undertake research on developing robust database on trade in services. The aim should be to make services trade data as accessible to researchers, businesses, and policymakers as merchandise trade data.

Besides IT and ITES services, there are several other areas of commercial services trade where India's potential is yet to be fully realized. One such area is the healthcare services sector. It has a potential to benefit substantially from demographic complementarities between India on the one hand and affluent and rapidly aging Asian countries such as Japan, Korea, Australia, New Zealand

and Singapore (Asher and Nandy, 2006). Hong Kong and Taiwan are also affluent and rapidly aging economies and may consider constructive cooperation with India.

The potential benefits of the Asian countries will arise not just from acute healthcare services, but from making generic drugs available at much lower costs. Pharmaceutical costs are between 15 and 20 per cent of total health budgets of most Health Organizations. There is therefore potential for substantial savings. India's tourism sector has the potential to generate significant additional income and employment. In 2005, international tourist arrivals were just under 4 million, though the average stay per visitor was over 20 days. India's domestic tourism increased from 67 million in 1991 to 366 million in 2004, and is also growing rapidly. However, in 2004, India had only 1892 approved hotels, with slightly less than 100,000 rooms (as compared to 1.2 million in China, and 4.4 million rooms in the U.S.). The demand-supply gap is expected to narrow, and market forces are likely to bring about lower hotel room rates in the next few years. India's tourism sector thus provides substantial business opportunities for Asian and other businesses.

India also hopes to expand its medical tourism industry. In 2005, India provided medical services to 200,000 patients from abroad. India is also executing medical services outsourced by the National Health Service (NHS) of UK. A recent study by India's Confederation of Indian Industry (CII) and McKinsey has projected that India could earn around US $ 2 billion through medical tourism by 2012 (www.medical-tourism-india.com). While there is some competition among India and some of the other Asian countries in this area, as in the IT and ITES sector, there are also likely to be complementarities. Moreover, India's rising medical needs will provide substantial opportunities for Asian countries to operate in India. Similarly, the healthcare industry of India also has plans to expand abroad. India's performance in providing affordable health services to its population is however quite modest, and needs to be substantially improved. Health insurance is an area of potential commercial opportunity for domestic and foreign insurance firms.

The Indian educational institutions are beginning to establish a presence in rest of Asia. This is exemplified by the Global Indian International School (GIIS) which has already established two campuses each in Singapore and Japan, and one in Malaysia. In mid 2007, GIIS will launch a campus in Auckland, New Zealand. The GIIS is involved in providing primary and secondary education. While it caters primarily to Indian diaspora, the GIIS also has attracted students from other nationalities. Similarly, the Delhi Public School (DPS) is expanding its presence in Asia. It is already operating in Indonesia, Nepal, Singapore and Sri Lanka. Other less well known but good quality Indian educational institutions are also setting up operations in Asia.

The Government of India's state of Bihar has taken the initiative to revive ancient Nalanda University as an institution of higher learning and cultural exchange between India and the rest of Asia (Velloor, 2007). The project envisages enlisting support of several nations in Asia, most notably Japan. This project also has the potential to provide a useful forum for India and ASEAN to forge deeper understanding. At the tertiary level, Melaka Manipal Medical College represents a low-key, but constructive engagement between India and Malaysia in the field of education. India's engineering and management institutes are gradually establishing their presence in rest of Asia. It is now common for the Indian management institutes to have a component in their postgraduate programs involving study visits to other Asian countries. India welcomes foreign educational institutions to set up operations in India. India needs to significantly increase and upgrade its tertiary education facilities, and needs to manage political economy of access to higher education opportunities. India is likely to continue to be a significant source of students for education export sectors of countries such as Australia, Singapore, New Zealand, and Malaysia. Indian policymakers have signalled their intentions to diversify the export basket of services with the appropriate policy and focus. India has the potential to host significant number of foreign students in its educational institutions at all levels. Presence of foreign educational institutions may help in this regard.

India is putting increasing emphasis on greater air and sea connectivity, including direct links with major cities in Asia. India has liberalized and deregulated its aviation and maritime transport services sector, resulting in increased competition that augurs well for facilitating greater economic linkages between India and the rest of Asia. India is setting up Services Export Promotion Council (SEPC) to increase the share of services in India's total exports. In addition to the above services, exports by the construction industry will also be emphasized.

India and Preferential Trade Agreements (PTAs)

Unsatisfactory progress in multilateral trade liberalization in recent years has been among the factors which has led to many Asia-Pacific economies towards negotiating regional and bilateral PTAs, with trading partners within and outside Asia, though some of the major FTAs such as EU, and NAFTA (North American Free Trade Agreement) pre-date this (Sen, 2006; Dent, 2006; and Aggarwal and Urata, 2006). This trend of proliferation of Asian FTAs has also led India to expand bilateral trade and investment linkages through economic partnership and preferential trade agreements (PTAs) with a number of Asian countries. The key motivations for entering into such deals have been both strategic and economic. India envisages PTAs as important foreign policy tools to forge new strategic alliances with the rest of Asia, and to contribute to regional security efforts.

The PTAs are also expected to strengthen India's market-based economic integration with its neighbours and geographically proximate regions, viz. SAARC, ASEAN, and East Asia. India also aims to increase cross-regional trade linkages with Latin American and Middle-Eastern countries, as indicated by the initiatives to form similar agreements with the MERCOSUR grouping, GCC, Egypt and Chile. India, Brazil and South Africa (IBSA) have been discussing a trilateral free trade agreement which will also involve the South African Custom Union (SACU) and MERCOSUR (RIS, 2006). The IBSA aims to contribute towards developing a sustainable and inclusive model of globalization. India has signalled its willingness to engage in more complex forms of economic cooperation. With India planning to expand bilateral trade and investment linkages through economic partnership and preferential trade agreements (PTAs) with a number of Asian countries, the pace of India's trade integration with the rest of Asia not just in merchandise trade, but also in commercial services, is likely to expand in the near future.

One of India's most representative and respected business associations, Confederation of Indian Industry (CII) has called for an internal debate on the FTAs (2006). In particular, it has argued that FTA negotiations should be undertaken after detailed analysis and study, which should include an assessment of the economic impact on various industrial sectors. It has also argued that the FTA negotiations should incorporate high degree of implementation integrity. The CII report also rightly emphasizes domestic reforms in taxation, infrastructure, and governance to enable the country in general and industry in particular to obtain maximum benefits and mitigate possible adverse impacts.

The above arguments have considerable merit and the Indian government should closely consult the CII and other such organizations before moving forward with new FTAs; and in ensuring maximum benefits for the country from the current agreements. India's growing web of PTAs with Asian countries indicates its willingness to engage the rest of Asia towards forming an Asian Economic Community that is inclusive in its approach. While services trade has only been bilaterally negotiated so far for the PTA with Singapore, very few of India's PTAs have an established dispute settlement mechanism being negotiated for cross-border investments. In this sense, India's PTAs, in its current state, raise significant concerns on the possibility of trade diversion from cheaper import sources, and also the fact that in spite of negotiating these agreements, most of them remain grossly underutilized due to lack of implementation integrity (Asher and Sen, 2005). As most of India's PTAs, which are in force, are undergoing further negotiations, there is a distinct possibility of their becoming more comprehensive in the future. This will involve inclusion of services and investments are likely to be added. In particular, India is discussing comprehensive bilateral agreements with Japan and Korea. An economic agreement with China is also under discussion.

It is striking that from the 16 countries included in Japan's proposal for a Comprehensive Economic Partnership in East Asia (involving ASEAN, China, Japan, Korea, India, Australia and New Zealand), it is only with Australia and New Zealand that India does not have PTA discussions currently. Our perception is that these two countries will find India quite receptive in engaging in such discussions and deepening economic linkages. This will require a mind-set change in the policy, business, and academic think tank communities of these two countries. After the recent deadlock in WTO talks, it has already been indicated by Indian policymakers that bilateralism is likely to emerge as one of the key instruments of its commercial trade strategy (Sen, 2006). It is beginning to undertake WTO-plus commitments on tariff reduction, which adds a new dimension to India's trade policy.

India offered to substantially reduce duties on ASEAN's imports of agricultural products for 94 per cent of ASEAN exports to India, by offering to reduce refined palm oil tariff from 90 per cent to 60 per cent; crude palm oil from 80 per cent to 50 per cent; black tea from 10 per cent to 5 per cent and on pepper from 70 per cent to 50 per cent. ASEAN's unhelpful tone and style of negotiations are however contributing to negative perceptions in India about the FTA negotiations. This is indicated by an editorial in the Business Line (August 31, 2006), a newspaper favorably inclined towards India's LEP, which stated that some of India's Asian neighbors "make financial demand without a commensurate *quid pro quo*". As indicated in Table 1, India's per capita income is about half that of ASEAN. Even though reduction in India's poverty rate has been about 1 per cent per year in recent years, the number of poor is still at an unacceptable level of 250 million persons. Most of the poor are in the rural sector engaged in agriculture. Tea, pepper, and coffee from Vietnam and Palm oil from Malaysia and Indonesia are perceived in India to be particularly sensitive products for the rural population. India has offered concessions, including staggered time frame for duty reductions, but ASEAN's proposal of only 60 sensitive items on the negative list is clearly unrealistic. India has been arguing with considerable logic for a dual approach based on value addition, and change in tariff heading in structuring Rules of Origin. ASEAN has argued for only value addition approach which will permit easy re-export of the third country products, undermining the spirit of the agreement. India's bilateral agreements with Singapore and Thailand have incorporated both the requirements. Both are ASEAN members.

India-ASEAN FTA which was scheduled to become operational in January 2007 is still under negotiation. In addition to the above issues, the enforcement aspects need emphasis. Internally, India needs to speed up its trade facilitation efforts. Reforms designed to make India a unified market, and measures to reduce overall transaction costs are needed. In particular, India needs to make it easier to start and to close businesses, and to substantially lower costs of seeking legal remedies for commercial disputes. India ranks 134 out of 175 countries in the case of doing business (World Bank, 2007). It must consciously address the current inefficiencies in this area; in particular India needs to implement a more modern bankruptcy law.

While India is engaging in sub-regional cooperation with selected low and middle income countries in South Asia and Southeast Asia through the BIMSTEC (Bay of Bengal Initiative for Mutli-sectorial and Technical Cooperation), it is observed by Asher and Sen (2006) that such cooperation is contingent upon domestic reforms and constructive engagement among the members of the grouping while there are a range of areas from energy security, tourism and infrastructure cooperation that would generate a win-win situation for all members, a more pragmatic mindset that does not regard economic cooperation as a zero sum game is needed. These countries need to undertake joint efforts to address common problems and challenges, particularly in enhancing connectivity through better infrastructure. They further note: "In order for BIMSTEC to be a credible sub-regional grouping, comfort levels among the BIMSTEC members would need to be enhanced, with greater focus on livelihood generation and protection and on enhancing capacities and improving governance. There have been some serious coordination problems involving BIMSTEC, that should not recur in the future...enlightened self interest of BIMSTEC members requires constructive cooperation for managing globalization and other challenges." (Asher and Sen, 2006).

Foreign Investment Flows

With economic reforms in 1991, both inward and outward investment policies in India have been gradually liberalized, increasing the receptiveness of the economy to foreign investment flows. India's Foreign exchange reserves stand at US $ 176 billion for the year 2006 (The Financial Express, December 22, 2006). Indian market capitalization has more than trebled in value over more than a decade to stand at US $ 643 billion (The Financial Times, 2006). As of December 2006, 1000 FIIs have invested US $ 46 billion in India's capital markets. Between 2000 and 2005, India received US $ 8.4 billion in private equity (Tucker and Leahy, 2006). A study by Bain and Company has projected that by 2010 India is likely to receive US $ 7 billion a year in private equity (Tucker and Leahy, 2006). India's FDI Inward stock was estimated at US $ 51 billion in 2005, and is projected to be US $ 109 billion by 2010. While that of FDI outward stock was US $ 11 billion in 2005, and is projected to be US $ 29 billion in 2010 (EIU, 2006). FDI share of GDP was 5.9 per cent in 2004. While official levels of FDI are estimated to be US $ 11 billion in March 2007 double that from the previous year's US $ 5.5 billion. India set up three national multi-commodity exchanges in 2002-03, all of which are ranked among the twenty largest in the world as measured in terms of number of contracts traded (UNCTAD, 2006). These demutualized organizations have focused on establishing hi-tech, low-cost, web-based trading. They are regulated by the Forward Markets Commission (FMC). As with Indian companies in general, these exchanges have been seeking international alliances and ventures. Some of the traded contracts have purely domestic focus, others such as precious metals, raw jute, and oilseeds, have the potential to take on international importance. Investment flows have already surpassed FDI inflows and have expanded significantly to about US $ 9.0 billion by the 2004-05 period. India's net FDI inflow in 2004 was US $ 5.3 billion.

Such inflow is projected to be US $ 11.6 billion annually for the 2006-10 period, 19th in the world (EIU, 2006). India is increasingly becoming an attractive destination for global investors. According to AT Kearney 2005 Survey, India was ranked as most favorable destination for global FDI after China. While China and India are ranked quite high in the FDI Confidence Index, some of the other Asian countries such as Japan, Singapore, Thailand and Korea are ranked below the global top 10 destinations. It is important to note that while India appears to be attracting much less amount of FDI inflows compared to that of China, the interest of foreign investors in India is relatively recent. FDI into China (and many other East Asian countries) is driven by capital-intensive manufacturing while in the case of India it is driven more towards skill and knowledge intensive areas involving service transactions in the Information and Communication technology, financial services and in research and development.

While the reflection of such investments in conventional merchandise and services trade data is relatively small in value terms, non-trivial importance of the knowledge-based work which is eventually incorporated into electronics, hardware and other products which provide large gross volume of merchandise trade is undertaken in India. Although India is yet to substantially attract FDI in heavy and light manufacturing, the success of India's automobiles and steel industry continues to improve investor perceptions. Malaysia's *Petronas* has acquired a 10% stake in Cairns India Limited. Korean company, Pohang Iron and Steel has recently invested 12 billion dollars in building a steel plant and building iron ore in the eastern state of Orissa. Global automakers like Volkswagen and BMW are planning to assemble cars in India for domestic consumption and export (Giridharadas, 2006). India produced nearly 8 million motor vehicles in 2005, of which 1.3 million were passenger cars. The auto industry sales are expected to increase from US $ 36 billion in 2005 to US $ 145 billion by 2016. The Korean and Japanese auto producers have specially aggressive plans for India, but Indian companies are also gearing up for global competition (Yee, 2006 a & b). At the same time Indian companies continue to invest significantly in Asia.

India's outward investment stock is estimated to be US $ 12 billion (IBEF) in 2006. This excludes the investments by the over 20 million Indian Diaspora. Southeast Asia in particular is expected to be the main beneficiary of India's FDI outflows, thus diversifying the region's source of investments and technology. Indian companies are poised to invest in Thailand (auto components sector), in Indonesia and Vietnam (motor vehicles and energy sector), Malaysia (herbal and medicinal plants), and in the Philippines (ICT sector), among others (Sen and Srivastava, 2007). India's national oil company is already involved in a joint venture to explore oil and natural gas in Myanmar and Vietnam. An Indian company, *Kirloskar Brothers Ltd* (KBL) has partnered with Laos in addressing the challenges of floods and drought in rice production. High quality, well-tested, but reasonably priced, pumps of KBL enabled Laos to increase its rice production by over 20 times, helping it to be self-sufficient in its key consumption commodity. The Indian companies have also invested in manufacturing companies in South Korea. An Indian company, Burrup Fertilizers, is the first such company in secondary processing of gas in Western Australia, with an investment of Australian dollar 630 million (Srinivasan, 2006). The two-way flow of investments between and India and rest of Asia is becoming an increasing reality. Philippines and Vietnam's IT companies can also invest in India, the way their Malaysian and Singapore counterparts have done. Recently, a Malaysian-owned company based in Thailand won a competitive contract to modernize a Zoo in Mumbai (The Indian Express, December 27, 2006). This suggests the increasing variety of economic linkages between India and ASEAN. More such market-based linkages can be expected to continue.

The Foundations of India's Competitive Advantage

Let us now turn briefly to some critical factors underlying India's competitive advantage in the global market place. The legal and institutional framework of a modern market economy goes back at least 150 years in India. This is a tradition not many developing countries can boast about, and a tremendous competitive advantage. A special aspect of this is the use of the English language. While the rest of the developing world is working hard to acquire this skill, India and Indians already have this tremendous comparative advantage. These features are among the major attractions for doing business in India (Asia-Pacific Executive Forum, 2004).

The second strategic advantage is India's vast pool of technical and scientific personnel. As we are already seeing in information technology and bio-technology, this pool gives India a great competitive advantage in a global economy increasingly driven by scientific knowledge and technology.

A third strategic advantage is India's huge home market, with a large middle class and its rapidly growing buying power. This allows our enterprises to reap economies of scale and reduce costs within the domestic market, thereby positioning them to penetrate global markets. Last, but not least, there is a remarkable change in the mindset of India's entrepreneurs and policy makers from an inward looking control ridden outlook to a confident, outward-oriented ambition to emerge as global players. Though intangible, the power of ideas should never be underestimated. As most of you are well aware, it is indeed imagination and ambition which drives us to success. It is this ambition to be global players which is driving much of India's recent successes.

The Key Challenges

Along with India's strategic strengths, it is important to take note of its strategic challenges. The most important among them, as we are well aware, is weak infrastructure. Poor roads and transport connectivity, unreliable power supply, and poor telecommunications have been a major impediment to growth, and greatly escalated costs. There has been significant improvement in the recent past, but there is still a long way to go. A closely related strategic challenge is the rapid depletion of water and other natural resources which could eventually bring India's high growth to a grinding halt if these are not urgently addressed. Another strategic disadvantage is the combination of restrictive labour laws for large enterprises and special incentives for small enterprises, which together undermine the scale economies and cost advantage of large enterprises, thereby eroding India's cost competitiveness.

Finally, there are the well-known inefficiencies and inertia in governance, corruption, and rent-seeking activities. All of these greatly undermine competitiveness through delays in decision making, and escalation of transaction costs.

Impact of Asian Energy Consumption Pattern on the Global Environment

Asia, to which Japan belongs, is expected to increase energy consumption at a rate fastest in the world because of its great population, accounting for about 50 per cent of the world population, and the anticipated rapid economic growth of the newly industrializing economies (NIES) and developing countries like China and India (http://www.nistep.go.jp/achiev/abs/eng/rep003e/rep003ae.html). The adverse effects of their energy consumption have already become evident, in the form of acid rain for example. Concern is expressed also over such global atmospheric environmental effects as greenhouse effect (NISTEP Report No. 4th Policy-Oriented Research Group).

In spite of importance of Asia in its effect on the global environment, accumulation of knowledge on its present energy consumption pattern, geoscientific features and environment is not sufficient to assist in formulating adequate measures to cope with the environmental problems foreseen in the future. Furthermore, a great diversity among concerned Asian nations in energy consumption and socioeconomic conditions will make environmental conservation even more difficult.

NISTEP has decided to study the present patterns of production and consumption of energy, emission of pollutants, and their future prospects, for 25 Asian countries east of Afghanistan and Pakistan, both countries inclusive, not limited to important countries in terms of these issues. Subsequently, NISTEP will analyze the outcomes of the study to identify scientific and technological issues that should concern the global environment in the future. For these purposes NISTEP set up in March this year (1989) the Study Committee on Asian Energy Consumption and Global Environment, drawing upon experts on such fields as economy, combustion, atmospheric environment, weather, tropical forests, and initiated the study.

The study group conducted a primary treatment of the data exerted from the Energy Statistics Yearbook of the United Nations, the World Energy Statistics and Balance by OECD/IEA and other energy-related statistics including the Yearbook of Forest Products by FAO. The interim report provides a preliminary summary of the present energy consumption patterns as a result of the above endeavor. The Energy Statistics Yearbook of the United Nations provides information on the energy consumption pattern of Asia necessary for analyzing global environmental problems, by country and by region and by degree of socioeconomic development. The World Energy Statistics and Balance by OECD/IEA, issued November last year (1988) as a bulletin and June this year (1989) as a formal report, provides for the first time a comprehensive coverage including developing countries.

Findings of the Study

(1) Consumption of energy is growing in Asia faster than any other regions of the world. Asia also depends heavily on coal which imposes a heavy load on the environment. These trends are becoming even more pronounced recently.

(2) Viewed from the standpoint of consumption by country, China, Japan and India are the major consumers of energy in Asia. Both China and India have a pattern of energy consumption in which coal is the primary source of energy; furthermore, their demands for energy are increasing. Overall, NIES and Japan are shifting their dependence from liquid fuel to natural gas and nuclear power, both of which give smaller environmental load than petroleum. However, the rate of solid fuel consumption is also increasing. The least developed countries (LDC) are introducing natural gas and developing hydroelectric generation. This trend should be highly valued from the viewpoint of global environmental conservation.

(3) On the subject of energy consumption by sector, Japan recently exhibits a tendency for decreasing the share of the industry sector while increasing the shares of the transportation and household sectors. By contrast, the ASEAN countries, LDC and NIES are increasing the share of the industry sector. The transportation sector is notably increasing its share in NIES.

(4) The forest is declining in Southeast Asia at the fastest rate, the rate even faster than the forest decline of Brazil. Charcoals are cited as major causes for the forest decline. Firewood and charcoal production accounts for the majority of timber production.

GLOBAL IMBALANCE: INDIAN PERSPECTIVES

I: Global Perspective on Global Imbalances

(a) Essential Feature of the Global Imbalances

It is useful to understand that in different countries the existence of a current account surplus or deficit is inevitable among economies at any given time. In particular, one of the arguments in favor of global integration is that capital may flow from developed economies to the capital-starved developing economies which implies that there would be current account deficits in the latter. The problem is not the existence of current account deficits or surpluses *per se*, but it is persistence of large current account deficit and large current account surplus, particularly in large and systemically important economies, which give rise to fears of unsustainably and disruptive unwinding (Reddy, 2006-http://www.un.org/esa/ffd/events/KeynoteReddy.pdf).

(b) Possible Causes of Global Imbalances

The current global imbalance is reflected in large mismatches in the current account positions in some countries and its mirror image in the form of domestic saving-investment mismatches. For instance, the US current account deficit was 6.4 per cent of GDP in 2005 and stood at US $ 805 billion. While the current account surplus of Japan and emerging Asia accounted for about 60 per cent of the current account deficit of the US. Now, with rising oil prices, the oil exporting countries also exhibit large current account surpluses. It is argued by some that since the late 1990s, the growth processes in many emerging market economies (EMEs), especially those from Asia, have come to rely heavily on external demand. Under such a scenario, it has been felt, many of these countries tried to maintain their external price competitiveness by keeping their currencies undervalued. The process, it is stated, in turn, led to large trade and current account surplus for the Asian EMEs and large trade and current deficits elsewhere in the world, most noticeably in the US. It is also clear that the sharp deterioration in the saving-investment balance in the US in the recent years along with sustained rise in consumption demand, could only be met by rising imports; hence rising large current account deficits in the US. The adverse shift in saving-investment balance in the US is reflected both in the high budget deficit since 2002 and the deterioration in net personal saving since 1998.

(c) The Emerging Consensus on Policy Responses

The global imbalance as it stands today may get corrected on its own and perhaps there could be chances of a less favorable outcome of disorderly correction. It is held that one scenario could be that an orderly private sector led adjustment in imbalances could materialize even without policy action. It is argued that, however slim the chances of a disorderly adjustment, in view of huge cost of disorderly adjustments, public policy cannot afford but strive for relatively orderly adjustment. In any case, it is felt that there is a need for better understanding of policy issues with a view to take appropriate policy actions as also to minimize the cost of adjustments if it were to take place in not very orderly fashion. We have viewed, like many others here, that the sustained and increasing imbalances in the current account positions across the globe could entail serious risks for the functioning of the international monetary system. Rebalancing is best seen as a process with many moving parts that involve all the major actors in the global economy. The successful execution of rebalancing will require a careful application of traditional macro policies — monetary, fiscal, and currency policies — as well as implementation of comprehensive micro agenda of structural reforms.

A significant part of the debate seems to be on relative weights to be accorded by each country to the various elements of the package and the aspects of coordination among the countries that are appropriate. As regards the current global initiatives to correct global imbalances, the Communiqué issued by the International Monetary and Financial Committee (IMFC) released on April 22, 2006 highlighted that action for orderly medium-term resolution of global imbalances is a shared responsibility, and will bring greater benefit to members and the international community than actions taken individually by countries.

Key elements of the strategy towards orderly resolution of the global imbalance suggested in the Communiqué are as follows:

- Raising national saving in the United States—with measures to reduce the budget deficit and spur private saving;
- implementing structural reforms to sustain growth potential and boost domestic demand in the euro area and several other countries;
- further structural reforms, including fiscal consolidation, in Japan;
- allowing greater exchange rate flexibility in a number of surplus countries in emerging Asia; and
- promoting efficient absorption of higher oil revenues in oil exporting countries with strong macroeconomic policies.

In the light of the above, the adjustments that are generally advocated in the individual economies and regions may be summarized as follows:

(i) A major challenge for US authorities could be to seek policies that balance between measures to boost personal saving coupled with measures to cut consumption. However, US policies would need to delicately balance a gradual withdrawal of fiscal stimulus without hurting the recovery. It should be noted that demand compression could result in another recession, which would not be in the interest of the global economy. A gradual realignment of the real exchange rate of the US dollar coupled with measures targeted towards fiscal consolidation is generally advocated. Having said that, proper calibration would hold the key to the success of such a policy mix and this is an important public policy issue.

(ii) The Euro area, which continues to depend largely on external demand, could pursue some structural reforms, especially product and labor market policies, to boost domestic demand and broad-base the recovery. While there are signs of recovery in investment, it is recognized by many that further progress would be helpful to foster better integration of labor, health care, product, pension and financial market reforms. It is recognized that structural reforms by their nature are complex and their impact at best could be only over the medium term.

(iii) We are already witnessing that the Japanese economy is on the way to recovery; the current account surplus has begun to narrow against the background of strengthening domestic demand, which is critical. Thus, the Japanese economy is expected to continue to take some concrete measures to strengthen its financial system, restructure the corporate sector, and reduce large fiscal imbalances.

(iv) As for the emerging economies, especially in Asia, some experts suggest that the growth strategy could be reoriented towards domestic demand to offset possible declines in exports to the US. There are already some signs of strengthening in domestic demand in this region. It is felt that improvement in the investment climate to support higher private investment in the emerging economies is important. It is argued by some that the exchange rate policy may require some attention of the policy makers in the region. However, some others consider that exchange rate adjustments may not serve the interests of output and employment in these countries, while effectiveness of such exchange rate adjustments by themselves in unwinding the imbalances is not conclusive.

(v) The oil exporting countries have recorded large trade surpluses, the investment of which in the domestic market and abroad would help rebalancing global demand. It is suggested that these countries could boost expenditures to some extent in areas where social returns are high like education, health, infrastructure and social security. It is felt that structural policies to strengthen legal and economic infrastructure in these countries may help promoting investment. However, it is also argued that in many oil exporting countries scope for domestic absorption is limited in the short run.

II. India's Perspective on Global Imbalances

(a) India's Role in Global Imbalances

Since Independence, India has moved from a moderate growth path of the first three decades (1950 to 1980) to a higher growth trajectory since the 1980s. Over the last two and a half decades, India has emerged as one of the fastest growing economies of the world, averaging about 6 per cent growth rate per annum and the ranking of the country in terms of size of the economy, especially in purchasing power parity (PPP) terms, has improved. In the last three years, we have averaged a growth rate of 8 per cent. Apart from registering impressive growth rate over the last two and a half decades, India's growth process has been stable. Studies indicate that the yearly variation in growth in India has been one of the lowest. During this period, we have faced only one crisis in 1991.

The crisis was followed by a credible macroeconomic structural and stabilization programme encompassing trade, industry, foreign investment, exchange rate, public finance and the financial sector. The Indian economy in later years could successfully avoid any adverse contagion impact of shocks from the East Asian crisis, the Russian crisis during 1997-98, sanction like situation in post-Pokhran scenario, and border conflict during May-June 1999. In this context, it is appropriate to view the evidence that the policies followed by India have not in any way contributed to the widening of the current global imbalances:

(i) Between 2001-02 and 2003-04, India registered modest current account surpluses, but this was more of a reflection of phase of business cycle, and with the turn around in the business cycle, India has registered a modest current account deficit in the last two years. In fact, going by the current indication and the projections of the tenth Five Year Plan, India is likely to maintain a modest and sustainable current account deficit in the near future.

(ii) It is observed that generally current account surplus accounted for a considerable proportion of reserve accumulation in most of the Asian EMEs and Japan during 2000-05. For India, current account surplus has been a minor source of reserve accretion. In our case, capital flows, as opposed to current account surpluses, played an increasingly important role in the accumulation of reserves.

(iii) Our approach aimed at market determined exchange rate with no predetermined target along with market interventions essentially to manage volatility has served us well. At the empirical level, the flexibility of Indian exchange rate policy is captured by marked two-way movement of Indian rupee against the major currencies including US dollar. Recent international research on viable exchange rate strategies in emerging markets has lent considerable support to the exchange rate policy followed by India.

(iv) The main driver of growth in India has been domestic demand. Impressive growth in exports and imports does strengthen the economy but the ratio of exports to GDP in India is lower than most EMEs.

(v) The overall improvement in GDP growth during the reform period has also been facilitated by improvement in the rate of aggregate domestic saving. For instance, in the high growth phase of last three years, the saving rate rose by 5.5 per centage points from 23.5 per cent in 2001-02 to 29.1 per cent in 2004-05. Gross domestic investment rate, for the first time, remained above 30 per cent in 2004-05, mainly on account of private investment growing at 19.7 per cent. With the Fiscal Responsibility and Budget Management Act in place, the fiscal situation in India has shown improvement in the recent years. The fiscal consolidation process envisages phased reduction in the key deficit indicators. Monetary policy, while being supportive of investment demand places emphasis on price and financial stability and has succeeded in containing inflation expectations. These factors give confidence to the possibility of sustaining the present growth momentum – GDP growth of close to 8 per cent per annum. India has, thus, been following policies which not only served it well but also contributed to global stability. As mentioned by our Finance Minister, Mr. P. Chidambaram, we do not expect any change in the basic framework of our policies both in terms of growth based on efficient use of capital and stability assured by sound macroeconomic policies.

(b) Possible Impact of Global Imbalances on India

As highlighted by our Finance Minister during the recent ADB annual meetings that apart from the impact on the real and external sectors, it is felt that the developments in the currency and capital market are intrinsically intertwined with the global imbalance and, therefore, in the eventuality of a disorderly correction, disruption in these markets in the form of large cross-currency volatility and sharp rise in interest rates are likely in the global economy. What could be the possible impact of less than orderly adjustment of global imbalances on the Indian economy?

India does not depend on the international capital market for financing the fiscal deficit and consequently to some extent adverse consequences of the global developments would be muted. However, there could be a spill-over effect of global developments on domestic interest rates and thus on fiscal also.

The fiscal position of the Government could also be indirectly impacted through the nature of management of foreign exchange reserves held by the Reserve Bank. Similarly, any abrupt adjustment in global imbalances may affect corporate, banks and households in India though the impact may be less than some other emerging economies. With respect to the impact on corporate, if there is widening of spreads due to a shift in investor confidence in the international markets, those corporate which have borrowed at variable rates may possibly suffer more than those, which have taken loans on a fixed rate basis. Corporate which have hedged against currency and interest rate risks may escape the adverse effects. It may be noted that the Reserve Bank has been urging banks to encourage corporate to hedge their foreign currency exposures. Further, exposure of the corporate sector as a whole to the external debt is limited by indicative ceilings on external commercial borrowings imposed by the Government and the Reserve Bank of India. The level of total external debt of India is currently less than the foreign exchange reserves.

Although banks in India have their deposit base predominately in rupees and their investment in foreign currency assets is not large, they have been financing investment in assets, home loans and the retail market as well as equities. Like in many EMEs, asset prices have risen sharply in India too. Should there be a reversal of capital flows, asset prices may decline but the banks' exposure to the risky assets have been severely restricted by Reserve Bank's regulatory actions. Likewise, the equity market has also seen a sustained uptrend but efforts have been made by the Reserve Bank to cap the banks' exposures. Further, banks in India have invested significantly in government debt and other fixed income securities. If a rise in international rates gets reflected in domestic interest rates, banks will have to mark down the value of their investment portfolio. To the extent a rise in international interest rates impacts the domestic interest rates, it would entail marked-to-market losses on the investment portfolios. However, the banking sector has acquired some added strength to absorb such probable shocks, largely aided by regulatory actions. As regards impact on the households, there is a risk that rises in interest rates in general could impact the housing market and expose the balance sheet of the households to interest rate risk, increasing the risk of loan losses for banks. The overall banking sector's exposure to housing loans being relatively small, adverse developments may not have any systemic implications on the banking sector.

(c) The Emergence of Oil as a New Factor

The emergence of large current account surpluses among the oil exporting countries is an important recent development. The current account surplus of the oil exporting countries increased from 6.2 per cent of their GDP in 2001 to 19.1 per cent in 2005. Less than third of the combined current account surplus of the oil exporting countries has been reflected in their foreign exchange reserves which rose by US $ 90 billion in 2005. The IMF (World Economic Outlook, April 2006) has highlighted that to the extent that higher net savings by oil exporters have driven down global interest rates, and that these lower rates have boosted demand in economies with market-based financial systems, such as the United States, the oil price shock may also have had an additional negative effect on the US external position.

The fact remains that the rising oil prices would result in further widening of global current account imbalances as according to consensus forecast the current account balance of the US is projected to deteriorate further in 2006. Other industrialized economies are projected to run a combined surplus led mainly by Japan and Germany. The aggregate current account surplus of the major oil exporting countries is expected to increase further in the near term. In this regard, it may be noted that India's oil import bill amounted to 2.9 per cent of GDP in 2001-02, but the bill climbed to 5.5 per cent of GDP in 2005-06, though in volume terms the increase has been marginal.

III. Future Agenda for Analysis

In view of complex nature of global imbalances and the way forward to minimize the risks of disorderly adjustments, it may be useful to explore possible agenda for further analysis. First, national balance sheets, as mentioned by Governor Mervyn King, could be given special attention to get a fuller picture of financial claims that countries have against other countries. Looking at the national balance sheets would also be useful to acquire a sense about the potential for adjustment, and they will give a sense of the possible impact of relative price changes on the value of assets and liabilities. The composition and size of the liabilities and assets of the national balance sheets are crucial as by viewing them together we could get a global picture. However, we should look deeper into the balance sheets in terms of disaggregating them into public and private sector components and the incomes generated in the process. A relevant observation here is the perceived higher returns to external assets held by US relative to US assets held by the rest of the world. A dis-aggregation enables analysis of the role of private and public sector in perpetuation as well as the resolution of imbalances. There could be dominance of bilateral claims of the private sector of one country to the public or the private sector of other country.

Second, following the experience of the East Asian crisis of 1997-98, where private sector vulnerabilities rather than public sector imbalances played a key role in precipitating the crisis, the third generation models have explicitly brought to the fore the role of balance sheet mismatches in causing financial crises. A country's balance sheet as evident from traditional macroeconomic aggregate could be quite sound, yet, analysis of composition and size of the liabilities and assets of the balance sheets of domestic entities may be useful in assessing vulnerability to the manner of unwinding of imbalances. It would therefore be useful to analyze the impact of global imbalances on various balance sheets within the country such as the government sector, financial sector including banks and financial institutions, non-financial private sector including corporate and households.

Third, as mentioned earlier, surplus of oil exporting countries has emerged as a new factor in the debate on the global imbalance. There are some indications that the oil surpluses are being deployed in more diversified avenues than official reserves. Oil exporters appear to have taken advantage of emerging investment opportunity in stock markets and real estate. Such inflows could have helped to keep long-term interest rates as also emerging market bond spreads low, even as policy rates are rising. An interesting issue would be the nature of their responses to unwinding of global imbalances.

Fourth, in a way global imbalance is a reflection of incomplete globalization. If there were complete globalization, the surplus in saving of one country could be utilized by a country which has deficit in saving as it happens among different States in India or the US. It could be argued that as the global economy integrates further, the resolution of the global imbalances might be smoother.

Fifth, what is the evolving role of viewing exchange rate regimes in influencing domestic economy? It is argued by some that the emerging evidence indicates that domestic price movements remain somewhat immune to considerable exchange rate movements. If so, the possibility of bringing about global rebalancing through exchange rate adjustment by itself may not be very encouraging. No doubt exchange rate would have an important role to play in global rebalancing, but the issue is its relationship with other components of the whole package like saving–investment, fiscal deficit, raising investment, structural reforms and domestic output as well as employment. The linkages among the various components described here could be very country specific. Sixth, there is wide diversity among the Asian economies in terms of saving and investment rates, fiscal deficit, drivers of growth (domestic versus external demand) and the degree of flexibility in their exchange rates. Thus, it may not be difficult to treat all of them as contributing to global financial imbalances in the same manner, nor would all the Asian economies be identically affected by the adjustment of global financial imbalances. Correspondingly, the policy response of each country to the issue would be tailored to the circumstances. More importantly, with growing integration among Asian economies, how would the process of rebalancing affect them depending on the manner in which dominant economies in Asia manage the process?

Seventh, our Prime Minister, Professor Manmohan Singh has suggested that given the potential for investment demand in the region, we must find ways of making better use of savings and finding investment avenues within the region. In this regard, an important issue would be generation of demand within the region so that the aggregate current account surpluses are absorbed in the region itself. This process of demand generation would help in orderly correction of the global imbalances. Eighth, one wonders whether there is a dissonance between the perception of financial markets and that of the policy makers in regard to global imbalances. The policy makers appear to give some signals of concern, but the response of the financial markets is often out of alignment with the signals. Interestingly, anecdotal evidence shows that analysts in financial intermediaries are sensitive to the downside risk of imbalances, but the conduct of the participants does not reflect the awareness. No doubt, this sense of dissonance is not new, as for example, stock markets went up after Mr. Alan Greenspan's statement regarding irrational exuberance. If such dissonance is true, and persists, what would be the effectiveness of public policy initiatives?

Ninth, is there an advantage in assessing the non-quantifiable factors to explain the persistence of what has been stated as a stable disequilibrium to describe the current status of the global economy? For example, signature value of United States in terms of confidence of financial markets as a lasting safe haven status could be a factor, though the issue is whether it will be valid interminably. The perception of continuing productivity gains in the US due to its proven flexibilities could be another. Lack of alternatives to deploy global savings, which are expanding may also be relevant. No doubt, these are not quantifiable, but do not cease to be relevant for analysis and assessment.

Finally, is it possible that there are several intermediate scenarios between orderly adjustments and disruptive or disorderly adjustments? A series of marginal adjustments, often in spurts, could take place which may appear random, but move towards gradual lessening of imbalances through an interactive and iterative processes encompassing markets, national policies and global cooperation. The agenda for analysis proposed here may facilitate exploration of such intermediate scenarios of unwinding global imbalances.

To conclude, the performance of the Indian economy since 1980, and in particular since the reforms in the 1990s, is in many ways an impressive success story both in terms of growth and stability. The Indian economy has responded well to the rising global competition with gradually increasing integration with the world economy. The current high growth phase of the Indian economy is also coinciding with rising domestic saving rates. While India by itself hardly contributes to the current global financial imbalances, any large and rapid adjustments in major currencies and related interest rates or current accounts of trading partners could indirectly, but significantly, impact the Indian economy.

Liberalization of Indian Foreign Trade with China Focus

Liberalization of the foreign trade sector has been seen as a cornerstone of the reform of the Indian economy. This has obvious parallels with China where Deng Xiaoping's policy of 'opening up to the outside world' saw a remarkable increase in foreign trade.

India is often compared with China, and with good reason. They are both huge countries and have been, through history, major centers of world civilization. They both suffered under, and were transformed by, the impact of the outside world, especially during the period of Western ascendancy. The Republic of India and the People's Republic of China came into being within two years of each other and both embarked on a course of planned development to restore their national economies. In particular they both emphasized import substitution and a policy of exporting in order to import goods and material needed for economic growth. Finally, they have both turned from planning and self-reliance to market-oriented and outward-looking policies. Comparative advantage has replaced self-sufficiency and they are both pursuing export-led growth.

However, although China and India are natural benchmarks for each other, there are considerable differences between the two. In this context the PRC cannot be discussed in isolation from Taiwan and Hong Kong. It seems unlikely that India will repeat the export growth of the PRC under the open door policy. The advantages that the PRC had, particularly the existence of Hong Kong and Taiwan, were unique and cannot be replicated.

It would appear that India should pay special attention to the quality of exports rather than the quantity and utilize the advantage it has of elite which is more familiar with the outside world than the Chinese, particularly those from the PRC, and which sees English, that international business language, as its own. These could be considerable advantages as India strives to win global markets.

India and China: Sharing a Common Heritage

India and China are natural points of comparison, not merely because they are of comparable size but also they seemed to represent two opposed models—'democracy' and 'totalitarianism' (Bhagwati, 1993). They also share a common historical heritage and much of their modern economic policy can be explained in terms of it. They were both colonized through foreign trade; both saw planning (Hanson, 1966; Bhattacharyya, 1966), an independent foreign trade position, self-reliance and import substitution as precursors of development. Both have now moved away from self-reliance into a relatively liberalized trade system based on comparative advantage, utilizing foreign capital (Beal, 2008).

The success, until recently at least, of the export-led economies of East Asia has led to a general acceptance that foreign trade is an important aspect of economic growth (OECD, 1994). It is certainly becoming an increasingly important part of the world economy. In 1820 exports accounted for only 1% of world product; that rose to 8.7% in 1913. The ratio fell during the inter-war period because of depression and protectionism, but grew again in the postwar period, especially after 1950, when the pax-Americana provided a security framework for expansion again, particularly in the market economies (Madison, 1995).

A stable foreign exchange system, underpinned by the strength and availability of the US dollar, led to great growth in world trade, roughly double that of the world economy itself. In 1950 merchandise exports were 7.0% of world GDP (down from 8.7% in 1913) but by 1973 this had risen to 11.2% and by 1992 to 13.5%. This average masks considerable differences amongst countries and regions. Large countries, for well-known reasons, tend to have a relatively small trade component. For instance, the export/GNP per centage for the United States in 1950 was a mere 3%, slightly above India's 2.6%, below Indonesia's 3.3% and way below Britain's 11.4% or the Netherlands' 12.5%. However, even for the United States the export ratio has grown sharply and in 1992 was 8.2%. And there were two regions in which the growth was most marked. One was Western Europe where proximity and the European Common Market led to rapid growth of trade amongst member countries. Some of the European economies had been traditionally trade-oriented although Britain, which started this period with the remnants of the imperial trading system (which had included India, of course, as the jewel in the crown), ended up with a lower export dependency than its fellow members (21.4% against an average of 29.7%) and far below the Netherlands' 55.3%.

The other region, and the one that had the most impact on the economic strategy of India and China, was East and Southeast Asia. The export dependency rose from 2.3% for Japan in 1950 to 12.4% in 1992. The rate of growth for the newly-industrialized economies (NIES) was much more pronounced. South Korea moved from 1.0% to 17.8%, Taiwan from 2.5% to 34.4% (Maddison does not give figures for Hong Kong or Singapore).

Whatever the balance of reasons between domestic political struggles and changes in the international environment, China did embark on a radical revision of its foreign trade strategy and with it the proportion of exports to GNP rose considerably. India, which had traditionally been a much more trade-oriented economy, both under the British and with independence, has become less trade-oriented than China over the last 20 years.

The shift in relative trade orientation was mirrored in share of world exports. In 1870 (when Taiwan was still part of Qing China), India's share of world exports was two and a half times that of China. By 1992, India's exports were only a quarter of those of China (here referring to the People's Republic of China) and her share of world exports had fallen ten-fold, from 5% in 1870 to 0.5% in 1992. If the balance of trade deficit had been a problem shared with India's peers then that might have been taken as an attribute of the inherent inequality of the North-South relationship. However, the East Asian NIES and then the People's Republic of China were developing large trade surpluses. Indeed these surpluses have become one of the main points of friction between these economies and the United States.

World exports grew some 10-fold between 1950 and 1992. In terms of constant 1990 US $ the rise was from $375,765 million in 1950 to US $ 3,785,619 in 1992. In 1950 Japan, which was still in its postwar depression and before the Korean War kick-started its economy, held just 0.9% of world exports compared with India's 1.5%. In 1992, although India's exports had grown 4-fold, her share of world exports had shrunk to 0.5% whereas Japan's had risen to 7.9%.

Although Japan is the world's second largest exporter her rapid export growth was emulated and surpassed by a number of East Asian economies. Even in South Asia, Pakistan and Bangladesh did considerably better than India, both raising their exports 10-fold and returning their 1950 share of world exports. The People's Republic of China (PRC) which had, until the late 1970s, followed a broadly similar policy of self-reliance and import substitution, had turned to a trade-oriented policy and seemed to be doing well.

It is worth noting that China's exports, and share of world 1992 exports, were twice that of India in 1973 that is during the Maoist policy of self-reliance. Nevertheless, as discussed below, it is policy shifts under Deng which saw the very rapid expansion of Chinese exports. The question arises: does the experience of the People's Republic of China in moving towards a more trade-oriented strategy have implications for India? Can India follow China through this open door into world markets?

Chinese foreign trade policy was greatly influenced in practice by the international geo-political situation as well as the state of the domestic economy. There are many differences between China and India in respect of foreign trade but three deserve special mention here. One is that the PRC has, generally speaking, been able to preserve a positive trade balance. The exceptions being the early 1950s, when it received relatively large amounts of Soviet aid, and again in the mid 1980s, when there was a surge in imports. This was brought under control and the PRC moved back into a surplus, and a very substantial one, on merchandise trade. Secondly, the PRC share of world exports held up much better than India's. The relatively high share in the 1950s, based primarily on trade with the Soviet Union, fell back slightly during the next two decades, which witnessed a huge growth in world exports. Then the 1980s, after the opening policy took effect, saw a very rapid increase in the PRC share. The change in policy may have led to an increase in exports, but the preceding period indicated that the PRC economy could, for whatever reason, produce products that could win a place in world markets.

A COMPARATIVE ANALYSIS OF EXPORT GROWTH IN INDIA AND CHINA

Since India and China have several comparable regional conditions, there is a similarity in their export patterns. For both the countries, agriculture and mining products jointly account for less than a quarter of the total export basket, while manufacturing (*Identifying Mutual Interest Areas at WTO: A Sino-Indian Joint Perspective*) 271 goods (http://works.bepress.com/cgi/viewcontent.cgi?article=1003&context=julien_chaisse) accounts for the remaining portion, the proportion of which is expanding. In India, manufactured goods (SITC, section 6) and miscellaneous manufactured articles (SITC, section 8) hold important positions, as they account for around 38.7 and 20.3 per cent of export respectively in early 2000. In case of China, although the export of manufactured goods (SITC, section 6) and miscellaneous manufactured articles (SITC, section 8) declined to some extent over the last decade, it has been more than compensated by machinery and transport equipment (SITC, section 7), whose export share increased from 15.5 per cent in 1992 to 35.6 per cent in 2001 (Chaisse and Chakraborty, 2008). In addition, the major export destinations of both neighbours include EU, Japan and the US. Since the initiation of economic reform in early 80s, China's export growth rate has increased tremendously, and India's performance in comparison seems quite modest. Throughout the 1990s, China's commodity export has grown at an average of 14.9 per cent, as compared to 9.9 per cent in case of India. The imports have grown at an average of 14.4 and 9.5 per cent for China and India respectively. While India's global market share was higher than China at the time of signing of GATT, thanks to the policy of self-reliance, the scenario reversed over the next decade. Since the mid-90s China's export and import shares have taken a sharp upturn, while India is lagging far behind, as seen in following Figure.

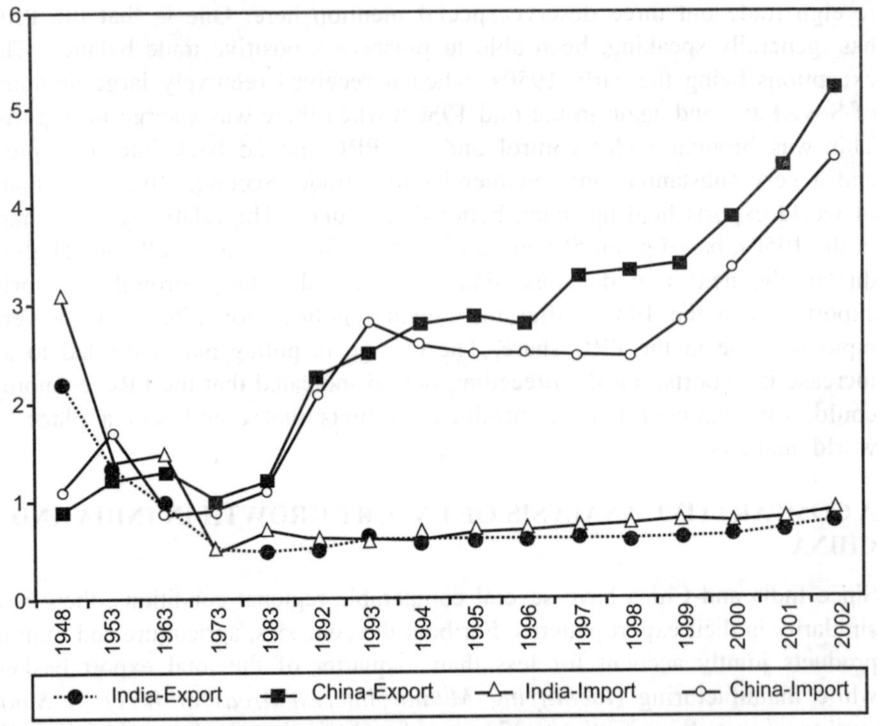

Export-Import Shares of India and China in World Commodity Trade

The increasing intensity of Chinese exports in global economy could also be demonstrated with the help of the following table. Table 3 shows the comparative export and import trends of India and China for major commodity groups. It becomes evident that while China's export shares in the world for all the mentioned commodity groups have steadily increased over the last twenty years, the same for India has remained stagnant. From the International Trade Statistics data (2003) it is further observed that during 1990–2002, the import share of China in the four principal markets, namely Canada, EU, Japan and US has increased by almost four times in all cases. On the other hand, India's import shares have marginally increased in case of Canada, EU and US, while decreasing to some extent in case of Japan.

THE FUTURE CONCERN AREAS

While China expects continuation of this spectacular performance in general and further increase in export growth rate of certain sectors, like textile and clothing products (Nordas, 2004), its trade potential might be limited by several

Table 3: Export and Import Shares of Major Commodity Groups in Global Market

Product	Country	Export 1980	Export 1990	Export 2000	Export 2002	Import 1980	Import 1990	Import 2000	Import 2002
Agricultural products	China	1.5	2.4	3.0	3.2	2.1	1.8	3.3	3.5
	India	1.0	0.8	1.2	1.1	–	0.4	0.7	–
Manufactures	China	0.8	1.9	4.7	6.2	1.1	1.7	3.5	4.9
	India		0.5	0.7		–	0.5	0.4	–
Iron and Steel	China	0.3	1.2	3.1	2.3	2.7	2.5	6.3	8.9
	India	–	–	–	–	–	–	–	–
Chemicals	China	0.8	1.3	2.1	2.3	2.0	2.2	5.0	5.7
	India	0.3	0.4	0.8	0.8	–	–	–	–
Office machines and telecom equipment	China	–	1.0	4.5	9.0	–	1.3	4.6	7.9
	India	–	0.06	0.04	–	–	0.2	0.3	–
Automotive products	China	–	–	0.2	0.4	–	–	0.6	1.1
	India	–	0.06	0.1	–	–	0.08	0.06	–
Textiles	China	–	6.9	10.4	13.5	–	5.0	8.3	8.5
	India	–	2.0	3.8	–	–	0.2	0.3	–
Clothing	China	4.0	8.9	18.3	20.6	0.1	0.0	0.6	0.6
	India	1.7	2.3	3.1	2.8	–	0.0	0.0	–

Source: Calculated from International Trade Statistics (WTO 2003c).

factors. A number of developed countries have often raised objections on the remaining WTO incompatibilities in the Chinese system. Most of the objections date back to the negotiation period in mid-90s. With the completion of the transitory phase in December 2004, China now needs to liberalize its domestic market appreciably. (*Identifying Mutual Interest Areas at WTO: A Sino-Indian Joint Perspective* 273). A number of areas of discontent between China and its trade partners have surfaced in the post-transitory phase, most of which correspond to textile trade (*New York Times*, 2005).

There is a high probability that in future China might be taken into, or need to move to, the dispute settlement body of the WTO over some of these issues. The future problems could be broadly classified under two categories, namely, conformity of Chinese Laws to WTO, and the trade barriers related disputes with other WTO members. The entire commitments made under WTO Agreements are required to be enforced by the Member States of the WTO, first by necessity to give effectiveness to the adopted rules, then to avoid potential conflicts between national and international laws. China is currently trying hard to bring its domestic policy in line with WTO rules, as Youngjin (2002) notes: A closer examination of the Chinese government's relentless efforts to expedite its legal reforms since its 'open door' policy in the late 1970's shows that, its predilection for a legal approach is not a fluke. Even before joining the WTO, China showed a strong readiness to abide by the WTO agreements in coming up with rhetoric against other countries' alleged protective measures...at first blush, China's rule-oriented approach seems inconsistent with the conventional wisdom that a country that has just acceded to the WTO tend to exercise moderation in invoking its trading rights conferred by the WTO agreements, given the substantial adjustment period necessary for implementing the new commitments accompanying a WTO membership. (Youngjin, 2002). However, the expected reform in China's legal system is yet to reach the desired level (Almstedt and Patrick, 2000), and Judge Wang Feirightly points out: If the Legislature does not strengthen our legal system after WTO accession we will have a hard time with TRIPs and it will be detrimental to the long term protection of intellectual property rights in China. We need judicial independence as well.... After the accession to WTO there will be a judicial revolution in China.... China will be a country ruled by law. (Panitchpakdi and Clifford, 2002).

The country reports published by the WTO *Trade Policy Review* are an efficient indicator of the WTO-compatibility of the current policies of any member. However, till date no report has been published on People's Republic of China. Therefore, the Chinese policies potentially prone to future disputes, as identified from the National Trade Estimate Report (USTR 2004), are summarized in Table 4.

Table 4: Looking Through Chinese Trade Policies

Policies Praised	Policies Where Further Reform Advocated
• Reduction in overall average tariff rate. • Various reform measures to enhance WTO-compatibility of domestic policies	• Slowdown in China's WTO implementation efforts since 2003 • Continuing use of regulations written in the 1980s on determining the origin of imports. • Allegation of manipulating various technical standards to limit imports. • Time-consuming and costly process for 'China Compulsory Certification' (CCC) mark. • Weak enforcement of IPRs. • Various barriers in service sectors. • Ineffectiveness of the current anti-competitive practices. • Existence of export subsidies and other administrative supports in certain sectors.

Source: Compiled from USTR (2004).

The report has been very critical of China on the grounds of manipulation of technical standards, weak enforcement of intellectual property rights (IPR), barriers in service sectors, inefficient anti-competitive practices, existence of various subsidies and support measures in certain sectors, etc. However, it was particularly unhappy about the general slowdown in China's WTO implementation efforts since 2003. The European Union has also raised concerns over enforcement of IPR, opening up of insurance and telecom sector, sanitary and phyto-sanitory measures and issues, etc. on various occasions (Lamy, 2003).

The potential areas of dispute concerning India could be identified by analyzing the two WTO *Trade Policy Reviews* on it. The first review on India was performed shortly after it joined WTO in 1998 (WTO, 1998) and the compliance level was not very appreciable at that point. The polices subject to criticism included complex tariff structure and tariff escalation, over-protective import regime, presence of indirect subsidies, inappropriate compliance with TRIPS, lack of transparency, prohibition in various service sectors, etc. However, India modified a number of its policies since then, many of which have been WTO-driven. The increasing WTO-compatibility becomes evident by judging the chronology of the cases it faced at the DSB. A total of seventeen cases have been filed against India so far. The fourteenth case (DS 279) has been filed in early 2003, whereas the earlier one (DS 175) was filed in 1999 (Chaisse and Chakraborty, 2003). In the 2002 review (WTO, 2002), the simplification in the tariff structure, complete elimination of quantitative restrictions, reduction in export restrictions, modification of TRIPS legislation, and reforms in telecommunication, financial and infrastructural services were praised. However, it had been quite critical of India on three points—first, sharp increase in the use of contingency measures; second, price and distribution controls in agriculture which were yet to be phased out; and third, certain commodity-specific entry restrictions. While no complaints on the second and the third issues have been registered at the WTO so far, the last three cases against India (DS 318 by Taiwan; DS 306 by Bangladesh; DS 304 by EU) were filed questioning the WTO-compatibility of its anti-dumping measures. In particular, the case filed by Bangladesh is worth mentioning, since a developing country has moved against India at the DSB for the first time. The major observations of the two reviews are summarized in Table 5.

While several domestic policies of the two countries are likely to be challenged by other members in the coming years, their exports are more vulnerable to various barriers, particularly in the post-transitory phase of WTO. Commenting on the state of trade liberalization, WTO Annual Report (2004) has noted that: Market access issues were the focus of attention in the early part of the year with deadlines set in all three areas: services, agriculture and non-agricultural market access... in general the negotiations did not move forward as far or fast as anticipated, with important spring deadlines in agricultural and non-agricultural market access and on dispute settlement being missed.... many Members apply tariffs at rates well below the bound levels set out in their Schedules which suggests they have considerable scope for tariff reductions (WTO, 2004).

Table 5: Looking Through Chinese Trade Policies

Policies Praised	Policies Where Further Reform Advocated
Trade Policy Review (1998)	
• Rapid reform in tariff rates over 1993-94 to 1997-98. • Overall economic reform measures. • Amendment in Copyright law in line with TRIPS.	• Complex structure of tariff regime and tariff escalation. • Import restriction on consumer goods. • Restrictive import licence and other procedural hassles on imports. • Presence of indirect subsidiles, export subsidies and other incentives. • Unfinished compliance with TRIPS. • Reform in case of agricultural products. • Transparency in decision-making. • Reform in services.
Trade Policy Review (2002)	
• Simplification of tariff structure. • Complete elimination of quantitative restrictions. • Reduction in export restrictions. • Review of FDI policy. • Move towards full conformity with TRIPS. • Significant reforms in certain key service sectors e.g. telecommunication, financial services and to some extent in infrastructural services.	• Increase in use of contingency measures on imports. • Wide range of price and distribution controls in agriculture. • Existence of certain commodity-specific entry restrictions.

Source: Compared on the basis of WTO Trade Policy Reviews on India (1998, 2002d).

Table 6 sums up the findings of an ESCAP study (ESCAP, 2000), which identifies the NTBs imposed on the exports of the South and South-East Asian countries in their principal markets (ESCAP, 2000). It is clearly observed that given the resemblance of their export basket, both China and India are subjected to similar types of barriers. Given the fact that the total value of China's commodity exports in 2001 was more than six times India's total export, its products are attracting higher volume of NTBs. Sally (2000), Mattoo and Subramanian (2003), and others have strongly advocated in favour of adoption of a proactive strategy by the developing countries at WTO forums to achieve common interest. Keeping the success achieved by China and India at the Cancun Ministerial (2003) in mind, it is extremely important for the two countries to continue on the path of a joint negotiating agenda in order to ensure better market access, which is not easily forthcoming. Critics were slightly skeptical about China's seriousness in joining any formal trade bloc or negotiating alliance after its WTO accession, as Panitchpakdi and Clifford (2002) note: China is unlikely to join any formal blocs, such as the so-called like-minded countries, an informal grouping that includes India and Brazil and the most important representative

Table 6: Non-Tariff Barriers Faced by China and India in Principal Markets

The United States	European Union	Japan
China		
• MFA Quota • Anti-Dumping Measures • SPS Measures • Packaging Quarantine • Label Requirements • Technical Standards • Environmental Regulations	• Anti-Dumping Measures • Various regulations on imports from China • Safeguards • Technical Standards • Environmental Regulations • SPS Measures	• Technical Standards • SPS Measures
India		
• Technical Standards • Environmental Regulations • SPS Measures • Anti-Dumping and Countervailing Measures • Government Procurement and Domestic Preference Legislation	• Anti-Dumping Measures • Technical Standards • SPS Measures • Child Labour	• Technical Standards • SPS Measures • Environmental Regulations

Source: Constructed from the analysis in ESCAP (2000).

of developing countries at the WTO. But it will help to balance the dominance of what is known as Quad, a grouping that includes the US, Japan, the European Union and Canada. However, China's role and its intentions will only be truly tested during a new round of trade negotiations (Panitchpakdi and Clifford, 2002).

Identifying Mutual Interest Areas at WTO: A Sino-Indian Joint Perspective

As per their prediction, China followed the track of independent proactive strategy up to Cancun, from which point it resorted to cooperation with other developing countries. In light of the similarity in NTBs on the exports and several other concern areas, it makes sense for China to follow a joint proactive strategy in collaboration with India at WTO forums on two aspects—namely, material and institutional. There is substantial scope for material collaboration in all major fields, given the similarity of export pattern. Here we focus on three areas: namely, agriculture, anti-dumping measures and intellectual property rights, in light of the serious consequences they pose to the export basket and domestic concerns of the countries. Finally, it has been mentioned earlier that the two countries are likely to get involved at the WTO dispute settlement system both as complainant and respondent. However, the working of the WTO dispute settlement mechanism for developing countries has been questioned on several occasions, and we attempt to identify the key points for joint negotiation by the two countries in this regard.

Competitive Advantage of International Standards

To be competitive on both a national and a global basis, organizations must adopt a forward-thinking approach in developing their management strategies. In this section, the International Standards such as ISO 9000 and ISO 14000 are compared to suggest how these standards may be used to move an organization toward that paradigm and thus enable it to compete more effectively in today's global marketplace.

Many of our current quality management and environmental management systems are reactive—that is, they have been developed in response to federal, state, or local regulations. International standards force companies to look at their processes in a new light and to take a more active approach to management. For example, if a company wishes to pursue the new environmental standard, ISO 14000, its environmental management system's pollution control policy will have to be revamped to focus on prevention rather than command-and-control. As the company moves in that direction it will truly become more competitive, and will do so on a global basis.

ISO 9000: A Key to Global Markets

First published in 1987 and revised in 1994, ISO 9000 is a series of standards and guidelines related to quality management and quality assurance. Because the standards are neither industry- nor product-specific, they may be used by either manufacturing or service industries. According to a December 1995 survey by Mobil Inc., more than 130,000 companies worldwide have been registered to ISO 9000.

While ISO 9000 does not specify precisely what kinds of quality processes must occur, or how, it does require that appropriate quality activities be defined, that processes be documented, and that proof be supplied that the company consistently adheres to both. ISO 9000 registration does not ensure a defect-free or quality product or service, but it does indicate that a basic quality system is in place, and that the registered organization is at least capable of providing its customers with quality products and services.

To become registered to ISO 9000, a company must hire an independent third party (known as a registrar) to conduct an on-site audit of its operations and verify that it is in compliance with the requirements of the standard. In the United States, it is recommended—though not required—that the registrar be accredited by the Registrar Accreditation Board (RAB).

The main strength of the ISO 9000 standards, and the reason they have been adopted worldwide, is that they assure customers who do business with registered firms that fundamental quality systems are in place within those organizations. For many international companies, ISO 9000 is seen as a key to doing business in global markets and improving competitiveness, particularly since for many regulated products in the European Union, ISO 9000 registration is a requirement.

The advantages of ISO 9000 registration, whether perceived or real, are nonetheless marked. For example, in a survey conducted by Dowling College of Long Island, about 41% of ISO 9000–registered companies in the New York City metropolitan area reported an increase in their European market share after registration.

In another survey, conducted by the newsletter *Quality Systems Update*, approximately 85% of companies claimed they had experienced external benefits as a result of registration to ISO 9000, and 95% noted internal benefits. The most significant external benefits reported in the survey were:

- Higher perceived quality (83.3%).
- Competitive advantage (70%).
- Reduced customer quality audits (56%).
- Improved customer demand (29%).

The internal benefits of registration included:

- Better documentation (88%).
- Greater employee quality awareness (83%).
- Enhanced internal communication (53%).
- Increased operational efficiency and productivity (40%).

ISO 14000

Whereas ISO 9000 deals with quality management, ISO 14000 is designed to provide a structure for the management of environmental compliance. The ISO 14000 series comprises numerous individual generic standards, which may be broadly classified according to the following six categories: Environmental Management Systems (EMSs), Auditing, Labeling, Performance Evaluations, Life Cycle Assessment, and Environmental Aspects of Product Standards.

The most familiar standard in the 14000 series is ISO 14001, entitled "Environmental Management Systems, Specification with Guidance for Use." Before being published in its final form, 14001 was widely distributed and closely studied as a draft international standard. Organizations will be able to register only to this one standard; all other standards in the series are guidelines to help companies set up, audit, and improve their environmental management systems.

Like ISO 9000, ISO 14000 is neither industry- nor product-specific. The anticipated benefits of registration to this new international standard include:

- Worldwide focus on environmental management.
- Promotion of a voluntary consensus standards approach.
- Harmonization of national rules, labels, and methods through minimization of trade barriers and complications and promotion of predictability and consistency.
- Demonstrated commitment to maintaining and moving beyond regulatory environmental-performance compliance.

ISO 14000 will provide multinational organizations with a single environmental management system that may be implemented wherever they operate, thus eliminating the need for multiple registrations, inspections, certifications, and labels, and doing away with conflicting requirements. As with ISO 9000, even though this is a voluntary standard, suppliers may find it hard to conduct international trade without being registered to it; in the future, ISO 14000 registrations may even become a legal prerequisite for entering the regulated European Union market.

Even before the environmental standards were published in their final form last spring, some companies had already begun to think about how ISO 14000 would fit into their existing systems. In a survey of companies with more than $ 1 billion in sales conducted by the Arthur D. Little consulting firm, 62% of respondents said that ISO 14000 certification would be essential to their future business success, while 70% felt that the most useful benefit of certification was as a demonstration of due diligence. Sixty-one per cent thought it would offer companies a potential competitive advantage in certain markets; 48% feared that lack of certification might be a non-tariff barrier; and 35% believed it might improve quality and reduce costs.

These survey results suggested a few of the ways in which international standards can help a company gain a competitive advantage. In encouraging companies to focus on continuous improvement and to develop a forward-thinking operating paradigm, the standards could have a revolutionary impact on the world's business community.

By implementing ISO 14000, any company can become truly competitive by:

- Decreasing costs through increased efficiencies.
- Creating and maintaining new market opportunities in areas such as Europe, which may eventually make registration to the standards a necessary condition of doing business within their jurisdiction.
- Demonstrating environmental leadership.
- Improving both its own corporate image and community goodwill.
- Enhancing credibility through registration by an independent third party accredited by the appropriate national body, such as the RAB in the United States, or the Japanese Accreditation Board.
- Streamlining/simplifying its EMS.

Addressing OHS Issues

Now that ISO 14000 has become a reality, another international standard—this one focusing on occupational health and safety (OHS) issues—is under consideration. Although it will likely be several years (at least) before such an OHS standard is published, a number of companies are already formulating their EMSs to include health and safety provisions in anticipation of international standards development by the International Organization for Standardization (ISO) as well as the American National Standards Institute (ANSI).

According to the chief executive of the RAB, an ANSI-sponsored public forum held in the spring of 1996 to solicit feedback on this topic found no great interest in an OHS standard among attendees. The consensus seemed to be that it was too soon. But consider this: there is certain logic to the idea of integrating quality, environmental, and OHS management systems, and it is not likely that such integration will occur at some point in the future.

The future of business is closely tied to the development and implementation of international standards such as ISO 9000 and ISO 14000. A mutual commitment to environmental and quality management systems may be expected to serve as a prerequisite for many business relationships. Internally, companies must be aware that certain system efficiencies, as well as opportunities, may be realized through the adoption of voluntary quality and environmental system standards.

Preparing for ISO 14000

So what can companies do now to prepare for upcoming ISO 14000 registrations? Many are conducting gap analyses—that is, evaluating their existing EMSs in relation to the requirements of the current ISO 14001 draft international standard. This enables them to develop road-maps for achieving registration by effectively integrating ISO 14001 into their present environmental, quality, and corporate management systems. Of the companies that have already performed gap analyses, roughly 41% feel that their existing EMS is either close or very close to meeting the ISO 14001 standard, according to a survey carried out by ML Strategies Inc.

A number of companies in almost every industry are adopting a wait-and-see attitude, holding off on seeking registration until such time as industry conditions demand it. As a result, the first of these companies to register will be those whose customers insist on it. But while these organizations delay taking action, many others will gain competitive advantage and get a jump on the future by registering before their customers require it.

South-East Asian Free Trade Agreement: Evolution and Challenges

After the Second World War, significant protectionist sentiment compelled the economies of South Asia to pursue import-substituting industrialization (ISI). While intra-regional trade is not a novel concept for the region, the economies of South Asia are new to the ideas of regionalism and regionalization. Several factors combine to make a negative case for a viable free trade agreement in the short-term. Even so, a reasonable case exists for the creation and gradual strengthening of SAFTA, as there are few benefits to dwelling on historical ill will. As these economies grow and economic complementarities begin to develop, the countries of South Asia may find that SAFTA can offer a potentially significant contribution to their progress.

A Reasonable Case for SAFTA

South Asia saw a far larger level of intra-regional trade half a century ago than it has seen in current times. Recent history demonstrates that hurdles in the path towards an active and functional free trade agreement are essentially political in nature. The countries of South Asia must strive to emulate the recent achievements of Southeast Asian economies, which have succeeded in achieving economic integration despite a history of rivalry and poor mutual relations. The pursuit of mutual economic interest must be prioritized over political harmony. South Asian policy makers must be responsible enough to realize that if regional welfare gains are to be achieved, animosity must be put aside. A legacy of tension has made the member countries excessively cautious in taking meaningful policy measures toward economic cooperation. Thus viewed, several factors combine to make a negative case for a viable free trade agreement in the short-term. Even so, a reasonable case exists for the creation and gradual strengthening of SAFTA, as there are few benefits to dwelling on historical ill will. As these economies grow and economic complementarities begin to develop, the countries of South Asia may find that SAFTA can offer a potentially significant contribution to their progress.

The trade-weighted average tariff is one of the standard measures of the tariff rate. This measure is regarded as more realistic and accurate than the average tariff. It weighs each tariff by the share of total imports in that import category—that is, if a country has most of its imports in a category with very low tariffs, but has many import categories with high tariffs but virtually no imports, and then the trade-weighted average tariff would indicate a low level of protection. The standard way of calculating this tariff rate is to divide total tariff revenue by the total value of imports. Many countries regularly report this data.

This argument does not necessarily conflict with the fact that poverty amelioration in India during the 1980s was greater than in the 1990s, although growth performance in the 1980s was relatively weaker. The reason is that the poverty elasticity of economic growth in India fell over this period—poverty elasticity indicates the extent to which poverty can be reduced with a 1% point increase in the GDP growth rate.

The definition of absolute poor is based on subsistence, the minimum standard that is needed to live. Robert McNamara defined it as "a condition of life beneath any reasonable standard of human dignity." There has been a long-standing debate in development economics regarding whether income or consumption poverty lines should be defined in absolute or relative terms. Most international organizations define the poverty line in an absolute way as the "level of income necessary for people to buy the goods necessary to their survival." In keeping with this concept, the dollar-a-day line, at 1985 purchasing power parity, is being used extensively among academics and policymakers.

Disagreements between India and Pakistan on SAFTA-related issues persisted even in 2006. In November 2006, India claimed that Pakistan was deviating from the SAFTA Agreement and was refusing to implement it in letter and spirit. The Indian Minister of External Affairs suggested that it would be difficult to operationalize SAFTA unless Pakistan implemented it earnestly. While Pakistan had expanded the basket of tradable goods under the positive list by 78 items, obstructions to trade continued.

Trade for Economic Development: China, India, and the Challenge of Specialization

The rise of China and India in the global economy has had important effects on Latin America and has been the subject of passionate public debate. Both these Asian giants have outperformed Latin America since the mid-1990s in terms of growth, exports, FDI attraction and innovation, giving rise to considerable pre-apprehension in the region. While there are many examples of business co-operation between Latin America and the Asian giants, and trade agreements are being signed between their governments, public opinion has at times seen Asia's increased presence as a threat to national industries. A closer look at the real impact in Latin America of the world's rapidly growing trade with China and India nevertheless offers a much more encouraging assessment.

Trade Competition Between Latin America and the Asian Giants

The United States, the European Union and Japan are where most third-market competition takes place between Latin America and the Asian giants. That competition is fiercest in the United States, which alone received 57 per cent of Latin American exports in 2006. China and India have been increasing their market shares in the United States — and, in the case of China, have already overtaken Mexico's share, for example.

Closer inspection shows, however, that only a few countries in Latin America face much trade competition with China and India, and that the latter do not constitute a significant threat to Latin America as a whole. The available data suggest that the export structures of most Latin American countries are very different from Chinese and Indian export structures, implying that they have little to fear from China's and India's export dynamism. Other emerging economies such as Thailand, Hungary and Malaysia are facing substantially tougher competition from Chinese exports. Mexico and Central America are the exceptions to this general pattern in Latin America of non-competition with China. Latin America's competition with India is similarly low, with El Salvador, Brazil and Argentina apparently facing the most exposure to competition, and emerging economies in other regions — notably Pakistan, Romania, Turkey and Bulgaria — facing much tougher competition with India. Not surprisingly, Latin American countries that export mainly commodities face the least trade competition with China and India, as the latter are net importers of these products. Paraguay, Venezuela, Bolivia and Chile thus suffer the least from Chinese and Indian trade competition.

Advantages of Outsourcing to India

There are numerous benefits to outsourcing operations and tasks to companies and suppliers based in India, especially as it could help to boost growth and reduce overall costs. Outsourcing can be used in a variety of ways by companies within a whole range of industries and sectors. It can be one of the most productive ways of lowering operating costs, reducing IT bills and, most importantly, meeting customers' needs. In recent years, the growth of outsourcing to India has increased rapidly as many leading companies take advantage of improvements in global communication technology by relocating back-office tasks such as payroll and data entry as well as purchasing and billing. It is estimated that up to two-thirds of Fortune 500 firms currently outsource some part of their operations overseas and that outsourcing levels are expected to increase rapidly as companies strive to improve performance and increase efficiency levels, especially as the global competitive marketplace continues to develop. In many cases, firms have quickly realized that outsourcing can lead to the development of successful competitive strategies.

Changes in IT provision mean that on shoring is no longer the only option for many firms, especially as it can prove costly to rely on local labour forces. Instead, opting to outsource work to India can lead to substantial reductions as it can often remove the need for expensive software development programmes and can help to considerably reduce labour costs – which are often one of the most expensive overheads for a small but successful business. Increasingly start-up businesses are opting to outsource areas of their operations from day one due to the potential savings and reduction in development costs as well as enabling capital to be used more productively.

Opting to outsource routine operations overseas can also enable firms to focus on core competencies and enables better development of products and services – instead of having to oversee and supervise mundane tasks, executives are able to concentrate on expansion, customers' needs and long-term growth plans. Establishing fixed costs for many outsourced business practices also means that companies are better placed to anticipate future costs and set realistic budgets, which is essential in ensuring a profitable business. Outsourcing to India can also play a key role in improving international economics by providing more employment opportunities as well as encouraging wage increases, funding local infrastructure improvement programmes and boosting living standards in the region.

Export Bonanza in Commodities

Equally significant is the fact that rapid growth in China and India is opening important export opportunities for Latin American countries. Thus, while Mexico's export structure suggests it is the most vulnerable amongst Latin America's large countries to Asian competition in third markets, especially in manufactures, Mexico is also one of the Latin American countries, together with Colombia and Venezuela that stands to gain the most from increased commodities exports to China and India. Indeed, of the 19 biggest Latin American and Caribbean exporters, 11 are specialized in commodities, and both China and India are prime importers of these products. Their heightened demand for oil and minerals has already substantially increased Latin America's export earnings, which have benefited both directly, from the increased volume of the region's commodities exports to China and India, and indirectly, from the increase in world prices for the region's commodities exports to Asia and elsewhere induced by strong Asian demand. Few countries in Latin America, in contrast to Southeast Asian developing countries, for example, appear likely to benefit from potential intra-industry trade growth with China and India, however. Mexico and Brazil may be partial exceptions in this regard, as they may have some potential to benefit from intra-industry trade in manufactures with the Asian giants.

Future Perspective

Latin America benefits today from stable macroeconomic environments and pragmatic policy making. Democracy is widespread, and is gaining strength from improving fiscal policies. Pension reform is promoting financial development, if not raising savings. Foreign direct investment is strong, and the region has become an important home, as well as host, to multinational corporations. Rapid development of telecommunications, to which foreign investors are major contributors, should help raise the productivity and living standards of many people. And trade with Asia, contrary to widespread fears, constitutes more of a bonanza than a competitive threat for the region as a whole. Indeed, the preservation of macroeconomic stability in the context of such a bonanza is itself an important achievement. The challenges Latin America faces today are no less impressive. Continuing high levels of poverty and inequality top the list. Together with policies to sustain growth, they call for less regressive and more efficient social and public expenditures that help build fiscal and development strength.

Implication of Globalization for Agro-based Industries in Asia-Pacific Region

The main implications of globalization may be divided into several broad categories: the increased movement of goods, capital, information and labour, and the emergence of international production networks. The implications of these trends for agro-industries in the Asian and Pacific region are also examined briefly in this section (http://www.unescap.org/tid/publication/indpub2325_chap1.pdf).

A. Increased movement of goods: trade liberalization

One of the core features of globalization is the liberalization of trade. Trade liberalization lifts protectionist measures and thus allows trade flows to increase. The most immediate consequence of increased trade flows may be related to an increase in competition. Even though trade liberalization can benefit economies in terms of raising GDP in the long run, producers may feel the consequential competition as a burden in the short run. It should be recognized that competition fuels a drive for efficiency and rationalization of production along the lines of competitive advantage. Therefore, there is a general consensus that the issue is not one of whether to open up and integrate with the global economy in a market-consistent manner, but when and how to do so.

In the Asian and Pacific region, virtually all countries have opened up or are in the process of opening up, their markets to trade, and pursue trade liberalization policies. An important example is China's accession to WTO in November 2001.

Protection of the agricultural sector is pursued by both developing and developed countries alike; in fact, it became one of the most difficult and controversial issues in the WTO negotiations and agreements in Cancún, Mexico. Nevertheless, most countries in the Asian and Pacific region are committed to liberalizing their markets; policies regarding trade are undergoing a process of liberalization and import tariff rates are gradually being lowered.

Globalization offers opportunities for agro-industries in several ways. Currently, the more developed countries in the region specializing in higher technologies import semi-industrial products and foodstuffs, which provide an opportunity for developing countries to produce and export goods and services to them.

Enterprises with economies of scale benefit from the expansion of resource markets, as they can engage in cross-border supply and production chains known as international production networks; they can set up extensive networks to provide input in a most economically efficient manner. Small enterprises in developing countries benefit from expanding output markets because they can act as suppliers in the aforementioned networks make technological advances and gain other benefits.

Expanding markets also augment the possibilities to diversify the agro-industrial sector. Producers need to not only consider the demand of the local market but also reduce risk by diversifying production based on the same resources that can be sold on local, national and international markets.

B. Increased capital flows

The rapid economic development of countries in Asia and the Pacific over the past decades has attracted huge amounts of foreign investment to the region. As information and communication technology (ICT) has enabled finance capital to become a tradable "goods", it is not surprising that WTO maximized efforts to apply the "national treatment rule" to the banking sector, as would be done for any other tradable goods.

The Asian financial crisis of 1997 discouraged foreign investment for a while, but the region has managed to build new confidence. As for the current recession, some countries have been able to avoid a downward economic spiral through high private domestic spending. However, the total volume of foreign direct investment (FDI) has declined and in general banks have been implementing a more conservative lending practice ever since the financial crisis. About half the global investment flows are directed towards Asia and the Pacific in spite of the declining trend of FDI at the global level.

Regarding the flows of FDI in the Asian and Pacific region, two interesting observations can be made. First, agro-based industries have attracted less FDI than sectors of higher risk and profitability; only a small proportion of total inflows are directed to the agro-based industries in the Asian and Pacific region. High value-added manufacturing and services sectors have attracted larger amounts of FDI. This illustrates one of the single most important considerations for investors: profitability. Second, most FDI in the Asian and Pacific region is directed towards the more advanced developing economies such as newly industrialized economies, South-East Asian economies and China and India, while the less developed countries of the region have had more difficulty in attracting FDI. This is related to the relatively difficult, expensive or time-consuming procedures and regulations in those countries.

Developing countries in the Asian and Pacific region have introduced various measures for the promotion of FDI. Some of these measures are the provision of infrastructure facilities (including land), the easing of bureaucratic procedures, permission to repatriate profits on investments and the provision of one-stop services. Other incentives that countries offer are financial packages such as tax holidays for a fixed period of time, discriminatory corporate tax concessions, preferential duty on imports of machines and equipment and foreign exchange facilities. A recent World Bank study (2003) put several recommendations forward to attract FDI; they include strengthening the legal regulatory system (to reduce statutory requirements, to limit smuggling and other criminal activities, etc.), improving government procedures in terms of transparency and inter-government-office cooperation and promoting information technology and the education of their workforce.

In the Asian and Pacific region, agro-based industries in rural areas have attracted less attention from institutional investors and venture capitalists owing to their relatively low productivity and the opportunities they offer for relatively lucrative investment in other sectors such as high technology. In many societies in the region, rural communities finance agro-industries of relatively smaller size through community savings groups or the private investments made by the local population (in many cases remittances from family members working in urban areas). The prospects for investment in Asia's rural-based agro-industries look good in view of the importance of SME promotion and development perceived by policy makers as well as the increased access to

SME financing schemes, such as micro-credit and other rural banking and financing mechanisms.

C. Increased flow of knowledge and information

The rapid advancements made in ICT are among the developments that fuelled global integration. ICT innovations and applications such as e-mail, satellite connections, fibre-optic cables, data compression and the commercialization of their use significantly boosted the efficiency of traditional industries as well as those of the financial and services sectors. Moreover, they have opened up a whole new area of services and products for further development.

Accelerated flows of information enable enterprises to respond faster to market opportunities. As access to information is accelerated, decisions can be made based on more information thus reducing the risk involved with these decisions. Owing to its ability to reduce risk, information has become a tradable good in itself and a thriving, lucrative service industry has evolved around it. For the agro-industry sector, ICT has encouraged the establishment of databases with useful information regarding technologies, R&D, markets, among others. Information is more efficiently stored and managed while its accessibility is enhanced by simultaneous developments in communications technology. The latter has further facilitated the establishment of networks around the globe, among them the developers of new technologies in agro-industries.

However, another technological development has had a great impact specifically on agro-industries. In the current age of knowledge-based economies, it is understandable that many societies with large agricultural sectors, as well as developed countries focusing on high technology, are pursuing advances in biotechnology. This high-end agro-industry is a rapidly growing field in the Asian and Pacific region, as many Governments regard the development of biotechnology as the key strategic area in their policies on agriculture, science and technology.

Biotechnology can be defined as the application of science and engineering to the direct or indirect use of living organisms, or parts or products of living organisms, in their natural or modified forms. Although biotechnology has drawn a great deal of attention because of cloning and the ethical complexities it involves, it also concerns many applications such as the genetic modification of crops to increase disease resistance or to increase the yield per plant. Biotechnology also offers solutions for the diagnosis and control of disease in crops and livestock, the utilization of crop residues and animal waste, and so on.

These applications of biotechnology can make an immense difference in the productivity and competitiveness of agro-industries in the region. The competition gap that this new technology may create could have a serious effect on agro-industries. National legislation and international agreements concerning biotechnology are only at the preliminary stages of development.

However, under the WTO agreement on trade-related aspects of intellectual property rights (TRIPS), the intellectual property rights of biotechnological inventions can be governed to some extent.

D. Increased movement of labour

The integration of production processes has also resulted in increased mobility of labour, especially in the light of the technology transfer required for specific production processes. However, in the agro-industrial sector the movement of human resources is not so much international as it is from rural to urban areas of a country.

The increased exposure of people to different countries and cultures has resulted in new eating habits besides the traditional ones. This requires a diversified input of agricultural raw materials. Examples are the import of grain into the Asian and Pacific region to meet the demand for bakery items, and the import by European countries of Asian spices to satisfy new tastes. The increased mobility of labour has had a very positive impact: as travelers acquire a taste for foreign foods, the opportunity for market creation and expansion is great for agro-based industries in particular.

E. International production networks

In most cases, within international production networks, a mutually beneficial deal is struck. An environment of trust is required as transnational corporations (TNCs) provide technical and market information and labour support, while the suppliers, in turn, invest in equipment and specialization according to TNCs' demands. From either side, such investments would not be worthwhile if the cooperation was not for a considerable duration. Hence, many countries regard their entry into international production networks as a great value in the development of their national economies.

Some are concerned about the disruption of the global supply chain. The size of TNCs gives them a dominant position in trade; even more serious is the situation in international production networks where TNCs simply internalize the supply chain as part of their global operations. Hence, consideration should be given to how the current trend of emerging international production networks could benefit SMEs and their entrepreneurs. In this regard many Governments have tried to facilitate ways to develop linkages between these networks and local SMEs. Producers in the agricultural sector usually represent the supply enterprises in such networks; however, the further they move up the value chain, the more diverse the input for their products becomes. Hence, they may end up with the demand-side of the relationship.

4

Global Competitiveness: Advantage India

The World Competitiveness: Definitions

World Competitiveness provides a frame of reference to assess how nations manage their economic future. It does not only measure Economic Performance, Wealth or Power, as mentioned in "World Competitiveness Yearbook" it is the result of a long history of thoughts and of a vast array of research. In this context, the World Competitiveness Yearbook (WCY) is based on the following academic definition of competitiveness, which has inspired the researchers on world competitiveness. Two types of definitions are currently used in the WCY (Stéphane Garelli, 2008):

I. A Condensed Definition

The "wholeness" described above is an important characteristic of competitiveness. Competence is the other. Nations and enterprises are in the "business" of managing a set of competencies and skills to reach prosperity for one and profit for the other. The combination of both concepts leads to the following condensed definition of competitiveness: *Competitiveness analyses how nations and enterprises manage the totality of their competencies to achieve prosperity or profit.*

This shorter definition has some limitations: for example, it doesn't take into consideration the fact that a nation—or an enterprise—is also dependent on purely physical attributes, such as location or the availability of natural resources, and on the legacy (positive or negative) it inherits from past policies. It would be more correct to say that it a competitive person, enterprise or nation strives it can outperform others. A high level of competitiveness in all areas is highly unlikely. This concept has led to the theory of specialization in international trade developed by David Ricardo. Its most recent illustration is the strategy of outsourcing or off-shoring undertaken by many global companies. Specialization therefore plays an important role in competitiveness. The World

Competitiveness Yearbook encompasses these two approaches: the rankings provide the benchmarking aspect to competitiveness while the country competitiveness profiles indicate how nations individually perform and specialize.

Finally, there is indeed in competitiveness a notion of "stretching" competencies. A company that succeeds will have aimed to achieve far more than it has done in the past. A nation that succeeds in competitiveness will have fully exploited all its resources and competencies. Hence, to sum-up competitiveness is about getting the best from the individual, the organization or the nation.

II. An Academic Definition

The "one-liner" definition mentioned earlier can be supplemented by a more academic definition, which has the merit to encompass all the aspects of competitiveness, especially when it deals with nations. '*Competitiveness of Nations is a field of Economic theory, which analyses the facts and policies that shape the ability of a nation to create and maintain an environment that sustains more value creation for its enterprises and more prosperity for its people*'. Fundamentally, what differentiates competitiveness of nations and competitiveness of enterprises is where the creation of economic value takes place in the society. However, a nation does not directly generate economic added value.

This academic definition is better understood by breaking it down into its individual elements:

"Competitiveness of Nations is a field of Economic theory" such as the theory of comparative and competitive advantage.

Competitiveness is thus one of the most powerful concepts in modern economic thinking. One of its key contributions to classical economic theories is that competitiveness encompasses the economic consequences of non-economic issues, such as education, sciences, and political stability or value systems. It is precisely because it is a multifaceted concept that it has led to a proliferation of definitions. This diversity should however be welcomed in order to refine such an important concept, which has the ambition to provide a dynamic and systemic approach to the creation of wealth for nations and the long-term prosperity of people. The IMD World Competitiveness Yearbook (WCY) looks at the relationship between a country's national environment (where the State plays a key role) and the wealth creation process (assumed by enterprises and individuals). The WCY focuses on the outcome of the interaction of four competitiveness factors, which generally define a country's national environment. These are:

- Economic Performance
- Government Efficiency
- Business Efficiency
- Infrastructure

On the basis of these four factors and more than 300 criteria, the WCY assumes that healthy performance in these dimensions creates a national environment that sustains World Competitiveness.

Historical Backdrop of Global Competitiveness

The concept of competitiveness is the result of a long history of thoughts, which has helped to define the various aspects of this more modern and complex concept. Among those who have made a decisive contribution are as follows (Stéphane Garelli, 2008):

1. The classical economists who have identified the four input factors: land, capital, natural resources and labor. (Adam Smith (1723 – 1790), *"An Inquiry into the Nature and Causes of the Wealth of Nations"*, 1776).
2. David Ricardo with his Law of Comparative Advantage, which already underlines how countries should compete (see David Ricardo (1772 – 1823), *"Principles of Political Economy and Taxation"*, 1817).
3. The Marxist economists, who have highlighted the impact of the sociopolitical environment on economic development—hence the communist idea that changing the political context should precede economic performance (Karl Marx (1818 – 1883), *"Capital: A Critique of Political Economy"*, 1867).
4. Max Weber, the German sociologist, who established the relationship between values, religious beliefs and the economic performance of nations. (see Max Weber (1864 – 1920), *"Ethic of Protestantism and the Spirit of Capitalism"*, 1905).
5. Joseph Schumpeter, who emphasized the role of the entrepreneur as a factor of competitiveness, underlining that progress is the result of disequilibria, which favor innovation and technological improvement. (Joseph Schumpeter (1883 – 1950), *"Capitalism, Socialism and Democracy"*, 1942).
6. Alfred P. Sloan and Peter Drucker, who have further developed the concept of management as a key input factor for competitiveness. (Alfred P. Sloan (1875 – 1965), *"My Years at General Motors", 1963; Peter Drucker, "The Age of Discontinuity"*, 1969).
7. Robert Solow, who has studied the factors underlying economic growth in the US between 1948 and 1982 to highlight the importance of education, technological innovation and increased know-how (Robert Solow, 1957), *"Technical Change and the Aggregate Production Function"*.
8. Nicholas Negroponte and numerous modern economists who are further refining the concept of "Knowledge" as the most recent input factor in competitiveness. (Nicholas Negroponte, *"Being Digital"*, 1995).
9. Finally, Michael Porter who has tried to aggregate all these ideas into a systemic model, called the Competitiveness Diamond. (Michael Porter, - *"The Competitive Advantage of Nations"*, 1990).

Ten Golden Rules of achieving Global Competitiveness as suggested by Garelli (2008) are as follows:

(i) Creditable and Predictable Legislative environment.
(ii) Work on a flexible and resilient economic structure.
(iii) Invest in traditional and technological infrastructure.
(iv) Promote private savings and domestic investment.
(v) Develop aggressiveness on the international markets as well as attractiveness for Foreign Direct Investment.
(vi) Focus on quality, speed and transparency in government and administration.
(vii) Maintain a relationship between wage levels, productivity and taxation.
(viii) Preserve the social fabric by reducing wage disparity and strengthening the middle class.
(ix) Invest heavily in education, especially at the secondary level, and in the life-long training of the labor force.
(x) Balance the economies of proximity and globality to ensure substantial wealth creation, while preserving the value systems that citizens desire.

Global Economic Trends and India : A Perspective Analysis

The latest reports of depression in the global economy are quite significant for India. Looking to the past trends, the global economy is an important determinant of India's economic growth prospects. J.P. Morgan's highly respected report on World Financial Markets stated at the beginning of 21st century that the world economy as a whole has been suffering from low growth (Venkitaramanan, 2001).

The latest global numbers published in the 'Hindu Lines' on August 6, 2001 showed a modest inflation outlook, reflecting below-trend global economic growth. Higher energy prices are fading as a source of industrial country inflation. There are also dramatic cuts in the prices of hi-tech equipment. Sustained low inflation will cause the continuance of lower interest rates and sustained easing of monetary policy. The report is, however, optimistic about a gradual return of trend growth in the US economy well in advance of other key economies. The dollar will continue to be strong.

The overall impact of the rising slowdown of global economy has been widespread and intense. Virtually all economies in the world are operating below their potential. There will be two effects of this slowdown. One has been referred to as lower inflation and the other is higher unemployment. Already, commodity prices are falling markedly during the past few months, and further declines are expected. The global economic environment is becoming highly disinflationary and, in Japan, deflationary. This should encourage consumption and ultimately aid recovery. The decline in growth of the global economy has been caused by a combination of global and country-specific factors. One universal cause has been the persistent rise in the energy prices during 1999-

2000. Another key factor to the reduction in growth has been the sharp and sudden downturn in hi-tech investment in the second half of 2000. This weakened growth, notably in the US and Europe, while brutally reducing the export performance of many Asian countries. This pervasive setback has contributed to the weakness of manufacturing sector in virtually every industrial country and driven many Asian economies, including Singapore, into recession.

Particular mention must be made of the rise and fall of demand for hi-tech equipment. In the US, the output of hi-tech equipment accelerated at an annual growth rate to 70 per cent in early 2000, before collapsing. The crisis worsened because not only was demand falling but the unit price equipment in the hi-tech sector also collapsed. US investment spending was sharply reduced, particularly on hi-tech equipment. The unexpected decline in the demand for hi-tech investment goods undermined stock prices, reversing the earlier surge in the value of new economy stocks.

One other factor responsible for straining the earlier growth and subsequent slowdown in the US has been the tightening of monetary policy. While the tightened monetary policy did help control inflation, it also contributed to subsequent economic slowdown. Similar was the experience in other countries, where major central banks contributed to the cycle, by first tightening their monetary policy and then relaxing it. The opinion of most observers is that the recent problems of the emerging economies, such as Brazil, Argentina and Turkey, will not have a contagion effect and will not spread to other economies, unlike the experience of 1997-98 East Asian crises.

It is worth noting that while global growth has slipped below 2 per cent in 2001, the Indian economy has been well above the global rate. The Indian economy has continued to grow at a rate ranging 5-6 per cent with a credible inflation record and with no perceptible strain on the Balance of Payments.

The J.P. Morgan report is significant for certain comparisons it offers between India and China. Chinese GDP grew 7.5 per cent, against India's 5.3 per cent. The consumer inflation of China in 2001 was 1.6 per cent, against India's 5 per cent. One important contributing factor to this is the low fiscal deficit in China at 2.7 per cent of GDP as against nearly 7 per cent in India. The trade balance was in surplus of $ 27.7 billion in China as against a negative figure of $ 9.1 billion for India.

The account balance during the reported period was significantly more robust in the Chinese case, standing at a surplus of $ 15.4 billion against a negative figure of $ 1.6 billion for India. The international reserves of China stood at $ 178.9 billion, against our $ 43.8 billion. The total external debt of China, as a percentage of exports, stood at 50 per cent, against 139 per cent in the case of India. India's major benchmark in global development has to be China.

The report stressed that Japan's weak economy may end-up with a weak yen. Both US and Japanese policy-makers made it clear at that time that they are prepared to accept a weak yen if that is the result of market reactions.

The devaluation of the yen would not be without impact on other currencies. It is quite possible that China may react with the devaluation of Yuan, which may well force the various Asia-specific countries to follow suit. This ought to have a serious repercussion on the world economy.

The India-specific forecast of J.P. Morgan has been that, given a modest growth outlook and benign inflation, public spending is likely to be stepped up to provide impetus to a sagging economy. Consequently, it was predicted that the fiscal deficit may well exceed the targeted 6.5 per cent of GDP. The report also had a forecast of a further bank rate cut of 50 basic points. Its forecast of the exchange rate is Rs. 50 for dollar by 2002 first half.

The decline in the world's major economies has its repercussions, unpleasant ones, on India's economy, in particular on its export prospects. The Government had to take a note of this trend and be ready to handle the adverse consequences of a continuing global economic slowdown. It could not have been 'business as usual'.

Indian Economy Overview

The Indian Economy is consistently posting robust growth numbers in all sectors leading to impressive growth in Indian GDP—especially in the 1st decade of the 21st century. The Indian economy has been stable and reliable in recent times, while in the last few years it has experienced a positive upward growth trend—barring, of course, occasional aberrations, primarily due to sharp rise in crude oil prices, geopolitical reasons etc.

A consistent 8-9% growth rate has been supported by a number of favorable economic indicators including a huge inflow of foreign funds, growing reserves in the foreign exchange sector, both an IT and real estate boom, and a flourishing capital market.

All of these positive changes have resulted in establishing the Indian economy as one of 'Recent Growth Trends in Indian Economy' (http://www.economywatch.com/indianeconomy/indian-economy-overview.html)

Growth in the manufacturing sector has also complemented the country's excellent growth momentum. The growth rate of the manufacturing sector rose steadily from 8.98% in 2005, to 12% in 2006. The storage and communication sector also registered a significant growth rate of 16.64% in the same year.

Additional factors that have contributed to this robust environment are sustained investment and high savings rates. As far as the percentage of gross capital formation in GDP is concerned, there has been a significant rise from 22.8% in the fiscal year 2001, to 35.9% in the fiscal year 2006. Further, the gross rate of savings is a proportion to GDP. The Indian Economic Survey for 2007-08 has set the target growth rate of GDP to be 9% for the period from 2007-2012 (http://exim.indiamart.com/economic-survey).

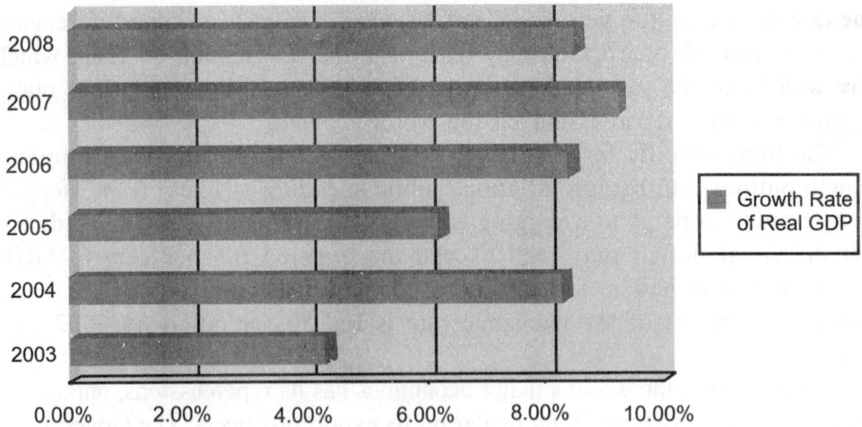

The Economic Survey of India is published by Central Statistical Organization which consists of general economic health of the country. It focuses on various micro and macro economic sectors with complete statistical data and analysis. Each year such survey is conducted to show the status of economic scenario of the country.

Highlights of Indian Economic Survey 2007-2008

These are some of the highlights of Economic Survey (2007-08) of India:

- Economy retards to 8.7% in the year 2007-08
- Agricultural growth at 2.6 pc in 2007-08 from 3.8 pc in 2006-07
- It appears difficult to sustain 9% rate of economic growth
- Inflation recorded to be 4.4 pc in 2007-08
- Retardation this year was expected
- Government plans an aim of 9 pc GDP growth during 11th Five Year Plan (2007-2012)
- Investment climate "full of optimism"
- It has been observed that labor force is rising at a greater pace than the employment growth
- 3 manufacturing sector to rise at 9.4 pc in present financial year which is less from 12 pc in 2006-07
- Unemployment rate rises by 1 pc in five years to 2005
- Subsidies might see an increment by Rs. 6,550 cr over Budget Estimate
- Fuel and power constitute the main subscriber to inflation
- The Budget figured for subsidies was Rs. 51,247 cr
- Inflation primarily decided by chief non-food items
- Losses over off-Budget subsidies
- Inflation was found to be less than 5.6 pc last year

Focus of Competitive Strategies in India

Meaning of Productivity

Broadly speaking, "Productivity means the ability of a nation, company or any business unit to harness its physical and human resources to generate the desired output". Simply put in a non-technical way, productivity refers to working "smarter" and not necessarily "harder". The productivity of human resources determines employee wages. The productivity of capital determines the return it earns for its holders" (Patel, 2006).

Meaning of Globalization

Globalization is a process of interaction and integration among the people, companies, and governments of different nations, a process driven by international trade and investment and aided by information technology. This process has effects on the environment, on culture, on political systems, on economic development and prosperity, and on human physical well-being in societies around the world.

Productivity for Global Competitiveness

In his book 'Competitive Advantage of Nations', Michael Porter observed, "The only meaningful concept of competitiveness at the national level is Productivity. Productivity is the prime determinant of a nation's long-run standard of living; it is the root cause of national per capita income.

Consequent on the on-going process of economic reforms and liberalization as well as coming into force of the WTO regime, which is compelling India to dismantle the lingering protective environment which have so far sheltered Indian economy in general and industry in particular, the twin concept of productivity and competitiveness have become more relevant than ever before. One can even go to the extent of saying that these are perhaps intractably linked to the country's economic future and survival as a viable entity in this era of globalized economy. For a developing country like India, Productivity in its new manifestation, as a culture of accepting and bringing about continuous change through teamwork having continued focus on the customer-need is an inescapable imperative. These concepts have come to acquire greater significance in the current context of changed economic environment. However, the increasing market-orientation and private sector development have thrown up a number of new challenges. In fact, it is influencing the mindset of all the constituents of the society. Productivity is the key to competitiveness, which in turn is an indicator of a country's potential for economic growth in the short to medium term.

The findings of the Global Competitiveness Report of the World Economic Forum reveal that India's competitiveness is relatively quite low, which is not surprising, given the continuing low productivity levels of different economic sectors in India.

It also indicates that although productivity levels have been growing in India for at least a decade and a half, the level of growth is lower than that required to keep pace with rest of the world. Hon. PM of India, Dr. Manmohan Singh, in a recent address to the industrialists, stressed the need to boost productivity and global competitiveness of the Indian industry. He lamented that 'India still had a long way to go in catching up with the newly industrialized economies of Asia. We have to move fast, move quickly and move efficiently to catch up with our neighbours in East Asia'.

The Reasons for Low Productivity

Firstly, I believe that the work culture that is prevalent in the country is one important factor contributing to low productivity. I do recognize that this complacency must change. We are finding that the global environment will not accept anything but the best in terms of speed of service, accuracy in delivery and consistency in approach. Anything less will mean that we lose our market position as well as our reputation. Our work culture will need a major revolution in order to match the high standards demanded by the global community.

Another factor is the lack of skills in our workforce. You will agree with me that productivity growth depends on the birth of new ideas, that is, innovation and invention, and the ability to turn such ideas into usable technology. Both, in turn, depend on maintaining an educated and skilled work force. We have the numbers in terms of a good pool of labour force but we lack the skills.

The steady outflow of skilled emigrants from managerial, professional, technical and clerical occupations is also taking its toll on our skill base.

Another problem that we face is the lack of up-to-date and appropriate technology. As is typical of developing countries, investment into research and development is very low. Hence, our ability to turn innovative ideas and new inventions into useable technology is weak. In fact, growing disparities in growth patterns amongst industrialized nations have been related to the ability of those nations to adopt new and highly productive equipment. Those that have been able to rapidly adopt new technology and make best use of its potential have reaped productivity gains whereas the others have lagged behind.

Consequences of Low Productivity

On a macro level, we will not achieve our economic vision of Growth in GDP. This means that many of our children and grandchildren will not get jobs.

- Unemployment will be higher. Incomes will be lower.
- Poverty will rise.
- Social problems will escalate.

- Ultimately, the people will bear the incidence of poor productivity. Consumers will pay the welfare loss as they purchase their basket of goods and services at higher prices and perhaps low quality.
- The owners of capital and labour will also bear the loss. The efficiency of capital is reduced.
- Firms become inefficient and are unable to raise the return on their current level of resources.
- As the cost of doing business for firms increases they are either forced to shut down or retrench workers.
- The first option will mean loss of capital and lower investment. The second option means firms reduce their labour force, which leads to unemployment and income foregone.
- The impact of the economic loss from lack of productivity will not be borne evenly. It will impact more on the low income earners and the poorer.
- Low income earners are the first to lose their jobs in a crisis. They are also the group that cannot protect the value of their assets as price increases.
- There is also inflationary impact of reduced productivity. Poor worker productivity will obviously cause workers to prefer inflation-indexed wage increments instead of productivity based wage increments.

Competitiveness of Enterprises

With globalization, enterprises are now faced with new competitiveness requirements. These are brought about by:

- The globalization of competition: With the spreading trade liberalization and deregulation, there is now closer integration of domestic and international markets. Thus, enterprises must not only face increased competition in their export markets but even in the domestic markets must cope with the competition from imported products that can now easily enter the country. The increasing significance of electronic commerce is also contributing to the rapid integration of markets.
- Better informed and more discerning customers: The advance in international communication, increased access to knowledge and information, and the increased integration of markets have led to internationalization of consumer's demands and preferences. This is resulting in very discriminating customers who are demanding more product differentiation and specialization. The fads and fashion not only spread rapidly across the globe but also shift and change very quickly. The rapid advance in information and production technology makes product obsolescence very fast. The product variety is thus increasing but the product life cycle is decreasing.
- Increasing number of competitors: With countries moving towards trade liberalization and adopting export oriented development—from import

substitution strategies—many of their enterprises are entering international and the liberalized national markets.

- Rapid advance in both soft and hard technology: This enables more enterprises to adopt production and organizational systems that improves the capacity to produce products and services at lower costs, improved quality and increased speed of delivery.
- Advances in new scientific fields: The fast developments in fields such as electronics, biotechnology, materials science, are resulting in the increased flow of new products and services that substitute for or totally replace existing ones. This further accelerates product obsolescence mentioned earlier.

An enterprise's competitive advantage is developed through improvements in the way it organizes and performs its sourcing, production and distribution activities (Porter, 1990). It acquires strong competitive position by creating and offering products and services of better or superior value to its customers. This it can achieve through better management and performance of what is called the value-chain of the enterprise: the sourcing and organizing of inbound inputs, the production operations which transform these inputs into products and services needed by the target markets, the organization and management of outbound distribution, marketing and sales, and the provision of after-sales services to ensure that customers enjoy the full value of its products and services.

Customer Orientation

The improvement of the enterprise's value chain starts from determining what the customer wants. Thus, with the more discerning and demanding customers of varied and rapidly changing requirements, enterprises have realized the importance of increasing their customer orientation.

They must always be able to meet the needs, desires and expectations of their customers. This may call for rapid product development, frequent changes in product models and types, a broader range of products, and even production according to specifications of a particular buyer. With the rapid change of technology, of the fast spread of communication and information, the needs and requirements of customers, whether it be industrial or end-consumers, is very dynamic and volatile. An enterprise must have the flexibility and competence to cater to this very dynamic market.

Flexibility and Agility

An enterprise develops and acquires the flexibility and competencies needed through strategies that involve: (a) the development and strengthening of internal core competencies and capabilities, simplifying structures, improving lateral interactions and coordination and improving internal communication; (b) the outsourcing of standard and specialized competencies through practices such as outright purchasing of standard parts and subcontracting of specialized parts and services, including the use of business service suppliers, temporary workers, home-work and geographical relocation of particular jobs and activities; and (c) the acquisition and quasi-internalization of complementary competencies and capabilities through various forms of cooperative relations with other enterprises such as partnership, networking and alliances (Palpacuer, 1997).

Human Resource Management

Enterprise competitiveness is based more and more on the quality of the human resource of the enterprise. Good human resource management (HRM) thus becomes an important cornerstone of an enterprises competitiveness strategy. Being an integral part of the strategic management of the enterprise, the various HRM policies, functions and practices should contribute to the creation and sustenance of the enterprise's competitive advantage. Thus, the development of the culture of productivity and creativity, the building-up of mutual trust and shared values, initiative and self-management, and multi-skilling and skills upgrading and continuous learning must always be priority goals of the various HRM functions of human resource planning, staffing, and allocation; human resource utilization; human resource development; and motivating and commitment-building.

Trust and shared values appear as central mechanism for work coordination and control in a flexible enterprise. When work is complex and constantly changing, direct control based on supervision becomes too expensive and unwieldy, and bureaucratic control based on work standardization and rigid systems and procedures and rules and regulations is not workable and can be counter-productive. Organizations must rely more on self-management. This form of internalized control is built on mutual trust and confidence, shared values, and common understanding and acceptance of the organization's or corporate objectives, philosophies, priorities and norms. In this sense, the importance of information sharing becomes very important. Committed, motivated and capable employees at all levels are essential to gaining sustained competitive advantage.

Developing Distinctive Competence and Proprietary Technologies

In an era of rapid technological development, enterprises gain competitive advantage through offering unique product and services, development of distinctive competence and proprietary technologies. A strategy towards productivity and competitiveness therefore is promoting organizational capacity and adaptability to exploit the full potential of new technology to improve efficiency, develop new products and services and unleash the creativity and innovation of the workforce. Efforts need not be just in research and development to develop cutting-edge technologies, but it must also be in the adaptation of already existing hard and soft technology to build-up distinctive technical competence and develop superior products and services. Introducing technology alone however, is not sufficient. More than ever before, people are the most important resource in the new knowledge-based economy. The benefits of new technology can only be fully realized if it is introduced together with new forms of work organization and continuous training.

For enterprises in the cutting-edge technology development, the importance of keeping ahead in proprietary technology is clearly demonstrated in the electronics industry. New terms of competition, called "Wintelism" is emerging based on experiences in the electronic sector. In what is called the Wintelist (code word derived from combination of Windows and Intel) era, competition is based on setting and evolving de facto product standards in the market. In the computer industry for example, manufacturers, whose systems are nearly identical, emphasize in their sales pitch use of components or software that have become market standards - "Intel Inside", or "Microsoft Windows Installed" - rather than unique features of their own brand. In the Wintelist era, firms located anywhere in the value chain can, potentially, control the evolution of key standards and in that way define the terms of competition not just in their particular segment in the value chain but in the final product market as well. For the Wintelist firms, ownership and manipulations of the de facto standards they have set are considerably more effective barriers to entry than the barriers of scale and vertical control over technology and production because they are harder to duplicate (Borrus and Zysman, 1997).

Better Supply-chain Management

The product or service that an enterprise sells to a customer is the result of a series of activities that involves bringing together the inputs required, manufacturing these inputs into the enterprise's products, transporting these products to wholesalers and distributors, bringing them to the customer through retailing and other outlets, and providing after sales services as required. The supply chain is made-up of segments: the up-stream segments made-up of suppliers of raw materials, components, services, consumables, etc., the internal supply-chain made-up of the various departments and units involved in the production of the products or services, and the down-stream segment made-up of distributors, wholesalers, retailers and providers of after-sale service. Improved value to customers can be achieved through the improvement in the various segments of the chain, as well as in completely redesigning the supply chain. An enterprise can significantly improve its internal productivity by focusing on those things it can do well and subcontracting or outsourcing the other activities to other firms who could do them better. In the situation where an enterprise relies on network of suppliers and service provider, the effectiveness and efficiency of the enterprise is very much affected and is very much dependent on the way it manages the supply chain. Improving collective productivity of an enterprise's supply chain requires (Pouter, 1997):

- Carefully analyzing the enterprise's business, its business and operations strategy, how it can deliver the best value to its customer, and then deciding what to out-source and what products or parts produce and/ or activities to undertake internally within the enterprise;
- Careful selection of suppliers and down-stream distribution and sales channels;
- Establishing close collaboration and cooperation with suppliers and service providers to ensure that they meet the volume, quality and time requirements;
- Assisting in building the competencies of the various parties in the supply chain; and
- Ensuring that wastes in time, materials, money and other resources are minimized throughout the enterprise's supply chain.

Networking and Alliances

One way for enterprises to improve their flexibility, acquire new technical and managerial competencies, increase leverage of their internal resources, and achieve speed in bringing product to market from market research, product development to distribution and retailing is through entering into networks and alliances with other enterprises. Through cooperation and collaboration with other enterprises—even with those in the same business and competitors—an enterprise could access new market opportunities and sources of needed inputs; concentrate and perform only those activities and functions that it can do most productively and quickly; have better access to new technology and innovation; learn and access new managerial practices and organizational systems; increase speed of the product cycle; and improve overall productivity. The networking relationships between and among firms can be formal or informal. It can be vertical relationships such as those formed by firms engaged in complementary activities and those that form supply chain relationships, and horizontal relationship involving firms engaged in similar or competing activities. Strategic alliances can be entered into, agreeing with other firms to combine efforts to pursue a competitive advantage that neither of the parties to the alliance could accomplish nor achieve alone. The partners in the alliance contribute complementary products, market presence, distribution networks, production facilities, skills and technologies, etc. Strategic alliance is usually limited in space (e.g. for activities in a specific country), in time (i.e. for a specific period only), and purpose (e.g. they may be on technology but not on markets, or vice versa).

To obtain maximum benefits and minimize the risks and hidden costs of networking and alliances, the enterprises entering into the relationship must undertake careful analysis. They must address a number of critical questions such as what the enterprise's core competencies are, its strength and weaknesses and what peripheral capabilities must it seek from the external environment; how the network will be governed, share influence and responsibilities; and where the competitive advantage will be created through networking.

Sustaining the Enterprise's Competitive Advantage

The sustainability of the competitive advantage of an enterprise is dependent on the nature of the major source of its present advantage over the competitors. There is a hierarchy or level of sources of competitive advantage in terms of sustainability. Lower-order sources of advantage such as low labour costs or cheap raw materials are relatively easy to imitate or acquire by competitors. Higher order advantages such as proprietary processes and technology, product differentiation based on unique product or services, brand reputation based on cumulative marketing efforts, and customer relationships protected by high costs to the customer of switching vendors, are more durable. These higher-order advantages are created through sustained and cumulative investment in physical facilities, human resource development, research and development, and/or marketing activities. Competitive advantage is therefore sustained through constant improvement and upgrading. In order to sustain its competitive advantage, an enterprise must become a moving target, creating new advantages at least as fast as competitors can replicate old ones. To remain competitive, an enterprise must constantly destroy old advantages to create new, higher-order ones (Porter, 1990).

Competitiveness of Nations

The concept "the international competitiveness of a country" is a relative term. What is of interest is not absolute performance, however that may be defined, but how well a country does relative to others. Furthermore, the concept usually has a double meaning, it relates both to the economic well-being of its citizens, normally measured through GDP per capita, and the trade performance of the country (Jan Fagerberg, Martin Srholec and Mark Knell, 2005).

Nations do not compete as enterprises do. Rather, nations compete in creating the conditions that attract and encourage investors—foreign and domestic alike—to invest in productive and competitive enterprises within their borders (and even for local enterprise to invest abroad, if that will enhance international presence and market proximity and responsiveness). A country competes through creating the policy framework that encourage and enable its enterprise to constantly upgrade them and keep on improving their productivity, and by putting in place programmes and incentive packages that help and enable its enterprises to develop competitive advantages and pursue competitive strategies for successful participation in international markets.

Reports that rank countries according to competitiveness are getting widespread attention by policy makers and economic actors in both developing and developed countries. The World Competitiveness Yearbook of the

International Institute of Management Development based in Lausanne, Switzerland (IMD, 1998) uses eight major groups of factors/principles to rank a nation's ability to encourage and sustain the competitiveness of its enterprises. Similarly, the Global Competitiveness Report published annually by the World Economic Forum also makes use of eight clusters of structural characteristics of national economies in constructing the competitiveness index used in ranking the competitiveness of the countries covered. The Report looks at international competitiveness as the ability of a nation's economy to make rapid and sustained gains in living standard (Sachs, J., Stone, G. and Warne, A., 1996). The competitiveness index thus aims to gauge the ability of a national economy to achieve sustained high rates of economic growth. It attempts to measure growth potential on a horizon of five to ten years, offering an assessment of economic conditions for medium-term growth. A detailed scrutiny of the clusters of factors—and the sub-factors within them—used by the two competitiveness reports show that, over-all, the two cover the same general issues that are deemed to influence "national competitiveness" (O'Neill, 1997). These factors are: (a) internationalization or openness of the economy, (b) domestic economy and government involvement and policies including legal and regulatory environment and institutions of civil society, (c) financial institutions including their size and transparency (physical infrastructure, environment and energy), (d) management skills, (e) science and technology capability and facilities, and (f) people including skills and access to education, unemployment levels, working hours, welfare and social services, equality of opportunity, quality of life, and attitudes to work.

Systemic Competitiveness

The most competitive countries therefore have what Esser *et al.* (1996) call systemic competitiveness. Industrial competitiveness is the result of the complex and dynamic interaction among factors at four social and economic levels in a national economy: at the meta, macro, meso and micro levels.

At the meta level are the socio-economic, cultural and political factors that are essential to competitiveness such as:

- development-oriented cultural values which include social recognition of economic success, priority for long-term investment in knowledge and skills acquisition, a positive work ethics and pride in work and performance, and propensity to save;
- a basic consensus on the necessity of industrial development and competitive integration into the world market; and
- the ability of the social actors to jointly formulate visions and strategies and to implement agreed upon strategies and policies; this implies mechanisms and institutions for entrepreneurs, employers, workers and other concerned members of the society to develop shared visions on areas such as which position should be targeted in the international division of labour, which comparative advantage should be developed in

the long run, and how profits and costs of market integration should be distributed among social groups, etc.

At the macro level, the key ingredient for competitiveness is a stable and predictable macroeconomic framework. Such a framework should lead to the creation of well functioning markets that are essential for the effective and efficient allocation of resources. This policy framework includes a realistic exchange-rate policy, a general foreign trade policy that stimulate local industries, competition policy, and a fiscal and budgetary policy geared for growth and stability. The macro framework should encourage or require the country's enterprises to be effective and efficient.

At the meso level, the key factors for competitiveness are specific policies and institutions that help industries to suit to their environment and create competitive advantage. There are two sets of meso level factors:

- Meso-level institutions, both private and governmental, which offer services and support to enterprises and help build the development of human capital and technological infrastructure; and
- Selective and targeted policies aimed to shape and strengthen competitiveness of certain sectors (industrial structure, trade patterns, technology development and acquisition, human resource development, supportive infrastructures, etc.).

An important element at the meso level is the legal and regulatory framework affecting the establishment and operations of enterprises. A legal and regulatory framework that imposes undue and excessive administrative and financial burden on enterprises affect adversely their capacity to compete. Another important element is effective channels and media of communication that facilitate the flow of information and exchange of ideas among key stakeholders and actors, relevant social groups, organizations and institutions.

At the micro level, factors that determine enterprise's competitiveness (in terms of costs, quality, product specificity, speed and responsiveness) are: entrepreneurial and managerial competencies; quality of the human resource; organization of production, including process and organizational innovations; organization of product development; organization of the value-chain; and cooperation networks and alliances, among others.

Strategies for Enhancing Productivity and Competitiveness

The following are seemingly some of the strategies suggested by Essar *et al.* (1996) that can enhance the productivity and attendant competitiveness for an organization:

1. An organization has to develop the ability to harness the creative energies of their own available workforce.

2. The need of the times is to focus on creating and encouraging human capital. It is this pool of creative minds that will help in throwing up innovative ideas.
3. Education and training are emerging as key drivers of competitiveness. As the global economy has become more complex, it has become evident that to compete and maintain a presence in global markets it is essential to boost the human capital endowments of the labour force, whose members must have access to new knowledge, be constantly trained in new processes and in the operation of the latest technologies.
4. Most macroeconomic research studies conclude that Information and Communications Technology (ICT) is a significant contributor to productivity growth and most relevant in knowledge and information – intensive service enterprises for attaining global competence.
5. The value of Knowledge Management relates directly to the effectiveness with which the managed knowledge enables the members of the organization to deal with today's situations and effectively envision and create their future.
6. However, heavy investments in ICT and automation alone may not increase productivity unless a total, integrated approach is taken. This requires complementary investments in organizational restructuring, workplace and work process redesign, and a mindset change among employees, who need to be computer literate.
7. Increasing productivity has to emerge as a new national priority, where the efforts of all converge to accelerate the process of economic growth and raise the standards of living of our people.
8. Our business organizations will have to improve their performance to ensure their survival and growth in a fiercely competitive world. This improvement will come about only if we focus on production of quality goods, in a cost effective manner and by generating enough surpluses to plough back into the business to further improve productivity. And this must occur continuously, to create an advantage in the market place, which is what productivity is all about. Productivity, thus, will have to become a mass movement and to be put on the national agenda.
9. Every organization has its own distinctive approach towards development. Connecting these initiatives, there should be a commitment to enlarge the scope of innovation and to create environment conducive to Productivity. Productivity may be the outcome of techno-managerial practices, but eventually is the result of a mindset. Basic to this approach is the conviction that there is no limit to improvement. Even the best can be improved. The crucial ingredient is the preparedness of the human mind to change. Therefore, workers, managers, policy makers and others should be ready to continuously and collectively work for productivity improvement, not only in every economic activity, but also in every human endeavor for the development of the society as well as the

country. Needless to mention, as we graduate further into knowledge era, traditional methods and principles will become increasingly ineffective and we will have to innovatively augment productivity both at micro as well as macro level to realize a global competitive edge. "Productivity for Global Competitiveness" has therefore been chosen as the theme for the "Productivity Week-2007" (12th – 18th February).

10. Among the most important institutions are the National Productivity Councils and National Productivity Organizations. By performing their various roles as productivity promoters, catalyst and mobilizer, capability builder, etc. they in fact influence and strengthen the productivity and competitiveness factors at the various levels.
11. Through spearheading programmes such as national productivity awareness and education campaigns they help develop the national values and attitudes that appreciate good work and quality performance and are supportive of learning, innovation and change.
12. Through mobilization of a tripartite and multi-sectoral national productivity drive, they create the mechanisms and institutions for national concerted efforts towards productivity improvement.
13. By initiating and assisting in the review and formulation of macro and micro economic policies, they help create the conducive and enabling policy environment.
14. By networking and helping other institutions, they help build a strong supportive institutional infrastructure.
15. And through their training, consulting and information services those help enterprises acquire the managerial and workers' capabilities to effect and implement the "high road" to productivity and competitiveness improvement.
16. Through their pioneering of new productivity improvement approaches and capability building in industry, they help improve the production processes and build the human competencies essential to continuing productivity and competitiveness improvement.
17. Through the promotion of participatory approaches to productivity improvement, they help improve the quality of jobs.
18. The specific roles and functions of a national productivity organization will vary from country to country and will depend on its assigned mandate, needs of its clients, stages in the countries' economic development, cultural and social environment, and the quality of its leadership.
19. However, despite the diversity across countries, it is possible and useful to identify the most common roles. These are:
    (a) Those dealing with attitudinal change and developing awareness among people involved in productivity improvement;
    (b) Improving the performance capability of enterprises through upgrading management competence, corporate organization and management systems, improving HRM and HRD and enhancing performance of the enterprise as a whole;

(c) Promoting productivity initiative among organizations through networking between research and educational institutions and enterprises, developing better cooperation between trade unions and employers, and promoting productivity improvement programmes to enterprises; and

(d) Helping create the policy and regulatory environment for productivity improvement through assessing economic and business policies and regulations and their impact on productivity and competitiveness, providing advisory services on upgrading various productivity factors such as energy supply, transportation, technology and removing systemic barriers hindering productivity improvement.

Report on Indian Economy: 2006-07

Overall Economy

The statistical updates released by the Central Statistical Organization (CSO, 2007) showed that Indian economy grew by 9.4% during 2006-07. In absolute terms, the GDP of the country at constant prices stood at Rs. 2848157 crores for 2006-07 showing an annual rise of 9.4% over the previous year. The revised annual rise in GDP was slightly higher than the 9.2% (for 2006-07) estimated in February 2007. In 2006-07, GDP growth was mainly fueled by industry and services that grew at 10.9% and 11.0% respectively contributed 26.6% and 54.9% to the total GDP growth. However, during the year 2006-07 agriculture and allied services failed to maintain the growth momentum of 2005-06.

Industrial Growth

Indian industry achieved an impressive growth in the last fiscal 2006-07. The overall industrial production grew at 11.3% in 2006-07 as against the growth of 8.2% in the previous fiscal. The growth was more manufacturing sector led, which grew by 12.3% in 2006-07 as compared to 9.1% a year ago. Mining and electricity sectors too pushed the overall industrial growth posting a high growth of 5.1% and 7.2% in 2006-07 respectively as against the 1.0% and 5.3% growth respectively in 2005-06. Data as per the use-based classification shows that basic and capital goods – a proxy for investment demand have clocked growths of 10.2% and 17.7% respectively in 2006-07 in contrast to 6.7% and 15.8% registered during the previous fiscal. However, the consumer durables saw a slight slowdown in 2006-07 on account of lower growths in both the consumer durables and non-durables. During the last fiscal production of consumer goods grew at 10% as against the 12% growth in the previous fiscal. In 2006-07, among the 16 industry sectors, 12 industry sectors swept past the growths recorded in the previous fiscal. Production growth slid for 2 industry sectors and remained low for the remaining sectors. The sectors that improved their performance were basic metals, transport equipment, cotton textiles, machinery and equipment, wood, non-metallic mineral products, rubber, metal products and parts, manmade textiles, basic chemicals, paper and food products.

Six Core Infrastructure Industries

During the year 2006-07 the six core infrastructure industries grew at a high of 8.6% as compared to the 6.2% increase a year before. This growth arrived on account of better production numbers across the six core industries. The four infrastructure industries, crude petroleum, petroleum refinery, power and coal posted growths of 5.6%, 12.6%, 7.3% and 5.9% respectively exceeding the growths recorded in the previous fiscal, maintaining the overall infrastructure growth. However growth in the production of finished steel and cement slowed during the fiscal 2006-07. Production of finished steel was observed to speed-up in the last two months of 2006-07 compared to the corresponding months of 2005-06.

Telecommunication

Telephone connections in the country crossed the 200 million mark and an addition of about 67 million phones was made during the year 2006-07. Today the total telephone connections in the country stand at 206.8 million, of which 139.8 million come from mobile phones and the remaining 40.7 million connections from the landline connections. March 2007 saw mobile phones making lowest ever addition during the year; additions of just 3.53 million phone connections due to insistence by the Government to ensure verification of subscribers. Tele density went up by 43% touching 18.31 in March 2007 against the density recorded in March 2006.

Stock-Market Trends

The mood of the market is such that negative news triggers the adverse index movements while the positives leave markets unchanged. It was observed that the attempt of the central bank's monetary tightening measures, hike in the CRR and the lending rates to curb inflation rose concerns among the investor community. The fall in both the indices BSE and NSE seen in the middle of March through April 2007 was in response to the growing concern over the expensive funds. The BSE index plunged by 4.7 percentage points during March end 2007 over the previous month's close and NSE too slipped by 4.9 percentage points. However the stock markets have shown resilience in May 2007 and the host of corrective measures by the Central Bank resulted into bringing inflation to desired levels.

Inflation Trends

The overall WPI based inflation for 2006-07 averaged at 5.4% as against the 4.4% in the 2005-06. The upper limit of the targeted inflation for 2006-07 was breached in the last quarter of 2006-07, primarily on account of rising prices of primary articles and manufactured items. However, inflation was found to average below the set range of 5-5.5% for 2006-07.

For the current fiscal (2007-08) RBI has kept the target inflation rate around 4.5%. The recent counter-inflation steps taken by the government helped in cooling the inflation rate that was soaring above 6%. The measures applied by the RBI have checked the prices of some items falling under the broad categories - primary articles and manufactured products, further helping in bringing down the inflation rate. The RBI employed monetary tightening measures to absorb the excess liquidity in the market impacting the prices of the manufactured items. The government has regulated exports of some identified commodities addressing the supply crunch in various primary articles. Monsoon would also help in easing the pressures on the supply side of some primary articles.

Monetary Indicators

The broad money growth for the last fiscal 2006-07 stood at 20.7% and was slightly lower than the growth of M3 during the same period a year ago. Bank credit to the government rose substantially during the year-end 2007 compared to the same period of last year. We observed slowdown in the bank credit to the commercial sector. However, the net foreign exchange assets of the banks spiked by 28.9%, as against 11.1% in the same period a year ago. Scale up in investments on government securities by 10% was also seen during the year. Impact of the hike in the rates of long-term deposits was reflected in the numbers on aggregate deposits that went up by 23% in 2006-07 compared to 18% in the corresponding period of the previous year. Credit off take decelerated during the year compared to last year.

Fiscal Management

Gross tax revenue collections grew at a rate much higher in 2006-07 than the previous year. Data up to March 2007 shows gross collections increased at 29.3% as against the 20% increase in the previous year. Corporation tax and income tax both contributed 45% to the total tax collected and grew at 41% and 35.4% respectively and this was much higher than the increase in the tax collected a year ago. Among the indirect tax collections from customs maintained the steady rise, growing at 32.7%, although collections from the central excise was not as much as in the same period of previous year. In 2006-07, the Government was seen to achieve the targeted fiscal deficit. It touched a level of Rs. 146348 crore representing 100.10% of the targeted. Comparing the numbers of 2006-07 with that of the previous year's, we see numbers of 2006-07 close to the targeted figure.

Foreign Trade

Indian trade numbers available for the year 2006-07 showed Indian exports growing at 20.9% as against the high growth of 24% in 2005-06 in US dollar terms. Quarterly trends in trade show Indian exports strongly growing in the first two quarters of 2006-07; however exports took a hit from the middle of quarter three. Indian merchandise exports was able to achieve the targeted, US $ 125 billion for 2006-07. Indian exports were reeling under pressure since the third quarter of 2006-07 due to rising prices of raw materials and later due to appreciating Indian Rupee hitting the Indian business community in quick succession. However we saw that Indian imports soared at 26.4% during the year, further widening the trade deficit. The strong Indian Rupee against the greenback came as a breather for the importer, reducing the import bill, whereas the appreciating Rupee took exporters in its grip.

Capital Flows

Capital inflows for the period April-February 2006-07 have swept past the inflows received during the entire 2005-06. Direct investment contributed US $ 17.1 billion during April-February period of 2006-07; this was much higher than US $ 7.7 billion received in the entire 2005-06. Portfolio investments however remained lower in 2006-07 than the investments in the previous year. During the year 2006-07, the amount raised by the Indian corporate through GDR and ADR route has been much higher (US $ 3.7 billion) than that was raised in the previous year (US $ 2.5 billion).

Foreign Exchange Reserves

Foreign exchange reserves crossed the US $ 200 billion mark in the first week of April 2007. Forex reserves stood at US $ 180 billion in December, 2006 and since then a surge in the Forex was observed. The main constituent of the Forex, Foreign Currency Assets touched US $ 195.8 billion in the second week of April 2007. Gold, SDRs and reserve position in IMF however did not show much movement. The increase in the foreign currency assets was largely due to the effect of appreciation in the non–US currencies held in reserves (Euro, Yen and Sterling). The piling up of reserves is a strain for the central bank, as it is seen that interest on securities exceeds the rate of return on reserves and therefore some steps need to be taken to ease the pressure due to forex buildup.

Trends in Exchange Rate

Appreciation in Indian Rupee against the greenback started in March 2007. This rise in Rupee value was on account of an inflow in the foreign capital, in the form of FDI, ECB and Portfolio investments. To maintain the exchange rate within a range the central bank has been buying dollars from the market but due to inflationary pressures, RBI slightly distanced itself from the forex market. RBI's adoption of passive approach has made Rupee appreciate to levels that are pro imports.

Indian Rupee began to appreciate since the middle of March 2007, it continued to slide below Rs. 44.00 and slip to an alarming below-forty one level towards the end of April 2007. It has been found that Indian Rupee against the Euro too behaved similar to its movement vis-à-vis US $, Indian Rupee attained a level of Rs. 55-54 in June 2007 from Rs. 58-57 in March 2007, appreciating by 6.5%. Indian Rupee against the Euro averaged at Rs. 55.11 in May 2007 up from an average of Rs. 57.00 in the previous month.

Outlook for 2007-08

- Available information indicates continuation of the growth momentum during 2007-08 at a strong pace with the impulses of growth getting more broad-based. Steady increases in the rate of gross domestic saving and investment, consumption demand, addition of new capacity as well as more intensive and efficient utilisation/capitalisation of existing capacity are expected to provide support to growth during 2007-08. For monetary policy purposes, the Reserve Bank, in its Annual Policy Statement (April 2007), placed the real GDP growth for 2007-08 at around 8.5 per cent, assuming no further escalation in international crude prices and barring domestic or external shocks. The Reserve Bank in its First Quarter Review of the Annual Statement of Monetary Policy in July 2007 retained its projection of real GDP growth at around 8.5 per cent, barring domestic and external shocks.
- In view of the lagged and cumulative effects of monetary policy on aggregate demand and assuming that supply management would be conducive, capital flows would be managed actively and in the absence of shocks emanating in the domestic or global economy, the Reserve Bank in its Annual Policy Statement noted that the policy endeavour would be to contain inflation close to 5.0 per cent in 2007-08. Assuming that aggregate supply management will continue to receive public policy attention and that a more active management of the capital account will be demonstrated, the outlook for inflation in 2007-08 in the First Quarter Review remained unchanged. Accordingly, it was indicated in the Review that holding headline inflation within 5.0 per cent in 2007-08 assumed priority in the policy hierarchy; while reinforcing the medium-term objective to condition policy and perceptions to reduce inflation to 4.0-4.5 per cent on a sustained basis (RBI Annual Report: 2007-08).

India's 'Look-East' Policy

Indian Prime Minister Atal Bihari Vajpayee's Southeast Asian tour to participate in the Association of Southeast Asia Nations (ASEAN) summit in Bali, Indonesia in October, 2003 marked the success of a decade-long shift in Indian foreign policy - known as the "Look East" strategy - initiated by former Prime Minister Narasimha Rao in the early 1990's (http://ipcs.org/IPCS-IssueBrief-No54.pdf). The political consensus that had then emerged, partly as a response to the end of Cold War, to liberalize the economy and participate in the new trend of globalization, is apparently continuing to win India new business partners and friends in its continuing war against militancy in the Indian state of Jammu and Kashmir.

Two broad agreements, for comprehensive economic cooperation and combating terrorism, have been signed. India has also consented to the ASEAN Treaty of Amity and Cooperation. Vajpayee went a step further to offer a unilateral "open skies" policy to specified Southeast Asian airlines, which will be free to operate daily flights to the Indian metropolitan centers, outside any bilateral aviation pact. Laying stress on better connectivity between India and ASEAN, Vajpayee said, "We could see how close we can get with an open skies arrangement." In this context he announced India's unilateral decision to connect all 10 ASEAN capitals with four metropolises in India through daily flights without further bilateral discussions (Sulatan Shahin, 2008). Apart from laying emphasis on the need for road links between the geographically contiguous India and ASEAN countries, Vajpayee also suggested the holding of an India-ASEAN motor rally. The framework agreement spells out a program for free trade agreements in goods, services, investment, areas of economic cooperation and an early harvest program. Negotiations on free trade agreements in goods will take due account of the economic sensitivities of the less developed economies of Cambodia, Laos, Myanmar, Vietnam and the Philippines.

And on Thursday, India and Thailand signed five agreements covering a wide range of issues, including a landmark free trade agreement following a one-to-one meeting between Vajpayee and Thai premier Thaksin Shinawatra in Bangkok. The agreement will allow for free trade on all goods by 2010. The two countries will also slash tariffs by 50 per cent on 84 products under an early harvest scheme to go into effect March 1 of next year. In addition, ways to combat terrorism and intelligence sharing were also discussed, with India offering to sell defence equipment to Thailand.

Taken together, these steps promise considerable improvement in economic and political cooperation between India and its Southeast Asian neighbors - extending from Myanmar to the Philippines. India is glad to have been present, thanks to its ASEAN associate membership, when the members agreed to create the eastern equivalent of the European Union in two decades. The Bali Concord II envisions a single Southeast Asian market, covering 500 million people and with annual trade that already touches US $ 720 billion. The concord calls for the creation of an ASEAN Economic Community modeled on the EU by 2020. If ASEAN evolves a free trade arrangement with China on similar terms - the abolition of all tariffs and trade barriers - the result will be the world's largest free trade zone (http://ipcs.org/IPCS-IssueBrief-No54.pdf).

India has already been able to take a small step towards taking advantage of this historic development. The early harvest program New Delhi has signed with ASEAN lays out a timetable for mutual trade concessions up to 2007. Skeptical Indian observers are hoping that it will lead to an across-the-board lowering of trade barriers, despite India's traditional reluctance in giving such concessions, and that the story of so-called free trade agreements with Sri Lanka and Singapore will not be repeated. In the case of Sri Lanka, India placed curbs on tea, textiles and rubber - the very items Sri Lanka could sell in the Indian market. As for Singapore, more than two years after agreeing to work out a free trade treaty, it has just been announced that the city-state will only now "study" the issue.

The slow pace of economic reforms and lack of better integration of its foreign and trade policies has made many analysts skeptical whether India will be able to effectively sustain its "Look East" policy, despite all the hype associated with the prime minister's annual trips to the region. Former External Affairs minister Yashwant Sinha has, however, maintained that India had embarked on the second phase of its "Look East" strategy. In a speech at Harvard University last month, Sinha pointed to a remarkable transformation in India's attitude towards Asia: "In the past, India's engagement with much of Asia, including Southeast and East Asia, was built on an idealistic conception of Asian brotherhood, based on shared experiences of colonialism and of cultural ties. The rhythm of the region today is determined, however, as much by trade, investment and production as by history and culture. That is what motivates our decade-old 'Look East' policy. Already, this region accounts for 45 per cent of our external trade."

Vajpayee's address at the ASEAN business summit struck the right chord by focusing on the country's areas of strengths and inviting ASEAN investors to take a fresh look at "India of the 21st Century ... [a] country on the move." He has set an ambitious target for India-ASEAN trade: it is to grow from $ 12.5 billion now to $ 30 billion in 2007. Addressing the meet on Tuesday, Vajpayee, seeking to partner ASEAN in the era of globalization, listed six strong points of the Indian economy, including a rich pool of English-speaking people, as well as the information technology revolution for enhancing India-ASEAN trade and investment.

The Prime Minister said, "India is conscious of the new ASEAN members. We are offering unilateral tariff concessions on items of export interest to Cambodia, Laos, Myanmar and Vietnam [lesser developed and newer entrants to ASEAN]. We are also seeking to incorporate an early harvest scheme to provide the incentive for a long-term engagement. If we proceed along this course, we can target a trade turnover of US $ 30 billion by 2007 and a free trade area within 10 years." Observing that India's trade and economic interaction with the ASEAN countries has been growing steadily, but not fast enough, Vajpayee said trade of less than $ 10 billion between the two did not do justice to the combined population of 1.5 billion people, producing $ 1.5 trillion worth of goods and services annually. Recalling his speech at the first India-ASEAN business summit a year ago for boosting business, he said, "Our trade has since grown by about 25 per cent, but my comments remain valid."

The business summit was also addressed by Chinese and Japanese Prime Ministers Wen Jiabao and Junichiro Koizumi and South Korean President Roh Moo-hyun. The powerful ASEAN comprises Indonesia, its current chairman, Singapore, the Philippines, Malaysia, Thailand, Cambodia, Laos, Vietnam and Myanmar and Brunei. Vajpayee said in spite of the recent stalemate at the Cancun World Trade Organization (WTO) Ministerial Conference, a rule-based and fair multilateral trading system should remain the goal. "But while we search for this ideal, regional trading arrangements offer immediate advantages, particularly for geographical contiguous regions. They can provide our domestic industry and agriculture with a valuable learning period, before being exposed to the far greater competition of global free trade," he said.

Observing that non-Asians viewed Asia as the principal market of the future, the Prime Minister said it would emerge as a manufacturing hub and a global provider of services. "Asian countries should work towards strengthening their mutual synergies, so that they are strategically placed to derive maximum benefit from the emerging opportunities. The India-ASEAN partnership should energize this process to move us closer to our shared goal of making this truly the Asian century," Vajpayee said.

Of special significance for India was the agreement to fight terrorism cooperatively. It has been facilitated by the fact that several ASEAN countries are facing the threat of terrorism. The Philippines, Indonesia and even Singapore have felt the impact of international terrorism. The Jemmah Islamiyah outfit is active in Indonesia, the Philippines, Singapore and Malaysia. Indonesia in the past year has witnessed two major terror attacks in Bali and Jakarta. The ASEAN countries have, therefore, become serious about dealing with terrorism and related crimes like money laundering and drug trafficking. They are looking to India for support to meet the challenges on this front. The ASEAN Regional Forum will remain the platform for a security dialogue in the region and it includes the US and the European Union. The declaration adopted at Bali provides for cooperation on information exchange, legal matters, and enforcement matters apart from institution building and training.

India's growing relations with the countries belonging to ASEAN and the BIMSTEC forum comprising Bangladesh, India, Myanmar, Sri Lanka and Thailand is beginning to free it from the straitjacket imposed by the South Asian Association of Regional Cooperation (SAARC). The latter is now largely moribund due to a standoff between India and Pakistan.

Incidentally, India is not alone in its desire to run away from South Asia. While India has been looking east in its desire to get away from its geographical location, Pakistan has been looking west since even before India initiated its "Look East" policy. It has also been seeking to enter into ASEAN. While Indian efforts appear to be meeting with success, however, the same cannot be said about Pakistan. India-Pakistan animosity has created irritations for ASEAN as well. But its spill-over effects in India-ASEAN relations have been contained. Though some of Pakistan's friends in ASEAN have been trying to upgrade its status, perhaps in the name of Muslim solidarity, India and its friends have managed to keep it out. ASEAN is obviously trying to avoid becoming another arena for the two South Asian neighbors obsessed with each other to vent their hostility, make wild accusations and create ever-new controversies.

It seemed that at last India's "Look East" policy has started paying dividends. ASEAN and India appear to have developed a clearer vision of the future of their relationship. They have set realistic targets for development of trade and investment at the Bali summit. Southeast Asian leaders have also identified areas of cooperation and collaboration on global issues, including those related to the future of the United Nations. ASEAN has also been trying to balance its trade and overall ties between its two giant neighbors - China and India (http://www.indianmba.com/Occasional_Papers/OP104/op104.html).

Things have been moving forward for India since 1997, when it began its formal interaction with ASEAN as a full dialogue partner. It is up to New Delhi to maintain the momentum this relationship has been developing. ASEAN will naturally look for concrete follow-up measures on the agreements signed. The negotiations for a free trade agreement will begin in January 2004, on goods, and take up services in 2005 so that the whole framework is in place by 2007. India is committed to lowering its peak tariffs to East Asian levels by 2005. India cannot afford to be niggardly about tariff concessions, if it doesn't want the new ASEAN to automatically gravitate towards China. Meeting goals being set now will be the test of the relationship and its measure of success. Taking stock of the substantive agenda spelt out at the first India-ASEAN summit in Cambodia last November, Vajpayee admitted that there have been doubts about the pace of implementation of certain proposals, but in his view progress has nevertheless been much more rapid than anticipated. As a mark of this forward movement, the India-ASEAN Vision 2020 (http://www.ris.org.in/EAS_Booklet.pdf) would be adopted at the third summit in Laos next year.

DRIVERS OF ECONOMIC GROWTH

The following are considered to be the key drivers of economic growth in so far as India is concerned:

- Quarter century of strong economic growth built a momentum of sustained growth; average 5% per annum.
- Services driven growth, where services account for nearly 60% of GDP today.

- More open economy (to external trade and investment); fall in applied tariffs from over 100% in 1991 to 12% in 2006.
- Budget deficit declined from 7 to 3.7 per cent of GDP from 1991 to 2001.
- Supportive international economic environment fuelled by growth of China and the US. India itself now contributing to global economic growth significantly.
- Demographic dividend of a young population.
- Working population nearly 60% of total.
- Household savings rose from around 15-16% of GDP in late 1980s to 22-24% in recent years.
- A growing "middle class" fuelling domestic consumption.
- 100 million with $ 10 to $ 40.
- 340 million with incomes above poverty levels but less than $ 10.
- Six-fold increase in sales of motor vehicles and a 10-fold increase in telephones since 1991.
- Strong companies in a modernized capital market.
- Market capitalization on the Bombay Stock Exchange rose fourteen-fold from $ 50 billion in 1990/91 to $ 680 billion in 2005/06.
- Share of interest outgo in gross profits dropped sharply from above 50 per cent in the late 1990s to 15 per cent in 2005/06.

Location Strategy for Competitiveness of Special Economic Zones in India – A Generic Framework

Competitiveness has emerged as an important discipline in the area of strategy and research efforts have brought many interesting perspective and frameworks at the country, industry and firm level. Seeing competitiveness from competence point of view, role of factors, internal to the firms such as firm's strategy, structures, competencies and capabilities and other tangible resources lead to competitive success of a firm. This is recognized as Resource Based View towards competitiveness. Location decision of a firm has been subject for empirical researches and literature suggests that location can be a contributing factor to the competitiveness of a firm. The impact of location on the firm performance has been the subject for research and special economic zones, as a specialized location, have provided ease to use business location along with advance infrastructure and other facilities to enhance competitiveness at the country level (Dhingra et al, 2008: http://www.iitk.ac.in/infocell/announce/convention/papers/Context%20and%20Human%20Resource-02-Tarun%20Dhingra,%20Ambalika%20Sinha, %20Tripti%20Singh.pdf).

Special Economic Zones (SEZ) have emerged as a popular strategy adopted by various countries, particularly the developing countries, to increase their trade competitiveness. Zones have gained currency in these dynamic times to experiment with the market economy and to impart outward looking orientation to the economy. The ever-increasing competition has also put firms on a look out to find new methods and strategies to remain competitive and to survive in these turbulent periods of time.

This study proposes a generic theoretical framework which identifies various variables subsequently leading to superior firm performance. Further related intermediate variables are identified to develop hypothesis for assessing the impact of location strategy on the competitiveness of the firm, established in an SEZ. The further scope of the paper lies in empirically testing the proposed framework by using structural equation modeling in a specific industry or a sector.

India as a developing nation has strategically identified economic zones for export promotion and trade development. Ministry of Commerce, Government of India, defines, "Special Economic Zone (SEZ) as specifically delineated duty-free enclave and shall be deemed to be foreign territory for the purpose of trade operations and duties and tariffs". The common goals and the characteristic shown by the export zones have been highlighted by Agarwal (2004), Madani (1999), Kundra (2000), and Kumar (1989). Zones share few common features worldwide: (a) Unlimited, duty-free imports of raw, intermediate inputs and capital goods necessary for the production of exports; (b) Less governmental red-tape, flexibility with labour laws for the firms in the zone than in the domestic market; (c) Generous and long-term tax holidays and concessions to the firms; (d) Above average (compared to the rest of the host country) communications services and infrastructure; and (e) Zone firms can be domestic, international or joint venture. The role of FDI is also prominent in EPZ activities.

Indian government idea to foster SEZ relies on two-pronged strategy:

1. Reduction in restrictions—Duty-free imports, liberalized foreign exchanges, and flexible labour laws etc.
2. Provision of incentives—Better infrastructure and generous long-term income tax concessions (IDFC, 2001)

Although India was one of the first Asian countries to recognize the potential of EPZ model in promoting exports. It established Asia's first EPZ at Kandla, in the state of Gujarat in 1965, but it couldn't produce remarkable success in terms of contribution towards exports because of inward looking orientation and regulatory mindset in its initial years. Out of all the SEZs, established in India, the most successful SEZs are Mumbai, Noida and Chennai which are prominent cities in India. This also suggests the locational advantage of existing industrial and infrastructure base for export competitiveness of SEZ. Right now India has 19 functioning SEZs contributing 5% to the national exports and more than 400 SEZ's have been principally approved by Government of India at various locations (Ministry of Commerce, 2007).

The emergence of SEZ as policy enclave for promotion of exports has highlighted the importance of location and its impact on firm competitiveness.

SEZ, as specialized locations, have provided efficiency in business transaction through advance infrastructure and other facilities to enhance trade competitiveness of the country. The early theories of industrial location concentrated on analyzing simple frameworks, where the location and spatial diversification were simply determined by an adjustment between location and weight distance characteristics of inputs and outputs (Weber, 1929). However global competition has made location decisions of firms an important strategic decision depending on several factors. Various recent empirical research and literature suggests that location can be a contributing factor to the competitiveness of a firm (Karakaya and Canel, 1998). Empirical studies suggest that SEZs, which are located in already developed area, where there are higher chances of pursuing agglomeration, are found to be more successful as compared to those which are located in semi- or undeveloped areas (IDFC, 2001). It seems that agglomeration and linkage effect of the SEZ are more difficult to exploit if SEZs are established in an area with poor or no industrial base. This raises few significant research questions regarding the location of a SEZ, viz.

- Does location imparts competitiveness to the firm in SEZ?
- What instrument the competitiveness of a firm in an SEZ?
- Does location of a firm in an SEZ leads to superior firm performance?

According to India's five-year economic plan up to 2012, the country needs to attract $ 500 billion worth of investments to upgrade its infrastructure to achieve a 9% average annual economic growth rate. Annual growth in the March quarter was 8.8%. Around 30% of the spending is expected to come from the private sector, with the rest split between the federal and state governments. IDFC, which is 20% government-owned and finances projects such as highways, ports and gas pipelines, started the India Infrastructure Fund in March 2007, with Citibank as the co-sponsor and anchor investor of the fund. Owners of infrastructure assets list them as trusts or funds to cash in their initial investments. Infrastructure funds have grown rapidly in markets such as Britain, South Korea and the United States, attracted by the steady, long-term income streams sought by investors to match pension liabilities. Other infrastructure funds listed in Asia include Singapore's CitySpring Infrastructure Trust and Macquarie International Infrastructure Fund, and Australia's Babcock and Brown Infrastructure Ltd. IDFC is also partly owned by sovereign wealth fund the Government of Singapore Investment Corp (GIC) and Malaysian state investment firm Khazanah Nasional, Thomson Reuter's data shows. IDFC also has investment banking and asset management units that deal with infrastructure investments. The firm competes with the likes of US investment banks such as JP Morgan and Goldman Sachs to attract foreign investor money into Indian infrastructure (Lounge, 2008).

Special Economic Zones (SEZs)

Special Economic Zones (SEZs) are growth engines that can boost manufacturing, augment exports and generate employment. The private sector has been actively associated with the development of SEZs. The SEZs require special fiscal and regulatory regime in order to impart a hassle-free operational regime encompassing the state of the art infrastructure and support services. The proposed legislation on SEZs to be enacted in the near future would cover the Concepts of the developer and co-developer, incorporate the provision of virtual SEZs, have fiscal concessions under the Income Tax and Customs Act, provide for Offshore Banking Units (OBUs) etc. A brief on the facilities available under the SEZ scheme is given as under:

Eligibility

7.1 (a) Special Economic Zone (SEZ) is a specifically delineated duty-free enclave and shall be deemed to be foreign territory for the purposes of trade operations and duties and tariffs.

(b) Goods and services going into the SEZ area from DTA shall be treated as exports and goods coming from the SEZ area into DTA shall be treated as if these are being imported.

(c) SEZ units may be set up for manufacture of goods and rendering of services.

Export and Import of Goods

7.2 (a) SEZ units may export goods and services including agro-products, partly processed goods, sub-assemblies and components except prohibited items of exports in ITC (HS). The units may also export by-products, rejects, waste scrap arising out of the production process. Export of Special Chemicals, Organisms, Materials, Equipment and Technologies (SCOMET) shall be subject to fulfillment of the conditions indicated in the ITC (HS) Classification of Export and Import Items.

SEZ units, other than trading/service unit, may also export to Russian Federation in Indian Rupees against repayment of State Credit/ Escrow Rupee Account of the buyer, subject to RBI clearance, if any.

(b) SEZ unit may import/procure from the DTA without payment of duty all types of goods and services, including capital goods, whether new or second hand, required by it for its activities or in connection therewith, provided they are not prohibited items of imports in the ITC (HS). However, any permission required for import under any other law shall be applicable. Goods shall include raw material for making capital goods for use within the unit. The units shall also be permitted to import goods required for the approved activity, including capital goods, free of cost or on loan from clients.

(c) SEZ units may procure goods required by it without payment of duty, from bonded warehouses in the DTA set up under the Policy and/or under Section 65 of the Customs Act and from International Exhibitions held in India.

(d) SEZ units may import/procure from DTA, without payment of duty, all types of goods for creating a central facility for use by units in SEZ. The Central facility for software development can also be accessed by units in the DTA for export of software.

(e) Gem and Jewellery units may also source gold/ silver/platinum through the nominated agencies.

(f) SEZ units may import/procure goods and services from DTA without payment of duty for setting up, operation and maintenance of units in the Zone.

Leasing of Capital Goods 7.3 SEZ unit may, on the basis of a firm contract between the parties, source the capital goods from a domestic/foreign leasing company. In such a case the SEZ unit and the domestic/ foreign leasing company shall jointly file the documents to enable import/procurement of the capital goods without payment of duty.

Net Foreign Exchange Earning (NFE) 7.4 SEZ unit shall be a positive Net Foreign Exchange Earner. Net Foreign Exchange Earning (NFE) shall be calculated cumulatively for a period of five years from the commencement of production according to the formula given in Appendix 14-II of the Handbook (Vol-I)

Monitoring of performance

7.5 (a) The performance of SEZ units shall be monitored by the Unit Approval Committee.

(b) The performance of SEZ units shall be monitored as per the guidelines given in Appendix 14-II of Handbook (Vol-I).

Legal Undertaking

7.6 The unit shall execute a legal undertaking with the Development Commissioner concerned and in the event of failure to achieve positive foreign exchange earning it shall be liable to penalty in terms of the legal undertaking or under any other law for the time being in force.

Approvals and Applications

7.7 (a) Applications for setting up a unit in SEZ other than proposals for setting up of unit in the services sector (except software and IT enabled services, trading or any other service activity as may be delegated by the BOA), shall be approved or rejected by the Units Approval Committee within 15 days as per procedure indicated in Annexure to Appendix 14-II of Handbook (Vol-I). In other cases approval may be granted by the Board of Approval.

(b) Proposals for setting up units in SEZ requiring Industrial Licence may be granted approval by the Development Commissioner after clearance of the proposal by the SEZ Board of Approval and Department of Industrial Policy and Promotion within 45 days on merits.

DTA Sales and Supplies

7.8 (a) SEZ unit may sell goods, including by-products, and services in DTA in accordance with the import policy in force, on payment of applicable duty.

(b) DTA sale by service/trading unit shall be subject to achievement of positive NFE cumulatively. Similarly for units undertaking manufacturing and services/trading activities against a single LOP, DTA sale shall be subject to achievement of NFE cumulatively.

(c) The following supplies effected in DTA by SEZ units will be counted for the purpose of fulfilment of positive NFE:

(i) Supplies effected in DTA in terms of Chapter 8 of the Policy.

(ii) Supplies made to bonded warehouses set up under the Policy and/or under Section 65 of the Customs Act.

(iii) Supplies to other EOU/SEZ/EHTP/STP units provided that such goods are permissible for procurement by units.

(iv) Supplies against special entitlement of duty-free import of goods.

(v) Supplies of goods and services to such organizations which are entitled for duty-free import of such items in terms of general exemption notification issued by the Ministry of Finance

(vi) Supply of services (by services units) relating to exports paid for in free foreign exchange or for such services rendered in Indian Rupees which are otherwise considered as having been paid for in free foreign exchange by RBI.

(vii) Supplies of Information Technology Agreement (ITA-1) items and notified zero duty telecom/ electronic items indicated in the Appendix 14-II of Handbook.

Supplies from DTA to SEZ shall be entitled for the following DTA supplier shall be entitled for:

7.9

(a)

(i) Drawback or DEPB in lieu of Drawback.

(ii) Discharge of Export performance, if any, on the supplier.

(b) SEZ units shall be entitled for:

(i) Exemption from Central Sales Tax.

(ii) Exemption from payment of Central Excise Duty on all goods eligible for procurement by the unit.

(iii) Reimbursement of Central Excise Duty, paid on bulk tea procured from the licenced auction centres by the Development Commissioner of concerned zone as long as levy on bulk tea in this regard is in force.

(iv) Reimbursement of Duty paid on fuels or any other goods procured from DTA as per the rate of drawback notified by the Directorate General of Foreign Trade from the date of such notification.

(c) Supplier of precious and semi-precious stones, synthetic stones and processed pearls from Domestic Tariff Area to the units situated in SEZ shall be eligible for grant of Replenishment Licenses at the rates and for the items mentioned in the Handbook (Vol. I).

(d) The entitlements under paragraphs (a) and (b) (ii) above shall be available provided the goods supplied are manufactured in India.

Export Through Status Holder 7.10 SEZ unit may also export goods manufactured/ software developed by it through a merchant exporter/status holder recognized under this Policy or any other EOU/SEZ/EHTP/STP unit.

Inter-unit Transfer 7.11 (a) SEZ units may transfer manufactured goods, including partly processed/semi-finished goods and services from one SEZ unit to another SEZ/EOU/EHTP/STP unit.

(b) Goods imported/procured by a SEZ unit may be transferred or given on loan to another unit within the same SEZ which shall be duly accounted for, but not counted towards discharge of export performance.

(c) Capital goods imported/procured may be transferred or given on loan to another SEZ/ EOU/EHTP/STP unit with prior permission of the Development Commissioner and Customs authorities concerned.

(d) Transfer of goods in terms of sub-paras (a) and (b) above within the same SEZ shall not require any permission but the units shall maintain proper accounts of the transaction.

Other Entitlements Other entitlements of SEZ units are indicated in the Appendix 14-II of the Handbook (Vol-I).

Sub-Contracting 7.12 (a) SEZ unit may subcontract a part of their production or production process through units in the DTA or through other SEZ/EOU/EHTP/STP, with the annual permission of Customs authorities. Subcontracting of part of production process may also be permitted abroad with the approval of the Development Commissioner.

(b) Sub-contracting by SEZ gems and jewellery units through other SEZ units or EOUs or units in DTA shall be subject to following conditions

(i) Goods, finished or semi-finished, including studded jewellery, taken outside the zone for sub-contracting shall be brought back to the unit within 30 days. No cut and polished diamonds, precious and semi-precious stones (except precious and semi-precious stone having zero duty) shall be allowed to be taken outside the zone for sub-contracting.

(ii) Receive plain gold/silver/platinum jewellery from DTA in exchange of equivalent quantity of gold/silver/platinum, as the case may be, contained in the said jewellery.

(iii) SEZ units shall be eligible for wastage as applicable for sub-contracting and against exchange

(iv) The DTA unit undertaking job work or supplying jewellery against exchange of gold/silver/platinum shall not be entitled to export benefits.

(c) All units, including gem and jewellery, may sub-contract part of the production or production process through other units in the same SEZ without permission of Customs authorities subject to records being maintained by both the supplying and receiving units.

(d) SEZ units other than gems and jewellery units may be allowed to undertake job-work for export, on behalf of DTA exporter, provided the finished goods are exported directly from SEZ units. For such exports, the DTA units will be entitled for refund of duty paid on the inputs by way of Brand Rate of duty drawback.

(e) Scrap/waste/remnants generated through job work may either be cleared from the job worker's premises on payment of applicable duty or returned to the unit.

(f) SEZ units engaged in production/processing of agriculture/horticulture products, may on the basis of annual permission from the Customs authorities take out inputs and equipments to the DTA farm subject to the procedure indicated in Appendix 14-II of the Handbook (Vol-I)

Exit from SEZ Scheme

7.13 (a) SEZ unit may opt out of the scheme with the approval of the Development Commissioner. Such exit from the scheme shall be subject to payment of applicable Customs and Excise duties on the imported and indigenous capital goods, raw materials etc. and finished goods in stock. In case the unit has not achieved positive NFE, the exit shall be subject to penalty that may be imposed by the adjudicating authority under Foreign Trade (Development and Regulation) Act 1992.

(b) SEZ unit may also be permitted by the Development Commissioner, as one time option, to exit from SEZ scheme on payment of duty on capital goods under the prevailing EPCG Scheme, subject to the unit satisfying the eligibility criteria of that Scheme and standard conditions for exit indicated in Appendix 14-II of Handbook (Vol-I).

Export through Exhibitions/Export PromotionTours/Export through show rooms abroad/Duty Free Shops

7.14 (a) SEZ, units may :

(i) Export goods for holding/participating in exhibitions abroad with the permission of Development Commissioner.

(ii) Personal carriage of gold/silver/platinum jewellery, precious, semi-precious stones, beads and articles.

(iii) Export of jewellery is also permitted for display/sale in the permitted shops set up abroad.

(iv) Display/sell in the permitted shops set up abroad or in the showrooms of their distributors/agents.

(v) Set up showrooms/retail outlets at the International Airports.

Personal Carriage of Export/Import parcel.

<u>7.15</u> (a) Import/export through personal carriage of gem and jewellery items may be undertaken as per the procedure prescribed by Customs. Import/export through personal carriage for units, other than gem and jewellery unit, shall be allowed provided the goods are not in commercial quantity.

Export/Import by post/courier

<u>7.16</u> (a) Goods, including free samples, may be exported/imported by airfreight or through Foreign Post Office or through courier, subject to the procedure prescribed by Customs.

Disposal of Rejects/Scrap/ Waste/Remnants

<u>7.17</u> (a) Rejects/scrap/waste/remnants arising out of production process or in connection therewith may be sold in the DTA on payment of applicable duty. No duty shall be payable in case scrap/waste/remnants/rejects are destroyed within the Zone after intimation to the Custom authorities or destroyed outside the SEZ with the permission of Custom authorities. Destruction as stated above shall not apply to gold, silver, platinum, diamond, precious and semi-precious stones.

Replacement/Repair of Goods

<u>7.18</u> (a) The general provisions of Policy relating to export of replacement/repaired goods shall apply equally to SEZ units, save that, cases not covered by these provisions shall be considered on merits by the Development Commissioner.

(b) The goods sold in the DTA and found to be defective may be brought back for repair/ replacement under intimation to Development Commissioner.

(c) Goods, or parts thereof, including gem stones and precious metal components for jewellery making, on being imported/indigenously procured and found defective or otherwise unfit for use or which have been damaged or become defective after import/procurement may be returned and replacement obtained or destroyed. In the event of replacement, the goods may be brought back from the foreign suppliers or their authorized agents in India or the indigenous suppliers. Destruction shall however not apply to gem stones and precious metals.

(d) Goods may be transferred to DTA/abroad for repair/replacement, testing or calibration, quality testing and R & D purpose under intimation to Customs authorities and subject to maintenance of records.

Management of SEZ

7.19 (a) SEZ will be under the administrative control of the Development Commissioner.

(b) All activities of SEZ units within the Zone, unless otherwise specified, including export and re-import of goods shall be through self certification procedure.

Setting up of SEZ in Private/ Joint/State Sector

7.20 (a) A SEZ may be set up in the public, private, joint sector or by state Government as per details indicated in Appendix 14-II of the Handbook (Vol-I).

Samples

7.21 (a) SEZ units may, on the basis of records maintained by them, and on prior intimation to Customs authorities:

(i) supply or sell samples in the DTA for display/ market promotion on payment of applicable duties;

(ii) remove samples without payment of duty, on furnishing a suitable undertaking to Customs authorities for bringing the goods back within a stipulated period;

(iii) export free samples, without any limit, including samples made in wax moulds, silver mould and rubber moulds through all permissible mode of export including through couriers agencies/post.

Sale of Un-utilized Material/Obsolete goods

7.22 (a) In case an SEZ unit is unable, for valid reasons, to utilize the goods, including capital goods and spares, it may dispose them in the DTA in accordance with the import policy in force and on payment of applicable duties or export them.

(b) Capital goods and spares that have become obsolete/surplus may either be exported or disposed of in the DTA on payment of applicable duties. The benefit of depreciation, as applicable, will be available in case of disposal in DTA.

(c) No duty shall be payable in case capital goods, raw material, consumables, spares, goods manufactured, processed or packaged and scrap/waste/remnants/rejects are destroyed within the Zone after intimation to the Custom authorities or destroyed outside the Zone with the permission of Custom authorities. However destruction shall not apply to precious and semi-precious and precious metals

(d) SEZ unit may be allowed by Customs authorities concerned to donate imported/indigenously procured computer and computer peripherals without payment of duty, two years after their import/procurement and use by the units, to recognized non-commercial educational institutions, registered charitable hospitals etc as per the details given in Appendix 14-II in Handbook (Vol-I).

Entitlement for SEZ Developer

7.23 (a) For development, operation and maintenance of infrastructure facilities in SEZs, the developer shall be eligible for the following entitlements

(b) Income tax exemption as per 80 IA of the Income Tax Act.

(c) Import/procure goods without payment of Customs/Excise duty.

(d) Exemption from Service tax.

(e) Exemption from CST.

India and the World Trade Organization: Key to Global Competitiveness

India is a founder member of the General Agreement on Tariffs and Trade (GATT) 1947 and its successor, the World Trade Organization (WTO), which came into effect on 1.1.95 after the conclusion of the Uruguay Round (UR) of Multilateral Trade Negotiations. India's participation in an increasingly rule-based system in the governance of international trade is to ensure more stability and predictability, which ultimately would lead to more trade and prosperity for itself and the 134 other nations which now comprise the WTO. India also automatically avails of MFN and national treatment for its exports to all WTO Members (http://www.indianembassy.org/Policy/WTO/overview.html).

Ministerial Conferences of WTO

In the Doha Ministerial Declaration, Ministers recognized "the case for a multilateral framework of competition policy to enhance the contribution of competition policy to international trade and development" and agreed that "negotiations will take place after the fifth Session of the Ministerial Conference on the basis of a decision to be taken, by explicit consensus, at that Session on modalities of negotiations" (Paragraph 23). The Doha Declaration also provides identical mandates for the other new issues.

The Doha Mandate for Trade and Competition Policy

The Doha Declaration implies that negotiations on competition policy would be launched after the Cancun Ministerial Conference, subject however, to an explicit consensus on the "modalities" of negotiations. This convoluted text was the result of manipulative maneuvers by the developed countries to insert language to commit WTO Members to start negotiations on a multilateral competition framework (MCF), and the attempts by developing countries to block such language. In the final moments of the Doha Conference - on the insistence of a number of developing countries - the Chair of the Conference provided a clarification of this mandate. He said that the reference to explicit consensus on modalities meant that it was a pre-condition for the commencement of negotiations and that any Member could prevent the start of negotiations by withholding the consensus.

The Doha Declaration further instructed WTO Members to focus on the clarification of six elements: i.e., core principles of transparency, non-discrimination and procedural fairness, provisions on hardcore cartels, modalities for voluntary cooperation and support for progressive reinforcement of competition institutions in developing countries through capacity building (Paragraph 25). This work would be undertaken in the Working Group on the Interaction between Trade and Competition Policy (established by the Singapore Ministerial Conference in 1996). Paragraph 25 also explicitly requires that "full account shall be taken of the needs of developing and least-developed country participants and appropriate flexibility provided to address them". Developing countries have thus interpreted this to be the central focus of the clarification process, which requires consideration of the need for appropriate flexibility for developing countries to develop and implement trade and competition policies that meet their development needs and interests.

Appropriate Forms of Competition Policy for Developing Countries

Competition law and policy, in appropriate forms, are undoubtedly beneficial including for developing countries. Whilst not denying the need for regulation to prevent abuse of monopoly power and other anti-competitive practices, the key question is what form of regulation is appropriate for developing country needs.

From a development perspective, there is a fundamental imperative to build, develop and re-enforce national capacity, especially through domestic enterprises developing the scales and co-ordination necessary to enable them to compete effeetively in the face of large-scale intrusion in the domestic economy, as a result of increasing liberalization. Development of domestic enterprise with sufficient economies of scale is crucial for diffusion of technology and adaptation of imported technologies to domestic circumstances; domestic economic integration with spill-over effects in different sectors of economic and employment creation. This requires protection from the 'free' and full force of the world market for the time it takes for the local capacity to build up. It also requires a vital role for the state, which has to play the role of nurturing and encouraging domestic firms. Therefore, competition policy should complement national objectives – and these objectives may range from a comprehensive national industrial policy, the promotion of certain vital sectors and the enhancement of capacity of domestic entrepreneurs and farmers.

There are different approaches to competition policy and law. The European and the US models of competition policy represent an approach (although with important differences) that puts competition policy at the forefront and seeks to control and regulate anti-competitive and monopolistic behaviour of large corporations. There are limitations of this approach, namely, the over-arching focus on competition *per se* in which other social and economic considerations are secondary and the failure to address areas in which competition can be subjected, and promoted by, co-ordinated support for domestic industries to counter-balance existing big companies.

The Japanese model of the 1950-1970s, which locates competition policy within an industrial policy and the overall national policy objectives, provides an interesting contrast. The Japanese model of that time represents a more flexible approach to competition policy, premised on the application of positive discrimination between the needs of domestic enterprise for the development of a domestic economy against the market access needs of foreign enterprises in the local economy. Whilst the Japanese approach, in terms of economic theory and development-friendly policy, would appear to be one more suited to developing country needs, the pressure in the WTO to negotiate a MCF would force developing countries to adopt a diametrically opposite model of competition policy.

With respect to the international economy, it would also be important to curb the mega-mergers and acquisitions taking place, which threaten the competitive position of local firms in developing countries. World Bank analysis highlights the fact that the most important restraints on competition are policy barriers to trade. Subsidies and trade barriers in agriculture, and trade barriers in clothing and textiles, in the developed countries have adverse effects on developing countries. In addition, anti-dumping actions have been a favoured vehicle of the developed countries to restrict competition from developing countries' products. Restrictive business practices of large firms also hinder competition. Yet, calls to address these issues also do not find favour with the promoters of a MCF in the WTO.

The main pre-occupation of the proponents of the MCF seems to be focused on the need for foreign firms to be accorded "national treatment". This implies that foreign firms and their products be given equal or even better treatment than that given to local firms. It would curb the right of developing country governments to provide advantages to local firms, and local firms themselves may be restricted from practices, which are to their advantage.

Clarification in the Working Group: Divergence, not Consensus

The most insistent proponent of a multilateral competition framework is the EU, which had been pushing for inclusion of competition in the WTO since 1996. The EU has since "lowered its ambitions" in light of the resistance to their original proposals for a competition agreement in the WTO, which did little to disguise their market access objectives. Nevertheless, current EU proposals still create problems for the majority of developing countries. The proposals have the three main features: (1) A prohibition on hard core cartels domestic legislation, (2) domestic competition laws shall be in conformity with the so-called core WTO principles of non-discrimination, transparency and procedural fairness, and (3) the multilateral competition framework is subject to the dispute settlement system.

Discussions in the Working Group reveal major differences between the proponents of a multilateral framework on competition policy, such as the EU and Japan, on one hand, and developing countries, including India and some African countries, on the other. There is also some divergence in the views of the EU as between and other developed countries, such as the US, Canada and Korea. The views and positions of WTO Members on the elements identified for clarification clearly indicate that the clarification process has not engendered a common understanding of the issues, much less any agreement, between them.

Core principles—Non-discrimination, Transparency and Procedural Fairness Principles

The proposal is for the principles of non-discrimination, transparency and procedural fairness principles to be made binding on all Members, in that they should be applicable to the entirety of a competition law that is adopted in a country. Developing countries have argued that these principles are not universally applicable to all issues, developed as they were in the context of the original purpose of the GATT as an agreement to facilitate reduction of barriers to international trade in goods. It is not self-evident that it is either appropriate or desirable for these principles to be applied to competition policy.

Transparency: The proposal is that this principle should cover all aspects of competition regime – from legislation, rules and institutional structures to decision-making processes, including decisions on sectoral exclusions and exemptions. This would represent an extension of the transparency requirement in the WTO (GATT, Article X) which is limited only to the publication of trade regulations and does not extend to decision-making. There may even be a case for narrowing this remits, as the requirement for publication of "judicial decisions and administrative rulings of general application", which would be unduly burdensome and potentially unworkable in the context of competition policy. There is also a questioning of the insistence of the proponents in excluding confidential information from transparency requirements, when such information will increase effectiveness in enforcement.

Non-discrimination: The current EU proposal is for the non-discrimination principle to be applicable only to *de jure* discrimination; i.e., applicable only to discrimination contained in the legislation, not to how legislation is applied in individual cases. The extension of the national treatment principle to a possible MCF may mean that "national treatment" has to be ensured for foreign firms (and their goods and services) vis-à-vis local firms in the domestic market. Such "equality" would only accentuate the inequality in market outcomes, since local firms are generally smaller than the large foreign firms and transnational corporations (TNCs).

Procedural fairness: A key component of this principle is the guarantee of rights of access to the system of appeal, including right to reasoned final decision providing detailed grounds on which such decisions were based, and the right of parties to be heard. The concern is that developing countries with dissimilar legal systems to developed countries or with insufficient resources will run the risk of not meeting the requisite standard of procedural fairness. Notions of fundamental fairness differ among legal systems and political and legal cultures, and there is as yet no broad consensus on the meaning of procedural fairness in the context of competition law enforcement.

EU Perspective

The EU has insisted on the regulation of hard core cartels in the proposed multilateral competition framework, and an obligation at national level for the enforcement of this prohibition. A fundamental problem with this proposal is that there is as yet no generally accepted definition of hard core cartels. Moreover, the assumption that all hard core cartels have adverse impacts for all countries in all markets at all stages of their development is questioned. The experience of some Asian countries in which cartelization was, for a time, an element of their industrial policies, challenges this assumption. In addition, nearly all developed countries have had exemptions (and continue to maintain some of them) on the basis of overriding economic or public interest grounds, or allow co-operation by small and medium-sized enterprises (SMEs) to countervail the market power of a dominant firm on the other side. Although the proponents envisage the possibility of allowing existing (and future) exemptions or exclusions, there has not been sufficient clarity on the scope of such exemptions/exclusions. Developing countries may not be able to define *ex ante* in their laws, which cartels would be exempted or excluded, and these exemptions and exclusions may change according to economic and socio-political exigencies. A multilateral obligation on hard core cartel prohibition will restrict the policy flexibility of developing countries.

Modus Operandi for Voluntary Cooperation

In contrast to the other proposals for binding obligations, the proposals for modalities on cooperation (i.e. among countries) are non-binding in nature. Developing countries have questioned the rationale of developed countries in proposing merely voluntary modalities for cooperation, whilst insisting on binding obligations for other aspects. Binding obligations in the WTO assumed in respect of domestic competition policy will clearly weigh more heavily on the developing countries. In contrast, best endeavour clauses on co-operation serve little purpose for developing countries, which would require much assistance in their enforcement efforts.

Locus Standi for the Developing Economies

Developing countries have raised the importance of their need to take certain policy measures affecting trade and competition, in line with their national developmental needs and objectives. These include measures such as those taken: (1) to maintain and enhance the competitiveness of domestic firms, particularly small firms, including aspects of industrial policy related *inter alia* to financial assistance, subsidies, local content policy and preferences in government procurement; (2) for promoting developing country products and services in developed countries, including reducing anti-competitive practices such as anti-dumping actions, subsidies (especially in agriculture) and tariff and non-tariff barriers; (3) at international level to curb anti-competitive effects of intellectual property rights, the practices of TNCs, including the need to address the monopoly or near monopoly in certain sectors/areas of production and the anti-competitive effects of corporate mega-mergers. Other issues include (1) Measures to formulate the obligations and responsibilities of foreign firms to the host country; and (2) Measures to formulate the obligation of the home governments to ensure the foreign firms fulfill their obligations vis-à-vis host countries.

The first Ministerial Conference held in 1996 in Singapore saw the commencement of pressures to enlarge the agenda of WTO. Pressures were generated to introduce new Agreements on Investment, Competition Policy, Transparency in Government Procurement and Trade Facilitation. The concept of Core Labor Standards was also sought to be introduced. India and the developing countries, who were already under the burden of fulfilling the commitments undertaken through the Uruguay Round Agreements, and who also perceived many of the new issues to be non-trade issues, resisted the introduction of these new subjects into WTO. They were partly successful. The Singapore Ministerial Conference (SMC) set up open-ended Work Program to study the relationship between Trade and Investment; Trade and Competition Policy; to conduct a study on Transparency in Government Procurement practices; and do analytical work on simplification of trade procedures (Trade Facilitation). Most importantly the SMC clearly declared on the Trade-Labour linkage as follows:

"We reject the use of labour standards for protectionist purposes, and agree that the comparative advantage of countries, particularly low-wage developing countries, must in no way be put into question. In this regard we note that the WTO and ILO Secretariat will continue their existing collaboration".

The Second Ministerial Conference of WTO, held at Geneva in May 1998, established a process to prepare for the Third Ministerial Conference and to submit recommendations regarding the WTO's future work program, which would enable Members to take decisions at the Third Ministerial Conference at Seattle.

The Geneva Ministerial Conference (GMC) Declaration had identified the following issues for the General Council's work, paragraphs 9(a) to 9(b) of the Declaration:

(a) (i) Issues, including those brought forward by Members, relating to implementation of Important Agreements and decisions
(ii) The negotiations already mandated at Marrakesh (Agriculture and Services) and ensure that such negotiations begin on schedule;
(iii) Mandated reviews already provided for under other existing agreements and decisions taken at Marrakesh;

(b) Recommendations concerning other possible future work on the basis of the work program initiated at Singapore Ministerial Conference consisting of:

(i) Trade and Investment;
(ii) Trade and Competition Policy;
(iii) Transparency in Government Procurement;
(iv) Trade Facilitation.

(c) Recommendations on the follow-up to the High-Level Meeting on Least-Developed countries;

(d) Recommendations arising from consideration of other matters proposed and agreed to by Members concerning their multilateral trade relations.

The 3rd Ministerial Conference held in Seattle during 30th November-3rd December, 1999 was being looked up by many, especially in the developing countries, as a launching pad for a comprehensive round of negotiations.

In the preparatory process in the General Council of the WTO (September 1998 to September 1999), new issues which were proposed for the negotiating agenda by some Members under paragraph 9(d) are as follows:

(a) Industrial Tariffs
(b) Global Electronic Commerce
(c) Trade and Labour Standards
(d) Trade and Environment
(e) Coherence in the interaction of WTO and other international organizations.

Outcome of the Seattle Ministerial Conference of WTO

The Indian delegation to the Third Ministerial Conference of the WTO was led by the then Union Minister of Commerce and Industry, Mr. Murasoli Maran. The delegation also included Members of Parliament, senior officials from different Ministries and representatives from the apex Chambers of commerce and industry (http://www.gao.gov/archive/2000/ns00086t.pdf).

The Seattle Conference attracted wide attention because of proposals by some countries to press for the launching of a comprehensive round of negotiations covering subjects as wide ranging as labour issues, coherence in global economic architecture, agriculture etc. Even before the commencement of the Conference there were widespread protests and demonstrations in Seattle by a number of anti-WTO groups ranging from environmental activists to labour unions. The inaugural session which was to be held in the forenoon of 30th November, 1999 had to be abandoned because of disturbances. The plenary which was to start in the afternoon on the same day had to be held under heavy police protection.

The Chairmen of various Working Groups tried to narrow down the differences in their respective groups with a view to arriving at a consensus in the draft Ministerial text that had been transmitted from the Geneva preparatory process. However, in view of the wide divergence of views, no group could present draft texts for inclusion in the Ministerial declaration acceptable to all the members.

As there was no prospect of reaching a conclusion on a large number of issues, it was decided after consultation among key members that it would not be practicable to adopt any Ministerial declaration. The Chairperson of the Conference made only a brief statement on 3rd December followed by brief reports by the Chairmen of the various groups. The Chairperson observed that divergences of opinion remained that would take time to be narrowed down. It was, therefore, decided to suspend the work of the Seattle Ministerial Conference.

While the above constituted the overall outcome, the deliberations and consultations which took place on several of the important issues are briefly outlined below subject-wise (these positions are indicative and not definitive since a number of delegations, including ourselves, made it clear that nothing was agreed until everything was agreed).

(a) **Implementation issues:** A good deal of discussions took place on this subject in Seattle, further to the extensive consultations held in Geneva earlier. The Working Group Chairman (Canada) came up with a final proposal (similar to what was mooted by the Secretariat) that meant a few immediate decisions at Seattle and establishment of a special mechanism to examine and make recommendations within one year, and in any case by the Fourth Ministerial Session, on other implementation issues. The Chairman's text also proposed negotiations in respect of Anti-Dumping and Subsidies Agreements. While India and most other countries were prepared to go along with the Chairman's text, the US had reservations and was opposed to any negotiations on anti-dumping and subsidies and could, at the most, agree to a few (not all) of the issues raised by the Committee on Anti-Dumping and Subsidies respectively. No consensus could, therefore, emerge.

(b) **Agriculture:** Mandated negotiations have to commence on 1.1.2000 on Agriculture. In the run-up to Seattle, however, the Cairns Group of countries supported by US sought to secure a more rigorous negotiating mandate that would speed up elimination/reduction of their export/ domestic subsidies. EC, Japan, Norway etc., resisted this to the very end. While EC appeared to display some flexibility on this issue, Japan put up stiff opposition on further inroads into elimination of domestic subsidies. As for India, our concerns relating to food security were adequately reflected.

(c) **Services:** No substantive negotiation took place in Seattle as there was hardly any divergence of views on the draft text which adequately takes into account India's concerns.

(d) **Investment and Competition Policy:** India, Malaysia, Hong Kong, China and Pakistan proposed the continuation of the study process launched at Singapore. EC and others stubbornly argued that they wanted negotiations to be launched right away. Given this, the talks broke off but a 'bridge proposal' which aimed at carrying forward the study process to prepare for negotiations to be launched by the Fourth Ministerial Conference began to take shape. While India, Malaysia, Hong Kong, China and Pakistan continued to oppose even the "bridge proposal", a number of other developing countries (including countries such as Zimbabwe, Sri Lanka and Egypt) showed inclination to agree to launch negotiations or to agree to the compromise proposal.

(e) **Market Access for non-agricultural items:** There was virtually no opposition for the launching of negotiations in this area except that a number of developing countries including ourselves pointed out the priority that we attached to the implementation issues and made it clear that agreeing to any text on this issue depended on progress in other areas. The text which evolved during the Green Room consultations left open the modalities to be followed for the tariff reduction exercise although the APEC countries wanted a specific reference to their Accelerated Tariff Liberalisation (ATL) initiative. EU wanted a common tariff reduction method to be adopted for all countries while certain others preferred a formula approach to be the main methodology. While our concerns were largely met in the draft text, the US insisted on avoiding any reference to peak-tariffs saying it was a politically sensitive issue. Several developing countries, including us, however, firmly opposed the substitution of 'peak tariffs' by any other phraseology. This matter still needs to be resolved.

(f) **Transparency in Government Procurement:** There were broadly three proposals on this subject at the Seattle Ministerial. First, that the Working Group should continue its work until the fourth Ministerial session. India and number of developing countries supported this proposal. Second, that the Seattle Ministerial should mandate commencement of negotiations based on the elements that had formed the basis of discussion in the Working Group with the objective of concluding an Agreement at the latest by the Fourth Ministerial session. A number of developed and developing countries such as Brazil and South Africa supported this proposal. Third, that the Ministers adopt at Seattle an Agreement on Transparency in Government Procurement based on the formulation proposed by the United States and the European Union. After further discussions in the open-ended Seattle Working Group on Singapore issues and other issues, its Chairman gave his understanding that there was virtual consensus among Members present on the second proposal. He noted that India was the only Member present that stated that it could not join such a consensus and urged India to reconsider its position. India had stated that it could only support further work in the Working Group aimed at arriving at a consensus on the elements of a Transparency agreement.

(g) **Trade and Environment:** Developed countries, particularly EU, were very keen on negotiations on environment related issues to accommodate concerns of their civil society. They wanted environmental considerations integrated throughout the negotiations in the new Round ('mainstreaming') which will also dilute the focussed mandate of the Committee on Trade and Environment (CTE) to that extent. USA was further keen that Members' right to set high environmental standards was not undermined by trade rules. The US and CAIRNS Group countries also called for the removal of environmentally damaging subsidies such as agricultural subsidies and fishery subsidies that contributed to over capacity. Developing countries sought adjustments in the TRIPS Agreement for preservation of biological diversity and reward for traditional knowledge. The proposal to mainstream environment and dilute the role of CTE and the US proposal regarding environmental standards were opposed by some developing countries including India while there was considerable support for removal of environment-related subsidies. The TRIPS related proposals were supported by some, but there was no consensus.

(h) **Intellectual Property:** Many members were willing to complete the negotiations on the establishment of a multilateral system of notification and registration of geographical indications for wines and possibly spirits, while there was an emerging consensus for an early decision on the ongoing discussions on inclusion of other products for the higher level of protection as has been provided to wines under Art 23 of TRIPS. Other work programmes proposed to be launched at Seattle included a proposal to make recommendations to the Fourth Ministerial Conference on the scope for protection for traditional knowledge and folkfore under the TRIPS Agreement, and review of Article 71.1, including enhancing the Agreement to respond to its objectives and principles as well as new developments elsewhere, and of Article 27.3(b) relating to life forms and plant varieties.

(i) **Other issues:** There were a few other issues which were less controversial. Subjects belonging to this category included E-commerce and trade facilitation. A proposal to set up a working group on transfer of Technology, supported by India also found wide support but was opposed by USA, while EC and some others preferred discussions on this issue within the Committee on Trade and Development. On the other hand, the proposed Working Group on Bio-technology, pursued by USA was hardly discussed because of strong opposition from many members, including India.

(j) Regarding transparency in the functioning of WTO, US and EU were keen for some kind of mechanism whereby civil society could participate in the WTO functioning, inter alia, through amicus curiae briefs in the trade dispute settlement mechanism. But this was sharply opposed by India and many other developing countries.

The Road Beyond Seattle

As earlier stated, no consensus could emerge as a result of the divergences that persisted on various issues and the Seattle Conference had to be suspended. For the present, it can only be said that the mandated negotiations in agriculture and services and mandated reviews would commence as scheduled from January 2000. The Ministerial Conference may resume its work only after the Director General of WTO has been able to consult with delegations and recommend its reconvening after making sure that the next time around there will be greater degree of consensus. In his statement after the Conference, Director General Moore said that it was "vital to maintain and consolidate what has already been achieved". However, there is no final agreed Conference document which records the progress already achieved.

Moves were already afoot to reconvene the Ministerial meeting. The European Union is in particular keen that this is quickly achieved with the launch of a comprehensive round of negotiations. The DG of WTO is also stated to be of the view that the Ministerial meeting should resume early. We have informed all those who have approached us that the contentious issues like labour standards should be off the table and further there should be narrowing down of differences on all issues before any attempt is made to reconvene the Ministerial meeting. The developments in the next few months are beings watched.

Environmental concerns are already built into the existing Agreements and there is also a Committee on Trade and Environment. Our objection is not to environmental standards per se but the possibility of misuse of environmental standards for protectionist purposes. We are opposing the enlargement of the mandate of the Committee on Trade and Environment and to what is called the mainstreaming of environment in all the agreements. US are very keen that they should have the right to lay down higher level of environmental standards in a non-discriminatory manner. It appears that many of the countries might have agreed to higher standards of environmental protection measures being implemented by any country so long as they are non-discriminatory and are not used for protectionist purposes.

On the issue of labour standards, however, there was considerable opposition to its inclusion in the agenda from many countries. A view point being advocated is that there should be no objection to a direction by WTO to ILO to make a study as it will not amount to giving negotiating mandate and that the developing countries can always say no to negotiations even at a subsequent stage. Even this limited scope was, however, not without some risks as was historically evident from the Post-Seattle scenario.

POST-SEATTLE SCENARIO

India took advantage of 'time out' to consolidate its position on issues of its interest in the WTO. Three-pronged efforts were launched which are as follows:

(a) On the one hand, India had, in the past, continued to highlight the areas of its concern at important bilateral and multilateral meetings, which have been as follows:

In his meeting with the Director General WTO on 12th January 2000 at New Delhi, Commerce and Industry Minister emphasised that globalisation has caused uneven growth, increasing the disparities between the richest and the poorest. This has to be addressed, inter alia, by addressing the implementation problems in existing Agreements and operationalising the special and differential clauses in favour of developing countries. A consensus could be reached only if the more controversial issues, such as non-trade related issues, could be eliminated from WTO.

In his statement at UNCTAD-X (Bangkok 13th February 2000), the Minister highlighted that "International rule making must ....permit flexibility and autonomy to developing countries to pursue their material development strategies on the basis of needs and aspirations of their people." He registered a strong protest on the part of the developing countries as to how issues extraneous to trade, such as labour standards, are sought to be put on the negotiating agenda, while, on the other hand issues such as the cross border movement of persons, a matter of great interest to developing countries is resisted by developed countries. On the margins of the UNCTAD Conference at Bangkok, he had also used this opportunity to have bilateral and plurilateral meetings with a view to evolve common stand on important WTO issues.

The UNCTAD Plan of Action has taken on board some of the important concerns of developing countries on implementation issues by inter alia recognising that "in the course of implementation of the WTO Agreements, most developing countries consider that certain imbalances and asymmetries exist" and that "these problems need to be addressed urgently so as to ensure that the multilateral trading system results in mutual benefits for all countries." India was also able to moderate the wording on global coherence as much as "coherence" has been diluted to "cooperation" in the critical portions of the UNCTAD-X Declaration and Plan of Action. India feels that strengthened 'coherence' between WTO and the UN organizations may lead to increased cross conditionalities which may narrow down our policy options for development. Thus our success in diluting the coherence brief in UNCTAD is significant.

(b) Under the second track of post-Seattle follow up Government has held consultations to appraise the situation arising out of the failure of the Seattle Ministerial Conference to reach consensus on major issues. A meeting of the Advisory Committee on International Trade was convened on February 3, 2000 to apprise the Committee of the important developments at and immediately after Seattle and seek the Committee's advice on the way forward. The gist of the Committee's advice to Government has been to ask Government to review the implementation issues and prioritise those which are of core interest; to ensure that our implementation demands are properly attuned to our autonomous programme of domestic economic liberalisation; to evolve a suitable response to a situation where even some of the developing countries are willing to accept some watered down version of a group on trade and labour in association with the WTO; and evolve our stand on environment so that we don't appear to be against protection of environment; to give adequate publicity to our positive record of adherence to ILO conventions and ongoing efforts for implementation of core labour standards; and to formulate a national consensus on biotechnology etc.

(c) The third strand of our post-Seattle approach has been to participate actively in the meetings of the General Council of the WTO and its subsidiary bodies to continue to emphasise the areas of our concern. India has participated actively in the General Council meetings held post-Seattle on 17th December, 1999 and on 2nd, 7th and 29th February, 2000.

On Cross-roads at Cancun

In the preparations for the Cancun Ministerial Conference, three options for a decision on competition policy were put forward by the Chair of the Working Group. The first option was to start negotiations on a binding multilateral agreement on competition. The second was to have a decision on modalities for a framework for cooperation in the WTO, without any binding rules (termed the "soft agreement" approach). The third was for the continuation of the clarification process in the Working Group. The first option was, of course, that preferred by the proponents of the multilateral competition framework. The third option was put forward by a number of developing countries, which had serious concerns regarding the implications of the MCF in the WTO.

Whilst the second option of a "soft agreement" appeared to be a formulation designed to strike a compromise between the first and the third options, it raised serious concerns that this might be a means by which the first option is re-introduced through the back door. The history of GATT and WTO negotiations demonstrate that a fairly innocuous proposal is often put forward as a means of gaining agreement, in order to push through the real objective of the proponents. The mandate for negotiating the TRIPS Agreement, which developed countries contrived to infer from the Punta del Este Ministerial Declaration of 1986, has been good illustration to recon for future learning. Furthermore, if the real intention was to develop non-binding rules or guidelines, it would be far more constructive to consider how the UN Set of Principles and Rules could be implemented in the context of UNCTAD, rather than duplicating the effort in the WTO.

In Cancun, one of the most important decisions for Ministers was, as to whether or not to launch negotiations on new WTO agreements on investment, competition, transparency in government procurement, trade facilitation. These four "new issues" are being pushed primarily by the EU, aided by the other Quad countries (Japan, Canada and the US) in varying degrees of force depending on the specific issue of their preference. Although most developing country governments have stated their objections against the launch of negotiations on the new issues, there are fears these governments may be pressured into agreement at Cancun. Prior to, and during, the Doha Ministerial Conference, manipulative negotiating tactics, undemocratic and non-transparent decision-making processes were used to push and pressure developing countries into a grudging acceptance of an expanded WTO mandate on the new issues (Peter Holms, 2008).

WTO Regime and its Impact

In analyzing issues relating to Indian industrial policy and the various strategies appropriate to face global competition it is important to consider the current international, institutional and technological scene, namely, the World Trade Organization (WTO), conditions imposed by the International Monetary Fund (IMF) for lending to countries and the roles of Information Technology (IT) and internet in global business. The attempts by several developing economies (DEs) to liberalize and integrate themselves with the global economy, has to be viewed in the context as also in larger perspective of the changing global institutional and technological environment (Siddhartan, 2005).

The WTO regime in 1995 has fundamentally changed the international trade scene. The WTO is the result of the Uruguay round of negotiations that began in 1986 in Punta del Este, Uruguay and concluded in Marrakesh on December 15, 1993. Two basic principles govern all WTO sections: national treatment and the most favoured nation status. National treatment to all firms prohibits the local host government from granting to the local firms favours, privileges and advantages that are not available to the foreign firms. Thus in matters relating to government purchases, licensing etc., local firms and foreign firms have to be treated on par. Likewise, the most favoured nation status prevents the host government from favouring firms from one WTO member country over firms from other WTO member countries. Till recently, India and several other Asian countries have been insisting on local content requirements from foreign firms. In this regard, in several cases, physical targets were fixed to promote domestic procurement and to increase the local content. To prevent the outflow of foreign exchange, trade balancing requirements were also imposed. These limit the imports of foreign firms to their earnings of foreign exchange through exports. In some cases, less stringent requirements like foreign exchange neutrality, namely, some balance between foreign exchange inflows (through exports and investments and other transfers) and outflows were enforced. WTO provisions prohibit all these measures. Consequently developing countries had to give up measures like local content, trade balancing and foreign exchange neutrality since January 2000. Studies (Kumar, 2002; Siddharthan and Rajan, 2002) have shown that these measures could reduce the quality of FDI inflows and inhibit the development of domestic component industries.

IMF Conditionality

It is important to distinguish the operations of IMF and the conditionality imposed by it from the operations of the WTO regime. While the WTO regulations apply to all member countries, the IMF conditionality affects only those member countries that borrow from IMF. By and large, IMF provides funds on the condition that the borrowing countries cut deficits, raise taxes and interest rates, liberalize trade and currency exchange rates and move towards making their currency convertible in both current and capital accounts. In some cases, the IMF fixes targets for each of these variables and monitors their performance. In addition to liberalization measures, it could also insist on privatization of government owned enterprises (Stiglitz, 2002).

The Impact of Information Technology

The emergence of the current generation of information technology tools, in particular the internet, has radically altered the nature of international transactions. Earlier market-seeking multinational enterprises (MNEs) invested in foreign locations mainly to exploit their firms' ownership advantages (Dunning, 1993; Caves, 1996). Currently, partly due to the WTO regulations and partly due to the vast changes in information and communication technology (ICT), MNEs are opting for efficiency seeking investments and especially non-equity alliances that often include acquisition of knowledge assets. This change in the MNEs' strategy has led to some notable consequences. Traditionally, design, engineering, and technological innovation were mainly conducted in the home country. Very little R&D was performed in the host countries and where it was performed, it was of an adaptive nature intended to modify the product or process to suit the resource conditions or tastes and preferences of the host country. By and large, the MNEs invested abroad to exploit the advantages that they possessed at home. However, unlike the earlier investments, some of the current investments are technology-augmenting investments aimed at exploiting host country resources (asset-seeking FDI). In the MNE's decision process the new factor considered is the skilled labour possessed in the form of a thin strata of educated labour in some developing countries. This applies already in industries such as software and pharmaceuticals (and it is arising in some manufacturing industries also), and in countries such as India and China (Kumar and Siddharthan, 1997; Siddharthan and Rajan, 2002; Belderbos, 2001; Florida, 1997; Kuemmerle, 1999). Most importantly, the new knowledge sharing methods adopted by MNEs need not be fulfilled by FDI. The internet revolution enables a range of non-equity alliances to substitute for FDI. The immobility of labour across nations that compelled international growth to take place either by trade or investment no longer applies to a range of professional and technical activities. The internet revolution has created virtual labour mobility. Professionals in home and host countries can transmit their labour services electronically and instantly across borders; they do not need to move geographically.

Investments in operations abroad are not necessary; outsourcing and networking serve as effectively. This has encouraged the creation of global R&D units that have removed the differences in the R&D performed by the home and host country R&D units. Consequently several MNEs have set-up strategic alliances with R&D units in a less developed country like India where they are performing innovative R&D aimed at pushing technological frontiers (Reddy, 1997; Siddharthan and Rajan, 2002). In the pursuit of efficiency, MNEs are also likely to source high-tech components from their strategic partners with whom they also share knowledge. In recent years, internet and e-commerce and in particular business to business (B2B) commerce, have assumed importance. The study by Freund and Weinhold (2004) found that internet stimulates trade. They show that internet reduces the fixed cost of entry into a foreign market and that helps firms from less developed countries and in particular small and medium enterprises (SMEs). Using data on bilateral trade from 1995 to 1999 and controlling for the standard determinants of trade growth, they find that the growth in the number of websites in a country helps to explain export growth in the following year. Accordingly the success of SMEs would crucially depend on their ability to network, which in turn would depend on the infrastructure facilities for B2B commerce. Thus IT has enabled SMEs to globalize. Given the context of the WTO regime and internet revolution, all the markets have become global and consequently all firms – small, medium and large - must have a global vision to succeed. Economic policies of developing have been responding to the altering international environment (Siddhartan, 2005).

5

Indian Economic, Industrial and Foreign Trade Policies Fostering Global Competitiveness

Indian Economy—A Historic Preview

The Economy of India, measured in US $ exchange-rate terms, is the twelfth largest in the world, with a GDP in excess of $ 1 trillion (2008). It recorded a GDP growth rate of 9.0% for the fiscal year 2007–2008 which makes it the second fastest big emerging economy, after China, in the world. At this rate of sustained growth many economists forecast that India would, over the coming decades, have a more pronounced economic effect on the world stage. Despite this phenomenal rate of growth, India's large population has a per capita income of $ 4,542, measured by PPP, and $ 1,089, measured in nominal terms. The World Bank classifies India as a low-income economy (http://en.wikipedia.org/wiki/Economic_history_of_India).

India's economy is diverse, encompassing agriculture, handicrafts, textile, manufacturing, and a multitude of services. Although two-thirds of the Indian workforce still earns their livelihood directly or indirectly through agriculture, services are a growing sector and play an increasingly important role in India's economy. The advent of the digital age, and the large number of young and educated populace fluent in English, is gradually transforming India as an important 'back office' destination for global outsourcing of customer services and technical support. India is a major exporter of highly-skilled workers in software and financial services, and software engineering. Other sectors like manufacturing, pharmaceuticals, biotechnology, nanotechnology, telecommunication, shipbuilding, aviation, tourism and retailing are showing strong potentials with higher growth rates.

India followed a socialist-inspired approach for most of its independent history, with strict government control over private sector participation, foreign trade, and foreign direct investment. However, since the early 1990s, India has gradually opened up its markets through economic reforms by reducing government controls on foreign trade and investment. The privatization of publicly owned industries and the opening up of certain sectors to private and foreign interests has proceeded slowly amid political debate. India faces a fast-growing population and the challenge of reducing economic and social inequality. Poverty remains a serious problem, although it has declined significantly since independence. Official surveys estimated that in the year 2004-2005, 27% of Indians were poor.

A Brief Indian Economic History

Economic history of India and Timeline of the economy of India

India's economic history can be broadly divided into three eras, beginning with the pre-colonial period lasting up to the 17th century. The advent of British colonization started the colonial period in the 17th century, which ended with independence in 1947. The third period stretches from independence in 1947 until now (http://en.wikipedia.org/wiki/Economic_history_of_India).

Pre-colonial

Assessment of India's pre-colonial economy is mostly qualitative, owing to the lack of quantitative information. One estimate puts the revenue of Akbar's Mughal Empire in 1600 at £17.5 million, in contrast with the total revenue of Great Britain in 1800, which totalled £16 million. India, by the time of the arrival of the British, was a largely traditional agrarian economy with a dominant subsistence sector dependent on primitive technology. It existed alongside a competitively developed network of commerce, manufacturing and credit. After the fall of the Mughals, India was administered by Maratha Empire. The Maratha Empire's budget in 1740s, at its peak, was Rs. 100 million. After the loss at Panipat, the Maratha Empire disintegrated into confederate states of Gwalior, Baroda, Indore, Jhansi, Nagpur, Pune and Kolhapur. Gwalior state had a budget of Rs. 30M. However, at this time, British East India Company entered the Indian political theatre. Until, 1857, when India was firmly under the British crown, the country remained in a state of political instability due to internecine wars and conflicts.

Colonial

An estimate by Cambridge University historian Angus Madison reveals that India's share of the world income fell from 22.6% in 1700, comparable to Europe's share of 23.3%, to a low of 3.8% in 1952. While Indian leaders during the Independence struggle, and left-nationalist economic historians have blamed colonial rule for the dismal state of India's economy in its aftermath, a broader macroeconomic view of India during this period reveals that there were sectors of growth and decline, resulting from changes brought about by colonialism and a world that was moving towards industrialization and integration. While the exact sectors of growth and decline is of questionable importance, the overall effect of the changes brought about by colonialism, and India's degree of industrialization and economic integration of India under the British rule on India's economy can be assessed from the kind of economy India inherited after the end of the colonial rule in India.

Independence to 1991

Indian economic policy after independence was influenced by the colonial experience (which was seen by Indian leaders as exploitative in nature) and by those leaders' exposure to Fabian socialism. Policy tended towards protectionism, with a strong emphasis on import substitution, industrialization, state intervention in labour and financial markets, a large public sector, business regulation, and planning. Jawaharlal, the first prime minister, along with the statistician Prasanta Chandra Mahalanobis, carried on by Indira Gandhi formulated and oversaw economic policy. They expected favourable outcomes from this strategy, because it involved both public and private sectors and was based on direct and indirect state intervention, rather than the more extreme Soviet-style central command system. India's low average growth rate from 1947–80 was derisively referred to as the Hindu rate of growth, because of the unfavorable comparison with growth rates in other Asian countries, especially the "East Asian Tigers".

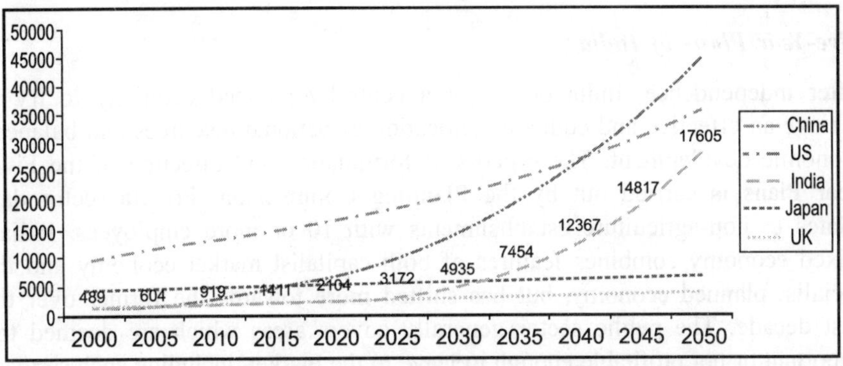

Fig. 1: GDP growth forecast for selected countries 2000-2050 (In Billion US$)

Goldman Sachs has predicted that India will become 3rd largest economy of the world by 2035 based on predicted growth rate of 5.3 to 6.1%. Currently, it is cruising at 8.5% growth rate. Since 1990 India has emerged as one of the wealthiest economies in the developing world; during this period, the economy has grown constantly, but with a few major setbacks. This has been accompanied by increases in life expectancy, literacy rates and food security. In 2003, Goldman Sachs predicted that India's GDP in current prices will overtake France and Italy by 2020, Germany, UK and Russia by 2025 and

Japan by 2035. By 2035, it was projected to be the third largest economy of the world, behind US and China. In its latest assessment dated January 22, 2007, of India's long-term economic outlook, which is titled, "India's Rising Growth Potential," Goldman Sachs suggests that India's influence on the world economy will be bigger and quicker than implied in its previously published BRICs research. (BRICs stand for "Brazil, Russia, India and China").

India's growth since 2003 represents a structural increase rather than simply a cyclical upturn. India's potential or sustainable growth rate is projected at an average of 8.4% until 2020. This is significantly higher than the 5.7% that was projected in the original BRICs paper of 2003. The implication of this is that India will overtake the G6 economies faster than envisaged in the earlier BRICs research. Indeed, India's GDP (in US $ terms) will surpass that of the US before 2050 to make it the second largest economy. India's contribution to world growth will also be increasing.

The recent growth spurt was achieved primarily through a surge in manufacturing productivity which can be sustained. The proximate cause is the increase in efficiency of private-sector firms in the face of growing competition. Restructuring has made India's private sector leaner, fitter, and more productive (http://www.hvacindia.org.in/DasBlogce/PermaLink, guid, 4f6e12f8-665b-4b5a-b59e-956320f62fd5.aspx).

State Planning and the Mixed Economy

Five-Year Plans of India

After independence, India opted for a centrally planned economy to try to achieve an effective and equitable allocation of national resources and balanced economic development. The process of formulation and direction of the Five-Year Plans is carried out by the Planning Commission. Private sector data relates to non-agriculture establishments with 10 or more employees. India's mixed economy combines features of both capitalist market economy and the socialist planned economy, but has shifted more towards the former over the past decade. The public sector generally covers areas which are deemed too important or not profitable enough to leave to the market, including such services as the railways and postal system. Since independence, there have been phases of nationalizing such areas as banking. More recently, there have been phases of privatizing such sectors.

Public Expenditure

India's public expenditure is classified as development expenditure, comprising central plan expenditure and central assistance and non-development expenditures; these categories can each be divided into capital expenditure and revenue expenditure. Central plan expenditure is allocated to development schemes outlined in the plans of the central government and public sector undertakings; central assistance refers to financial assistance and developmental loans given for plans of the state governments and union territories. Non-development capital expenditure comprises capital defence expenditure, loans to public enterprises, states and union territories and foreign governments, while non-development revenue expenditure comprises revenue defence expenditure, administrative expenditure, subsidies, debt relief to farmers, postal deficit, pensions, social and economic services (education, health, agriculture, science and technology), grants to states and union territories and foreign governments.

India's non-development revenue expenditure has increased nearly five-fold in 2003–04 since 1990–91 and more than ten-fold since 1985–1986. Interest payments are the single largest item of expenditure and accounted for more than 40% of the total non-development expenditure in the 2003–04 budgets. Defence expenditure increased four-fold during the same period and has been increasing due to growing tensions in the region, the expensive dispute with Pakistan over Jammu and Kashmir and an effort to modernize the military. Administrative expenses are compounded by a large salary and pension bill, which rises periodically due to revisions in wages, dearness allowance etc. subsidies on food, fertilizers, education and petroleum and other merit and non-merit subsidies account are not only continuously rising, especially because of rising crude oil and food prices, but are also harder to rein in, because of political compulsions.

Public Revenues

India has a three-tier tax structure, wherein the constitution empowers the union government to levy income tax, tax on capital transactions (wealth tax, inheritance tax), sales tax, service tax, customs and excise duties and the state governments to levy sales tax on intrastate sale of goods, tax on entertainment and professions, excise duties on manufacture of alcohol, stamp duties on transfer of property and collect land revenue (levy on land owned). The local governments are empowered by the state government to levy property tax, octroi and charge users for public utilities like water supply, sewage etc. More than half of the revenues of the union and state governments come from taxes, of which half come from indirect taxes. More than a quarter of the union government's tax revenues are shared with the state governments.

The tax reforms, initiated in 1991, have sought to rationalize the tax structure and increase compliance by taking steps in the following directions:

- Reducing the rates of individual and corporate income taxes, excises, customs and making it more progressive
- Reducing exemptions and concessions
- Simplification of laws and procedures
- Introduction of Permanent account number to track monetary transactions

- 21 of the 29 states introduced Value added tax (VAT) on April 1, 2005 to replace the complex and multiple sales tax system

The non-tax revenues of the central government come from fiscal services, interest receipts, public sector dividends, etc., while the non-tax revenues of the States are grants from the central government, interest receipts, dividends and income from general, economic and social services. Inter-State share in the federal tax pool is decided by the recommendations of the Finance Commission to the President.

General Budget

India's union budget for 2005–06 had an estimated outlay of Rs. 5,14,344 crores ($ 118 billion). Earnings from taxes amount to Rs. 2,73,466 crore ($ 63 b). India's fiscal deficit amounts to 4.5% or 1,39,231 crore ($ 32 b). The fiscal deficit is expected to be 3.8% of GDP, by March 2007.

Natural Resources

India's total cultivable area is 1,269,219 km² (56.78% of total land area), which is decreasing due to constant pressure from an ever-growing population and increased urbanization. India has a total water surface area of 314,400 km² and receives an average annual rainfall of 1,100 mm. Irrigation accounts for 92% of the water utilization, and comprised 380 km² in 1974, and is expected to rise to 1,050 km² by 2025, with the balance accounted for by industrial and domestic consumers. India's inland water resources comprising rivers, canals, ponds and lakes and marine resources comprising the east and west coasts of the Indian ocean and other gulfs and bays provide employment to nearly 6 million people in the fisheries sector. India is the sixth largest producer of fish in the world and second largest in inland fish production. India's major mineral resources include Coal (fourth-largest reserves in the world), Iron ore, Manganese, Mica, Bauxite, Titanium ore, Chromites, Natural gas, Diamonds, Petroleum, Limestone and Thorium (world's largest along Kerala's shores). India's oil reserves, found in Bombay High off the coast of Maharashtra, Gujarat, and in eastern Assam meet 25% of the country's demand. Rising energy demand concomitant with economic growth has created a perpetual state of energy crunch in India. India is poor in oil resources and is currently heavily dependent on coal and foreign oil imports for its energy needs. Though India is rich in Thorium, but not in Uranium, which it might get access to if a nuclear deal with US comes to fruition. India is rich in certain energy resources which promise significant future potential - clean/renewable energy resources like solar, wind, biofuels (jatropha, sugarcane).

Physical Infrastructure

Development of infrastructure was completely in the hands of the public sector and was plagued by corruption, bureaucratic inefficiencies, urban-bias and an inability to scale investment.

India's low spending on power, construction, transportation, telecommunications and real estate, at $ 31 billion or 6% of GDP in 2002 had prevented India from sustaining higher growth rates. This had prompted the government to partially open up infrastructure to the private sector allowing foreign investment which has helped in a sustained growth rate of close to 9% for the past six quarters. India holds second position in the world in roadways' construction, more than twice that of China. As of 2005 the electricity production was at 661.6 billion kWh with oil production standing at 785,000 bbl/day. India's prime import partners are: China 8.7%, US 6%, Germany 4.6%, Singapore 4.6%, Australia 4% as of 2006 CIA FactBook. As of 15 January 2007, there were 2.10 million broadband lines in India.

Financial Institutions

India inherited several institutions, such as the civil services, Reserve Bank of India, railways, etc., from its British rulers. Mumbai serves as the nation's commercial capital, with the Reserve Bank of India (RBI), Bombay Stock Exchange (BSE) and the National Stock Exchange (NSE) located here. The headquarters of many financial institutions are also located in the city.

Indian economy is largely dependent upon its four commanding centres which behalf four of its major sectors: Manufacturing Mumbai, Commerce Delhi, Exports Kolkata and Services Bangalore. Other important cities are Chennai, Ahmedabad, Hyderabad and Kanpur. The RBI, the country's central bank was established on 1 April 1935. It serves as the nation's monetary authority, regulator and supervisor of the financial system, manager of exchange control and as an issuer of currency. The RBI is governed by a central board, headed by a governor who is appointed by the Central government of India.

The BSE Sensex or the BSE Sensitive Index is a value-weighted index composed of 30 companies with April 1979 as the base year (100). These companies have the largest and most actively traded stocks and are representative of various sectors, on the Exchange. They account for around one-fifth of the market capitalization of the BSE. The Sensex is generally regarded as the most popular and precise barometer of the Indian stock markets. Incorporated in 1992, the National Stock Exchange is one of the largest and most advanced stock markets in India. The NSE is the world's third largest stock exchange in terms of transactions. There are a total of 23 stock exchanges in India, but the BSE and NSE comprise 83% of the volumes. The Securities and Exchange Board of India (SEBI), established in 1992, regulates the stock markets and other securities markets of the country.

Sectors

Agriculture

India ranks second worldwide in farm output. Agriculture and allied sectors like forestry, logging and fishing accounted for 16.6% of the GDP in 2007, employed 60% of the total workforce and despite a steady decline of its share in the GDP, is still the largest economic sector and plays a significant role in the overall socio-economic development of India. Yields per unit area of all crops have grown since 1950, due to the special emphasis placed on agriculture in the five-year plans and steady improvements in irrigation, technology, application of modern agricultural practices and provision of agricultural credit and subsidies since Green revolution in India. However, international comparisons reveal that the average yield in India is generally 30% to 50% of the highest average yield in the world.

The low productivity in India is a result of the following factors:

- Illiteracy, general socio-economic backwardness, slow progress in implementing land reforms and inadequate or inefficient finance and marketing services for farm produce.
- The average size of land holdings is very small (less than 20,000 m^2) and is subject to fragmentation, due to land ceiling acts and in some cases, family disputes. Such small holdings are often over-manned, resulting in disguised unemployment and low productivity of labour.
- Adoption of modern agricultural practices and use of technology is inadequate, hampered by ignorance of such practices, high costs and impracticality in the case of small land holdings.
- Irrigation facilities are inadequate, as revealed by the fact that only 52.6% of the land was irrigated in 2003–04, which result in farmers still being dependent on rainfall, specifically the Monsoon season. A good monsoon results in a robust growth for the economy as a whole, while a poor monsoon leads to a sluggish growth. Farm credit is regulated by NABARD, which is the statutory apex agent for rural development in the subcontinent.

Industry

India is fourteenth in the world in factory output. They together account for 27.6% of the GDP and employ 17% of the total workforce. However, about one-third of the industrial labour force is engaged in simple household manufacturing only.

Economic reforms brought foreign competition, led to privatization of certain public sector industries, opened up sectors hitherto reserved for the public sector and led to an expansion in the production of fast-moving consumer goods.

Post-liberalization, the Indian private sector, which was usually run by oligopolies of old family firms and required political connections to prosper was faced with foreign competition, including the threat of cheaper Chinese imports. It has since handled the change by squeezing costs, revamping management, focusing on designing new products and relying on low labour costs and technology.

Indian companies have been listed in the Forbes Global 2000 ranking for 2008. The 10 leading companies are (http://www.forbes.com/lists/2008/18/biz_2000global08_The-Global-2000_IndName.html):

World Rank	Company	Logo	Industry	Revenue (billion $)	Profit (billion $)	Assets (billion $)	Market (billion $)
193	Reliance Ind.	Reliance Industries Limited	Oil and Gas Operations	26.07	2.79	30.67	89.29
198	Oil and Natural Gas Corporation	ओएनजीसी ONGC	Oil and Gas Operations	18.90	4.11	33.79	54.11
219	State Bank of India		Banking	15.77	1.47	188.56	33.29
303	Indian Oil Corporation	इंडियनऑयल IndianOil	Oil and Gas Operations	42.68	1.82	25.39	16.36
374	ICICI Bank	ICICI Bank	Banking	9.84	0.64	91.07	29.85
411	NTPC	एनटीपीसी NTPC	Utilities	7.84	1.60	20.34	41.57
647	Steel Auth. of India Ltd	सेल SAIL	Materials	7.88	1.45	8.05	26.37
738	Tata Steel	TATA TATA STEEL	Materials	5.83	0.97	11.48	14.63
826	Bharti Airtel	Airtel Express Yourself	Telecomm. Services	4.26	0.94	6.61	39.16
846	Reliance Comm.	RELIANCE Communications Anil Dhirubhai Ambani Group	Telecomm. Services	3.13	0.65	13.08	29.63

Source: Wikipedia: http://en.wikipedia.org/wiki/Economic_history_of_India

Services

India is fifteenth in services output. It provides employment to 23% of work force, and it is growing fast, growth rate 7.5% in 1991–2000 up from 4.5%

in 1951–80. It has the largest share in the GDP, accounting for 55% in 2007 up from 15% in 1950. Business services (information technology, information technology enabled services, business process outsourcing) are among the fastest growing sectors contributing to one third of the total output of services in 2000. The growth in the IT sector is attributed to increased specialization, availability of a large pool of low cost, but highly skilled, educated and fluent English-speaking workers. On the supply side and on the demand side, increased demand from foreign consumers interested in India's service exports or those looking to outsource their operations. India's IT industry, despite contributing significantly to its balance of payments, accounted for only about 1% of the total GDP or 1/50th of the total services.

Banking and Finance

The Indian money market is classified into: the organized sector (comprising private, public and foreign owned commercial banks and cooperative banks, together known as *scheduled banks*); and the unorganized sector (viz. non-banking financial companies (NBFCs)). The unorganized sector and microcredit are still preferred over traditional banks in rural and sub-urban areas, especially for non-productive purposes, like ceremonies and short duration loans. Prime Minister Indira Gandhi nationalized 14 banks in 1969, followed by six others in 1980, and made it mandatory for banks to provide 40% of their net credit to priority sectors like agriculture, small-scale industry, retail trade, small businesses, etc. to ensure that the banks fulfill their social and developmental goals. Since then, the number of bank branches has increased from 10,120 in 1969 to 98,910 in 2003 and the population covered by a branch decreased from 63,800 to 15,000 during the same period. The total deposits increased 32.6 times between 1971 to 1991, compared to 7 times between 1951 to 1971. Despite an increase of rural branches, from 1,860 or 22% of the total number of branches in 1969 to 32,270 or 48%, only 32,270 out of 5 lakh (500,000) villages are covered by a scheduled bank. Since liberalization, the government has approved significant banking reforms. While some of these relate to nationalized banks (like encouraging mergers, reducing government interference and increasing profitability and competitiveness), other reforms have opened up the banking and insurance sectors to private and foreign players.

Regional Imbalance

One of the critical problems facing India's economy is the sharp and growing regional variations among India's different states and territories in terms of per capita income, poverty, availability of infrastructure and socio-economic development. The five-year plans have attempted to reduce regional disparities by encouraging industrial development in the interior regions, but industries still tend to concentrate around urban areas and port cities. After liberalization, the more advanced states are better placed to benefit from them, with infrastructure like well-developed ports, urbanization and an educated and skilled workforce which attract manufacturing and service sectors. The union and state governments of backward regions are trying to reduce the disparities by offering tax holidays, cheap land, etc., and focusing more on sectors like tourism, which although being geographically and historically determined, can become a source of growth and is faster to develop than other sectors.

External Trade and Investment: Global Trade Relations

India currently accounts for 1.2% of World trade as of 2006 according to the WTO. Until the liberalization of 1991, India was largely and intentionally isolated from the world markets, to protect its fledging economy and to achieve self-reliance. Foreign trade was subject to import tariffs, export taxes and quantitative restrictions, while foreign direct investment was restricted by upper-limit equity participation, restrictions on technology transfer, export obligations and government approvals; these approvals were needed for nearly 60% of new FDI in the industrial sector. The restrictions ensured that FDI averaged only around $ 200M annually between 1985 and 1991; a large percentage of the capital flows consisted of foreign aid, commercial borrowing and deposits of non-resident Indians.

India's exports were stagnant for the first 15 years after independence, due to the predominance of tea, jute and cotton manufactures, demand for which was generally inelastic. Imports in the same period consisted predominantly of machinery, equipment and raw materials, due to nascent industrialization. Since liberalization, the value of India's international trade has become more broad-based and has risen to Rs. 63,080,109 crores in 2003–04 from Rs. 1,250 crores in 1950–51. India's major trading partners are China, the US, the UAE, the UK, Japan and the EU. The exports during April 2007 were $ 12.31 billion up by 16% and import were $ 17.68 billion with an increase of 18.06% over the previous year.

India is a founding-member of General Agreement on Tariffs and Trade (GATT) since 1947 and its successor, the World Trade Organization. While participating actively in its general council meetings, India has been crucial in voicing the concerns of the developing world. For instance, India has continued its opposition to the inclusion of such matters as labour and environment issues and other *non-tariff barriers* into the WTO policies.

During the year 1950-51, the overall external trade of India reached Rs. 1214 crore. Since 1950, India is experiencing a persistent growth in external trade (external trade is the sum of total exports and imports, including re-exports). In fiscal year 2005-06, external trade in India touched Rs. 1085325 crore. During the period 2005-06, export of merchandise commodities in India touched US $ 103 billion (Rs. 454800 crore). In the previous year (2005-06), India's export volume of merchandise commodities reached Rs. 375340 crore with a growth rate of 21.17 %. India is showing this positive trend, despite a higher demand for capital goods. During the last four years of 10th Five Year Plan India is experiencing a sustained 20% growth rate and consequently India's contribution to global exports increased from 0.66% in 2002 to 0.9% in 2005. India's imports also exhibited a good result with an increase from Rs. 501065 crore in 2004-2005 to Rs. 630527 crore in 2005-06 (http://www.economywatch.com/indianeconomy/trade-scenario.html).

Balance of Payments

Since independence, India's balance of payments on its current account has been negative. Since liberalization in the 1990s (precipitated by a balance of payment crisis), India's exports have been consistently rising, covering 80.3% of its imports in 2002–03, up from 66.2% in 1990–91. Although India is still a net importer, since 1996–97, its overall balance of payments (i.e., including the capital account balance), has been positive, largely on account of increased foreign direct investment and deposits from non-resident Indians; until this time, the overall balance was only occasionally positive on account of external assistance and commercial borrowings. As a result, India's foreign currency reserves stood at $ 285 billion in 2008, which could be used in infrastructural development of the country if used effectively. India's reliance on external assistance and commercial borrowings has decreased since 1991–92, and since 2002–03, it has gradually been repaying these debts. Declining interest rates and reduced borrowings decreased India's debt service ratio to 4.5% in 2007. In India, External Commercial Borrowings (ECBs) are being permitted by the Government for providing an additional source of funds to Indian corporate. The Ministry of Finance monitors and regulates these borrowings (ECBs) through ECB policy guidelines.

India's balance of payments position has remained comfortable during 2007-08. The merchandise trade deficit, on balance of payments basis, increased from US $ 16.9 billion in April-June 2006 to US $ 21.6 billion in April-June 2007. Net surplus on the invisibles account exhibited buoyancy during the first quarter of 2007-08, led by exports of software, business services and private remittances, and continued to finance a large part (78.2 per cent) of the merchandise trade deficit. Despite large merchandise trade deficit, higher net invisible surplus contained the current account deficit (US $ 4.7 billion) during the first quarter of 2007-08 at broadly the same level (US $ 4.6 billion) as in the first quarter of 2006-07. The current account deficit was financed by capital flows that have remained large during 2007-08.

During 2007-08 (up to October 19, 2007), net inflows by FIIs amounted to US $ 21.2 billion as compared with outflows of US $ 933 million in the corresponding period of 2006-07. FDI inflows were US $ 6.6 billion during April-July 2007 (US $ 3.7 billion a year ago). On the other hand, non-resident Indian deposits registered net outflows amounting to US $ 148 million during April-July 2007 as against net inflows of US $ 1.6 billion during April-July

2006. During 2007-08 (April-December), growth of merchandise exports moderated, while imports posted a high growth rate. Non-oil imports registered high growth due to robust growth in capital goods. Oil imports registered a sharp deceleration from the strong growth recorded during the corresponding period of the previous year. Net surplus under invisibles (services, transfers and income taken together) exhibited buoyancy during the first quarter of 2007-08, showing an increase of 36.4 per cent. Exports of services and higher transfer receipts comprising mainly remittances remained the key drivers of the net surplus. Amongst services, both software and business services continued to record robust growth. Private transfers during April-June 2007 increased by over 45 per cent over the corresponding quarter of 2006-07 (http://www.indiaonestop.com/economy/balanceofpayments/economy-macro-balance%20of%20 payments.htm).

Foreign Direct Investment (FDI) in India

India's recently liberalized FDI policy (2005) allows up to a 100% FDI stake in ventures. Industrial policy reforms have substantially reduced industrial licensing requirements, removed restrictions on expansion and facilitated easy access to foreign technology and foreign direct investment FDI. The upward moving growth curve of the real-estate sector owes some credit to a booming economy and liberalized FDI regime. In March 2005, the government amended the rules to allow 100 per cent FDI in the construction business. This automatic route has been permitted in townships, housing, built-up infrastructure and construction development projects including housing, commercial premises, hotels, resorts, hospitals, educational institutions, recreational facilities, and city- and regional-level infrastructure (Economy Watch: http://www.economywatch.com/policywatch/fdi-policy.htm).

A number of changes were approved on the FDI policy to remove the caps in most sectors. Restrictions will be relaxed in sectors as diverse as civil aviation, construction development, industrial parks, petroleum and natural gas, commodity exchanges, credit-information services and mining. But this still leaves an unfinished agenda of permitting greater foreign investment in politically sensitive areas such as insurance and retailing. FDI inflows into India reached a record US $ 19.5 bn in fiscal year 2006/07, according to the government's Secretariat for Industrial Assistance. This was more than double the total of US $ 7.8 bn in the previous fiscal year. The FDI inflow for 2007-08 has been reported as $ 25 bn.

TRADE POLICY MAKING IN INDIA

Trade policy making in India has been perceived as confused, contradictory and ill-conceived. While several authors have attributed this to the need to deal with an internal clientele being used to a protectionist environment on the one hand and the advantages of openness in trade on the other, very few have recognised the changes in negotiating stances that India has been taking in recent years (Narayan, 2005).

BACKGROUND 1952 TO 1991

Any analysis of India's existing trade agreements as well as its position on important WTO issues has to bear in mind the economic and policy environment from which these strategies have evolved. On a historical perspective, the period 1947 to 1991 was an era of protectionism based on a development strategy anchored on the concept of large-scale import substitution. The Planning Commission in its first Five Year Plan (1951-1955/56) document had the following to say on matters concerning trade:

"The expansion of trade has, under our conditions, to be regarded as ancillary to agriculture and industrial development rather than as an initiating impulse in itself. In fact, in view of the urgent needs for investment in basic development, diversion of investment on any large scale to trade must be viewed as a misdirection of resources."

Trade and trade policy were not of primary importance and the latter would be determined automatically by whatever was needed to augment and make more favourable, conditions under which domestic industry and agriculture had to operate. Over the years, this gave rise to architecture of permits, permissions and licences to provide protection to domestic industry. At the same time, overseas investments, flow of technology and trade was strictly controlled by bureaucratic mechanisms, a complicated tariff structure and quantitative restrictions. The Chief Controller of Imports and Exports was a powerful figure that could decide the incentives for exporters, the concessions for importers and thus, alter terms of trade. It has been argued that the two outstanding features of the tariff regime were that the development of a large confusing system of exemptions and the lack of economic and/or welfare rationale in the tariff structure.

In the international arena, India has been a founder member of GATT since 1948. However, India's approach to trade issues in the multilateral context was conditioned by its political perception as a spokesperson of the developing world rather than as a negotiator for any trade or commodity bloc. During these years, India did not leverage its position to gain advantage in trade or improve relations for itself or for the developing countries it professed to represent.

By the 1970s, the Quantitative Restrictions regime and the licence/permit systems had developed into a very complex, costly, administrative system. A process of liberalisation that began in 1980 was slow and fragmented. This was also the period that saw strong debates between trade reformists and government views. Reformists argued that a semi-managed exchange rate should be used to manage trade flows. They also argued that as long as import of consumer manufactures remained banned, industrialists would have strong incentives to raise capital intensity of production, as this was the cheapest way to replace these imports. It was further argued that restricting the imports of capital goods and essential raw materials was inhibiting productivity and creating unnecessary economy wide inefficiencies.

LIBERALISATION PHASE 1991 TO 1996

India's balance of payment position worsened to crisis point in 1991. This led to a change in attitudes and policies. The Eighth Five Year Plan document (1992/3-1997/8) has the following comments on the 1991 crisis. The excerpt is long, but describes the situation better than any other source.

"The Balance of Payment situation has been continuously under strain for over almost a decade. During the Seventh Plan period the ratio of the current account deficit to GDP average 2.4 % – far above the figure of 1.6% projected for this period in the Plan documents. This deterioration in the Balance of Payments occurred despite robust growth in exports in the last three years. The already difficult Balance of Payments situation was accentuated in 1990-91 by a sharp rise in oil price and other effects of the Gulf War. With the access to commercial borrowings going down and the non-residents deposits showing no improvements, financing the current account deficits had become extremely difficult. Exceptional financing in the form of assistance from IMF, the World Bank and the Asian Development Bank had to be sought. While the immediate problems have been resolved to some extent, it is imperative that during the 8th Plan steps are taken to curb the fundamental weakness in Indian's Balance of Payments situation so that it does not cause serious disruption to the economy."

The events described above finally tipped opinions in favour of reform, and the policy environment became more amenable to change. Internal trade became freer as the licence or permit system loosened its control of economic activity and increasing emphasis was placed on the need for a more competitive export sector. Slowly but surely, the two biggest events in Indian economic history – the emergence of a market-based reform project and an incremental re-introduction to the global economy – began to take shape. But even in these circumstances, the policy for reform was not led by trade strategy. Rather, the effort was to liberalise licensing, reduce restrictions on production and investment, and open up financial markets, and correct fiscal, monetary and currency rate policies. Trade policy reform was slower in coming, and emerged more from restructuring of tariffs and import duties rather than from a clearly articulated vision. This was due to the focus on getting the financials of the country right in the first instance. India prided itself on never having been an external debt defaulter, and policy makers were concerned about keeping up this image. Trade policy, was thus, at best, only a secondary issue.

Consequently, India's stand in the Uruguay round of trade initiatives strongly suggests that reforms process did not immediately translate into a greater willingness to engage in trade negotiations. On the domestic front, the Uruguay

Round of negotiations seems to have played almost no role at all in moulding or accelerating the liberalization process. Initially India was unhappy with the invitation to new round in the first place and opposed the inclusion in the GATT agenda of services, intellectual property and trade related investments. A group of developing countries including Brazil got together into Like Minded Group, to articulate their objections. However, the position weakened soon and, in the end, India stood alone in its opposition to a new round. Thus, though India engaged in the preliminaries, its absence became conspicuous during the Round itself.

"In the view of unfriendly observers, India has been a pirate: it has made sporadic forays designed to throw negotiation into disarray...However, whether hostile or not, all observers agree that India has not taken any bold initiatives to give a new direction to the proceedings in any of the negotiation groups".

There appear to be three reasons for Delhi's reluctance to give anything away in the discussions. First, India was such a small player in international trade that any reciprocal tariff concessions would almost certainly result in a net welfare loss. Second, import substitution had resulted in such a wide variety of industries in India, some of them inefficient, that any reciprocal concessions to economies that a small industrial base would hurt India more than it would the other economy. Thirdly, several internal policies had a distorting effect on the export sector. For example the textile and garment sector was reserved for the small industries sector. The Indian textile industry thus was characterised by a wide array or technologies and production techniques. In short, market access negotiations in the UR were not attractive and India's attitude to other issues was well known. This made Indian unattractive bargainers, which resulted India being left alone or ignored.

At the same time, there were several forays that India made to get some advantage to itself. About the middle of the round of negotiations, with help from Argentina (Carlos Correa) and Brazil (Ricuperco), India participated in an organised pushback on TRIPS. It also took advantage of those situations, particularly in mode 4, where IT professionals could gain access. And even in the area of Agricultural strategies, India's effort to protect its producers and markets was largely successful. In some sense, its marginalisation in the main discussions provided ample time and space to campaign the cause of special and differential treatment and to concentrate on items of its defensive interests. By declining to aggressively seek concessions from its major trading partners, India had found a way to deflect attention from its major own protection levels, and thus effectively prevented UR negotiations from interfering with its reform process at home. This desire to minimise external pressures to liberalize, arising potentially from the WTO and bilateral agreements has remained an important feature of the Indian trade strategy.

CHANGES 1996 TO 2004

India saw two coalition Governments in 1996 and 1997, which were therefore the years of some political instability. The political environment in 1996 and 1997 put trade and reform issues on the backburner. It was only in 1998 that Parliament had occasion to examine the implications of the Marrakesh agreements. A Parliamentary Standing Committee of the Commerce ministry, headed by the eminent left wing economist and parliamentarian, Ashok Mitra—the Secretary General, FICCI, went into the implications of the agreement for the country. Membership of the committee spanned across the political spectrum, and contained several eminent figures including one who would be a future Minister for Commerce. The report of this committee was tabled in both houses of the Parliament in December 1998. The report starts with the leftist concern that the Marrakesh agreement calls upon the member countries to surrender some of their sovereign rights to the decisions and wishes of the WTO. It also expresses concern over the lack of transparency in the negotiations, absence of consensus building inside and outside Parliament, and the lack of consultation with the States. The Committee makes the following broad observations:

1. Developing countries in general have failed to extract any significant leverage out of the WTO system.
2. India failed to extract concessions pertaining to its interests in the agreement on IT products.
3. Global free trade over which WTO presides is quite some distance from the concept of fair and equitable international trade, and that the balance is tilted in favour of the developed world.
4. India should reiterate its reservation with reference to Articles 70.8 and 70.9 of the TRIPS in ministerial meetings.
5. There is need to introduce transparency in the government actions in respect of WTO related issues. There is also need to improve coordination between various ministries dealing with WTO issues.

The tabling of the report of the Committee resulted in several very important developments. First, in accepting the multilateral structure, the Committee committed the Parliament and the nation to the process of globalisation of trade. The acceptance of the framework of the WTO was a signal victory for the managers of Government policy, and from this point, there would be no turning back in engaging with the world on trade.

Second, Commerce Ministers from that day have been careful in reporting to Parliament a step-by-step account of the negotiations and the stance taken by the Government. There have been several Parliamentary questions, call attention notices and debates on issues involving the WTO. Industry associations and interest groups became active in trying to understand, and to debate, the positive as well as negative issues of the agreements. In short, we see the report as the beginning of a stage of transparency in negotiations that persists even today.

Third, administrative coordination between ministries improved. In the run up to the Seattle negotiations, issues and strategies were discussed not only within ministries, but also with industry and trade groups. The delegation to Seattle included a large delegation from industry that was consulted regularly. It also included Members of Parliament from the opposition. In Seattle, it was clear that India had put a lot of thought behind the negotiations.

EVOLUTION OF TRADE POLICY PROCESSES

Other changes were seen as well from 1999. The consultation process encompassed an active effort to communicate. During that year, over 30 seminars were held in different parts of the country. There were talk shows and media briefings. The Ministry of Industry conducted workshops in most states on the TRIPS agreement and the implications of the product patent regime. The debate on multilateralism became much more inclusive. The Ministry of Commerce and Industry lost some of its secretiveness.

Trade policy in India is primarily the responsibility of the Ministry of Commerce and Industry (MoCI) and it plays a major role in defining and setting policy. The MoCI occupies a privileged and exclusive space in Indian politics, and formulates policy largely in isolation earlier, that is, without consulting other government branches, often taking instructions directly from the Prime Minister. The MoCI also negotiates bilateral agreements. However, the consistency of domestic and external policies is addressed at the cabinet with the assistance of advisory committees. Inter-ministerial consultations always include the Ministry of Finance (MoF), and the Ministry of External Affairs (MoEA). Ministry of Textiles (MoT), Ministry of Agriculture (MoA) are involved in the process on specific agenda. A small group of ministers, consisting of the Ministers for Commerce, Finance, External Affairs, Agriculture, assists the Prime Minister at stages leading up to the ministerial. The cabinet is invariably consulted on negotiating stances and strategies, and the Prime Minister is kept informed daily on the progress of the negotiations. After each of these, the Commerce Minister briefs Parliament.

India's trade policy can be said to consist of three levels: (i) its multilateral negotiating position at the international level; (ii) the framing and operation of import-export policy at home ('traditional' trade agenda), and (iii) sectoral policy affected by trade agreements ('new' trade agenda). The first level deals mainly with trade agreements, WTO, Free Trade Agreements (FTAs), etc. The second one focuses on changes in the tariff level, duty drawback, subsidies, incentives for exporters and the concession for importers, etc, and in a sense is a support mechanism for its exporters to deal with uncertainties of the exposure to globalisation. The last level deals with emerging sectoral trade agreements such as General Agreements on Trade in Services (GATS). Though the structure remained the same, there was more interaction and more thinking on issues. That this resulted in greater maturity in handling the WTO agenda can be evidenced from several subsequent developments.

The negotiations and the failure of movement at Seattle demonstrated to the Indian public and legislators the weaknesses of a consensus bound arrangement, that lack of consensus could derail the transactions. Introduction of labour standards and Singapore issues was strongly resisted by several, India including and leading several groups. At Doha, the stand that India took, considered intransigent by all, won domestic legitimacy to the MOC in the process of negotiation, and the acceptance of Parliament and States. That India was an important client to be consulted, was evident subsequently from the discussions on agriculture, and way forward could be found only after several countries, including India, had agreed on the approach.

TRIPS

One of the most interesting examples of these has been the handling of the obligations under TRIPS. Product patents for pharmaceuticals and agro-chemicals had been done away with in the 1970 Indian Patents Act, which provided for process patenting enabling the patented drugs to be developed and marketed in India without fear of infringement action. A healthy indigenous industry, strong in chemistry, developed, and was opposing introduction of product patents that would affect its growth. Commitments under TRIPS required that product patents should be introduced by 1 January 2005, and that a system of Mailbox for applications started by 1997. This latter did not happen in time, and the US took India to the dispute settlement panel, where India lost the case as well as the subsequent appeal. The Parliamentary Committee report deals at length on this case, has strong language about the arm-twisting by the US, but finally recommends appropriate legislation, which happened in April 1999. In some sense, this served as a wake up call. The Ministry of Commerce and Industry engaged in looking at options for 2005; internally, there was a call to local industry for shaping up and getting prepared for competition; tariff concessions to Pharma industry including major income-tax deductions for research and development were announced; and India decided to take the debate international. At Cancun and at Doha India pressed for implementation of TRIPS clauses that provided for technology transfer and for compulsory licensing provisions. The South African case of drug delivery for AIDS patients came up as a strong argument against protecting multinational Pharma companies' interests. India took up at WHO and other forums, the inequities to poor nations of a high drug cost product patent regime. There was sufficient groundswell of support for this position in the country and the Patents Amendment Law was on the brink of not being approved, even as late as December 2004. The required legislation was put through as Ordnance on the last day of the year, and finally accepted by Parliament, after much protest by the left, a few months later. The Government, in this strategy, was able to cater to requirements of local industry, and to use the emotions of the critics to push through a legislation that is barely adequate to meet international standards. In fact, some of the clauses of the legislation can be said to be TRIPS non-compliant; but the US has decided against taking the matter up for dispute settlement at the WTO. In effect, not only has India been able to take advantage of all the flexibilities in TRIPS, but has also been able to push the boundaries further than would have been considered possible. In short, the strategy adopted for handling internal dissension, demands of local industry, and its international commitment, can be considered quite clever and effective.

AGRICULTURE

The agreement on agriculture is another area where there has been maturity in dealing with diverse, often, contradictory, requirements. At Marrakesh, agriculture was put on the backburner for later discussions, for it suited Japan to do so. This was convenient for India, and post 1999, in Doha and at Cancun, India has been able to spearhead the demand for reduction of subsidies by the developed nations. At Doha, inept handling by the US of the concerns of African countries gave India the policy space needed to sensitise internal interests. It was always clear that India would have to give up some subsidies in agriculture, in return for market access for its products. The framework agreement, already moulded in the earlier Government, was inked within months of the new Government assuming power. It provides for flexibility to choose sensitive products for continued protection, and for an adequate time frame to decide on the products that would have to be given up. The battle now is for the numbers: to persuade US, EU and Japan to give up more in real terms, not just in nominal terms. The policy makers and the political parties, already accept that agriculture subsidies will be reduced.

DEALING WITH WTO PROCESSES

India has also leveraged the structural advantages of the WTO agreements. At Doha, interventions by India accounted for the inclusion of Public Health concerns in TRIPS. Interventions in Geneva have been pointed and effective. Before the dispute settlement board, there has been considerable success, and some failures. India won the dispute on shrimp fishing against the US and against Turkey on textiles. India defended steel exports to US before adjudication proceedings in the US. Patents issued in the US for items in realm of public knowledge in India, like the medicinal uses of neem, were effectively contested.

India emerged a major user of the provisions of anti-dumping and safeguards between 1999 and 2002. Over 300 cases were taken up, and dozens of anti-dumping notifications issued, several against imports from China. In 2003, as a conscious decision to liberalise trade further, recourse to anti-dumping measures was reduced.

ITAT

The agreement on hardware for IT products was one that could have caused some concern. The agreement required India to reduce tariffs on inputs and products for the IT industry to zero by 2005. The agreed list contained several goods that were used by the entertainment industry, for the manufacture of televisions etc. with a large indigenous manufacturing pace, it was important to find a soft landing for these agreements. Work on this started as early as 2002. Tariffs for selected inputs were reduced, that would help local industry to add greater value. Tax concessions and excise duty concessions were announced, and simultaneously, the concept of countervailing duty on imported products, to the extent of local duties, was also introduced. Customs tariffs were reduced progressively by 5% every year, starting with input materials, and finally in the budget of 2005, all tariffs in the agreement were reduced to zero. The benefits for the computer and the telecom industry have been quite significant. At the negotiations, India has been able to take an effective position against those of the Singapore issues that it considers to be not in its interest. In the services sector, for example, issue of access for its professionals is being pushed effectively at various forums.

REGIONAL TRADE INITIATIVES

As a further proof of moving forward, India has, in the last few years engaged itself more openly in advocating regional trade. The initialling of the South Asian Free Trade Agreement may have more to do with politics than with trade, but the FTA with Thailand has opened up opportunities for bilateral trade that did not exist before. In the next few months, the Comprehensive Economic Cooperation Agreement with Singapore would be signed. India is engaging with ASEAN, China and even exploring possible bilateral sectoral arrangements with the US.

The confidence that has developed in trade policy making has had much to do with the performance of the economy since 2000 and the policy measures for liberalisation. Tariff reduction has been doggedly pursued year after year, and from average values of around 47% even five years ago, the country is at around 17% today. Peak rates are down to 15%, except for agricultural products. Exports as well as imports have been growing year on year, at an excess of 25%. Reforms in the financial sector, including dematerialising of stocks, an open architecture for trade, introduction of futures and derivatives trading and commodity futures, have made investments in India interesting and profitable. Inward remittances and the growth of the software industry afford opportunities for the services sector that can be exploited only through an open architecture for trading. The young middle class is an eager consumer of global products, and manufacturing facilities for televisions and mobile phones are getting constructed. Industry and consumers are realising that openness in trade is a good thing, and that inherent competitiveness is good for the economy and for the consumer.

WAY FORWARD

At this stage of its development India is looking forward to engage more progressive not only at the multilateral level but also at the bilateral and regional level. The integration of South Asian countries into a trading block may take some time to realize, but would be pursued at a pace that would be acceptable to all constituents. Participation in ASEAN trade is of importance and India would pursue this opportunity vigorously. Regional trade pacts with China and with Japan are in the area of consultation. Trade with China will continue to grow. At the multilateral level India's primary concern would be agriculture and services. On the issue of reduction of agricultural subsidies India would be seeking enlargement of its list of sensitive products and exert greater pressure on reduction in tariffs by the developed countries. Non-tariff barriers to agricultural trade including phyto-sanitary conditions, and environmental issues would be taken up strongly to increase market access of Indian agricultural products.

In the area of services India would seek to extend opportunities for cross border service. It would seek greater flexibility in movement of technically qualified personnel and greater opportunities for its skilled manpower to work in different countries. It would seek that the agenda for negotiations in the WTO is not enlarged to cover all of the Singapore issues. It would ensure that public health concerns are highlighted and opportunities for its pharmaceutical products to provide cheaper drug delivery to rest of the world. At the same time, it would continue the process of reform and liberalization by opening up FDI in more sectors including retail, real estate and infrastructure. Irrespective of the political composition of the country and succeeding governments, progress along the path will perhaps be always be a balance of management of internal constituents and external opportunities.

India's Economic Reforms: Challenges and Prospects

The remarkable growth transformation since 1980s was made possible by gradual unshackling of the economy and liberalizing many sectors of the economy. The policies of centralized planning, state intervention and trade protection were gradually replaced by liberalization of trade, industrial de-licensing, rationalization of taxes, and current account convertibility of the rupee and the easing of foreign investment norms. The process of reforms gained momentum in the 1990s in response to the balance of payment crisis that surfaced in 1990-91 (http://www.isasnus.org/jan28conference/papers/Paper%20-%20S%20Narayan%20-%20India's%20Economic%20Reforms.doc).

The economic reforms in 1990s had a significant impact on the Indian economy. At a generic level, the reforms played a facilitative role and created a competitive environment for Indian companies. Industrial delicensing provided flexibility to firms in investment decisions. This led to a surge in private investment. The share of private investment in total industrial investment went up from 56 per cent in the 1980's to almost 75 per cent by the end of 1990's. Trade reforms lowered tariffs and removed barriers on imports. This increased import competition for traded goods and also allowed firms to rationalize their input decisions. This enhanced the productivity of Indian manufacturing and permitted them to not only stay competitive in the new environment but also become globally competitive. Many sectors were also opened up for Foreign Direct Investment (FDI) and higher equity participation. The Indian firms were permitted to access international capital markets. Capital market reforms, together with the removal of restrictions on firms to tap capital markets, brought down entry barriers. Telecom sector benefited from the entry of private players and improved access to capital.

Challenges

Most of the reforms implemented did not require legislative changes and could be carried out through administrative fiat. These reforms, as we have seen, made India competitive and notched up the GDP growth rates. But the high growth achieved in the mid nineties could not be sustained, as the momentum of reforms petered out. The 'Second Generation Reforms' would involve crucial structural, legislative and administrative changes in major sectors and require wider consensus building, particularly due to coalition governments. The major second generation reforms are listed below:

- Power sector reforms. Implementation of the Electricity Act, 2003.
- Providing flexibility of entry and exit to firms. This would involve amendment of the labour laws.
- De-reservation of the small-scale sector. This will permit the exploitation of scale economies.
- Fiscal consolidation - keeping the deficits and debt under check. Encouraging FDI flows.
- Reducing tariff barriers to the international level.
- Reducing unemployment and alleviating poverty.
- Bringing up human development, etc.

Infrastructure Bottlenecks

Successive Indian governments have put considerable emphasis on infrastructure; there is a considerable gap between demand and available supply. India not only lags behind the developed countries but also its developing country peers with respect to infrastructure supply. The reforms that India has had so far, by and large, failed to address the critical issue of improving the supply and lowering the costs of non-tradable inputs like infrastructure which cannot be procured from just anywhere. All the infrastructure sectors need sufficient funds for expansion and maintenance of existing facilities. According to the tenth five-year plan the cumulative investment requirement during 2001-02 to 2005-06 has been estimated at Rs. 7500 billion. Of this, 40 per cent of the investment is required in the power sector, 11 per cent in telecom and around 14 per cent in roads and railways. With Rs. 1819.4 billion already invested during 2001-02 to 2002-03, there still exists a target of Rs. 5680.6 billion to be met in the next three years.

Power

There is a virtual consensus on the fact that the power situation in the country is not very sound. It would be no exaggeration to say that Indian industries pay inordinately high prices (when they do) for inordinately low quality power (when they receive it). This immediately imposes a severe constraint on production and would inevitably affect the investment decisions of new entrepreneurs. Despite a rapid expansion of generation (from 1300 megawatts in 1947 to 112,000 megawatts in 2003) and simultaneous growth in transmission and distribution, the sector has not been able to keep pace with the growth in demand, resulting in chronic shortage. Under-investment in the sector has stemmed largely from the poor financial health of the state electricity boards (SEBs) that have traditionally played the key role in generating and supplying power. This, in turn, is due to uneconomic tariffs for the agricultural sector, lower slabs for domestic consumption and high transmission and distribution (T&D) losses that are often due to theft and poor billing and collection efficiency.

Transport

The transport is another sector, which is not only relatively expensive by any mode but also because of infrastructural constraints hugely unpredictable in terms of transit time. One of the critical problems in Indian railways has been the decline in share of its internal resources, which has deteriorated its financial position. This decline is due to the loss of its freight market share to road transport, and the relatively higher freight rates in order to subsidise ordinary passenger segments. Besides this, there is a large speed differential between freight and passenger services that reduces the traffic throughput in the system. Also there is an urgent need for better port connectivity and better infrastructure for handling larger vessels. Focus on providing hinterland connection to various ports through railways and roads will reduce congestion levels at many ports. Though the average turnaround time for ships has improved, it is still lower compared to international standard. Rural road infrastructure is also very poor because of bad connectivity, which in turn takes longer time to travel and market agricultural products across the country.

Labour Laws and Labour Market Rigidities

The Indian labour market does not seem to function with a reasonable degree of efficiency. Subject to the constraints that all employees have certain rights that must be protected, market efficiency implies that workers will be hired or retrenched as the demand for their particular skills expands or contracts. However, in the present scenario, an employer, employing more than 100 workers, has to seek permission to lay off workers—from the state government. This effectively means permanent employment. For practical purposes, once a worker is hired his costs have to be borne by the employer whether he is contributing to revenues or not. In a risky business and uncertain market environment, and there is no question that the policy changes have all contributed to enhancing business risk, this is a huge deterrent to hiring and growth of firms beyond the limit. Labour market rigidities constrain large industrial investments and therefore preserving the extreme fragmentation of the industry and limiting its growth potential. The new government has explicitly ruled out the relaxation of job security regulations that would make the market more flexible. Elimination of job security regulations for the industrial sector would significantly impact the effective cost of labour which would make all labour-intensive manufacturing far more competitive.

Reservation for Small-Scale Industry (SSI)

The policy of reservation of commodities for production by the small-scale sector is another area. It supports and sustains weak and inefficient producers, it hinders the assimilation of technology, it perpetuates sub-optimal scales of production. Reservation of small scale production constrains large industrial investments and therefore preserving the extreme fragmentation of the industry and limiting its growth potential. Though exemptions based on export obligations which are by all accounts hardly monitored are one way in which back-door entry by large producers into the manufacture of reserved products is affected, this back door entry is less competitive than any front door entry.

Despite many persuasive arguments to the contrary, particularly the fact that most of the commodities, which are reserved, are freely importable, the government has not been able to terminate this policy. Though there is some back-door liberalization, with a few products being de-reserved every now and then, for many products, this is a binding constraint on scale of operations, which typically means lower quality, use of inferior materials and localized marketing. De-reservation would allow producers of these to build up to scales for national and global competitiveness, which would give a huge boost to the manufacturing sector as a whole, because of linkages.

Fiscal Consolidation

Government finances remain an area of major weakness. Some reforms in this area have already been initiated, however, results are awaited. The government is facing a severe resource constraint, which prevents it from making the kinds of investments - both in physical and social infrastructure - that are consistent with its growth and human development objectives. This has resulted in a legislative mandate to curb government consumption expenditure, the Fiscal Responsibility and Budget Management Act of 2002, which should compel the government to re-orient both the tax and expenditure systems towards growth and income-enhancing activities.

Lower FDI Flow

India has experienced lower FDI inflows in relation to the size of the economy. This contrast is sharp in comparison to China and other East Asian economies. The key deterrents to FDI in India are bureaucratic bottlenecks, slow reforms and poor infrastructure. But market size and potential, labour force skills, and competitive wages are the key advantages that India has. However, India has not been able to leverage its competitive advantage, due to a lack of concerted effort. The challenge is that India has to remove the above impediments in order to attract more FDI in the country.

Tariff Barriers

India earlier had one of the most restrictive trade regimes. Not only were there physical barriers to trade (through quotas), tariff rates also were very high. As a result of tariff reforms, import-weighted average tariff came down from a high of around 56 per cent in 1990 to around 28 per cent in 2001 for all products put together. According to World Development Indicators, the reduction in tariffs for manufactured products was much sharper from about 71 per cent in 1990 to 29 per cent in 2001. Despite these reductions, India's tariff rates are among the highest in the South and East Asian countries.

Unemployment and Poverty

Currently around 60 per cent of the workforce is employed in agriculture, about 17 per cent in industry and while the rest in services. It is difficult to expect services to absorb such a large overhang from agriculture - industry must also contribute. The government has drastically reduced its intake of people; the private sector just does not seem inclined to take up the slack for the reasons mentioned earlier. The slow growth in employment and the rising number of young people looking for jobs is another critical issue for any government wishing to be re-elected. Reforms in labour markets that promote employment and the development of social security systems will allow the economy to significantly increase its utilization of its most abundant resource - unskilled and semiskilled labour.

Reduction of poverty is another area of challenge. There is a considerable controversy about the impact of growth and reforms on poverty and income distribution. According to official household surveys, the proportion of population below the poverty line fell from around 51 per cent in 1978 to 36 per cent in

1994 and further to around 26 per cent in 2000. However, various researchers have adjusted and corrected the methods to show either greater or lesser poverty reduction. Though the last decade has seen a substantial reduction in the absolute incidence of poverty but India has to go a long way to alleviate poverty.

Human Development

There has been a continuous improvement in the Human Development Index since 1980s. At the national level, the index has improved by nearly 26 per cent in the eighties and by another 24 per cent in the nineties. Despite improvement in human development parameters in the past two decades, India ranks 127th in the world, compares very unfavorably with other countries.

Political Instability

From an economic policy perspective, despite the many changes in the composition of the government, the overall direction of these reforms did not change fundamentally. Apprehensions were expressed that the reforms process of the present UPA government would be derailed because of the fragility of the new coalition (UPA), with Congress at the helm of affairs being critically dependent on outside support by Left. Though the underlying reformist tendencies of the economic administrators are still active and their agenda is being pursued, the pace of reforms has slowed down compared to the early 1990's. Public opposition from the Left is a regular phenomenon and one of the reasons for the slow pace of reforms. There are persistent demands for obtaining consensus on economic reforms, particularly those which are likely to impose high short-term costs on entrenched political interests. Public sector jobs, subsidies on various commodities and services and so on are prominent examples of the pressures that any government has to contend with. This is in sharp contrast to China, where the issue of consensus-building does not arise and the state is able to push reforms in the desired direction at a faster pace.

India — A Diversified Global Manufacturing Hub

In comparison with its Asian peers, manufacturing in India makes a relatively lower contribution to the GDP. The contrast is particularly sharp in relation to China where the share of the manufacturing sector in overall GDP was around 36 per cent in 2002, compared with a mere 16 per cent in India (Gupta, 2004).

It is general understanding that the major barriers to India's emergence as a diversified global manufacturing centre, a role, which is entirely compatible with its varied resource endowments - labour, natural resources and agricultural products - are in the policy realm. The two most important of these are infrastructure and labour market inflexibility. Power is a sector that impacts on the prospects of virtually all manufacturing activity, so the likelihood that India will develop as a global manufacturing hub, depends critically on the growth of the power sector. Dealing with both these issues may not in and of itself unleash a boom in manufacturing activity; however, it is unlikely that anything will happen in this sector unless these two problems are squarely dealt with.

Prospects

Future prospects for the Indian economy depend on a number of factors ranging from the pace of economic reforms to the performance of the global economy. India has a number of inherent advantages, and reforms can translate these advantages into high growth rates in the long run. Population and income demographics play a critical role in the production process as well as from the consumption side.

Rising Level of Per Capita Income

Over the past decade, per capita incomes have risen at the faster pace in the country's history due to higher GDP growth and falling birth rates. With the income growth fast outpacing population growth, nominal per capita income has grown by 3.6 times between 1990-91 and 2002-03. The present level of per capita income may still be a very low level by international standards, but it is an impressive change and this has had very interesting effects on consumer behaviour.

Growing Middle Class

The survey conducted by the National Council of Applied Economic Research (NCAER) showed that middle class segment has grown by 2.5 times between 1995-96 and 2001-02. This survey also mentions that the middle class is expected to show a significant bulge in future. The middle class is defined as households with income between Rs. 2,00,000 and 10,000,00. Bulging middle class together with rising income will give a thrust to consumption in future.

Larger Number of Working Population and Reducing Dependency

The age dependency ratio in India was expected to show a significant decline. Dependency ratio is defined as the ratio of non-working population (< 15 years and > 64 years) to working population (15-64) years. India will have an advantage of lowest dependency ratio. Low dependency ratios promote consumption of goods and services, due to lower burden of caring for the aged and bringing up children. Higher population in the working age group implies greater supply of labour, and an increasing concentration of population in higher income group translates into higher consumption levels.

India's current share of working population in total population is low, but the size of population puts India in the second spot after China in terms of number of people in the working age. Among comparator countries, the share of working population to total population will decline in China, Thailand, Brazil and Russia. India, Malaysia and Philippines will have larger and increasing share of working population in the years to come. India, with a faster rate of increase, will emerge as a major source of labour supply, due to the sheer size of its population. The rising share of working population is both an opportunity as well as a challenge. The opportunity is in terms of availability of human capital and challenge is in provision of productive employment to the bulging working population. Also, much will depend upon the education levels and skill sets of the working population.

Availability of Qualified Manpower

There has been a steady improvement in the literacy rate from around 52 per cent in 1991 to around 65 per cent in 2001. A very significant advantage that India has is the high pool of educated and technical staff together with low wage rates. As India's 60 per cent of the labour force is in agriculture, India will also remain a key supplier of low skill labour in times to come.

In terms of skill sets and availability of qualified labour, India is quite well placed. India ranks very high in terms of availability of skilled labour in general and engineers in particular. This fact is brought out by the Global Competitiveness Report's finding, which puts India in the third place in the availability of scientists and engineers. India, however, does not rank very high in the quality of education system. It ranks 36 in terms of quality of overall education among the 102 countries surveyed in the Global Competitiveness Report (http://www.kfuriconsulting.com/GlobalCompetitive.pdf).

Certain Niche Areas where India can make Competitive Advantage

Economic liberalization and increased globalization has effectively changed the Indian industrial landscape. Increased opportunities, greater access to resources and knowledge and the forces of competition have transformed the Indian industrial landscape quite dramatically. India currently is a service hub of the world where it enjoys dominant position in a variety of service and knowledge-based activities.

There is no question that India has potential comparative advantage in many manufacturing activities. First there is the substantial natural resource endowment. Secondly there is the oft-repeated abundance of relatively low-cost labour, much of which are endowed with craft skills emerging from the tradition of occupational castes. India has a competitive advantage in some sectors like pharma, auto and auto ancillaries, textiles, gems and jewellery, etc.

Although India's growth performance does not match that of other fast growing East Asian countries and China, in recent years India has emerged as one of the fastest growing economies not only in the region but also in the world. It is expected that India would be a high performer in the years to come. Some studies attribute the Indian reforms introduced in the early 1990s to the balance of payments crisis in 1991 when India was left with just two weeks' import cover (Bhaumik *et al.,* 2002). The 1991 crisis could have acted as a catalyst for the reforms. But the entire reform process cannot be attributed to the crisis. India has been deregulating its economy since the year 1985 in response to the changes in the international environment discussed in the previous section. Factors like the success of the Chinese and East Asian liberalization measures, Uruguay round of negotiations that started in 1986 and that was nearing completion in the early 1990s, the collapse of the Berlin wall in 1989, the turmoil in the erstwhile Soviet Union and the ongoing IT revolution contributed significantly to the introduction of liberalization measures in India and other Developing Economies (DEs). In fact most countries went in for liberalization in the 1990s and India was no exception.

Nevertheless, the measures introduced in the year 1991 were not on par with the earlier reform measures. The year 1991 was a landmark or a watershed. A statement on Industrial Policy was introduced in July 1991 that aimed at letting entrepreneurs make investment decisions on the basis of their own commercial judgement. Under the industrial license and permit regime this freedom was not given to entrepreneurs. The statement also declared that the role of the government would be changed from one of only exercising control to that of providing help and guidance by making essential procedures fully transparent and by eliminating delays. This statement is a major departure – a paradigm shift – from the earlier role of the government. Towards this objective the government introduced a series of "measures to unshackle the Indian industrial economy from the cobwebs of unnecessary bureaucratic control" (Industrial Policy Statement 1991, Page 9). They covered several areas – industrial licensing policy, foreign investment, foreign technology agreements, public sector and the MRTP Act. These decisions include the abolishing of industrial licensing for all projects except for a short list of industries attached in Annexure II; liberalization of the granting of import licences for capital goods; removal of the requirement of industrial approvals for locating industries in cities with less than one million population; approval of FDI up to 51 per cent in priority industries and for trading companies; automatic approval for foreign technology agreements in high priority industries subject to lump-sum payments being less than one crore rupees and royalty being less than 5% for domestic sales and 8% for exports; freedom to hire foreign experts; and the amendment of the MRTP Act to remove the threshold limit of assets of MRTP companies and dominant undertakings. In addition, import duties have drastically come down over the years. The peak tariff in 1991-92 (excluding high tariff items like alcohol, agricultural products and automobiles) was 150 per cent and it has come down to 20 per cent in 2003-04.

In addition to these measures, the government introduced a fiscal squeeze during 1991-92 and 1992-93 accompanied by exchange rate depreciation. In July 1991 the rupee was valued by 19 per cent and the depreciation process continued. This resulted in a virtual 40 per cent devaluation in nominal terms and 25 per cent in real terms over 1991–1993 (Joshi and Little, 1996). Two important intentions of the 1991 Industrial Policy Statement, namely, transparency in enforcement of rules and regulations and elimination of delays continue to remain important even now as seen from the policy statements of the Prime Minister and Finance Minister in 2004.

During the years 2000 and 2001, India announced important policy initiatives relating to Science and Technology and Information Technology. These policy statements and enactments will have far reaching effects on Indian industry's competitive advantages.

Indian Science and Technology Policy

India announced a new Science and Technology policy Statement on October 29, 2001 with the objective of revitalizing the scientific enterprises in the country and raising the standards of the science and technology (S&T) institutions in India in order to meet the challenges of the technologically sophisticated world. The government discovered that the university system was under strain and the science departments had difficulty in attracting good students and faculty. Most good students opted for business management and other related areas that offered better avenues for employment. Another important component of the policy is to enhance the linkages between the Indian national laboratories and teaching institutions and universities. This will be mutually beneficial to all. Several colleges face a resource crunch and consequently are unable to provide high quality laboratory facilities to their students and teachers. By teaming up with better equipped national laboratories they would be able to do better research. Scientists from the national laboratories will also benefit by interacting with young and energetic students. Furthermore, to promote innovative activities the policy requires every technical department of the government to earmark a part of its budget for this purpose.

The policy also encourages the development of India's indigenous resources by enhancing research on traditional medicine and by applying globally acceptable norms of validation and standardization. A purposeful programme to enhance the Indian share of the herbal medicine market has been initiated. In this context an IPR (intellectual property rights) system to protect innovations arising out of traditional knowledge has been evolved and incorporated in the law.

International Collaborations

The Industrial Policy of India encourages international collaborative programmes between academic institutions and national laboratories in India and their counterparts in all parts of the world. It lays special emphasis on collaborations with developing countries of the South with whom India shares many common problems. The document lists several policy objectives. They include greatest autonomy for R&D institutions and science laboratories, interaction between industry and public institutions in science and technology and international collaborations.

IT Act, 2000 and the Booming Software Industry

The enactment of the IT Act of 2000 is an important landmark in India's entry to e-commerce and internet-based transactions. The Act provides legal recognition for transactions carried out by means of electronic data interchange and other means of electronic communications, like, e-commerce, which involve the use of alternatives to paper-based methods of communication and storage of information. The Act facilitates electronic filing of documents with government agencies. In particular the Act provides for authentication of electronic records by affixing digital signatures. It allows the use of asymmetric crypto systems and makes provisions for verifying electronic records.

The IT Act 2000 also ushers in Electronic Governance by according legal recognition to electronic records and digital signatures. The law provides for the filing of any form, application or document, the issue of licence or permit and the receipt or payment of money using electronic records and digital signatures. Furthermore, it also makes provision for the recognition of foreign certifying authorities. Thus the digital signatures certified by these authorities will be valid as per the Act. In other words the Act puts the necessary legal framework in place for Indians to participate and benefit from the IT and internet revolution. This section has mainly presented the important reforms introduced since 1990. The impact of these reforms and the need for further reforms will be discussed later at the appropriate places.

FDI Inflows: India and the East-Asian Economy

The nature and character of FDI flows, particularly in the WTO regime, is likely to be very different from the flow during the pre-WTO regime. In the earlier regime one of the important reasons for FDI inflows was to jump tariffs and exploit the host country markets (Caves, 1996 and Dunning, 1993). In some of the earlier studies, effective rates of protection emerged as the most significant variable explaining FDI inflows (Lall and Siddharthan, 1982). FDI inflows are mainly analyzed using the Ownership – Location – Internalization (OLI) paradigm, which states that MNEs enjoy ownership advantages in terms of technology, brand names and other intangible assets and they prefer to exploit them in a foreign location if internalization advantages are large. That is, ownership advantages could be exploited in three ways: (1) by producing goods in the home country and exporting them to third countries, (2) licensing their technology and brand names to third parties, and (3) investing in foreign locations (FDI) and producing the goods in the host country.

The decision to produce goods in a third country instead of exporting to that country or licensing their intangible assets to their partners will depend on internalization advantages and the international trading environment. Here, one of the important motives for FDI happens to be host market exploitation. The WTO regime has drastically altered the international trading environment. With the reduction of tariffs and abolition of quantitative restrictions, exports have emerged as a viable option to market seeking FDI. Furthermore, the intellectual property regime has made licensing of technology less risky (UNCTAD, 2006).

Under these changed circumstances, the importance of host market seeking FDI will decline. At present, partly due to the WTO regulations and partly due to the vast changes in the communications and information technology, MNEs are deciding on efficiency seeking investments and are using the host country as a platform to export to third countries. This change in the MNEs' strategy has led to some notable consequences. In the case of host country market exploiting FDI, the MNEs carried out most of their designing and innovative R&D in the home country. Very little R&D was performed in the host countries and where it was performed, it was of an adaptive type intended to modify the product or process to suit the resource conditions or tastes and preferences of the host country. By and large, the MNEs invested abroad to exploit the advantages that they possessed in their home. Unlike the earlier investments, some of the current investments are by way of technology augmenting investments aimed at exploiting the host country resource (including knowledge base and human skills) advantages (Kumar, 1998, 2000, 2002; Kumar and Siddharthan, 1997; Belderbos, 2001; Florida, 1997; Kuemmerle, 1999; Siddharthan and Rajan, 2002). Consequently, MNEs will locate plants in third countries because it is more efficient to produce in that location. The determinants of efficiency seeking FDI are very different from those of market seeking FDI.

The WTO regime will also affect the investment behaviour of domestic firms (both large and medium sized). In the global regime, Indian firms may not invest in India if it is not efficient to produce that product in India. They may prefer to produce it in China, Malaysia or Thailand and import it into India. Already there is some evidence of this happening from newspaper and media reports. Therefore, it is not enough to study the changes in the Indian business environment over the years and analyze their changing trends. It is important to study the Indian business and investment environment in relation to India's main competitors in our neighborhood like China, Malaysia, Thailand and other ASEAN countries.

The share of the DEs in the FDI inflows was more than 30 per cent during the first half of the 1980s. They sharply declined in the second half of the 1980s and the DEs' share came down to about 15 per cent during 1989. It started increasing after that and reached over 30 per cent only during 1992. During 1997 it reached its peak of about 40 per cent and started declining again. Currently the DEs' share in FDI inflows is about 25 per cent. It turns out that the MNEs are mutual invaders and they prefer to invest in high income developed countries that are also home countries of MNEs rather than investing in DEs. The share of DEs is modest and FDI to DEs also flows to relatively high growth countries like China and East Asian countries. Likewise technology has also been flowing into technology rich countries (Siddharthan and Rajan, 2002). Developed countries make more than 85 per cent of the royalty payments and DEs make very little technology payments.

Economic Survey of India-2007

India's key challenges to sustaining high growth

Over the past two decades, India has moved away from its former dirigiste model and become a market-based economy. This process started in the mid 1980s and gathered substantial momentum at the beginning of the 1990s. Direct tax rates were significantly reduced, pervasive government licensing of industrial activity was almost eliminated, and restrictions on investment by large companies were eased. Furthermore, financial markets were reformed, with banks restored to health, entry barriers lowered, equity markets transformed and new supervisory bodies introduced. The process of reform has continued in this decade with a further opening of the economy to competition. The number of industries reserved for very small firms has been significantly reduced, and foreign suppliers have been encouraged to enter the market by a progressive lowering of tariffs to an average of 10% in 2007. The rules governing foreign direct investment have been markedly eased, notably in the manufacturing sector. Last but not least, fiscal discipline has been improved by the passage of fiscal responsibility laws for the central government and all but three of the 28 state governments (Economic Survey of India, 2007).

These reforms have had a major beneficial impact on the economy. By 2006, the average share of imports and exports in GDP had risen to 24%, up from 6% in 1985. Inflows of foreign direct investment increased to 2% of GDP from less than 0.1% of GDP in 1990, with outflows of foreign direct investment picking up substantially at the end of 2006. The combined fiscal deficit of central and state governments has been reduced from 10% of GDP in 2002 to just over 6% of GDP by 2006, with the ratio of debt to GDP falling from 82% in 2004 to 75% by March 2007. There has been a massive increase in output, with the potential growth rate of the economy estimated to be around 8½ per cent per year in 2006. GDP per capita is now rising by 7½ per cent annually, a rate that leads to its doubling in a decade. This contrasts to annual growth of GDP per capita of just 1¼ per cent in the three decades from 1950 to 1980. Faster growth has resulted in India becoming the third largest economy in the world (after the United States and China and just ahead of Japan) in 2006, when measured at purchasing power parities, accounting for nearly 7% of world GDP. Moreover, with increased openness and rapid growth in exports of merchandise and IT related services, its share in world trade in goods and services had risen to slightly over one per cent in 2005, when measured at market exchange rates.

Past reforms have brought higher growth in GDP per capita.

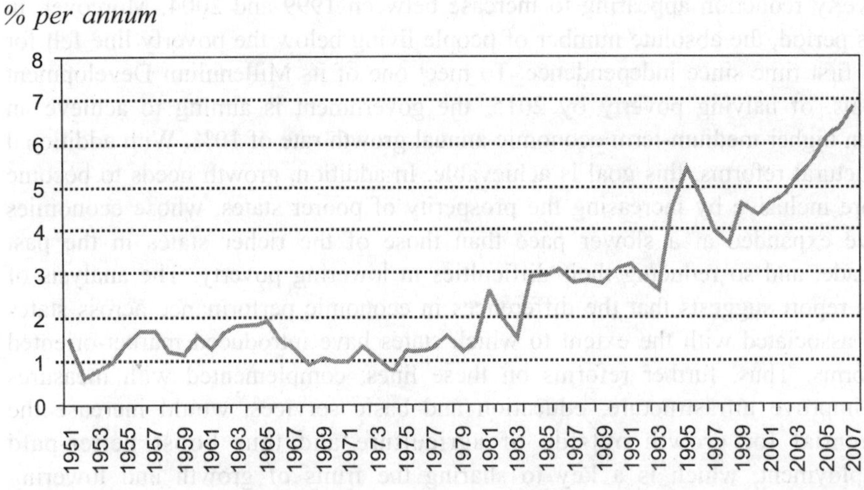

The current expansion, which started in 2003, has not led to an imbalance between supply and demand, despite annual GDP growth reaching 9% in 2006. The non-agricultural GDP deflator, a broad measure of prices, has shown little tendency to accelerate and increased by less than 5% year on year in 2006. Some measures of inflation have moved above the authorities' goal of keeping the annual inflation rate in the range of 5-5½ per cent, reflecting sharp increases for food in other commodity prices. However, the monetary authorities are acting to ensure that such increases do not become entrenched and announced, in April 2007, that monetary policy will aim at achieving an inflation rate of 4-4½ per cent per year over the medium term. In this respect, they are being helped by the appreciation of the currency. The current account balance has moved into a deficit, but only similar in relation to GDP to that of the second half of the 1990s and, moreover, is being financed by foreign direct investment. Such a benign outcome has been helped by increased domestic saving including the recent fiscal consolidation.

The Fiscal reforms enacted in 2004 have permitted a significant reduction in the extent to which the government pre-empts national savings to finance consumption. The fiscal deficit, which has been reduced substantially, is on track to meet the legislated target of a combined central and state government fiscal deficit of 6% of GDP by fiscal year 2008. Already, the reduction in government dis-saving contributed almost half of the increase in the net national saving rate between 2001 and 2005, which has now reached almost 22% of GDP, with the gross saving rate being some ten percentage points higher at 32%. Faster economic growth will require that a greater share of output be devoted to investment for both business expansion and infrastructure. This implies the need to raise savings further by continuing the fiscal consolidation strategy. At the same time, it is necessary to improve the quality of spending.

Increased growth since the mid 1980s has helped to substantially reduce the national poverty rate to 22% of the population in 2004, with the speed of poverty reduction appearing to increase between 1999 and 2004. Moreover, in this period, the absolute number of people living below the poverty line fell for the first time since independence. To meet one of its Millennium Development Goals, of halving poverty by 2015, the government is aiming to achieve an even higher medium-term economic annual growth rate of 10%. With additional structural reforms, this goal is achievable. In addition, growth needs to become more inclusive by increasing the prosperity of poorer states, whose economies have expanded at a slower pace than those of the richer states in the past decade, and so reducing their difficulties in lowering poverty. The analysis of this report suggests that the differences in economic performance across states are associated with the extent to which states have introduced market-oriented reforms. Thus, further reforms on these lines, complemented with measures to improve infrastructure, education and basic services, would increase the potential for growth outside of agriculture and thus boost better-paid employment, which is a key to sharing the fruits of growth and lowering poverty.

Key proprieties for future reforms

The next round of reforms needs to focus on a number of key areas that have the potential to further boost economic growth, while ensuring that the expansion becomes more inclusive. Recent reforms have made a number of sectors of the economy more dynamic, especially in the service sector. However, there are still a number of barriers to growth in product, labour and financial markets, and the provision of infrastructure, where reform is needed both at the central and state levels. While the optimal policy would be to remove these bottlenecks across the country, the creation of Special Economic Zones that aim to reduce a number of these barriers locally might demonstrate the benefits of such reforms and so act as a catalyst for more generalized change, but care needs to be taken as to the extent of tax concessions that are granted. Furthermore, taxation policies need to be reformed in order to create a truly national market and improve incentives and release resources for reducing bottlenecks in infrastructure, which are a key constraint on growth. In addition, education needs to be delivered more efficiently so as to improve human capital formation. There are undoubtedly further challenges facing the economy, but this report focuses on these areas which are a key to boosting growth further.

Market-oriented reforms – which started in the mid 1980s and were followed by more fundamental reforms since the early 1990s and renewed in the 2000s – have lifted the Indian economy on to a significantly higher growth path, helping to reduce poverty. This success should encourage policymakers to continue with this strategy by, in particular: further reducing restrictions in labour and product markets; improving infrastructure, human capital formation and general public services; and further reducing tax distortions. Speeding up such reforms would help the government to achieve its objective of further raising India's sustainable growth path and at the same time make growth more inclusive.

The Indian economy has undergone a remarkable transformation over the past two decades. The growth rate of average incomes has increased from 1¼ per cent prior to 1980 to 7% by 2006. Between 1999 and 2004, the absolute number of people living under the national poverty line has fallen for the first time since Independence. Faster growth has been brought about by a paradigm shift in economic polices that has opened the economy to foreign trade and markedly reduced direct tax rates and government influence over most investment decisions. Despite this favorable performance, there is still much room for improving policy settings to further raise growth potential. This chapter first looks at India's past reforms and the main sources of its improved growth performance and then identifies a number of key challenges that could make growth faster, more sustainable and more even across the country: (i) making goods and service markets more competitive; (ii) enhancing employment in the formal sector through broad-ranging labour market reforms; (iii) further liberalizing the banking sector; (iv) improving public finances to achieve more rapid growth through a more ambitious fiscal consolidation, reducing subsidies and further reducing tax distortions; (v) improving infrastructure and facilitating urbanization by involving private players more intensely; and (vi) upgrading the quality of educational outcomes through institutional reforms.

India's growth pattern and obstacles to higher growth

India's growth performance has improved significantly over the past 20 years, but it has been uneven across industries and states. While some service industries, notably the information and communications technology (ICT) sector, have become highly competitive in world markets – yielding considerable gains for employees and investors – manufacturing industries have lagged and improved their performance only recently. A divergence in performance has taken place, with firms in those states and sectors with the best institutions gaining, and those in the more tightly regulated states and sectors falling further behind. As a result, the competitive landscape is uneven across sectors and states and a high degree of concentration continues in different industries. While this is partly the result of the legacy of licensing, change has been politically difficult, making it harder for the manufacturing sector than for the service sector to expand. The need for further institutional reforms is urgent, focusing on product and labour market regulations at the central and state levels.

Reforming India's product and service markets

The degree of competition in product markets has been found to be an important determinant of economic growth in both developed and developing countries. This chapter uses the OECD's indicators of product market regulation to assess the extent to which the regulatory environment in India is supportive of competition in markets for goods and services. The results indicate that although liberalization has improved the regulatory environment to international best practices in some areas, the overall level of product market regulation is still relatively restrictive. In addition, estimating the product market regulation indicators for 21 Indian states shows that the relatively more liberal states have higher labour productivity, attract more foreign direct investment, and have a larger share of employment in the private formal sector in comparison to the relatively more restrictive states. The chapter goes on to review various aspects of India's product market regulation and suggests a number of policy initiatives that would improve the degree to which competitive market forces are able to operate.

Improving the performance of the labour market

Over the past decade, labour market outcomes have improved in India, with net employment rising markedly for the economy as a whole. However, these gains have arisen primarily in the unorganized and informal sectors of the economy, where productivity and wages are generally much lower than in the formal organized sector. It is only India's organized sector that is subject to labour market regulation, and here employment has fallen. The role of employment protection legislation in affecting employment outcomes is controversial both in the OECD area and in India. This chapter looks at the impact of employment protection legislation and related regulation on the dynamics of employment in the organized sector of the economy, using newly constructed measures of national regulation and state labour reforms. We find that while reforms have taken some of the bite out of core labour laws, more comprehensive reforms are needed to address the distortions that have emerged.

Reforming the financial system

This section examines the performance of India's financial sector and compares its structure to that of other emerging economies. The financial sector went through a period of considerable re-organization during the last 15 years. New regulators were introduced for all sectors of the market and this has boosted the development of highly efficient equity and commodity markets. The health of the banking sector has also improved and competition within the sector has increased. Nonetheless, costs remain high in a sector that is still dominated by public sector banks. The corporate bond market is still underdeveloped, as is the foreign exchange market. Considerable scope exists for improving efficiency in the financial sector by opening it to more foreign direct investment and removing a number of regulatory constraints that impede the development of a full set of financial markets.

Improving the fiscal system

This chapter examines areas of government spending, taxation and fiscal federalism where further reforms are desirable to reduce economic distortions and improve the provision of public services. As to government spending, it finds that a large share is used to subsidise commercial undertakings, agriculture and food distribution and that there is much room to improve the quality of spending and target it better to reduce poverty. On taxes, which have undergone major reforms since the early 1990s, it points to the large number of loopholes and suggests that a broadening of the tax bases would allow further reductions in tax rates and make the system simpler and more efficient. Reforms of indirect taxes should focus on creating a common market within India so that goods can move between states without border controls. India's federal structure has led to a well-developed system of tax-sharing and transfers, both through constitutionally empowered bodies and delivered through the annual budget. Overall, this transfer system has worked well; moving resources towards the poorest states, but the system has become very complex and, in the past, weakened fiscal discipline. Furthermore, it has not been able to create an effective local government system; this would be important for improving accountability and responsiveness to citizens' needs as three-quarters of the population live in states with over 50 million inhabitants.

Removing infrastructure bottlenecks

With high rates of economic growth and low public sector investment, India's infrastructure is in short supply and potentially a major constraint on future growth. To alleviate fiscal constraints and improve infrastructure productivity, the government is turning increasingly to the private sector to finance and run infrastructure projects. In some infrastructure sectors in which the regulatory environment is conducive to private sector involvement, performance has improved significantly. However, although infrastructure policy is moving in the right direction in some sectors, there are still a number of ways in which the regulatory environment could be improved further. This chapter outlines a range of policy initiatives that would increase private sector participation and improve infrastructure service delivery to international standards. It begins by discussing the role of public-private partnerships in the provision of infrastructure services before moving on to review the regulatory environment in a number of infrastructure sectors with a focus on regulatory settings that constrain competition.

Improving human capital formation

The provision of high-quality education and health care to all of the population is considered a core element of public policy in most countries. In India, the government is active in both education and health but the private sector also plays an important role, notably for health, and to a lesser extent in education. At present, the quality and quantity of the outputs from education, and also from public health care, are holding back the process of economic development. Steps are being taken to draw more children into primary education and the chapter considers ways to keep children in school. The chapter also considers institutional changes that may help to improve the performance of the educational system and so boost human capital formation.

INDIAN FOREIGN TRADE POLICY: 2004-09

On August 31, 2004 the Government spelt out a bold vision to double India's share in world trade within five years, and to focus on the generation of additional employment in the process. The current trade figures indicate that India is not only on the right path but approaching the goal at an accelerated pace (http://www.helplinelaw.com/docs/foreign-trade-polocy/sup-05.php).

India to be a major gainer from emerging global trends

In the fast changing international trading scenario, outsourcing of manufacturing activities in the skill intensive sectors has become an essential business strategy for the developed countries. India with its large skilled work force, growing domestic market, raw material availability and the emergence of a mature supply base is set to gain enormously from this trend since the Indian advantage goes well beyond the low wage rates. While there is no doubt that knowledge-based industries such as information technology offer India a smooth route to world markets, great potential and opportunities exist in the manufacturing sector also.

FTP strategy is on the right track

When the Five-year Foreign Trade Policy (FTP) was announced on August 31, 2004, the Government took cognizance of the fact that a bold and clearly delineated approach was needed to tap such opportunities. The Foreign Trade Policy articulated two basic objectives that would enable India to achieve these goals. The first objective was doubling our percentage share of global merchandise trade within five years. To achieve this, an average annual growth rate of about 16% was envisaged. The DGCI&S trade statistics show that the actual growth of the merchandise trade in the very first year of the policy period has been of the order of 24%, which has far surpassed the target we set for ourselves. This growth has been unprecedented in India's economic history, and if we can maintain the momentum, the Government is confident that India will cross the 150 billion dollar milestone substantially earlier than the target date.

FTP as a generator of employment

The second objective of the FTP was providing thrust to employment generation particularly in semi-urban and rural areas. The FTP announced special focus initiatives in the employment intensive areas of agriculture, handicrafts, handlooms, gems and jewellery and leather and footwear sectors. The employment generation has been encouraging not only in these sectors, but in other sectors across the board. A study commissioned by the Ministry reveals that exports generated an incremental direct employment of 10 lakh jobs in the year 2004-05, over the previous year. The total employment generated during the year corresponding to export activity valued at 78 billion was 1 crore jobs - 86 lakhs of direct employment, and 14 lakhs of indirect employment in the logistics, transport and related sectors. The study further reveals that if we achieve our target of 150 dollars over the next four years, we shall be adding a further 1 crore jobs: 85% of it direct employment, and 15% indirectly associated jobs.

A policy of partnership

The FTP provided a road map that could help Indian companies become globally competitive and simultaneously aimed at giving Indian consumers world class products and services. Specific sectoral initiatives have helped in creating more jobs, higher exports and an enhanced level of confidence for Indian products and services in the global economy. Government is committed to resolving all outstanding problems and disputes pertaining to the past policy periods through the Grievance Redressal Committee set up last year, for condoning delays, regularizing breaches by exporters in bonafide cases, resolving disputes over entitlements, granting extensions for utilization of licences etc. The atmosphere of partnership between Government and Business will be enhanced and taken forward.

Changing International Trade Dynamics

The dynamics of global trade and the opportunities provided by the multilateral trading platform necessitate a continuous realignment of our international trade strategies and priorities. While India's international trade will continue to function under the overall framework of the Foreign Trade Policy 2004-09 announced on 31st August 2004, some fine-tuning needs to be done to take into account the changing international trade dynamics. In order to achieve our Foreign Trade Policy objective of becoming a major player in world trade, a comprehensive view needs to be taken for the overall development of the country's foreign trade. Coherence and consistency among trade and other economic policies of both the Union and the State Governments is important for maximizing the contribution of such policies to development. State Governments are increasingly required to partner with the Union Government in the process. Some States have formulated export policies recognizing the need to focus on the removal of impediments in promoting trade, employment and economic activity. But a lot needs to be done to coordinate this. It should therefore be the imperative of the Central Government to engage the State Governments in providing an enabling environment for boosting international trade, by setting up an Inter State Trade Council. It is hoped that the Council would provide an appropriate institutionalized dialogue mechanism on the subject.

REMOVAL OF EXPORT CESS

The Department of Commerce has taken a consistent stand from a policy perspective that taxes and duties should not be exported. The cess levied under the different Commodity Board Acts is a tax on exports, which is a handicap and a major irritant to our exporters and erodes the competitiveness of Indian agriculture exports. Department of Commerce proposes to abolish cess on export of all agricultural and plantation commodities levied under various Commodity Board Acts.

EXPORT PROMOTION CAPITAL GOODS SCHEME

a. For providing a thrust to the Agricultural sector, concessional duty imports made by agro units under the EPCG Scheme shall be allowed to fulfill the export obligation over a longer period of time with a reduced export obligation i.e. 6 times the duty saved over a 12 year period instead of the normal window of 8 times the duty saved in 8 years.
b. To promote capacity expansion and quality up-gradation in the SSI sector, import of capital goods at 5% Customs duty shall now be allowed subject to a fulfillment of an export obligation equivalent to 6 times the duty saved on capital goods imported under the EPCG Scheme over a period of 8 years. (At present the export obligation under the EPCG Scheme is 8 times the duty saved and reducing the export obligation for small manufacturing units to 6 times shall provide an impetus to industries to modernize their plant and machinery which will enhance our overall export competitiveness in the medium term.)
c. To create modern infrastructure in the retail sector, concessional duty benefits under EPCG scheme shall be extended for import of capital goods required by retailers having a minimum covered shopping area of 1000 sq metres. The retailer shall fulfill the export obligation under the Scheme from payments received against 'counter sales' in free foreign exchange through banking channels as per RBI guidelines.
d. With a view to accelerate exports under the Scheme and to incentivize fast track companies, firms making 75 % or more of the exports under

the EPCG Scheme (including average level of exports) in half or less than half the original export obligation period, shall be freed from the balance export obligation.

e. Payment received in Rupees for the Port Handling services are counted for export obligation discharge under the EPCG Scheme. This facility is now being extended to include minor ports including ICD's and Container Freight Stations (CFS) also. This will enable augmentation of the facilities available at the secondary ports with modern equipment and thereby reduce cargo handling turnaround time and related transaction costs.

f. The present requirement of submitting an Installation Certificate for machinery imported under EPCG Scheme will now not be required for units which are not registered with Central Excise. In lieu of a Central Excise Certificate, a Chartered Engineer Certificate will now suffice. Firms importing spares under EPCG shall also be required to submit a Chartered Engineer certificate only instead of a certificate from Central Excise authorities.

g. The facility of clubbing of EPCG licences has been further liberalized and restrictive conditions relating to same licensing year and same products/services have been deleted. Henceforth, all EPCG licences issued under the same Customs Notification can be clubbed. This will considerably reduce paperwork both for the exporter and the licensing authorities and lead to easier monitoring.

SERVICE EXPORTS

a. To enable the Service providers to upgrade the infrastructure in their associate companies, the goods imported under the 'Served from India' Scheme shall be transferable within the Group companies and managed hotels subject to Actual User condition.

b. At present, Hotels and Restaurants are required to submit a Chartered Accountant certificate that the entire duty benefits availed under the 'Served from India' Scheme have been passed on to the consumer. From now on, only a declaration will be submitted by the Hotels and Restaurants that the duty benefits shall be passed on to the consumer and no CA certificate will be required to be submitted.

AGRI-EXPORTS

a. Benefits under 'Vishesh Krishi Upaj Yojana' shall also be extended to exports of poultry and dairy products in addition to export of flowers, fruits, vegetables, minor forest produce and their value-added products.

b. Procedural guidelines for the Scheme have also been notified and the exporter has been given the flexibility to obtain duty credit certificates in split form that will make utilization of the licences easier.

GEM AND JEWELLERY EXPORTS

a. Entitlement for Duty Free imports of Gems and Jewellery samples have been enhanced to Rs. 3 lakhs in a financial year or 0.25% of the average of the last three years exports turnover or gems and jewellery items, whichever is lower. Earlier this limit was Rs. 1 lakh.
b. Supply of gold of 0.995 and above purity shall also be allowed for release by nominated agencies for export purposes. Earlier this facility was only available for supply of gold in the domestic market.
c. The notional rate for fixing the US $ rate for calculating gold jewellery exports shall now be based on a certificate which is not older than 7 working days from the date of shipping. The present provisions mandated that the notional rate certificate issued by the nominated agency should not be older than 3 working days.
d. Exporters of plain/studded/precious metal jewellery will be allowed to import plain/studded/precious metal jewellery (gold jewellery of 18 carats and below/platinum and sterling silver jewellery) for the purposes of exports.

PACKAGE FOR MARINE SECTOR

a. Duty free import of specified specialized inputs/chemicals and flavoring oils as per a defined list shall be allowed to the extent of 1% of FOB value of preceding financial years export. Use of these special ingredients for seafood processing will enable us to achieve a higher value addition and enter new export markets.
b. To encourage the existing mechanized vessels and deep sea trawlers to adopt modern technology for scientific exploitation of our marine resources in an eco-friendly manner and boost marine sector exports, it is proposed to allow import of monofilament long line system for tuna fishing at a concessional rate of duty.
c. The present system of disposal of waste of perishable commodities like seafood after inspection by a customs official is very cumbersome and leads to development of unhygienic conditions. To overcome this, a self removal procedure for clearance of waste shall be applicable, subject to prescribed wastage norms.

ADVANCE LICENSING SCHEME

a. No safeguard and antidumping duty shall be levied on inputs under Advance Licence for deemed export supplies made to ICB projects. With this different categories of Advance licences i.e. advance licence for physical export, advance licence for intermediate supplies and advance licence for deemed exports have been merged into a single category for procedural facilitation and easier monitoring.

b. The scope of Advance Licence for Annual requirement has been extended to all categories of exporters having past export performance. Earlier, the option was limited to Status Holders only. The earlier limit of obtaining Advance Licence for Annual requirement has also been enhanced to 300% of FOB/FOR value of exports made in the previous year from 200%.
c. Clubbing of advance licences for export regularization purpose has been allowed even for licences pertaining to 1992-97 period.
d. Units registered under BIFR shall be allowed export obligation extension as per the rehabilitation package or a period upto five years reckoned from the date of issuance of the advance licence, whichever is higher.
e. Transfer of Duty Free material imported or procured under Advance Licence from one unit of the company to another unit of the same company to be allowed with prior intimation to the jurisdictional central excise authority. Earlier prior permission of the jurisdictional central excise authority was required.
f. In cases the Bank Guarantee/LUT has been redeemed under the Advance licence, the Licensee may be allowed to get duty free inputs processed from any manufacturer under actual user condition subject to central excise procedures relating to job work.
g. Removal of requirement of ARO for taking supplies from EOU/EHTP/STP/BTP units and allowing direct debit of the advance licence by the Bond Officer of these units. A detailed procedure in this regard shall be prescribed by the CBEC.

DUTY-FREE REPLENISHMENT CERTIFICATE

a. List of Sensitive Items has been pruned down to nine items. Brass scrap, Additives, Paper/Paper Board and Dye Stuffs shall be removed from the Sensitive List of items prescribed for import of items under DFRC.
b. Provision for re-credit on account of rejections of items imported under DFRC shall be similar to the facility available to DEPB and Advance Licence. While allowing re-credit, 95% of the value of the DFRC shall be credited.

DEPB

DEPB benefits shall be available for supply of goods from DTA to SEZs for the period 1.04.2003 to 11.05.2004.

EXPORT-ORIENTED UNITS

a. Duty free spares up to 5% of the value of Capital Goods imported for excavation purposes in the Granite sector will be allowed to be removed to the quarries.

b. The de-bonding procedure for EOUs has been simplified. A self-assessment procedure along with time bound disposal of applications of such exiting EOUs will be put in place.
c. Capital Goods will be allowed to be transferred or given on loan basis to other units under intimation to both Excise and Development Commissioner.
d. Transfer of samples to other EOUs on returnable basis within a period of 30 days to be allowed.
e. EOUs to be permitted to claim IT exemption in respect of income on export proceeds realized within a period of 12 months from date of export.

TARGET- PLUS SCHEME

a. The Target-plus Scheme aimed at rewarding incremental exports would continue in the year 2005-06 with such modifications as will be notified, separately for preventing misuse, if any.

BANK GUARANTEE

Quantum of Bank Guarantee in respect of "Other Manufacturer Exporters" category is being reduced from 25% to 15%. Units in Agri Export Zones (AEZs) shall also be eligible to submit a Bank Guarantee of 15%. In addition, only a 15% Bank Guarantee shall be required for 'established service providers' who have free foreign exchange earnings of Rs. 50 lakhs or more during the preceding financial year and have a clean track record.

Procedural Simplification to liberalize Transaction Costs

Importers and exporters have to fill multiple application forms at various stages of their business activity to meet the procedural requirements of different Departments/Ministries under different Acts. It is our endeavor to simplify procedures and reduce the documentation requirements so as to reduce the transaction costs of the exporters and thereby increase their competitiveness in the international markets. With this in mind, a Committee to look into procedural simplification and reduction of transaction costs was set up under the Chairmanship of Director General of Foreign Trade. The Committee has submitted its report and some of the key recommendations made are:

a. Internal process re-engineering to enable greater delegation and simplification of forms and documents;
b. EDI linkage of all community trade partners like DGFT, Customs, Banks, Export Promotion Councils etc to facilitate web-based filing, retrieval and verification of documents;
c. A fast track mechanism for clearances, examination, testing, quarantine, packaging etc. to be set up by all agencies to facilitate import/export of perishable cargo;

d. Laying down time limits for giving approvals/sanctions for different import and export activities by different agencies to ensure a transparent system of working in Government Departments and ensure continuous improvement in quality of services rendered.

As a first step towards this exercise, the DGFT has devised a single common application form called 'Aayaat Niryaat' (Import-Export) Form. This 50-page set of forms, as against the 120-page set currently in existence, provides availability of information on DGFT related documentation at a single place and has a web interface for on-line filing by the exporter and retrieval of documents by the licensing authorities.

EDI INITIATIVES

a. DGFT shall strive to move towards an automated electronic environment for filing, retrieval and authentication of documents based on agreed protocols and message exchange with other community trade partners including Customs and Banks. Increased use of information technology for interacting with the trade through video conferencing, doing away with manual filing of documents by using digital signature and introducing a Special Purpose Vehicle for electronic licence utilization and transfer mechanism is also envisaged. In addition, online web-based information shall be made available for all Export and Import related policies and procedures on the DGFT website to enable the international trading community to access information from a single source.

b. A time frame of six months for complete EDI linkage between Customs and DGFT has been specified. After completion of this project the manual submission of shipping bills and related documents will be done away with and verification of licences shall be done online which shall considerably reduce transaction costs.

c. Facility of issuing Importer Exporter Code number (IEC) online is also being provided by linking the DGFT database with the Income Tax PAN Database and use of digital signature technology. To add transparency in the system, other e-governance initiatives are also being planned to provide delivery of services to the user community without any human interface with the DGFT offices.

TRADE FACILITATION

a. To enable the users to make commercial decisions in a more professional manner, DGCI&S trade data shall be made available with minimum time lag in a query based structured format on commercial criteria.

b. All DGFT offices shall continue to provide facilitation to exporters in regard to developments in international trade i.e. WTO agreements, Rules of Origin and SPS requirements, anti-dumping issues etc. to help the exporters strategize their import and export decisions in an internationally dynamic environment.

c. To promote export of 'Minor Forest Produce' products Shellac Export Promotion Council has been designated as a nodal EPC for minor forest produce.
d. All EPCs shall open a separate Cell to involve and encourage youth and women entrepreneurs in the export effort.
e. Handloom—Government has decided to develop a trademark for Handloom on lines similar to 'Woolmark' and 'Silkmark'. This will enable handloom products to develop a niche market with a distinct identity.
f. Tea—In order to maintain quality and retain the brand equity of Indian teas, the Government has issued a new Tea (Distribution and Export) Control Order, 2005 which prescribes strict norms for tea. All teas, whether imported or exported, would be required to conform to the specifications cited in the new Order. Tea has been classified for the purpose of issue of non-preferential Certificate of Origin into three categories:
    i. Tea wholly produced or obtained in India will only be classified as "India tea."
    ii. Where the Indian tea content in the export is not less than 90% by weight, it will be classified as "India tea (not less than 90% by weight of tea)".
    iii. In case of tea not wholly produced or obtained in India and where the content of Indian tea is less than 90% by weight, it will be classified as "Blended tea of different origin and packed in India". The new Order also prescribes a minimum value addition norm of 50% on export of all imported tea and stipulates a time period of 6 months from the date of import for the export of imported tea.

COMPREHENSIVE FOREIGN TRADE POLICY

To take an integrated view of the overall development of India's foreign trade a comprehensive Foreign Trade Policy (CFTP) for 2004-2009 was announced on 31st August 2004 and its Annual Supplement was released for the year 2005-06 on 8th April 2005. The basic objective of this policy is to double India's share in world trade and to make exports an effective instrument of economic growth by giving thrust to employment generation through a number of policy initiatives. These include simplification of procedures, reduction in transaction cost, neutralization of incidence of levies and duties on inputs used for exports and development of global hubs for manufacturing, trading and services. Some of the major initiatives taken recently including measures announced in the Annual supplement to the FTP in April 2005 are given below:

Package for Marine Sector

- Duty-free import of specified specialized inputs/chemicals and flavoring oils as per the defined list shall be allowed to the extent of 1% of FOB value of the preceding financial years export which will enable seafood processing exporters to achieve a higher value addition and enter new export markets.
- Import of monofilament long line system for tuna fishing will be permitted at a concessional rate of duty so as to encourage the existing mechanized vessels and deep sea trawlers to adopt modern technology for scientific exploitation of India's marine resources.

Gems and Jewellery

- Duty-free imports of gems and jewellery samples are enhanced to Rs. 3 lakhs in a year or 0.25% of the average of the last three years exports.
- Supply of gold of 0.995 and above purity is allowed for release by the nominated agencies for export purposes.
- Exporters of plain/studded/precious metal jewellery are allowed to import plain/studded/precious metal jewellery (gold jewellery of 18 carat and below, platinum and sterling silver jewellery) for the purposes of exports.
- Import of gold of 18 carat and above is allowed under the replenishment scheme.

Vishesh Krishi Upaj Yojana

The benefit of Vishesh Krishi Upaj Yojana is extended to exports of poultry and dairy products in addition to export of flowers, fruits, vegetables, minor forest produce and their value-added products. Under the scheme, exports of these products qualify for duty-free credit entitlement equivalent to 5% of FOB value of exports. The entitlement is freely transferable and can be used for import of a variety of inputs and goods.

Duty-Free Replenishment Certificate (DFRC)

Import of fuel under DFRC entitlement shall be allowed to be transferred to marketing agencies authorized by the Ministry of Petroleum and Natural Gas. Brass scrap, additives, paper/paper board and dye stuffs are removed from the sensitive list of items, prescribed for import of items under DFRC. The provision for re-credit on account of rejections of items imported under DFRC has been made similar to the facility available to DEPB and Advance Licence. While allowing re-credit, 95% of the value of the DFRC shall be credited.

Duty Entitlement Pass Book (DEPB)

To remove the uncertainty of the exporters, the DEPB scheme which accounts for more than 55% of the total exports would be continued until replaced by a new scheme. The new scheme will be drawn up in consultation with exporters. DEPB benefits shall be available for supply of goods from DTA to SEZs for the period 1.4.2003 to 11.5.2004.

Export-Oriented Units (EOUs/EHTP/STP/BTP)

Units undertaking to export their entire production of goods and services, except prohibited items of exports, can be registered under the Export-Oriented Unit (EOU) Scheme, Electronic Hardware Technology Park (EHTP) Scheme, Software Technology Park (STP) Scheme and Biotechnology Park (BTP). Such units may be engaged in manufacture of goods including repair, remaking, reconditioning, re-engineering, agriculture, including agro-processing, aquaculture, animal husbandry, bio-technology, floriculture, horticulture, pisciculture, viticulture, poultry, sericulture and rendering of services. EOU/EHTP/STP units are permitted import duty free on all types of goods, including capital goods required by it for its activities or in connection therewith, provided they are not prohibited items of imports in the ITC (HS). The units are also permitted to import goods required for the approved activity, including capital goods, free of cost or on loan from clients. These units have to be net positive foreign exchange earners.

Deemed Exports

"Deemed Exports" refers to those transactions in which the goods supplied do not leave the country and the payment for such supplies is received either in Indian rupees or in foreign exchange. The following categories of supply of goods by the main/sub-contractors are regarded as "Deemed Exports" provided the goods are manufactured in India:

- Supply of goods against Advance Licence/DFRC.
- Supply of goods to Export-Oriented Units (EOUs), Software Technology Parks (STPs) or Electronic Hardware Technology Parks (EHTPs) and Bio-Technology Parks (BTP).
- Supply of capital goods to holders of licences under the Export Promotion Capital Goods (EPCG) Scheme.
- Supply of goods to projects financed by multilateral or bilateral agencies/funds as notified by the Department of Economic Affairs, Ministry of Finance under International Competitive Bidding in accordance with the procedures of those agencies/funds where the legal agreements provide for tender evaluation without including the customs duty.
- Supply of capital goods, including in unassembled/disassembled condition as well as plants, machinery, accessories, tools, dies and such goods which are used for installation purposes till the stage of commercial production and spares to the extent of 10% of the FOR value to fertilizer plants.

- Supply of goods to the power and refineries not covered in the above.
- Supply of goods to any project or purpose in respect of which the Ministry of Finance, by a notification, permits the import of such goods at zero customs duty.
- Supply of marine freight containers by 100% EOU (Domestic freight containers manufacturers) provided the said containers are exported out of India within 6 months or such further period as permitted by the Customs.
- Supply to projects founded by UN agencies.
- Supply of goods to nuclear power projects through competitive bidding.

Deemed Exports are eligible for the Advance Licence/DFRC, Deemed Export Drawback, and Exemption from/Refund of Terminal Excise Duty benefits.

Board of Trade

The Board of Trade was reconstituted with 39 members to advise the government on policy measures connected with India's foreign trade promotion. The Board is to prepare and implement short-term and long-term strategies in response to emerging national and international trade scenarios. An eminent person from trade and industry, Shri Kumarmangalam Birla has been nominated as President of the Board. Two meetings of the Board of Trade have already been held and the third meeting is going to be held shortly. Five Working Groups have been set up on various subjects which include evaluation of various export promotion schemes, trade facilitation, manufacturing sector, identification of specific sectors and strategies for enhancing competitiveness of exports and promoting SEZs and EOUs. Besides, there are four sectoral study groups on textiles; pharmaceuticals; chemicals and allied sectors; and impact of Regional Trade Agreements (RTAs) and Free Trade Areas (FTAs) on Indian industry and exports.

Inter-State Trade Council

The Inter-State Trade Council has been set up to ensure a continuous dialogue with State Governments and Union Territories which inter alia advises the Government on measures for providing a healthy environment for international trade in the States with a view to boost India's exports.

Trade Facilitation

- To enable the users to make commercial decisions in a more professional and quick manner, DGCI&S trade statistics are made available with minimum time lag in a query based structured format.
- All DGFT offices provide facilitation to exporters in regard to developments in international trade, i.e. WTO agreements, Rules of Origin

and SPS requirements, anti-dumping issues etc., to help the exporters strategize their import and export decisions in an internationally dynamic environment.

- To promote export of Minor Forest products, the Shellac Export Promotion Council has been designated as the nodal EPC for minor forest produce.
- All EPCs shall open a separate Cell to involve and encourage youth and women entrepreneurs in the export effort.
- Government has decided to develop a trademark for Handloom on lines similar to 'Woolmark' and 'Silkmark'.
- In order to maintain the quality and the brand equity of Indian teas, Tea (Distribution and Export) Control Order, 2005 has been issued wherein Tea has been classified for the purpose of issue of non-preferential Certificate of Origin into three categories. It also prescribes a minimum value addition norm of 50% on export of all imported tea and stipulates a time period of 6 months from the date of import for the export of imported tea.

Other Measures

- Import of 0.177 bore air guns and air pistols were made free for shooters registered with Rifle Clubs or District/State/National Rifles Associations since 4th July, 2005.
- Two types of planting seeds have been made freely importable since 26th July 2005.
- Due to the reporting of the outbreak of the Highly Pathogenic Avian Influenza (Fowl Plague), imports of certain livestock and livestock products have been prohibited.
- Import policy of marble rough and finished products has been amended.
- To fulfill India's commitments under the Rotterdam Convention, two items namely, Tetra methyl lead and Tetraethyl lead has been restricted since 31.10.2005.

India's FDI Policy: Some Highlights

The strong macro-economic fundamentals, growing size of the economy and improving investment climate has attracted global corporations to invest in India. A major outcome of the economic reforms process aimed at opening up the economy and embracing globalization has led to tremendous increase in Foreign Direct investment inflows into India. According to AT Kearney Report, India ranks second in the world in terms of attractiveness for FDI. A.T. Kearney's 2007 Global Services Location Index ranks India as the most preferred destination in terms of financial attractiveness, people and skills availability and business environment (http://www.atkearney.com/main.taf?p=5,3,1,160&utm_source=pr&utm_medium=atk).

Similarly, UNCTAD's World Investment Report, 2005 (http://www.unctad.org/en/docs/wir2005_en.pdf) considers India the 2nd most attractive investment destination among the Transnational Corporations (TNCs). The positive perception as a result of strong economic fundamentals driven by 16 years of reforms has helped FDI inflows grow at about 20 times since the opening up of the economy to foreign investment since August 1991 (Fig. 2).

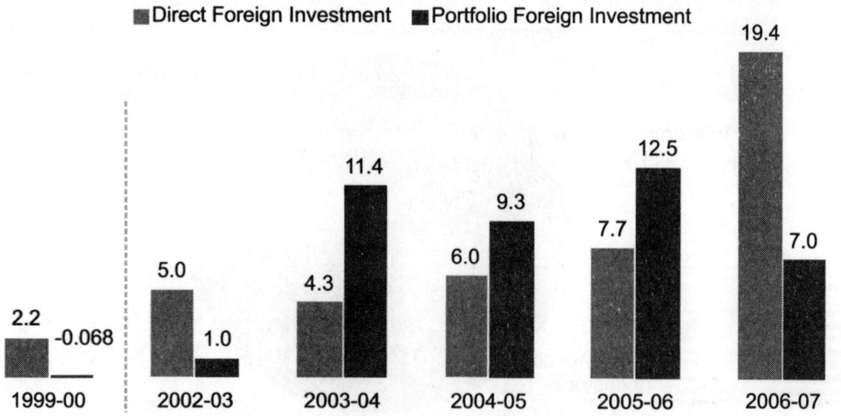

Fig. 2: Foreign Investment (In billion $)
Source: Reserve Bank of India

Direct Foreign Investment

The major sources of FDI in India are through both the equity route, which accounted for 82% of the total FDI inflows in India. Reinvested earnings of FDI companies accounted for 15% of the total Direct Investment. Acquisitions accounted for 32% of total FDI. Mauritius has been the major route for FDI inflows into India due to the Mauritius's stature with India as a tax haven and most volume of FDI inflows through Mauritius has been from the USA and the major investor (FDI) in India for the last 16 years has been USA (Fig. 3).

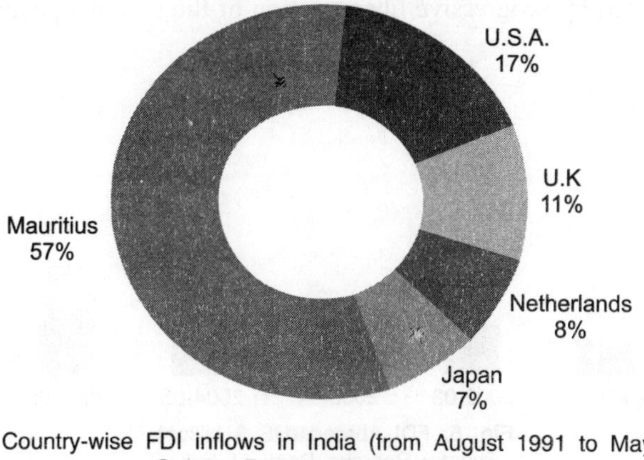

Fig. 3: Country-wise FDI inflows in India (from August 1991 to May 2007)
Source: Reserve Bank of India

Sectors that have attracted major portion of FDI are manufacturing industries and services such as Financial and Business Services. During the year 2006-07, the major recipient of FDI was Financial and business services (US $ 4.4 billion during 2006-07). Manufacturing was the next largest recipient of FDI at US $ 1.6 billion. Overall, during the period August 1991 to May 2007, manufacturing attracted the major portion of FDI inflows in India (Fig. 4).

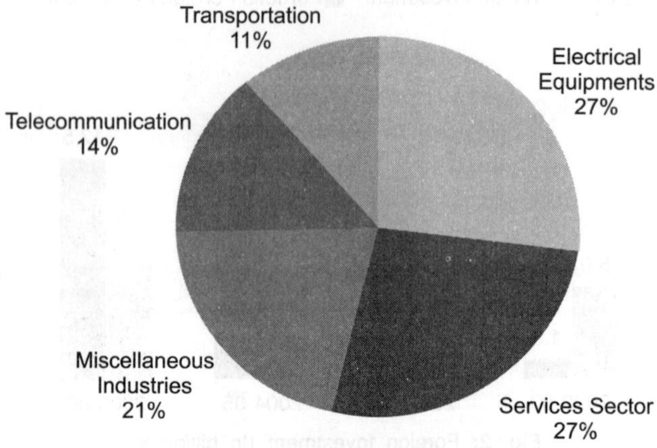

Fig. 4: Shares of Major Sectors in FDI inflows
(From August 1991 to May 2007)
Source: Reserve Bank of India

Overseas FDI by Indian Corporations

Increasing competitiveness of Indian industry due to globalization of Indian Economy has led to emergence and growth of Indian multinationals. This is evident from the FDI overseas from India, which increased by 13.5 times during the last 7 years (Fig. 5). The year 2006-07 witnessed large overseas acquisition deals by Indian corporate to gain market shares and reap economies of scale, supported by progressive liberalization of the external payments regime.

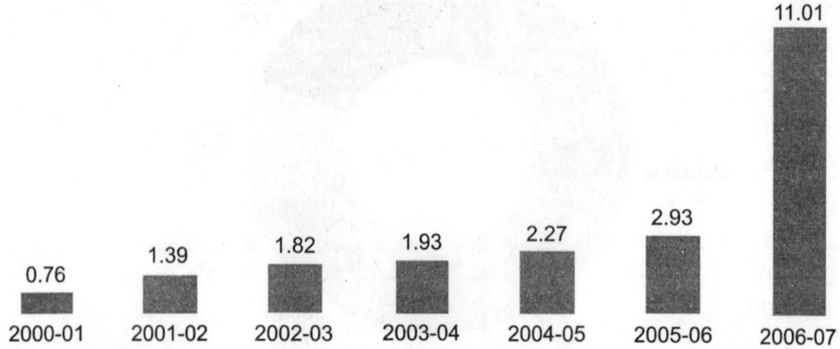

Fig. 5: FDI Abroad (US $ billion)
Source: Reserve Bank of India

Overseas investment that started off initially with the acquisition of foreign companies in the IT and related services sector has now spread to other areas such as manufacturing including auto components and drugs and pharmaceuticals.

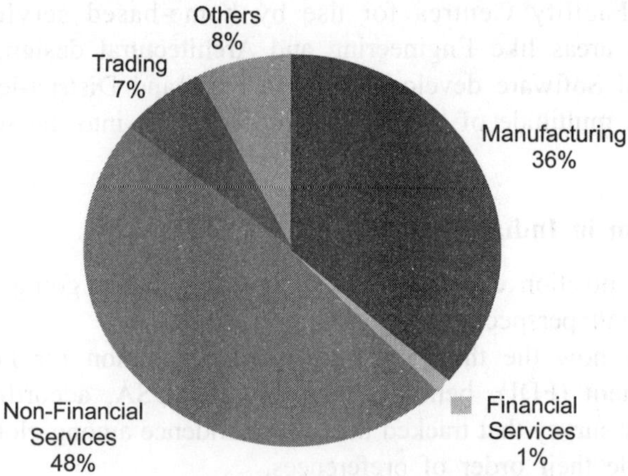

Fig. 6: Sectoral share of FDI Abroad
(1 April 2003 to 31 March 2007)
Source: Reserve Bank of India

SERVICES EXPORTS

Services Exports Services include all the 161 tradable services covered under the General Agreement on Trade in Services where payment for such services is received in free foreign exchange or in Indian Rupees which are otherwise considered as having been paid for in free foreign exchange by RBI. A list of services is given in Appendix-10 of Handbook of Procedures (Vol. I). All provisions of this Policy shall apply mutatis mutandis to export of services as they apply to goods, unless otherwise specified.

Export Promotion Service exporters are required to register themselves with the Council for Services: Federation of Indian Exporters Organization. However, software exporters shall register themselves with Electronic and Software Export Promotion Council.

In order to give proper direction, guidance and encouragement to the Services Sector, an exclusive Export Promotion Council for Services shall be set up.

The Services Export Promotion Council shall:

(i) Map opportunities for key services in key markets and develop strategic market access programmes for each component of the matrix.

(ii) Co-ordinate with sectoral players in undertaking intensive brand building and marketing programmes in target markets.

(iii) Make necessary interventions with regard to policies, procedures and bilateral/multilateral issues, in co-ordination with recognized nodal bodies of the services industry.

Common Facility Centres: Government shall promote the establishment of Common Facility Centres for use by home-based service providers, particularly in areas like Engineering and Architectural design, Multi-media operations, and Software developers etc. in State and District-level towns, to draw in a vast multitude of home-based professionals into the services export arena.

The FDI boom in India

The following position explains the FDI boom in India, going by the future economic growth perspective:

* India is now the third most favoured destination for Foreign Direct Investment (FDI), behind China and the USA, according to an AT Kearney survey that tracked investor confidence among global executives to decide their order of preferences.
* India's share of global FDI flows rose from 1.8 per cent in 1996 to 2.2 per cent in 1997.
* FDI in India in 1997-98 was lower at US $ 5,025 million compared to US $ 6,008 million in 1996-97 because of a decline in portfolio investment. Although foreign direct investment (FDI) increased by 18.6 per cent from US $ 2,696 million in 1996-97 to US $ 3,197 million in 1997-98.
* International developments continue to attract capital flows into India in 1998-99 as well.
* Mauritius, as in the previous two years, was the dominant source of FDI inflows in 1997-98. U.S.A. and S. Korea were, respectively, the second and third largest sources of FDI.
* S. Korea increased its flow of investment in India from a meager US $ 6.3 million in 1996-97 (0.2 per cent of total FDI) to US $ 333.1 million in 1997-98 (10.4 per cent share).
* There has been a sharp rise in the number of FDIs approved in 2004.
* During the first seven months of 2004, between January and July, Rs. 5,220 crore worth of FDI was approved.
* Almost a third share of the investment in India is by NRIs.

According to the latest Reserve Bank of India figures, outflows through various NRI deposits schemes amounted to $ 903 million since May 2004, as against net inflows of $ 1.2 billion in the corresponding period last year.

A recent international agency report has explained that the Indian economy will become one of the world's largest by 2050 A.D. With a GDP growth rate of 8 per cent since 2003 starting with a rebound in the Indian agriculture initially but now followed with a boom in production and service sectors similar to that of China.

In the last couple of months there has been a series of announcements of huge investments by giant foreign and NRI companies. Bill Gates in recent visit to India announced that the Microsoft will invest around $ 1.7 billion over the next few years in India. Intel, the world's largest computer chips company has planned to invest over $ 1 billion in India. CISCO has announced plans to spend $ 1.1 billion over the next few years in India. And for Microsoft, India is emerging as a big market to exploit as Microsoft doesn't have much in stake in China. Purchasing of shares to the tune of $ 1.5 billion in Bharti Telecom by Vodafone is another big FDI inflow into the country. To be a genuine competitor of China in FDI, India should attain an annual growth rate of 10%. So far India has not attracted more then $ 3-4 billion annually when compared to FDI inflows of $ 55-60 billion for China. The number of foreign and NRI equities which have invested in India between Aug. 1991–Nov. 2002 is 15761 with a total foreign investment of Rs. 283447 crores. However things are changing and improving in India too. FDI investment in India has nearly doubled to $ 2.9 billion during April–July 2006 from $ 1.5 billion for the same period last year (2007) representing a growth rate of 259%. According to the RBI, it is inferred that India has received $ 50.1 billion since 1991 of which $ 16 billion or 32% of it came since April 2004.

The negative side of this bouncing FDI and NRI inflow is the constraints of Indian economic growth which are internal and not external. Ups and downs in Indian agriculture play a major role in constraining Indian growth rate coupled with unhealthy infrastructure like pot-holed roads, incomplete flyovers, undeveloped airport facilities etc are the main constraints in the growth of the Indian economy.

However a very reassuring development has been the tremendous boost up which the recent budget has given to industrial infrastructure and FDI investment in India. Positive side of the story is the tremendous resilience of the economy, rapid growth of Indian agriculture, boost up to infrastructural facilities, the tremendous global outsourcing boom in India and a well-regulated and deep capital market. Looking at the current rate of FDI inflow India can attract a record of $ 12 billion FDI inflow this fiscal year. The Commerce Minister of India feels it is possible though he has a note of caution, "There is competition not only just from China but also from others like Thailand, Malaysia and so on. We can't lose focus on attracting investments since we can't get inflows by giving lectures but work on ways to get investors."

If a comparative analysis of the Indian and Chinese economics is done some interesting comparison emerges as to why India lags behind China in so many areas and a lot needs to be done if India has to catch up with China. The comparative analysis is given as below:

Basis of Comparison	China	India
Total population	1272 billion	1033 billion
Savings rate	50 per cent	26 per cent
Labour force	757 billion	451 billion
Annual GDP	US $ 1159 billion	478 US $ billion
Share of agriculture in GDP	15 per cent	27 per cent
Share of industry in GDP	52 per cent	27 per cent
Share of service sector in GDP	33 per cent	48 per cent
Rail routes	56.7 thousand sq kms	62.5 thousand sq kms
Motor vehicles per 1000 people	8	7
R&D expenditure	0.1 % of GNP	0.6 % of GNP
Internet host	0.6 per 10000 people	0.8 per 10000 people
Education expenditure	2.3 per cent of GNP	3.2 per cent of GNP
Female adult literacy	85 per cent	45 per cent
Undernourished people	9 per cent of the total population	23 per cent of the total population

Thus, it is noticed that the overall scene of Indian economy with a booming stock touching almost the 14000 mark, a buoyant Rupee of Rs. 43.44/Dollar and a healthy growth trend of the major sectors of the Indian economy the environment is very positive for FDI and NRI inflows. However compared to China it is still behind even though it is marching ahead. A lot more needs to be done. The Indian bull is no doubt energetic now however it has to run fast to overtake the Chinese dragon which is possible if friendly ground is created.

Conclusion

It is generally said that future is always uncertain. This saying is correct to some extent. But at the same time it is also said that exceptions are always there. This exception is about India's certain higher rate of growth in the coming future. The future of Indian economy is brighter because of its huge human resources, rapidly upcoming service sector, availability of large number of competent professionals, vast market for every product, increasing impact of consumerism, absence of controls and licences, interest of foreign entrepreneurs in India and existence of four hundred million middle-class people. Even today, India is producing largest number of billionaires in a year, take over by Indian multinationals is amazing, the craze of Indians to go abroad is rapidly diminishing, and the Rupee is becoming stronger and stronger in relation to Dollar. India's say in the international diplomacy and political affairs has now become meaningful, thousands of foreigners are working as executives in India, packages are becoming lucrative and competitive and annual rate of growth is highest after China. This present picture gives some reflections of the future. But this is all in the absolute sense and not in the relative terms.

A country can only grow if the government policies allow more participation and is able to attract more and more foreign direct investment in India. Today, India provides highest returns on FDI than any other country in the world.

India is poised for further growth in manufacturing, infrastructure, automobiles, auto components, food processing sectors, real estate development etc. In this context it is also worth mentioning that savings rate has also increased from 23% to 31% over the last year to this year. India's continuing ambivalence on FDI, as a result, exacts a heavy toll on the economy. Undoubtedly, India is ceding billions of dollars of FDI to its neighbours each year. While China achieved actual FDI inflows of around $ 45.3 billion in 1997, India settled for a mere $ 3.2 billion. India therefore stands to win in the next few years.

Export-Oriented Units (EOUs), Electronics Hardware Technology Parks (EHTPs), Software Technology Parks (STPs) and Bio-Technology Parks (BTPs)

Eligibility : Units undertaking to export their entire production of goods and services (except permissible sales in the DTA), may be set up under the Export Oriented Unit (EOU) Scheme, Electronic Hardware Technology Park (EHTP) Scheme, Software Technology Park (STP) Scheme or Bio-Technology Park (BTP) scheme for manufacture of goods, including repair, re-making, reconditioning, re-engineering and rendering of services. Trading units, however, are not covered under these schemes.

Export and Import of Goods:

(a) An EOU/EHTP/STP/BTP unit may export all kinds of goods and services except items that are prohibited in the ITC (HS). Export of Special Chemicals, Organisms, Materials, Equipment and Technologies (SCOMET) shall be subject to fulfillment of the conditions indicated in the ITC (HS). Procurement and supply of export promotion material like brochure/literature, pamphlets, hoardings, catalogues, posters etc. up to a maximum value limit of 1.5% of FOB value of previous years exports shall also be allowed.

(b) An EOU/EHTP/STP/BTP unit may import and/or procure from DTA or bonded warehouses in DTA/international exhibition held in India without payment of duty all types of goods, including capital goods, required for its activities, provided they are not prohibited items of import in the ITC (HS). Any permission required for import under any other law shall be applicable. The units shall also be permitted to import goods including capital goods required for the approved activity, free of cost or on loan/lease from clients. The import of capital goods will be on a self certification basis. Goods imported by a unit shall be with actual user condition and shall be utilized for export production.

(c) State Trading regime shall not apply to EOU manufacturing units.

(d) EOU/EHTP/STP/BTP units may import/procure from DTA without payment of duty certain specified goods for creating a central facility which will be used by software units. These software units can be EOU/DTA units who will use the facility for export of software.

(e) An EOU engaged in agriculture, animal husbandry, aquaculture, floriculture, horticulture, pisciculture, viticulture, poultry or sericulture may be permitted to remove specified goods in connection with its activities for use outside the bonded area.

(f) Gems and jewellery EOUs may source gold/silver/platinum through the nominated agencies on loan/outright purchase basis. The units obtaining gold/silver/platinum from the nominated agencies, either on loan basis or outright purchase basis shall export gold/silver/platinum within 90 days from the date of release.

(g) EOU/EHTP/STP/BTP units, other than service units, may export to Russian Federation in Indian Rupees against repayment of State Credit/ Escrow Rupee Account of the buyer subject to RBI clearance, if any.

(h) Procurement and export of spares/components upto 1.5% of the FOB value of exports may be allowed to the same consignee/buyer of the export article.

India's Balance of Payment

India has a chronic deficit on current accounts. What bridges the gap between payments and receipts are mainly external aid (especially non-project assistance), tourism earnings, and remittances from Indians working abroad. Heavy imports of food grains and armament purchases caused a decline in India's foreign exchange reserves in the mid-1960s. An economic recovery from 1968–69, however, eased the problem, and by September 1970, foreign exchange reserves amounted to $ 616 million, as compared with $ 383 million by December 1965. Reserves declined to $ 566 million by the end of 1972 but increased to $ 841 million as of December 1975, despite massive deficits on current accounts, attributable to the quadrupling of oil import prices during 1973–74. Foreign exchange reserves declined from $ 6,739 million at the end of 1979 to $ 3,476 million as of November 1982 but subsequently rose to $ 5,924 million by March 1987.

The Gulf-War crisis worsened the ratio of current account deficit to GDP. Foreign exchange reserves plummeted because of export losses in Kuwait, Iraq, and other nations. Remittances from Indian workers fell, and sudden price increases for oil imports caused an estimated loss to India of over $ 2.8 billion in earnings. By November 1993, however, India's foreign exchange reserves had risen to $ 8.1 billion, the highest level since 1951. A substantial reduction in the trade deficit, increased inflows from foreign institutional investors, a stable exchange rate, and improved remittances all contributed in the recovery of reserves. Although export growth remained strong, the current account deficit tripled from 1993–94 to 1995–96. The increase was attributed to a continuing surge in imports and higher debt service requirements. However, between 1995 and 1998 the current account deficit shrank to about 1% of GDP due to increased textile exports and a liberalizing trade regime. India's total external debt in 2001 was estimated at $ 100.6 billion. In 2000, the external debt-GDP ratio stood at around 20.7%, down from 41% in 1991/92. In the early 2000s, India's exports to East and Southeast Asia increased, including to Japan and South Korea. High growth rates were registered for textiles, chemicals and related products, engineering goods, and leather and manufactures.

The US Central Intelligence Agency (CIA) reports that in 2001 the purchasing power parity of India's exports was $ 44.5 billion while imports totaled $ 53.8 billion resulting in a trade deficit of $ 9.3 billion.

The International Monetary Fund (IMF) reported that in 2000 India had exports of goods totaling $ 43.1 billion and imports totaling $ 55.3 billion. The services credit totaled $ 18.3 billion and debit $ 19.9 billion. The following table summarizes India's balance of payments as reported by the IMF for 2000 in millions of US dollars.

Current Account	**-4,198**
Balance on goods	-12,193
Balance on services	-1,582
Balance on income	-3,876
Current transfers	13,453
Capital Account	**...**
Financial Account	**9,616**
Direct investment abroad	-335
Direct investment in India	2,315
Portfolio investment assets	...
Portfolio investment liabilities	1,619
Other investment assets	-1,136
Other investment liabilities	7,152
Net Errors and Omissions	**670**
Reserves and Related Items	**-6,087**

Source: IMF (2000)

India: Commerce and Industry Competitive Advantage Analysis

India at the moment is attracting abundance like never before in history. Recently the International Monetary Fund said "buoyant global economic outlook has prompted it to revise" upward India's GDP growth rate by 0.6% to 9% for 2007. India today really is capital's favorite destination. Consider the case of private equity investments in India in 2006. According to Venture Intelligence a total of 302 deals worth $ 7.5 billion were reported. In the first half of 2007, 168 deals have been reported at $ 5.6 billion. In terms of investment in 2006, the top destination was China. China received around $ 900 million. London came second with a little more than $ 800 million. India came at number three with $ 746 million.

The India investment attraction can be simply be gauged from the fact that just in the second quarter of 2007 venture capital firms have invested about $ 112 million across 19 deals in India during the second quarter of 2007. The prominent Venture Capital firms already have offices already set in India to identify potential winners and as the India success story grows so is the attraction of newer players. Consider the case of Clearstone Venture Partners, a leading early stage venture capital firm. With US $ 650 million of committed investment capital, Clearstone sees India a favorable destination.

Besides innovation, probably the biggest fuel for entrepreneurial growth is venture capital investments. VC investments have been only growing in India. In 2006 venture capital firms invested $ 508 million over 92 deals in India. The amount invested during 2006 was significantly higher than that during the previous year (which had witnessed 44 deals totaling $ 268 million). In 2007, the VC score board so far reads 39 deals worth $ 242 million in its kitty. India today has come to the forefront as a global resource for industry in manufacturing and services. Its pool of technical skills, its base of English speaking populace with an increasing disposable income and its burgeoning market have all combined to enable India emerge as a viable partner to global industry.

Investment opportunities in India are today perhaps at a peak. Supported by India's natural strengths, the country offers investment opportunities in excess of $ 500 billion in diverse sectors over the next five years. The Government of India is committed to enabling foreign investors discover India as a partner - with whom they can work in synergy to achieve their objectives of growth and profitability.

This report on India's commerce and the competitive advantages garnered by its industry presents an in-depth and comprehensive study of the knowledge resource required to understand India in entirety as an investment destination. The report presents a historical perspective of India and the geographical, demographical facets of the country which add up to make the physical identity of India. The report also delves into the economic factors such as GDP, balance of payments, apart from the fiscal and monetary policies of the Government of India.

The commercial laws which govern the conduct of international trade in and out of India and the flow of investments which act as the precursors to the various schemes and trade promotion programs being run by the government are described in the report. The various industry forums act as policy guidance tools and catalyze the industry growth. Some of the highlights of India's Export-Import Trade performances during 2005-2007 are illustrated below (Table 1):

TABLE 1: HIGHLIGHTS OF INDIA'S EXPORT-IMPORT PERFORMANCE (2006-07)

Values in US$ Millions

Rank	*Name of Commodity*	*Apr 2005 - Feb 2006*		*Apr 2006 - Feb 2007*					
		Export Value of Goods		Export Value of Goods		% Growth	% Growth	% Share	% Share
		Value (INR in Crore)	Value (US$ in Million)	Value (INR in Crore)	Value (US$ in Millions)	Value (INR in Crore)	Value (US$ in Million)	Value (INR in Crore)	Value (US$ in Million)
(1)	(2)	(3)	(4)	(5)	(6)	(7)	(8)	(9)	(10)
1	India Export of Gems & Jewellary	61,369.32	13,867.33	62,586.53	13,785.00	1.98	-0.59	12.26	12.26
2	India Export of Petroleum (Crude & Products)	47,016.18	10,624.02	76,683.05	16,889.83	63.10	58.98	15.02	15.02
3	India Export of RMG Cotton Incl. Accessories	25,535.86	5,770.21	27,520.53	6,061.54	7.77	5.05	5.39	5.39
4	India Export of Machinery and Instruments	19,773.71	4,468.17	26,512.59	5,839.53	34.08	30.69	5.19	5.19
5	India Export of Drugs, Pharmcutes & Fine Chemls	19,553.87	4,418.49	21,833.63	4,808.97	11.66	8.84	4.28	4.28
6	India Export of Manufactures of Metals	16,674.57	3,767.87	20,156.05	4,439.47	20.88	17.82	3.95	3.95
7	India Export of Transport Equipments	16,374.62	3,700.09	19,064.44	4,199.04	16.43	13.48	3.73	3.73
8	India Export of Cotton Yarn, Fabrics, Madeupsetc	15,638.97	3,533.86	16,682.33	3,674.37	6.67	3.98	3.27	3.27
9	India Export of Iron Ore	14,505.39	3,277.71	15,074.03	3,320.13	3.92	1.29	2.95	2.95
10	India Export of Prmry & Semi-Fnshd Iron & Stl.	11,641.69	2,630.62	17,856.68	3,933.02	53.39	49.51	3.50	3.50
11	India Export of Plastic & Linoleum Products	11,239.89	2,539.82	13,132.29	2,892.45	16.84	13.88	2.57	2.57
12	India Export of other Commodities	10,157.94	2,295.34	22,636.02	4,985.70	122.84	117.21	4.43	4.43
13	India Export of Electronic Goods	8,454.86	1,910.51	11,453.82	2,522.76	35.47	32.05	2.24	2.24
14	Inorganic/Organic/Agro Chemls	7,726.50	1,745.92	8,584.59	1,890.80	11.11	8.3	1.68	1.68

(Contd.)

(1)	(2)	(3)	(4)	(5)	(6)	(7)	(8)	(9)	(10)
15	India Export of Manmade Yarn, Fabrics, Madeups	7,691.74	1,738.07	8,765.30	1,930.60	13.96	11.08	1.72	1.72
16	India Export of Marine Products	6,401.16	1,446.44	6,417.69	1,413.53	0.26	-2.28	1.26	1.26
17	India Export of Dyes/Intmdtes & Coar Tar Cheml	6,029.60	1,362.48	9,207.34	2,027.96	52.70	48.84	1.80	1.80
18	India Export of Non-Ferrous Metals	4,923.14	1,112.46	14,323.19	3,154.76	190.94	183.58	2.81	2.81
19	India Export of Processed Minerals	4,433.27	1,001.76	5,182.24	1,141.42	16.89	13.94	1.02	1.02
20	India Export of other Ores and Minerals	4,152.38	938.29	6,390.75	1,407.59	53.91	50.02	1.25	1.25
21	India Export of RMG Anmade Fibres	4,078.58	921.62	3,645.04	802.84	-10.63	-12.89	0.71	0.71
22	India Export of Oil Meals	3,960.66	894.97	4,710.21	1,037.45	18.92	15.92	0.92	0.92
23	India Export of Rubr Mfd. Prdcts Excpt Footwr	3,603.10	814.18	4,209.44	927.15	16.83	13.88	0.82	0.82
24	India Export of Paper/Wood Products	3,420.08	772.82	4,102.55	903.61	19.95	16.92	0.80	0.80
25	India Export of Carpet (Excl. Silk) Handmade	3,279.38	741.03	3,572.51	786.86	8.94	6.19	0.70	0.70
26	India Export of Footwear of Leather	3,169.30	716.15	3,886.61	856.05	22.63	19.53	0.76	0.76
27	India Export of Rice (other than (Basmati)	2,929.21	661.90	3,668.38	807.98	25.23	22.07	0.72	0.72
28	India Export of Residl Chemicl & Allied Prdcts	2,865.65	647.54	3,016.44	664.39	5.26	2.60	0.59	0.59
29	India Export of Gls/Glswr/Cermcs/ Reftrs/Cmnt/	2,856.98	645.58	3,450.60	760.01	20.78	17.73	0.68	0.68
30	India Export of Rice-Basmati	2,718.14	614.20	2,477.56	545.70	-8.85	-11.15	0.49	0.49
31	India Export of Leather Goods	2,648.14	598.39	2,849.61	627.64	7.61	4.89	0.56	0.56
32	India Export of Finished Leather	2,532.20	572.19	2,794.80	615.57	10.37	7.58	0.55	0.55
33	India Export of Meat & Preparations	2,474.31	559.11	2,925.45	644.34	18.23	15.24	0.57	0.57

(Contd.

(1)	(2)	(3)	(4)	(5)	(6)	(7)	(8)	(9)	(10)
34	India Export of Cashew	2,389.86	540.02	2,255.92	496.88	-5.6	-7.99	0.44	0.44
35	India Export of Cotton Raw Incld. Waste	2,233.23	504.63	5,027.31	1,107.29	125.11	119.43	0.98	0.98
36	India Export of Iron & Stl Bar/Rod Etc.	2,229.39	503.77	3,394.22	747.59	52.25	48.40	0.66	0.66
37	India Export of Cosmetics/Toiletries Etc.	1,965.51	444.14	2,248.64	495.27	14.41	11.51	0.44	0.44
38	India Export of Spices	1,894.59	428.11	2,718.26	598.71	43.48	39.85	0.53	0.53
39	India Export of Handcrfs (Excl. Handmade Crpts)	1,867.24	421.93	1,539.14	339	-17.57	-19.65	0.30	0.30
40	India Export of Natrl Silk Yarn, Fabrics, Madeup	1,744.91	394.29	1,799.35	396.32	3.12	0.51	0.35	0.35
41	India Export of Paints/Enamels/ Varnishes Etc.	1,690.16	381.92	1,682.52	370.58	-0.45	-2.97	0.33	0.33
42	India Export of RMG of othr Textle Matrl	1,595.12	360.44	1,855.51	408.68	16.32	13.38	0.36	0.36
43	India Export of Tea	1,589.85	359.25	1,859.71	409.61	16.97	14.02	0.36	0.36
44	India Export of RMG Wool	1,508.88	340.95	1,530.53	337.11	1.44	-1.13	0.30	0.30
45	India Export of Leather Garments	1,402.70	316.96	1,316.37	289.94	-6.15	-8.53	0.26	0.26
46	India Export of Coffee	1,391.80	314.5	1,717.29	378.24	23.39	20.27	0.34	0.34
47	India Export of RMG Silk	1,032.17	233.23	1,062.41	234.00	2.93	0.33	0.21	0.21
48	India Export of Ferro Alloys	1,008.15	227.81	1,417.38	312.19	40.59	37.04	0.28	0.28
49	India Export of Pulses	985.36	222.66	716.65	157.85	-27.27	-29.11	0.14	0.14
50	India Export of Fresh Fruits	938.58	212.09	1,167.26	257.10	24.36	21.22	0.23	0.23
51	India Export of Guergum Meal	929.61	210.06	1,016.15	223.81	9.31	6.55	0.20	0.20
52	India Export of Machine Tools	916.16	207.02	964.67	212.47	5.30	2.64	0.19	0.19
53	India Export of Tobacco Unmanufactured	887.42	200.53	1,108.72	244.2	24.94	21.78	0.22	0.22
54	India Export of Misc Processed Items	886.47	200.31	997.64	219.74	12.54	9.70	0.20	0.20
55	India Export of Castor Oil	862.98	195.00	992.84	218.68	15.05	12.14	0.19	0.19
56	India Export of Fresh Vegetables	823.33	186.04	1,322.54	291.3	60.63	56.57	0.26	0.26
57	India Export of Aluminium othr than Prdcts	798.88	180.52	1,191.20	262.37	49.11	45.34	0.23	0.23

(Contd.)

(1)	(2)	(3)	(4)	(5)	(6)	(7)	(8)	(9)	(10)
58	India Export of Leather Footwear Components	723.21	163.42	883.08	194.5	22.11	19.02	0.17	0.17
59	India Export of Dairy Products	703.71	159.01	475.70	104.78	-32.40	-34.11	0.09	0.09
60	India Export of Sesame Seeds	659.18	148.95	703.45	154.94	6.72	4.02	0.14	0.14
61	India Export of Project Goods	596.72	134.84	412.62	90.88	-30.85	-32.6	0.08	0.08
62	India Export of Wheat	556.95	125.85	35.86	7.9	-93.56	-93.72	0.01	0.01
63	India Export of Coir & Coir Manufactures	541.16	122.28	586.88	129.26	8.45	5.71	0.11	0.11
64	India Export of Sports Goods	532.61	120.35	529.22	116.56	-0.64	-3.15	0.10	0.10
65	India Export of Processed Fruits & Juices	517.71	116.99	635.35	139.94	22.72	19.62	0.12	0.12
66	India Export of Jute Hessian	460.71	104.10	349.66	77.01	-24.10	-26.02	0.07	0.07
67	India Export of Other Cereals	437.07	98.76	562.21	123.83	28.63	25.38	0.11	0.11
68	India Export of Groundnut	430.08	97.18	698.25	153.79	62.35	58.25	0.14	0.14
69	India Export of Processed Vegetables	426.99	96.48	539.67	118.87	26.39	23.20	0.11	0.11
70	India Export of Comp. Software in Physical Form	372.00	84.06	210.85	46.44	-43.32	-44.75	0.04	0.04
71	India Export of Sugar	368.89	83.36	2,651.86	584.09	618.87	600.71	0.52	0.52
72	India Export of Wollen Yarn, Fabrics, Madeupsetc	341.44	77.15	342.13	75.36	0.20	-2.33	0.07	0.07
73	India Export of Manmade Staple Fibre	335.84	75.89	790.07	174.02	135.25	129.31	0.15	0.15
74	India Export of Saddlery and Harnes	299.58	67.69	335.89	73.98	12.12	9.29	0.07	0.07
75	India Export of Poultry Products	298.82	67.52	262.00	57.71	-12.32	-14.54	0.05	0.05
76	India Export of Floor Covering of Jute	288.26	65.14	276.05	60.80	-4.24	-6.66	0.05	0.05
77	India Export of Tobaccoo Manufactured	274.75	62.08	372.28	82.00	35.5	32.07	0.07	0.07
78	India Export of Residual Engineering Items	273.87	61.89	320.57	70.61	17.05	14.09	0.06	0.06

(Contd.)

(1)	(2)	(3)	(4)	(5)	(6)	(7)	(8)	(9)	(10)
79	India Export of Floricltr Products	272.45	61.56	356.68	78.56	30.92	27.61	0.07	0.07
80	India Export of Spirit & Beverages	232.82	52.61	226.53	49.89	-2.71	-5.16	0.04	0.04
81	India Export of other Jute Manufactures	227.82	51.48	249.70	55.00	9.60	6.83	0.05	0.05
82	India Export of Footwear of Rubber/ Canvas Etc.	223.00	50.39	212.21	46.74	-4.84	-7.24	0.04	0.04
83	India Export of Coal	220.5	49.83	339.25	74.72	53.85	49.96	0.07	0.07
84	India Export of Jute Yarn	210.05	47.46	229.39	50.53	9.21	6.45	0.04	0.04
85	India Export of Shellac	145.64	32.91	133.05	29.30	-8.65	-10.96	0.03	0.03
86	India Export of Silk Carpet	95.05	21.48	118.28	26.05	24.45	21.30	0.02	0.02
87	India Export of Fruits/Vegetables Seets	75.67	17.10	97.65	21.51	29.04	25.78	0.02	0.02
88	India Export of Mica	69.07	15.61	69.07	15.21	0	-2.53	0.01	0.01
89	India Export of Niger Seeds	53.70	12.13	56.61	12.47	5.42	2.76	0.01	0.01
90	India Export of Mollases	26.93	6.09	119.37	26.29	343.22	332.02	0.02	0.02
	Total	**404,719.56**	**91,452.54**	**510,488.44**	**112,437.68**	**26.13**	**22.95**	**100**	**100**

Source: DGFT, GOI.

TOP IMPORT PRODUCTS

Values in US$ Millions

Rank	*Name of Commodity*	*Apr 2005 - Feb 2006* Export Value of Goods		*Apr 2006 - Feb 2007* Export Value of Goods		% Growth	% Growth	% Share	% Share
		Value (INR in Crore)	Value (US$ in Million)	Value (INR in Crore)	Value (US$ in Millions)	Value (INR in Crore)	Value (US$ in Million)	Value (INR in Crore)	Value (US$ in Million)
(1)	(2)	(3)	(4)	(5)	(6)	(7)	(8)	(9)	(10)
1	India Import of - WHEAT	–	–	1,417.61	312.24	–	–	0.19	0.19
2	India Import of - PETROLEUM, CRUDE & PRODUCTS	175,945.00	39,757.45	236,601.84	52,112.76	34.47	31.08	32.10	32.10
3	India Import of - ELECTRONIC GOODS	52,093.43	11,771.30	65,281.46	14,378.58	25.32	22.15	8.86	8.86
4	India Import of - GOLD	42,742.00	9,658.21	58,704.81	12,930.03	37.35	33.88	7.97	7.97
5	India Import of - MACHRY EXCPT ELEC & ELECTRONIC	39,209.91	8,860.08	56,216.24	12,381.91	43.37	39.75	7.63	7.63
6	India Import of - PERLS PRCUS SEMIPRCS STONES	38,229.69	8,638.58	30,061.51	6,621.20	-21.37	-23.35	4.08	4.08
7	India Import of - OTHER COMMODITIES	23,551.34	5,321.78	18,258.34	4,021.49	-22.47	-24.43	2.48	2.48
8	India Import of - ORGANIC CHEMICALS	18,839.31	4,257.03	22,405.24	4,934.87	18.93	15.92	3.04	3.04
9	India Import of - IRON & STEEL	17,413.25	3,934.79	24,413.75	5,377.25	40.20	36.66	3.31	3.31
10	India Import of - COAL,COKE & BRIQUITTES ETC.	15,332.59	3,464.63	18,363.64	4,044.69	19.77	16.74	2.49	2.49
11	India Import of - METALIFERS ORES & METAL SCRAP	15,086.80	3,409.09	34,051.38	7,499.99	125.70	120.00	4.62	4.62
12	India Import of - TRANSPORT EQUIPMENTS	12,995.64	2,936.56	18,123.59	3,991.81	39.46	35.93	2.46	2.46
13	India Import of - INORGANIC CHEMICALS	8,975.21	2,028.08	9,808.64	2,160.40	9.29	6.52	1.33	1.33
14	India Import of - ARTFCL RESNS, PLSTC MATRLS, ETC.	8,946.43	2,021.58	10,532.56	2,319.85	17.73	14.75	1.43	1.43

(Contd.)

(1)	(2)	(3)	(4)	(5)	(6)	(7)	(8)	(9)	(10)
15	India Import of - VEGETABLE OILS FIXED (EDIBLE)	7,916.45	1,788.84	8,732.09	1,923.29	10.30	7.52	1.18	1.18
16	India Import of - PROFSNL INST, ETC EXCPT ELCTRNC	7,816.48	1,766.25	9,484.26	2,088.96	21.34	18.27	1.29	1.29
17	India Import of - NON-FERROUS METALS	7,287.55	1,646.73	10,830.59	2,385.49	48.62	44.86	1.47	1.47
18	India Import of - FERTILEZERS MANUFACTURED	7,031.26	1,588.82	11,728.69	2,583.30	66.81	62.59	1.59	1.59
19	India Import of - ELEC MACHRY EXCPT ELECTRONIC	5,969.75	1,348.96	7,988.29	1,759.46	33.81	30.43	1.08	1.08
20	India Import of - MANUFACTURES OF METALS	4,816.91	1,088.45	6,431.91	1,416.66	33.53	30.15	0.87	0.87
21	India Import of - MACHINE TOOLS	4,229.03	955.61	6,036.84	1,329.65	42.75	39.14	0.82	0.82
22	India Import of - MEDICINAL & PHRMACUTICL PRODTS	4,128.27	932.85	5,284.68	1,163.98	28.01	24.78	0.72	0.72
23	India Import of - CHEMICAL MATRL & PRODCTS	4,090.10	924.22	5,480.34	1,207.07	33.99	30.6	0.74	0.74
24	India Import of - WOOD AND WOOD PRODUCTS	3,747.36	846.77	4,101.95	903.48	9.46	6.70	0.56	0.56
25	India Import of - COMP.SOFTWARE IN PHYSICAL FORM	3,610.95	815.95	3,952.49	870.56	9.46	6.69	0.54	0.54
26	India Import of - OTH TXT YRN, FABS, MADEUP ARTL	3,326.96	751.78	3,748.26	825.57	12.66	9.82	0.51	0.51
27	India Import of - PROJECT GOODS	3,322.87	750.85	7,472.79	1,645.92	124.89	119.21	1.01	1.01
28	India Import of - NON-METLC MNRL MNFS EXCL PERLS	2,460.62	556.01	3,251.70	716.20	32.15	28.81	0.44	0.44
29	India Import of - PULSES	2,325.93	525.58	3,374.58	743.27	45.09	41.42	0.46	0.46
30	India Import of - PULP AND WASTE PAPER	2,288.44	517.11	2,578.60	567.95	12.68	9.83	0.35	0.35
31	India Import of - M-MADE FMNT/ SPUN YRN(INC.WAS)	2,244.97	507.28	2,340.27	515.46	4.25	1.61	0.32	0.32
32	India Import of - SILVER	2,153.16	486.54	742.11	163.45	-65.53	-66.41	0.10	0.10

(Contd.)

(1)	(2)	(3)	(4)	(5)	(6)	(7)	(8)	(9)	(10)
33	India Import of - CASHEW NUTS	2,018.10	456.02	1,733.16	381.74	-14.12	-16.29	0.24	0.24
34	India Import of - PAPER BOARD & MANUFACTURES	2,017.25	455.83	2,780.81	612.49	37.85	34.37	0.38	0.38
35	India Import of - DYENG, TANNG, COLRNG MATRLS	1,995.10	450.82	2,453.17	540.32	22.96	19.85	0.33	0.33
36	India Import of - PRNTD BOOKS, NWSPAPRS, JRNLS ETC	1,768.55	399.63	2,230.29	491.23	26.11	22.92	0.30	0.30
37	India Import of - NEWSPRINT	1,726.52	390.13	2,225.05	490.08	28.88	25.62	0.30	0.30
38	India Import of - SYNTHC & RECLMD RUBBER	1,396.69	315.6	1,888.52	415.96	35.21	31.8	0.26	0.26
39	India Import of - FRUITS & NUTS EXCL CASHEW NUTS	1,277.48	288.67	1,751.54	385.79	37.11	33.64	0.24	0.24
40	India Import of - FERTILIZERS, CRUDE	1,276.30	288.4	1,488.21	327.79	16.6	13.66	0.20	0.20
41	India Import of - COTTON YARN & FABRICS	1,125.42	254.31	1,332.47	293.48	18.40	15.41	0.18	0.18
42	India Import of - LEATHER	934.06	211.06	1,178.67	259.61	26.19	23.00	0.16	0.16
43	India Import of - SILK YARN & FABRICS	893.94	202.00	838.32	184.64	-6.22	-8.59	0.11	0.11
44	India Import of - OTHER CRUDE MINERALS	838.77	189.53	979.52	215.74	16.78	13.83	0.13	0.13
45	India Import of - WOOL, RAW	809.03	182.81	959.52	211.34	18.60	15.60	0.13	0.13
46	India Import of - PRIMRY STEL, PIG IRON BASD ITMS	735.19	166.13	1,571.52	346.13	113.76	108.35	0.21	0.21
47	India Import of - SILK, RAW	705.57	159.43	607.79	133.87	-13.86	-16.03	0.08	0.08
48	India Import of - SUGAR	651.00	147.10	3.27	0.72	-99.5	-99.51	0	0
49	India Import of - SPICES	631.71	142.75	669.88	147.55	6.04	3.36	0.09	0.09
50	India Import of - COTTON RAW: COMB./UNCOMB./WASTE	594.97	134.44	566.81	124.84	-4.73	-7.14	0.08	0.08
51	India Import of - SULPHR & UNROSTD IRON PYRTS	572.76	129.42	453.74	99.94	-20.78	-22.78	0.06	0.06

(Contd.)

(1)	(2)	(3)	(4)	(5)	(6)	(7)	(8)	(9)	(10)
52	India Import of - ESSENTIAL OIL & COSMETIC PREPN	564.11	127.47	720.03	158.59	27.64	24.41	0.10	0.10
53	India Import of - SYNTHETIC & REGENERATED FIBRES	306.65	69.29	407.35	89.72	32.84	29.48	0.06	0.06
54	India Import of - NATURAL RUBBER	251.99	56.94	649.19	142.99	157.63	151.12	0.09	0.09
55	India Import of - MADEUP TEXTILE ARTICLES	239.81	54.19	279.65	61.59	16.61	13.66	0.04	0.04
56	India Import of - RAW HIDES & SKINS	235.9	53.31	290.51	63.99	23.15	20.04	0.04	0.04
57	India Import of - READYMADE G-MENTS (WOVN & KNIT)	219.87	49.68	298.92	65.84	35.96	32.52	0.04	0.04
58	India Import of - WOOLEN YARN & FABRICS	202.29	45.71	137.77	30.35	-31.89	-33.62	0.02	0.02
59	India Import of - WOOLEN AND COTTON RAGS ETC.	177.63	40.14	145.01	31.94	-18.36	-20.43	0.02	0.02
60	India Import of - CEREAL PREPARATION	117.34	26.52	124.31	27.38	5.94	3.26	0.02	0.02
61	India Import of - TEA	98.02	22.15	118.37	26.07	20.76	17.71	0.02	0.02
62	India Import of - JUTE, RAW	73.19	16.54	110.94	24.43	51.58	47.75	0.02	0.02
63	India Import of - OIL SEEDS	40.06	9.05	82.43	18.16	105.77	100.57	0.01	0.01
64	India Import of - OTHER CEREAL	26.24	5.93	10.07	2.22	-61.63	-62.60	0	0
65	India Import of - VEGETABLES AND ANIMAL FATS	13.34	3.01	10.66	2.35	-20.08	-22.10	0	0
66	India Import of - MILK AND CREAM	13.19	2.98	26.16	5.76	98.38	93.37	0	0
67	India Import of - CEMENT	11.12	2.51	46.85	10.32	321.16	310.52	0.01	0.01
68	India Import of - RICE	0.01	0	0.41	0.09	4,008.85	3,905.02	0	0
	Total	**572,686.81**	**129,407.30**	**736,971.94**	**162,321.83**	**28.69**	**25.43**	**100**	**100**

Source: DGFT, GOI

India Export-Import Trade Statistics

Top Exports Products

Sources: Ministry of Commerce, Government of India

Insurance Sector Poised for 200% Growth

Indian insurance sector is likely to register unprecedented growth of 200% and attain a size of Rs. 2000 billion by 2009-10, in which a private sector insurance business will achieve a growth rate of 140% as a result of aggressive marketing technique being adopted by them against 35-40% growth rate of state-owned insurance companies.

The aforesaid findings are made by The Associated Chambers of Commerce and Industry of India (ASSOCHAM) on 'Insurance in Next 2 Years', saying that in the last couple of years, the insurance sector has grown by CAGR of around 175% and the trend will emerge still better because of potential factor. Currently, the insurance sector size is estimated at Rs.500 billion. On account of intense marketing strategies adopted by private insurance players, the market share of state-owned insurance companies like GIC, LIC and others have come down to 70% in last 4-5 years from over 97%.

The private insurance players, despite the sector is still regulated, has been offering rate of return (RoR) to its policy holders which is estimated at about 35% as against 20% of domestic insurance companies. This factor is mainly responsible for hike in private insurance market share which will grow further which is why the ASSOCHAM estimates that its growth rate could even exceed 140%.

Secondly, the state-owned insurance companies such as LIC and GIC have limited number of policies to offer to their subscribers while in case of private insurance companies, their policy numbers are many more and the premium amount as well as the maturity period is much competitive as against those of government insurance companies. Interestingly, said Mr. Dhoot that the private sector insurance players have started exploring the rural markets in which until recently, the state-owned companies had the monopoly.

The Chamber has projected that in rural markets, the share of private insurance players would increase substantially as these have been able to generate a faith among their rural consumers.

Estimating the potential of the Indian insurance market from the perspective of macro-economic variables such as the ratio of premium to GDP, ASSOCHAM reveals that India's life insurance premium, as a percentage of GDP is 1.8% against 5.2% in the US, 6.5% in the UK or 8% in South Korea.

ASSOCHAM findings further reveal that in the coming years, the corporate segment, as a whole will not be a big growth area for insurance companies. This is because penetration is already good and companies receive good services. In both volumes and profitability therefore, the scope for expansion is modest. The Chamber has suggested that insurer's strategy should be to stimulate demand in areas that are currently not served at all. Insurance companies mostly focus on manufacturing sector; however, the services sector is taking a large and growing share of India's GDP. This offers immense opportunities for expansion opportunities.

To understand the prospects for insurance companies in rural India, it is very important to understand the requirements of India's villagers, their daily lives, their peculiar needs and their occupational structures. There are farmers, craftsmen, milkmen, weavers, casual labourers, construction workers and shopkeepers and so on. More often than not, they are into more than one profession.

The rural market offers tremendous growth opportunities for insurance companies and insurers should develop viable and cost-effective distribution channels; build consumer awareness and confidence. The ASSOCHAM found that there are a total 124 million rural households. Nearly 20% of all farmers in rural India own a Kissan Credit cards. The 25 million credit cards used till date offer a huge database and opportunity for insurance companies. An extensive rural agent network for sale of insurance products could be established. The agent can play a major role in creating awareness, motivating purchase and rendering insurance services.

There should be nothing to stop insurance companies from trying to pursue their own unique policies and target whatever needs that they want to target in rural India. ASSOCHAM suggests that insurance needs to be packaged in such a form that it appears as an acceptable investment to the rural people.

Insurance Sector Opens up in India

The eagerly awaited Insurance Regulatory and Development Authority (IRDA) Bill to open the insurance sector in India to private and foreign players, was passed by the Lok Sabha on December 2, 1999 and by the Rajya Sabha on December 7, 1999. The Bill seeks to grant statutory status to the interim Insurance Regulatory Authority and amend the 1938 Insurance Act, the 1956 Life Insurance Corporation Act and the 1972 General Insurance Business (Nationalization) Act to end the public sector monopoly. The IRDA Bill incorporates the recommendations made by the Parliamentary Standing Committee on Finance (India Economic News, 1999).

Salient Features of Insurance Sector Reform Bill:

- The bill sought to regulate, promote and ensure orderly growth of the insurance industry and provides for solvency norms and specifies that the funds of policyholders would be retained within the country.
- The minimum capital requirement for life and general insurance has been retained at Rs. 100 crore ($ 23.02 million) and for reinsurance firms at Rs. 200 crore ($ 46.04 million) as provided in the earlier IRA Bill.

- It has been stipulated that the aggregate foreign holding in an Indian insurance company shall not exceed 26 per cent of the paid-up equity. Moreover, to provide a level playing field, it has been proposed that the Indian promoters would also be required to bring down their equity holding to 26 per cent after a period of 10 years from the commencement of business.
  The Bill has proposed solvency margins of Rs. 50 crores (US $ 11.51 million) for life and general insurance and Rs. 100 crores (US $ 23.02 million) for reinsurance companies.
- IRDA, in addition to other functions, would supervise the functioning of the Tariff Advisory Committee (TAC) and specify the percentage of premium income of the insurers to be set aside to finance schemes for promoting and regulating professional organizations in the insurance sectors.
- The four amendments, made in the Insurance Bill by the Lok Sabha, are as under:
  - The Insurance Regulatory and Development Authority (IRDA) should give priority to health insurance.
  - Policyholders' funds will be invested in the social sector and infrastructure. The percent may be specified by the IRDA and such regulations will apply to all insurers operating in the country.
  - Insurers will be expected to undertake a certain per cent of business in rural areas, and cover workers in the unorganized and informal sectors and economically backward classes.
  - In the event of insurers failing to fulfill the social sector obligations, a fine of Rs. 25 lakh ($ 0.06 million) would be imposed the first time. Subsequent failures would result in cancellation of licenses.

IRDA has also notified Micro-Insurance regulations facilitating insurers to tap the potential of rural markets. As per these regulations like Non-Government Organizations (NGO), Micro Finance Institutions (MFI) and Self-Help Groups (SHG) have been recognized as micro-insurance agents. It is envisaged that micro-insurance would facilitate penetration of insurance to rural and remote areas. He said that Micro-Insurance being an integral part of overall insurance system, attempts to offer the target specific insurance products at a relatively lower cost, for a lower coverage of amount.

Foreign equity upto 26% is allowed in the insurance sector. The entry of foreign partners has resulted in the sector attracting FDI of US $ 543 million as on 31st March, 2007. The private companies have created a niche for themselves. They have been able to increase their share in the insurance market in competition with their counterparts in the public sector. As a part of the reform process, premium rates for non-life insurance products have been de-tariffed w.e.f. 1.1.2007. Insurance Regulatory and Development Authority has granted registration to 37 insurance companies, which include 17 life insurance (including on PSU), 19 non-life insurance (including four PSU, one AICL and one ECGC) companies and one re-insurance company. At present seventeen insurance companies are operating in the general insurance side and seventeen insurance companies on the life side.

India offers a stable investment climate as well as a huge market with a growing middle class. Investor confidence in India is at an all time high today. A.T. Kearney in 'The FDI Confidence Index 2005' has ranked India as the 2nd most attractive investment destination just behind China whereas 'World Investment Report, 2005' ranked India as the 2nd most attractive investment destination among Transnational Corporations (TNCs).

FDI is now permitted in 21 activities through the auto-route. These include FDI in development of township, housing, built-up infrastructure and construction development projects, exploration and mining of diamonds and precious stones and insurance.

6

Sectoral Investment Opportunities in India for Achieving Global Competitiveness

A series of sectoral reforms, consequential to major economic reforms, initiated by the Government of India in 1991, has paved the way to create new business opportunities, particularly for the private investors and entrepreneurs in the country. This, over the years, has created fierce competitive environment among the private players to compete for market share. Leveraging on the policy of economic liberalization, many foreign investors, particularly the MNCs, are increasingly getting attracted to invest in India, mainly as Joint ventures with equity participation. Equally, many emerging Indian MNCs are also investing overseas into similar ventures in the forms of Greenfield operation, Merger and Acquisition, Strategic alliance etc. as the long-term growth strategy. But the key driving force in such endeavours will be to acquire global-level competencies mainly in the shape of high professional and managerial skills, blended with benchmarking high quality standards with six-sigma approach to match with global competitiveness.

Measured by global competitive standards and recent performances, India has demonstrated global leadership in Telecom and ITES, Textiles, Gems and Jewellery, Automotive Engineering, Manufacturing, Pharma, Biotechnology, Agribusiness, Retails, Oil and Natural Gas, Energy Transport and Power, Infrastructure, Port and Shipping, Banking and Insurance, Medico-Tourism, Hospitality, Technical and Management Education as evident from the fact that many lead Indian companies have transformed into MNCs to go global. In the given scenario, India has little choice but to enhance Global competitiveness to dominate the global market. The following sections are exclusively dedicated to highlight the state of Indian competitiveness in response to emerging investment opportunities in India and abroad—both by the Indian companies as well as foreign investors in potential sectors.

Competitiveness in Indian Service Sector

Overview of Services

Over the years, India, by virtue of exploitation of core competencies in IT/ ITES sector, amply backed up by conducive National Policy—such as IT Act, has gained global recognition as the Global leader in the sector—more prominently so in other inter-related Service Sector just as well. Most of the developing economies are in rapid transit towards becoming 'service economies' and therefore 'competitiveness of service sector' is emerging as a crucial factor influencing the overall competitiveness of a country, and India is no exception to this, where the share of services is increasingly getting higher in the total GDP, and also the growth rate of India's 'service exports' is higher than the world average, hence for India, out of the three pillars of competitiveness, one is certainly its service sector (Dugar, 2008).

About 58% of Indian GDP now comes from Services sector and large FDI has started flowing into this sector in India. IT/ITES appears to be largest and fastest growing services sector with estimated revenue of $ 34 billion. However, Indian economy has largely been regulated from time of independence till 1995 i.e. a few years after official milestone of economic liberalization in the country of 1991.

To enhance the competitiveness of the services sector, the high level group set up by the Planning Commission, Government of India has recommended that the education system must be reformed and expanded. The skill deficit in almost all service sectors must be eliminated through concerted action and the physical infrastructure, including the urban infrastructure and civic amenities, brought to world standards. The Working group, chaired by Planning Commission member Anwarul Hoda, noted: "Shortages exist equally at the level of managers and supervisors, and of skill categories. In some categories, the numbers being turned out by the institutions are extremely inadequate, while in other, the quality of trainees is poor and they need to undergo 'finishing' process so that they become employable." It has, therefore, recommended the establishment of the private sector led development councils for each sub-sector, broadly on the model of the Construction Industry Development Council (Jainath, 2008).

Urban infrastructure

Of particular interest to the services sector, is the quality of urban infrastructure, including sewerage, drainage, water supply, solid waste management and urban transportation. This is important in any city for smooth movement of people and goods. All cities must have an integrated traffic and transportation plan, the implementation of which should be monitored by a Unified Metropolitan Transport Authority, as envisaged in the National Urban Transport Policy. In large cities, a major requirement is provision of mass rapid transit systems, connecting various parts of the cities, including the railway stations and airports. The competitiveness of the services sector is affected if too much time of the worker is taken in commuting between residence and the workplace. In view of the increasing congestion and rising costs in existing metros, it is necessary for the State governments to promote new townships. Trade in IT and ITES being a main driver of growth in India's trade in services in recent years, this sector has been dealt with in detail. India has become a leader in IT and BPO offshore segments, accounting for an estimated 64 per cent of offshore IT spends and 41 per cent of offshore BPO spends in 2007.

Tourism

With tourism accounting for 5.83 per cent of the GDP and 8.27 per cent of employment in the country, it calls for special attention. It has been estimated that the shortfall in tourist accommodation in the country will be 1.50 lakh rooms by 2010, of which more than one lakh will be in the budget category. As land prices and availability were the main bottlenecks, the State governments could arrange for long-term lease of lands for hotel development. Similarly, the Indian Railways could speed up the proposal for development of budget hotels in its land on a PPP basis. Beach tourism was of particular interest and the Coastal Regulation Zone requirements have posed a major barrier. The Government has provided special incentives and tax breaks for development of convention centres and promotion of Meetings, Conference and Exhibitions (MICE). There has been considerable focus on health, medical education, and medical insurance too. The group emphasized the need for early implementation of the National Commission for Enterprises in the unorganized sector for a health insurance scheme for BPL families — about five crore families in five years.

Financial services

The projected shortage of manpower in financial services, notably banks and insurance, has been underlined in the Working group report, which calls for consolidation among players and leverage of the synergistic benefits. The growth of the financial services sector will be hampered by shortage of qualified people, unless there was investment in educating and training professionals. There is need for vocational training to equip those with high school and graduate level qualifications with skills for financial sector jobs. On bank jobs, the Working group specifically recommended: Individual banks should be given the freedom to determine their recruitment, placement, promotion, performance evaluation, and compensation policies, including performance bonuses and stock options. These are essential tools in attracting, retaining, and leveraging human capital, which is a key competitive differentiator.

Some of key features need to be addressed in Indian services sector businesses are:

1. Attitude towards employees, their compensation, reasonable job stability. Even now a good part of Indian business treats employee like that from regulates manufacturing system based on quotas and permits. Human resource is still considered as one of factors of production and most unwelcome and of least value as a factor.
2. Attitude to customer is also indifferent and casual having same mindset of regulated rationed economic development with shortages and Public Distribution order. Thus neglecting very essential difference in services and manufacturing sector that the former passes on intangible benefits and is based on personal relationship, service attitude and intense people processes. Creating credibility of services offering and post-sales service guarantee are major challenges.
3. Need for change to develop a global attitude in operations and marketing in services (World class operations and marketing).
4. Market forces and economics, rather than ideology will drive the 21st century.
5. Large amount of funds are required in infrastructure growth and capital assets required for various sectors like Hospitals, Hotels, Roads, Airports and Tourism packages. These required investments can be mobilized by encouraging FDI.
6. Focus on marketing backed by ITES technology for netter marketing and customer care, an important component in services marketing.

As compared to China, India has distinct advantages in services competencies based on inherent Indian cultural system and genes (for example-Traditional hospitality of Rajasthan and its majestic past make it a distinct place for Heritage and Conventional tourism) and high IQ and English-speaking erstwhile British colony. For example, Indian origin nurses are considered one of the best in world markets, particularly UK and US. US government has separate class of Visa for Nurses. It is also true for priests and ITES too. India can become important services outsourcing center providing both know-how and export of trained personnel. Healthcare is one of important sectors, which India can tap both offshore and by way of exporting skilled Medicare personnel. In USA alone the 8% of GDP on health care will rise to 18% or so due to rising population of senior citizens and the same is also true in Japan.

Any planning for boosting services exports without strong and well developed domestic market may have serious consequences in long run and not sustainable. The Key labor wage differential and high education level of English speaking Indians can be leveraged for sectors like R&D outsourcing. Moving high up in value chain is imperative for Indian services industry in a few years time, as other nations including China will be catching up with us fast.

Service Excellence

Excellence can be defined as the quality or state of being outstanding or superior since customers have rising threshold of satisfaction levels and hence excellence. Excellence will deliver memorable personal experiences including customer Delight. Since it is often difficult to standardize pricing in personalized need for services products and customer is not able to find value of the service product—reliability, loyalty programs, credibility and efficiency of service providers is vital for ensuring service excellence. It is a constraint that several top service organizations in India in various sectors like share registry and brokerage, insurance, higher education, medical care and public services are far from above mentioned quality components for excellence. In services as well as manufactured goods it is the value delivery and communication of this value proposition to customer is very important for growth and profitability. It would always be rewarding for organizations to develop the evaluation criteria by which customer can judge and appreciate the value. This is one area which needs well-designed systems and communication with customer. In multi-ethnic, multi-religion and multi-lingual society like in India it is quite daunting and challenging for creating such components of service excellence.

Factors Affecting Prosperity in Indian Service Sector

In just over a decade, India has grown into one of the world's leading economies. Out of an economic crisis that saw the country's gross domestic product (GDP) growth reduced to just 1.1 per cent in 1991, India now enjoys a current growth rate of 8 per cent annually, making it second only to China as the world's fastest-growing economy. Today, the country, which had long been one of the richest nations on earth prior to the 1800s, is once again becoming a global economic powerhouse—the world's fourth-largest economy after the United States, China, and Japan (as measured by GDP at purchasing power parity) in 2005. What is particularly impressive about India's recent growth is the distinctive way in which it has been achieved. Typically, poorer countries grow through low technology, labor-intensive processes that accelerate with the strong export of manufactured goods, which has been the primary driver for growth in China. By contrast, a large proportion of India's growth comes from high technology processes requiring skilled labor, in which exports of services have played a key role. This growth pattern has resulted in services becoming the largest component of the Indian economy—contributing 51 per cent of GDP—making India's situation unique in the developing world.

India has achieved dramatic success with a service-driven economy on the strength of its enough of the right ingredients to make it the right environment at the right time to do so. Those ingredients—changes that eased its regulatory environment, an available supply of skilled workers who, very importantly, spoke fluent English, and the minimum physical infrastructure—have helped India become an outsourcing destination of choice for many global technology services companies since the mid-1990's. A more important question, however, is whether India will continue to have enough of the right ingredients to continue its growth and further build an innovative services sector that is integrated into global services supply chains. Despite its recent successes India faces several internal and external pressures that could decelerate growth if not managed effectively. Its physical infrastructure, for example, is strained to capacity at the same time that other countries—notably, China, Brazil, Russia, Korea, Indonesia etc. are investing judiciously to create attractive environments that could enable them to surpass India as the leading service economy in the developing world.

New Regulatory environment

A key component in the recent growth of India's services sector was the country's move toward a more market-oriented regulatory environment in the early 1990s. During the previous decade, the country had achieved solid annual growth rates of 5.5 per cent, fueled by high rates of investment that required heavy borrowing from foreign sources. India's "new" regulatory environment focused on foreign trade. Import tariffs were cut in half from 56 per cent in 1990 to 28 per cent in 2004. Many restrictions on private companies were lifted, and a variety of anticompetitive regulations were removed. That, and the country's sizable educated workforce—India has a middle class of 300 million, equal to the entire population of the United States—many of whom speak English fluently, were largely sufficient to support an influx of new services industries, particularly in the information technology (IT) sector.

For India to further integrate itself into the global economy, and into global services supply chains, its regulatory environment must be better harmonized with prevailing global standards and practices. Among the most important of these are practices related to its capital markets. As Indian organizations move from state-run operations to private sector enterprises, they will need to participate in local and global capital markets to obtain the financing necessary to drive their growth. That may be difficult for them to do in a comparatively over-regulated and less-than-transparent business environment. To make themselves more attractive to investors, Indian companies need to focus on the business basics: world-class governance, monitoring more than just financing, effectively identifying and managing risk, and fostering an environment of innovation.

Good corporate governance practices are critical to building strong domestic capital markets in emerging economies. India's *Companies Act* outlines several important governance requirements, and the pace and tempo of adherence to them have increased significantly as a result of initiatives undertaken by the regulator, the Security Exchange Board of India. Since 2000, the Institute of Chartered Accountants of India (ICAI) has been working to bring Indian Accounting Standards in line with global standards, which will help ensure that Indian companies provide investors with information that is as transparent, and which measures performance in the same way, as that of companies from other jurisdictions.

Several factors facing professional services organizations in India—including limits on the number of individuals who may form a partnership, the number of audits an individual may perform, mandatory rotations of auditors for certain companies, and limits to the audit firms' ability to organize themselves and utilize their international networks—all constrain these firms' ability to meet demand. This is important because, as more global companies seek to establish operations, joint ventures, or other partnerships in India, they will require increasingly sophisticated professional services support for their operations.

Focus on critical infrastructure gap

India's economic development is somewhat restrained by inadequate infrastructure. One reason why importing, exporting, and transporting goods is as slow and difficult in India is the lack of sufficient networks over which to move them. Despite the fact highways are used to transport 80 per cent of goods in the country, they comprise only 2 per cent of the country's roads. The technological revolution that has occurred in global shipping, which has resulted in containerized shipping and consolidation among shippers, in turn resulting in port consolidation, has passed by India. The country cannot handle the large capacity vessels that account for one-quarter of global container capacity, and its inefficient ports are a key factor in its extended imports and exports. India also lacks a solid power grid—daily temporary blackouts are commonplace in many cities—and the country continues to have difficulty ensuring a sufficient supply of safe drinking water.

India's human infrastructure also presents challenges, particularly since an important ingredient in the current success of the country's services industries is the continuing rich supply of intellectual capital. Over 350,000 new engineers graduate each year and the large numbers of English-speaking graduates—3.1 million—helped the country attract IT outsourcing opportunities from global companies seeking to tap into a talent market that is available at a fraction of the cost of other countries. Indeed, opportunities for skilled workers are so good that many expatriate Indians are returning home to take advantage of the improved work environment and quality of life.

But while India continues to have enough talented workers to meet most of the needs of its services sector, these workers represent just a small portion of the population. Most Indians lack the skills to participate in a service economy, and continue to be employed in low-skilled, rural occupations. Three-quarters of the population leave school before finishing the eighth grade, and almost 40 per cent of the population is illiterate. Most adult Indians—almost two-thirds during the 1990s—are not employed, primarily because very few adult females are in the workforce. Just imagine the contributions to the Indian economy that could be made if an additional 10 per cent of the population—some 110 million people—became literate, or if more women joined the workforce (Delloite, 2007).

Building the infrastructure

In 2002, India invested just US $ 18 billion in its power and transport infrastructure, an amount equal to about 6 per cent of its GDP (by comparison, China invested US $ 128 billion in the same year, or about 20 per cent of GDP). The Indian government recognizes that much more needs to be done—it estimates that US $ 320 billion needs to be invested in roads, ports, and other infrastructure if India's current economic growth is to be sustained. The challenge, though, is to find the necessary funding. For example, of the US $ 4.3 billion capital investment required to upgrade India's railway network, just one-quarter will come from government. The remainder is to be attracted from the private sector. Private-public partnerships, therefore, will be critical to helping India address its infrastructure and other challenges. Such partnerships allow business and government to combine their complementary skills and share the responsibility for and the costs of completing projects quickly to address fundamental developments, such as infrastructure, education, talent development, and clean water supply. Since 2000, India has also started developing special economic zones (SEZs), similar to those in China, to help it encourage export reprocessing. While the SEZs could provide India with significant benefits, their effect may not be as dramatic as in China since Indian SEZs do not allow the free importation of components and raw materials. One of the easiest ways to boost infrastructure development may simply be to simplify India's regulatory environment. According to the International Monetary Fund, India's current tough regulatory regime is an important reason why the country is unable to generate adequate infrastructure spending.

Innovative Technology for building higher competitiveness

India has become the world's sixth most important offshore research and development location, and the country has a global reputation for being a leading jurisdiction for business process outsourcing (BPO) and call centers. As reported by various media outlets, global technology leaders such as Hewlett-Packard, Nokia, Ericsson, Motorola, Microsoft, IBM, and others are all investing in operations in India. Dell, for example, established a major production center that will employ 20,000 to serve the local Indian market, in which there was a demand for 5 million PCs in 2006 alone. And cell phone companies continue to enjoy one of the world's fastest growing markets in India, which is expanding at a rate of more than 50 per cent annually, or 5 million new subscribers each month. Technology industries also have a limited ability to help India address its employment problems. Despite their global reputation, India's IT industries are no more than "niche" employers—just 0.25 per cent of the Indian workforce works in IT. On the other hand, India has yet to tap into many of the technological benefits taken for granted in other countries. A lot of the supply chain functions, like logistics, are often carried out by people who are not very skilled or educated.

Planning an approach to innovation

According to the World Intellectual Property Organization, India's applications under the Patent Cooperation Treaty regime are increasing significantly, up 31 per cent in 2004 over 2002. New developments include those by Tata Motors—India's largest automobile company—which is using the country's low-cost engineering skills to develop a car that can be assembled on demand for customers at roadside garages. Ranbaxy Laboratories Limited developed an innovative drug delivery system for ciprofloxacin, which it then licensed to Bayer. It was reported in December 2006 that Intel, Microsoft, LANDesk, IBM, Cisco, and Lenovo jointly announced their launch of an innovation center in India. One particularly innovative solution to help India address its need for investment is provided by the 'Grameen Bank'.

India, over the years, will hopefully develop further innovations as it continues to address the regulatory, infrastructure, and other emerging challenges, typical of a fast-growing economy. How well it does so, however, will depend on how committed it is to building a modern business environment. While some of India's recent success occurred by design—its easing of various business regulations—much more was due to fortunate happenstance: the availability of a large English-speaking workforce and the development of global technology infrastructure. Further expanding its market economy will require much more proactive measures. China, for example, is already investing significantly more to create a more globally competitive business environment. While India's democratic government may make it harder to quickly enact changes and weather any short-term hardships related to those changes, it must nevertheless be as diligent as China in implementing a systematic, planned approach to building its economy if India is to sustain its current success.

Future Outlook of the Indian IT Industry

With a moderate degree of competitive advantage working to their favour, the top Indian IT companies can make inroads against the weaker competition. Put differently, though there may be new entrants it is certainly impossible for them to create another TCS, Infosys or Wipro. However, the competition from global players such as IBM and Accenture is accelerating at a great pace. The *comparative advantage* of low-cost labour that the Indian IT industry had been enjoying over other countries is now getting eroded with global MNCs setting up their shops in India. The rule of thumb in such a scenario would be to remain competitive and become *operationally efficient*. Apart from organic growth, Indian IT companies may also pursue the mode of inorganic growth. The trend has already started with few acquisitions been made by the biggies in the recent past. With industry maturing, there would be more consolidation activities to be witnessed. In such a case, only few players will concentrate the market.

Small and Medium Enterprises (SMEs): Issues in the changing Global economic environment

Problems facing the SSI sector

The SSI sector confronts several problems despite its strategic importance in any industrialization strategy and its immense potential for employment generation.

The problem which continues to be a big hurdle for the development of the sector is lack of access to timely and adequate credit. The Abid Hussain Committee on SSIs (1997) examined the problems of the SSI sector and recommended a package of policies to restructure the industry in the context of current global economic changes. The Expert Committee was of the view that the existing institutional structure for delivering credit to SSEs needs a thorough overhaul. It endorsed the recommendations of the Nayak Committee and urged the RBI to implement the same. The Committee recommended restructuring of financial support through SFCs and SIDCs, tapping of other sources of funding for SSEs, extending credit rating services to small units, and addressing the credit needs of tiny units to ensure that they are not bypassed by the commercial banking system. The overall credit availability for SSIs during 1991-1996 amounts to only 13% of the value of production (AIMA, 1997).

The Nayak Committee had recommended a desirable norm of 20% of the value of production to be made available by way of working capital through term-lending institutions and commercial banks. A norm of 75% was set for fixed capital assets whereas actual availability is only 55%. Lack of finance has been one of the major causes of sickness in the SSI sector, blocking access to technological modernization and other growth possibilities. There is an urgent need to enlarge flow of credit to the SSI sector from institutional sources. The creation of a facilitating environment for SSIs will centre on access to credit. The Ninth Five Year Plan (1997-2002) estimates additional working capital funds at Rs. 1420 to 1460 billion for the small sector. Lowering interest-rates, specifying a time-frame to clear loan applications and adherence to norms set down by the Nayak Committee are some of the minimum measures that need to be taken (Raju, 2008).

Competitive Strategy of SME Sectors

The SMEs' limited capacity to acquire information and use sources is a major factor explaining their low level of involvement and performance on export markets. Nonetheless, a small amount of applied research has been undertaken on this subject. We present the results of an inquiry into the impact of information search and competencies on the competitive strategy and export performance of 346 exporting manufacturing SMEs. The research model postulates that the performance of these SMEs is determined by their general competitive strategy, which in turn is explained by the ability of the business to acquire and manage foreign market information.

In the context of market globalization, the relatively low level of export involvement by small and medium-sized manufacturing enterprises, and the need to support economic growth through access to foreign markets, is of concern to both government and researchers. This is especially true for small market countries, such as Denmark, Belgium, Norway, and Canada, which must compete against economies such as the United States and Japan. Theoretical and empirical research findings published in the last 10 to 20 years on the factors that explain SMEs involvement in exporting all agree on one point: the limited ability of these businesses to acquire information and knowledge about foreign markets and to manage foreign activities is largely responsible for their relatively low level of exporting commitment and poor performance (Reid, 1984; Seringhaus, 1987; Christensen, 1991). Most SMEs simply do not make the effort, or are afraid of tackling international markets; but some of them limit their international activities because of their poor control over these activities, mainly as a result of a lack of information (Julien *et al.,* 1997). This problem is especially important because information is becoming a crucial resource in the knowledge economy and global market, not only for large enterprises, but also for SMEs. A better understanding of SMEs' information search would allow not only finding ways of helping these firms to develop and consolidate their activities abroad, but also to see how other firms with the potential or desire to begin international activities could improve and benefiting from their information practices.

Government Initiative for Boosting SME Sector

The importance and contribution of the SME sector to the economic growth and prosperity is well established. Their role in terms of employment creation, upholding the entrepreneurial spirit and innovation has been crucial in fostering competitiveness in the economy. Towards meeting the National developmental objective of a growth rate of over 8% on a sustained basis, it is imperative for the industrial sector to grow at a faster pace supported by a vibrant SME sector. Towards this, Government's policy initiatives like enactment of the new Micro-, Small and Medium Enterprises Development Act, 2006, pruning of reserved SSI list, advising FIs to increase their flow of credit to the SME sector, are all initiatives towards boosting entrepreneurship, investment and growth. There is an urgent need to enlarge flow of credit to the SSI sector from institutional sources. The creation of a facilitating environment for SSIs will centre on access to credit. The Ninth Five Year Plan (1997-2002) estimated additional working capital funds at Rs. 1420 to 1460 billion for the small-scale sector. Lowering interest-rates, specifying a time-frame to clear loan applications and adherence to norms set down by the Nayak Committee are some of the minimum measures that need to be taken. In the context of market globalization, the relatively low level of export involvement by small and medium-sized manufacturing enterprises and the need to support economic growth through access to foreign markets are of concern to government.

In order to improve the performance of Small and Medium Enterprises and to enable them to compete globally, Government has set up SMEs Renewal Fund for Technology Upgradation (RFTU), Creation of Quality Consciousness, and Promotion of Branding for Improved Marketing, Adoption of Improved Management Practices and Capacity Building. It is proposed to continue the scheme. State Government will have to set up Centre for Competitiveness to assist the small and medium scale industry to reap benefits of new technology, providing technology information services, consultancy and advisory services in agri-food processing and bio-technology sector. The Centre would undertake sectoral studies with the help of specialized organizations so that the industry in the region can regain its competitive edge. The centre will be funded from SME Renewal Fund. State Government will encourage the existing Small Scale Industrial units to undertake modernization and/or technology upgradation to meet the challenges of WTO regime.

Impact of WTO on SME Sector

The emerging challenges to the small-scale sector are to come from the impact of the Agreements under WTO to which India is a signatory along with 134 member countries. The setting up of the WTO in 1995 has altered the framework of international trade towards non-distortive, market-oriented policies. This is in keeping with the policy shift that occurred worldwide since the early 1980s in favour of free market forces and a tilt away from State regulation/ intervention in economic activity. This is expected to lead to an expansion in the volume of international trade and changes in the pattern of commodity flows. The main outcomes of WTO-stipulated requirements will be brought about through reduction in export subsidies, greater market access, removal of non-tariff barriers and reduction in tariffs.

There will also be tighter patent laws through regulation of intellectual property rights under the TRIPS Agreement which lays down what is to be patented (both products and processes), for what duration (20 years instead of the present 7 years under India's 1970 Patent Law), and on what terms. The responses by trading countries and the reframing of domestic economic policies which will result from the impact of WTO and the repercussions on the global economy of all these changes are highly uncertain as they involve several unforeseeable factors. However, there are certain indications of the shape of future trade patterns.

Increased market access to imports (of around 3% of domestic production to be raised to 5%) will mean opening up the domestic market to large flows of imports. The removal of quantitative restrictions (QRs) on imports has been speeded up to 2001. At present, 714 items are in the restricted category but imports of these items will soon be freed from all restrictions as announced in the recent EXIM policy. Increased market access under WTO requirements will also mean that our industries can compete for export markets in both developed and developing countries. But the expected surge in our exports can come about only if the SSI sector is restructured to meet the demands of global competitiveness which is the key to the future of small industries in the present context.

The SME sector in India faced a series of challenges due to the impact of the agreements of WTO (World Trade Organization), which India signed along with the other 134 member countries. The framework of international trade was diverted towards market-oriented policies in 1995 while setting up the WTO. In fact, this alteration of the framework was in accordance with the policy shift, which took place in the early 1980s. Apart from encouraging the free market forces, the impacts of WTO also resulted in greater market access, reduction in tariffs and export subsidies and removal of non-tariff barriers. In addition, the patent law became tighter under the TRIPS Agreement. The duration of patent was extended to 20 years from 7 years. Since the whole procedure of patent is quite expensive, this law was a big blow for the small and medium scale industries. However, there were certain positive sides as well. It increased the market access of the small and medium scale industries to imports. This enabled the SME sector to compete for export markets in the developed as well as in the developing countries (Mancha, 2008).

Indian Textiles and Garment Sector

The textile and garment sectors play an extremely significant role in India in terms especially of share in value added, foreign exchange earnings, and employment. With the impending dismantling of quotas in 2004 under mandate from the Agreement in Textile and Clothing of the WTO, the focus has clearly shifted to the future of the Indian textile and clothing exports.

A study conducted by ICRIER revealed that India's competitive performance in the US and EU markets for MFA (ATC) product categories, that are important in Indian export basket, and have found that Indian exports to the EU and the US are, on the whole, export-competitive. It has also delineated the changing landscape in the international trading environment which is likely to significantly impact global textile and clothing trade. To enhance the competitiveness of the industry, the study has highlighted areas requiring government policy intervention. The study concludes that while there is little doubt regarding the immense potential that the Indian industry—specially garment sector—has, several policy reforms are needed urgently in order to unlock this latent capability. Besides, from the emerging nature of global trading environment, it appears that market access would become an increasingly important aspect of translating competitiveness into export performance. The study provides significant inputs to policy-makers, industry captains as well as academicians towards unleashing the immense potential of the Indian textile and garment industry and enables the industry to realize its rightful place in the global economic space (Bardan, 2008).

Indian textile industry contributes about 20 per cent to the world spindleage of 166.36 million and three per cent to the world rotorage of 7.81 million and has the second highest spindleage in the world after China. It has also the highest loomage (including handloom) in the world and contributes about 64 per cent to the 8.9 million world loomage. It is the largest producer of jute, second highest producer of silk, third largest producer of cotton and cellulosic fibre/yarn and fifth largest producer of synthetic fibres/yarn. Despite the textile industry's strong presence in the world textile economy in terms of production of textile products, its share in the global trade is a meagre 3.11 per cent, while China with a comparable raw material base enjoys a trade share of 13.75 per cent. The reason for such low share lies in the fact that our export products are predominantly low value items and our insignificant presence in manmade textiles which predominate the world textile trade with a 70 per cent share. The world textile trade will be integrated by the end of 2004 as a result of the process of gradual phasing out of the tariff barriers by WTO, as envisaged. Consequently competition in domestic and global market has intensified and is likely to reach the level of the 'survival of the fittest' in the next few years. Besides, there is an implied threat, particularly from export-led economies, that our domestic market may face destabilization, albeit the fact that the free market offers unbridled opportunities. Modernization, productivity, quality and price will decide who will survive in post-MFA regime (http://www.expresstextile.com/20040415/annspecial21.shtml).

India's textile and apparel industries have grown at a steady pace in the last decade, but there is some apprehension about the immediate term outlook. India's exports of textiles and apparel have grown at a steady pace throughout the nineties. The same holds true for domestic consumption as well. However, there is no dearth of those who believe that a large part of this growth, particularly in apparel exports, has arisen because of the quantitative restraints applied by developed world importers including the U.S. and EU (JTN, 2001).

Global Competitiveness of Capital Goods

The study conducted by CWC on the "global competitiveness of Indian Capital Goods Industry" is based on application of measures of competitive performance and analysis of competitiveness issues. As a prelude to competitiveness analysis, the report seeks to define and classify Capital Goods, which have often been subject to non-uniform representation. The study formulates strategic goal to achieve global competitiveness, and identifies the actionable strategic initiatives and implementation plan to address the diagnosed lacunae in Indian Capital Goods industry (http://dipp.gov.in/first_new/globalrep/cap_good.pdf).

Capital Goods Definition, Classification and Selection

Capital Goods has been defined for the purpose of this study as any "product/ equipment of high value, durable (economic asset life of 3 years), used as plant and machinery for agricultural, industrial and commercial (transportation etc.) purpose in production/service delivery process". CWCe have adopted "use-based" classification to segment Capital Goods. From the list of classified segments, CWC have short-listed five most representative segments based on market size of the segment and its user industry, and IIP weightage of the segment. The five representative segments identified are as follows:

- Textile Machinery
- Machine Tools
- Electrical and Power Equipment which includes Boilers, Turbines, Diesel Engines, Transformers, Switchgear, Motors and Generators
- Earthmoving and Construction Equipment
- Process Plant Equipment which includes Pressure Vessels, Cooling Towers, Furnaces and Heat Exchangers

Competitiveness Analysis of Indian Capital Goods sector

The study of the performance of the Capital Goods sector reveals that its fortunes are inextricably linked with that of the overall Indian industry. High degree of correlation between the performances of the two sectors is further accentuated by high elasticity of Capital Goods industry to changes in industry growth. The Capital Goods value added contributes a fairly constant proportion (9-12 per cent) of the total manufacturing value added, thus establishing that manufacturing as the key end-user sector of Capital Goods drives the performance of the latter. Another key determinant of the demand for Capital Goods is the gross investment undertaken in the economy. The apparent consumption of Capital Goods constitutes a constant share (17-21 per cent) of the total Gross Domestic Investment in the country. On the supply side the output of Capital Goods is determined by investments in Capital Goods sector and capacity utilization. The investments in the Capital Goods sector have declined with the decline in the relative profitability of the Capital Goods sector with respect to other sectors. The export performance corroborates the inward focus of Capital Goods industry as less than one-tenth of its sales is directed to exports. Except for few segments within the Capital Goods sector, almost all of them have single digit exports as per centage of sales figures. Based on the study of industrial development trajectory and share in world exports of Capital Goods, we have chosen to compare Indian Capital Goods sector's competitiveness vis-à-vis three reference countries – China, Korea and Taiwan, and three benchmark countries – Japan, Germany and USA (PWC, 2008).

The India Advantage: Automotive Industries

India has the potential to become one of the top 5 automotive economies by 2025 based on its present growth potential. Steered here by the country's high engineering skills, established production lines, a thriving domestic automobile industry and competitive costs, global auto majors are rapidly ramping up the value of components they source from India. The industry is poised to jump from exports of US $ 1.8 billion in 2004-05 to US $ 5.9 billion in 2008-09. According to the Automotive Component Manufacturers Association of India, more than a third (36 per cent) of Indian auto component exports head for Europe, with North America a close second at 26 per cent.

In 2006, components worth US $ 2 billion were exported by Indian companies, 75 per cent of which were bought directly by car companies. The original equipment manufacturers (OEMs) include firms like General Motors, Ford Motor Company, Cummins International, Bosch, Volkswagen, BMW, MAN (trucks) and JCB (earthmoving equipment) amongst others. Over 20 OEMs have set up their International Purchase Offices (IPO's) in India to the components. This number is expected to double by the year 2010 (http://tacogroup.com/TACOedge/india.htm). India enjoys a cost advantage with regard to castings and forgings. The manufacturing costs in India are 25 to 30 per cent lower than its western counterparts. India's competitive advantage does not come from costs alone, but from its full service supply capability.

India—The Hub of Automotive R&D Base

India is slowly but steadily emerging as a major R&D base thanks to some innovative steps taken by the Industry as well as increased focus of Government initiatives. Global MNC's are shifting Automotive Design Centers into India as it is an excellent base for Prototyping, Testing, Validating and Productionizing of Auto-Components. India also has world renowned IT Skills with excellent Automotive Domain Knowledge. Some examples of the Global Design and research centers in India are General Motors, DaimlerChrysler, Ford, Caterpillar, Delphi, Bosch, Honda, Suzuki, Intel etc. The Government has set up a Core Group on Automotive R&D and produced a Technology Roadmap for this sector. The Vision is to enable an R&D program conducted cooperatively among industry, academia and government so as to promote technologies that will enhance energy security, environmental quality and economic growth towards establishing a globally competitive transportation industry (Intec.net, 2008).

The recommended Technology Program has identified three major areas:

1. Advanced Materials and Manufacturing: (Materials: High strength steels, aluminium, composites and plastics, manufacturing: Near-net-shape, flexible low cost manufacturing).
2. Alternate Propulsion: (Direct injection of alternate fuels in IC Engine (Straight vegetable Oils, Hydrogen), Hybrid Electric Vehicles: Drives and control systems, batteries and ultra capacitors).
3. Automotive Infotronics: Intelligent subsystems, control networks, sensors and Telematics.

It is also recommended to set up Centers of Excellence in the following fields:

- Centre of excellence in Combustion modeling and diagnostics
- Centre of excellence in Automotive Safety
- Centre of excellence in Recyclability and Manufacturing

Indian Manufacturing and Global Competitiveness

Call it the downside of explosive growth, but India's manufacturers face a daunting array of opportunities in the transition from being solely a low-cost manufacturing center to competing on the basis of innovation. This transition is being fueled by rapid growth in what for India are nascent industries—an opportune time for change. The challenge in catching up in R&D competitiveness is to do it right. Acquisition of a recognized brand or established company is one of the ways to compete with multinationals on their home turf. In some cases, such as pharmaceuticals, India has among the best manufacturing infrastructures in the world, and the stage is already set for a foray into research. Finally, global competitiveness involves reliability. India's manufacturing exports have risen impressively in the past decade or so and found to be directly linked to the world GDP and inversely related to real effective exchange rate (REER). Indian manufacturing industries have certain inherent strengths and advantages in having a relatively inexpensive, adequate and skilled labour force, cost-effective and competitive prices of goods produced, large manufacturing base and proximity to fast growing Asian markets.

India is one of the leading producers and exporters in a number of commodities and enjoys significant advantages in terms of lower labour costs as compared to other economies. Nevertheless, India's competitiveness is lost on account of lower labour productivity and higher input and material costs. To improve the competitiveness of the Indian manufacturing goods, issues like further diversification of export basket, upgradation of export quality, improvement in productivity, increased technology intensity in production, enhanced R&D activity, encouraging business environment, less cumbersome regulatory environment, flexible labour laws, removal of infrastructural bottlenecks and SME related issues need attention of all concerned (Lakshmanan *et al.,* 2007).

Competing in global manufacturing and service networks

Despite its modest 17 per cent share of domestic GDP, Indian manufacturing has the potential to become a world power. To fully exploit its potential, the Indian government has created the National Manufacturing Competitiveness Council (NMCC). The NMCC has begun to develop a national strategy with regard to technology and academic leadership. Similarly, companies have so far been unable to tap the full potential of emerging markets such as India, with only 29 per cent of executives in a global survey indicating their companies have actually achieved higher margins in these markets. Talent management has emerged as a crucial factor, as has the ability to move beyond successful developed-economy strategies that may not be optimal in the context of a multinational strategy. For Indian manufacturing, growth strategies can be viewed through the lens of the Four Forces framework of enablers, which encompasses modularity of products and supply chains, connecting technologies, economic integration, and resource management. National competitiveness—a prerequisite for corporate and industry competitiveness—tends to emerge from savvy decisions by governments and the private sector in these four areas.

Operational excellence in Indian manufacturing

Most activity in the manufacturing cycle constitutes waste: inefficiencies abound. Lean manufacturing is a key to pushing prices lower while maintaining profits and quality and, happily, India is uniquely positioned to pursue excellence in this area. From customized machines that can perform operations more efficiently to low-cost automation, which would take advantage of the skills of legions of talented design engineering people in India, process improvement is both feasible and essential. Operational excellence in Indian manufacturing often involves considerations foreign to planners in developed countries. Backward integration can be a wise move in India, where irregularities in power delivery can wreak havoc on a tightly run production facility. Reliance, for example, has a captive power plant, which it runs on an economical scale.

Global policy issues affecting Indian manufacturing

It's hard not to talk about China when speculating about India's growth potential, because both countries have enjoyed the spotlight in manufacturing over the last decade. But in fact there are major differences, and while services are presumed to be the key to India's continued growth, China has surpassed India in service exports. On the other hand, India may be poised to occupy the manufacturing space vacated by China due to its wage advantage. Much of the future of Indian manufacturing may hinge on the plight of Indian infrastructure—currently the biggest obstacle on the road to growth. Most infrastructure remains in the public sector, even as the Indian government has begun to reduce its borrowings and therefore may be tightening funding. The software and IT industry has been very good to India, and in many ways it has been more glamorous than the types of investments required for an infrastructure conducive to manufacturing.

Collaborating across the supply-chain

Supply chains appear to be an almost bottomless well for improvement, even with outsourcing having already moved from new idea to accepted practice. More recently, dynamic supply chains have emerged to offer a new dimension of supply chain efficiency and, simultaneously, complexity. Dynamic supply chains are agile, ad hoc networks that work together as the situation dictates. They make supply chain optimization—never a paper-and-pencil exercise to start with—even more of a complex science. Additional wrinkles, such as reverse supply chains, which retrieve a used product from a customer and repair or dispose of it, point to a world where supply chain management may be the forefront of competition. Another consideration is how the rise of outsourcing has placed an increased importance on negotiation, and how companies can best approach that arena alone and collectively.

Growth Strategies for Indian Manufacturing Industry

One can look at competitiveness at various levels—at the level of individual corporate firms, at the industry level and at the national level. Of course, these three are not independent but are highly correlated. An individual firm's competitiveness is dependent on the competitiveness of the environment in which the vertical industry and the national economy operate. Excellent logistics and IT infrastructure are becoming prerequisites for global competitiveness among manufacturing and service companies. The need of the hour for India is to meet local and global markets under open and fair economic conditions. It is possible for India to achieve very dynamic growth based upon labor-intensive manufacturing, which combines the vast supply of Indian labor, including skilled managerial and engineering services, with foreign capital, technology and markets. But to succeed, India must follow a balanced approach of developing its manufacturing capabilities, service infrastructure and operational capabilities, follow the right economic and trade policies, and finally develop the right kind of resource management skills. The Four Forces framework provides a basis for creating a competitive global manufacturing network in this context.

Scale and Innovation

For Indian companies, it is a problem of plenty as far as opportunities go. Typically, companies react to opportunities by going low-cost, expanding geographically or through mergers and acquisitions, or innovating continuously. The low-cost story is becoming less applicable in Indian manufacturing because of rising wages and firming interest rates. As for geographic expansion, most manufacturing companies do not necessarily have the managerial capability to run profit centers in other parts of the world. Also, few Indian companies are cash-rich. Most would therefore end up acquiring very small companies that might not add value. Mergers and acquisitions, again, are often difficult to accomplish for Indian manufacturing companies. That leaves innovation, which has not yet been fully exploited.

An ongoing Deloitte benchmark study of more than 35 Indian manufacturing companies against 140 multinational companies that have manufacturing operations in India has shed light on what Indian manufacturing companies are doing right and what they need to change. Companies across the spectrum agree that innovation is probably the manufacturing industry's most underexploited strategy. If the Indian manufacturing industry is to remain competitive over the next 15 years, it will need to focus on its innovation capabilities. The opportunity for dramatic improvement and transformation of business models in Indian manufacturing is significant. With average annual growth rates of nearly 20 per cent among the companies benchmarked based in India, companies are presented with an unprecedented chance for re-inventing themselves. Growing at that rate, just five or ten years down the road, the vast majority of investments in the business will be new investments. As opposed to the multinational companies that have stopped depending on the well-being of the economy or just the market in which they operate, Indian companies seem to consider those two as the main drivers for business in the foreseeable future. Indian companies lag behind their global competitors in research and development. This is, however, something that will start to change in the coming months and years as these companies look to launch products and services on a continual basis.

The best-performing companies in the global benchmark research, called "complexity masters," are far better at synchronizing innovation across the enterprise. They invest in better processes and technologies for optimizing the entire life cycle of products and services. The result is far better performance with profit levels up to 73 per cent higher than the competition. Many domestic Indian manufacturers as well as multinationals operating in India have a hard time keeping up and building the capabilities needed to succeed. In Indian manufacturing, the most worrying evidence is that of the lack of visibility into strategic information. This makes it difficult to take the right decisions in strategy, planning and execution. The other major challenge is that of flexibility. Indian companies will face increased complexity and constraints on flexibility as they continue their domestic and global expansion. In fact, the average Indian company is not lean at all.

Indian manufacturers lack the technology support for looking at the life cycle data of the products. Without this data, innovating on the product portfolio is difficult, if not impossible. Indian manufacturers are far behind multinationals in India when it comes to adopting leading technologies—despite the low cost of technology in India compared to the more developed countries. This low rate of technology adoption poses a real risk to Indian manufacturers' futures, limiting their participation in global value chains where these technologies are required. In the absence of lean processes or visibility, a lot of management time goes into day-to-day issues and firefighting with very little time left over for future planning and innovation. Despite a lackluster record when it comes to R&D, Indian manufacturing has recorded high growth, creating a unique opportunity for innovation. In fact, India is the top destination in the world for R&D investment. The cost of innovation in India is typically one-third that in developed markets; it is among the lowest globally. Manufacturers need to seize this opportunity to innovate with respect to products, processes, technologies and business models.

Summit on Indian Manufacturing Competitiveness

The second summit on India's manufacturing competitiveness was held on August 2-4, 2006, at the Indian School of Business, Gachibowli, Hyderabad, campus.

Manufacturing is the backbone of the Indian economy. Global competitiveness in manufacturing fosters growth, productivity, and employment, and strengthens the agriculture and service sectors. Rapid advances in worldwide distribution systems and information technology, combined with a lowering of trade barriers, has led to the proliferation of global manufacturing and service networks designed to take advantage of low-cost wage structures and reach local markets.

The 2006 Summit on Indian Manufacturing Competitiveness: Global Manufacturing and Service Networks explored the challenges and opportunities of global supply chain management in India, and the successes of Indian enterprises operating in global industries. The Summit helped set the agenda to take the manufacturing industry to the next level of competitiveness, and focus on lessons learned from developed and emerging economies across North and South America, Western Europe, Central and Eastern Europe, and Asia-Pacific. An annual event, the Summit provides a continuing forum for leading industry experts, business executives, and academic researchers from around the world to share experiences, ideas, and industry- and firm-specific research focused on the growth of manufacturing sector, as India begins to exploit its industrial potential (ISB, 2006).

The study of the competitiveness of global manufacturing and service networks demands expertise from diverse fields such as manufacturing operations, innovation and product development, sourcing strategies, supply chain network design and optimization, systems development and implementation, service network management, international trade, finance, and economics, international logistics and transportation. Topics addressed at the conference included:

- Global sourcing strategies
- Logistics in emerging markets
- Infrastructure supply chains
- Distribution systems in emerging markets
- New technologies for enhancing supply chain visibility
- Value chain synchronization
- Service innovation and service networks
- Differential pricing of products and services
- Integrated manufacturing and service networks
- Foreign direct investment and International trade
- Trade documentation automation
- Design of special economic zones (SEZs) in China, India, and other emerging markets
- Manufacturing networks in automotive, pharmaceuticals and food.

The National Manufacturing Competitiveness Council (NMCC) has been set up by the Government to provide a continuing forum for policy dialogue to energize and sustain the growth of manufacturing industries in India. The NMCC is expected to suggest various ways and means for enhancing the competitiveness of manufacturing sector including identification of manufacturing sectors which have potential for global competitiveness; current strengths and constraints of identified sectors, and recommend National level industry/sector specific policy imitative as may be required for augmenting the growth of manufacturing sector.

The National Common Minimum Programme had identified the need to have a continuing forum consisting of representatives from Government, the Industry and the Academicia for policy dialogue to energize and sustain the growth of the manufacturing industry. Food processing, Textiles and Garments, Engineering, Consumer goods, Pharmaceuticals, Capital goods, Leather and IT hardware are among the priority items specifically mentioned in the Common Minimum Programme.

Since 1991, the Indian economy is being progressively liberalized and its integration to the global economy is deepening. On one hand, the liberalization and globalization have provided unprecedented opportunity for the growth and expansion of the industry in general and the manufacturing in particular. On the other hand the Indian industry has to not only face stiff competition from free imports but also continue its efforts to grow its export capability through competitiveness. There is a continuous need to benchmark the Indian manufacturing sector against the best in the world and enhance competitiveness of the manufacturing sector.

Indian Gems and Jewellery

The Gems and jewellery (G&J) market essentially comprises of sourcing, processing, manufacturing and selling of precious metals and gemstones, such as, Gold, Platinum, Silver, Diamond, Ruby, and Sapphire etc. The G&J market is a significant contributor to the Indian economy, based on the size of the domestic market and through its contribution to the country's exports (http://www.bharatbook.com/Indian-Gems-Jewellery-Market.asp). India is the largest consumer of gold (around 20 per cent of global consumption) and also the largest diamond processor (around 90 per cent by pieces and 55 per cent by value of the global market). India's G&J industry is highly unorganized and fragmented with 96 per cent of the total players being family owned businesses. The gold processing industry has around 15,000 players, with only 80 having revenues over US $ 5 million. India is also home to around 450,000 goldsmiths, 100,000 gold jewellers along with 6,000 diamond processing players and 8,000 diamond jewellers. The value chain of the industry starts from sourcing and mining of the metals and extends to jewellery retail. While India is not a major miner of previous metals and stones, the country's inexpensive and well skilled workforce makes it a world leader in processing of diamonds. The country's jewellery retail sector is also expected to evolve with a shift among consumers towards branded jewellery, driven by greater quality consciousness (Bharat Book Bureau-http://www.bharatbook.com/Indian-Gems-Jewellery-Market.asp).

There are a few major players in the G&J segment, with Rajesh Exports being the most dominant name. Other key players in the field include Gitanjali Gems, Suhashish Diamonds, Su-Raj Diamonds, Viabhav Diamonds and Tanishq. Many of these players are focused on developing strong brands, large retail operations, strengthening their core manufacturing operations and building a strong international presence.

India's large population and rapid economic growth offer significant opportunities for growth of the industry. The emergence of jewellery retail chains provide customers with convenience and assurance of quality. The entry of foreign players is also likely to increase competition and provide consumers with greater choice. Apart from the above, there are other factors that contribute to a favorable outlook for the industry.

The 'Indian Gems and Jewellery Market' report provides a snapshot of the Gems and Jewellery industry in India. It covers an overview of the size and growth of the sector along with the market structure and various segments of the market including Gold, Silver and Diamonds. Additionally, the report will give a picture of the value chain of the sector from mining to retailing of jewellery. This will help the client in determining the market dynamics and future prospects of the industry.

About the Industry

The Indian Gems and Jewellery (G&J) market contributes significantly to the Indian economy through its vast domestic and export market. India apart from being the largest consumer of gold is also the largest diamond processor in the world. The Indian G&J market is predominantly focused on sourcing, processing, manufacturing and selling of precious metals and gemstones. Although, the gold processing industry in India has 15,000 players, there are only 80 players with revenues over US $ 5 million. As a result, there is high growth potential for Indian gems and jewellery in the global market. India is not a major miner of precious metals and stones, however the country's inexpensive and skilled workforce are one of the best in the world for processing of diamonds (Res. and Markets-2008).

Importance to Economy

The GJ industry has an important role in the Indian economy. While a predominant portion of gold jewellery manufactured in India is for domestic consumption, a predominant portion of rough, uncut diamonds processed in the form of either polished diamonds or finished diamond jewellery is exported. With an estimated consumption of 722 tonnes during calendar year or CY2005 (including jewellery consumption of 587 tonnes), India is the largest consumer of gold in the world. India is also estimated to hold nearly 14,000 tonnes of gold, accounting for nearly 9% of the world's cumulative mine production. Apart from its historical religious significance, gold is valued as an important savings and investment vehicle. The GJ industry also contributes around 15% of India's exports. As the table 1 below shows, exports of GJ aggregated Rs. 688.30 billion (US $ 15.55 billion) during FY2006, accounting for 15.1% of India's exports. Ignoring minor year-on-year variations, the share of GJ in India's exports has grown over time from 4% in 1972-73 (ICRA, 2006).

Table 1: Indian Gems and Jewellery Exports and Imports

FY	Exports billion		% of total export	Imports billion		% of total imports	Trade Balance billion	
	Rs.	US $		Rs.	US $		Rs.	US $
1973	0.79	0.10	4.0%	0.42	0.05	2.2%	0.38	0.05
1995	141.31	4.50	17.1%	51.17	1.63	5.7%	90.14	2.87
1996	176.44	5.27	16.6%	70.45	2.11	5.7%	106.00	3.17
1997	168.72	4.75	14.2%	103.84	2.93	7.5%	64.88	1.83
1998	198.67	5.35	15.3%	124.21	3.34	8.1%	74.46	2.00
1999	249.45	5.93	17.8%	158.20	3.76	8.9%	91.25	2.17
2000	325.09	7.50	20.4%	235.56	5.44	10.9%	89.54	2.07
2001	337.33	7.38	16.6%	219.63	4.81	9.5%	117.70	2.58
2002	348.45	7.31	16.7%	220.45	4.62	9.0%	128.00	2.68
2003	437.01	9.03	17.1%	293.41	6.06	9.9%	143.68	2.97
2004	485.86	10.57	16.6%	327.57	7.13	9.1%	158.29	3.44
2005	618.34	13.76	16.5%	423.38	9.42	8.4%	194.96	4.34
2006	688.30	15.55	15.1%	404.69	9.14	6.4%	283.61	6.41

The bulk of the Indian GJ exports comprise import of rough diamonds, cutting and polishing in India, and re-export. As per data released by the Gems and

Jewellery Export Promotion Council (GJEPC), cut and polished diamonds (CPDs) accounted for 71.1% of India's GJ exports of Rs. 733 billion during FY2006, followed by gold jewellery (23.2%), rough diamonds (3.4%), and others (2.3%). Thus, two items viz. CPDs and gold jewellery account for around 95% of India's GJ exports.

With negligible production of gold and diamonds, the Indian GJ industry is almost entirely dependent on imported raw materials. During FY2006, imports of pearls, precious and semi-precious stones aggregated Rs. 404.69 billion (US $ 9.42 billion), accounting for 11.2% of India's non-bulk imports, and 6.4% of total imports. The Indian GJ industry is also a major earner of foreign exchange, with a trade surplus of Rs. 283.61 billion (US $ 6.41 billion) during FY2006, as compared with an overall trade deficit of Rs. 1,757.27 billion (US $ 39.69 billion). The GJ industry has contributed significantly to the shift in India's exports. They, along with chemicals and allied products, engineering goods, ready-made garments, textile yarn, fabrics, made-ups have been the main drivers within the manufactured product exports during the last decade. With the increase in exports in recent years, the GJ industry has also accounted for an increased share of gross bank credit (GBC) of scheduled commercial banks (SCBs). With GBC of Rs. 198.66 billion in March 2006, the industry accounted for 3.61% of industry GBC of SCBs in March 2006, as compared with 2.7% in March 2000.

Future Outlook

The future of the industry is quite promising. More and more buyers across the world are turning to India as their preferred source for quality jewellery. The Gems and Jewellery Export Promotion Council (GJEPC) is looking at exploring new markets, such as Latin American countries. The industry also plans to make India a trading centre for cut and polished diamonds, and is closely working with the Government of India in this regard. The long-term prospects looks good with jewellery exports expected to touch US $ 16 billion in 2010 according to industry estimates.

Emerging Opportunity in the Indian Food-chain

India is one of the fastest growing economies in the world and one of the largest in terms of Purchasing Power Parity. Global brands are re-starting the hype of a decade ago, as they envisage how to take advantage of the massive population and rapidly growing income and consumption to create new business streams, sales and profits. But several challenges remain before companies can grab the big prize in India - fragmented chains, poor infrastructure plus policy and regulation issues make it difficult for retailers to make their move. However, things are improving as the Indian government start to make effective and coherent efforts to bring about change in the perishables supply chain (Res. and Market, 2005). But several challenges remain before companies can grab the big prize in India - the fragmented chain to handle perishable commodities in India, other polices and regulations and physical infrastructure being far behind what European or American companies are accustomed to.

In the past few years, the Indian government has made several attempts, to create positive changes to enable the perishables chain, including fresh and processed produce, but most has paled in view of the scale of the challenges and the scope of the opportunities. However, more recently, various departments and ministries have begun to make more effective and coherent efforts to bring about change in the perishables supply chain in India. The timing, then, is ripe for Indian and international firms to participate in this process of change. International companies known to be looking at entering the Indian market include McDonald's and Metro - case studies are presented to describe how these major retailers have structured their operations around the unique mix of opportunities and challenges in India.

Potentials of Food-Processing Industries

The food processing industry is coming of age; it is ranked fifth among industries of India. Nearly one third of the entire Indian food market share comprises of processed food. With policy measures from the government, the food processing industry accounts for 13% of the country's exports. The industry's size is estimated at US $ 70 billion; including US $ 22 billion of value-added products. Indians spend half of their household expenditure on food items at present. The industry would create 9 million employment opportunities from the current 1.6 m and investment of Rs. 1,50,000 crore in the coming 10 years.

With over 1 billion population and 350 million strong urban middle class and changing food habits, the processed food market is promising a huge potential to be tapped. A joint study by CII and AC Nielsen (market research firm), to understand demand drivers for processed food brings forth the changing Indian meal patterns: Working lunch seems to be replacing conventional meals in the day, with a need for no fuss packaging. In addition to this, the study says, Indians are willing to spend on global cuisines. Multi-cuisine restaurants are mushrooming even in small cities and towns. This reasons the array of foreign investors coming to India which is driving the growth of the industry. Like investments to offer Indians the real taste of Italian pasta; conglomerates from Emilla Romagina are looking at major Indian cities to set up Italian food processing plants. Most recent one was the proposal from West Midlands of UK to the Ministry of Food Processing Industries of India. Other foreign food companies like McDonald's, Pizza Hut, Cadbury's, Tropicana, Pepsi, Coke, HLL, Nestle, etc. are already earning huge returns by processing Indian food for domestic and global markets. Besides foreign investors, food processing sector is a major attraction for Indian corporate houses to invest. Reliance, Godrej, Bharti, ITC, Hero, Ballarpur Industries, DSCL, Tata and

Mahindra and Mahindra are prominent corporate houses with end-to-end integrated operations in the food chain.

Government's Initiative

Food processing has been declared as a priority sector. The National Food Processing Policy has been revised for an integrated approach in 2004-05 to facilitate speedy growth. The aim of the policy is to simplify procedures to comply with the need and growth of the sector. Under infrastructure development, Agro-Food Parks are identified in various Indian cities. Proposals to set up 20 Mega Parks and 50 Food Parks adopting the French Food Park as a model are undertaken by the Ministry of Food Processing Industry.

Tapping the industry's export potential is one of the major concerns. Presently, current exports of Indian processed food are worth Rs. 2500 billion. Agri-Export Zones (AEZs) are earmarked with nearness to highways, airports and marketing centers from the areas of food processing. The Policy urges private companies to grow processable varieties under contract farming. Under the AEZ scheme, state governments and private firms are entitled privileges of Special Economic Zones, like tax holidays up to 10 years and duty free imports of capital-goods to set up processing units.

To provide financial credit without any bottlenecks NABARD in the present plan is given with a corpus of Rs. 1100 million in single window clearing. This loan is for setting up new unit or to modernize an existing food processing units. Further, the government will give 25% subsidies for Greenfield projects up to the corpus of Rs. 100 crore for Mega Food Parks and up to Rs.105 crore for Food Parks.

For holistic approach, R&D initiatives to work on emerging challenges of the food processing technology and food engineering are underway. The industry's revenues can be increased if quality rules of SPS, VHT and the Codex international standards are approved. The Thanjavur paddy processing center will be added to the nationalized list of research institutes. Likewise, Indian packaging Industry is working on low cost and competitive packaging solutions. Packaging costs 20-70% of processed food.

Growth Potential

Over the past decade money spent by Indians on ready to eat food outside home has more than doubled. While 5 billion US $ is spend on ready to eat food this year research estimates it to double up in over five years. This year, the growth in sales (domestic and export) of processed food is more than 150%, most remarkable are the two sectors which showed remarkable growth in sales. Processed poultry's sales grew by 64%, and spirits and beverages by 75%. Food process outsourcing is presenting good prospects in multi-cuisine hotels and restaurants abroad for processed or semi-processed Indian seafood, dairy and Indian curries. 'Made in India' brands like Amul Dairy, Cobra Beer,

Bikanervala Foods, MTR Foods, ITC's Kitchen of India, Satnam Overseas' Basmati rice are finding prime global retail shelf-space. Convenience, variety and health issues are key drivers for quality of packaged food. With clear demand in the future if India can harness its production to the quality its dream to become the world's food basket is sure to come true (Chintala, 2008).

New Opportunities in Indian Retail Segment

The up-market retail sector seems set for a virtual explosion with the entry of a whole host of domestic players while foreign companies are waiting and watching eagerly on the sidelines. With India being one of the biggest emerging markets, it is no wonder that retail giants like Wal-Mart and Carrefour are eager to make an entry. India is estimated to have around 15 million retail outlets, making it the country with the highest retail outlet density in the world. It also tops AT Kearney's list of emerging markets for global retailers. Currently the value of the retail market is estimated at around $ 270 billion with a growth rate of 5.7 per cent per annum according to the India Retail Report 2007 (Indian Retail, 2008). For the time being, however, domestic giants like Reliance, Pantaloon, ITC, RPG, Rahejas and the Bharti group have jumped into the fray. The fact is that big retail chains have a lot to offer both the farmer and the consumer. On the other hand, the vibrant Indian trading community is going to be hard hit. Farmers are keen for big retailers to come in as they help in both marketing and processing of output without their having to go to middlemen in the mandis. Consumers similarly are reaping a bonanza as prices at these shops are at rock bottom rates since big retailers can afford to buy directly from the farmers.

No wonder that there have been reports of farmers protesting in Jharkhand against efforts to stop big retailers from buying tomatoes directly from them. In contrast, there were reports from another city of small retailers protesting in front of a Reliance Fresh showroom saying it was ruining their business. Politicians, of course, are entering the fray to oppose the entry of large retail chains, but clearly economic forces are now going to play a larger role. In this context, some of the data on the retail sector in India makes for interesting reading. For instance the CII-AT Kearney retail study shows that retailing is the largest contributing sector to the country's GDP. Besides, the retail sector contributes about 10 per cent to the GDP compared to 8 per cent in China, 6 per cent in Brazil and a matching 10 per cent in the US. As for job potential, the retail industry is the second largest employer after agriculture, employing about 6-7 per cent of the total work force.

Data clearly shows that the retail sector is not only extremely large but provides a huge amount of jobs in this country. The entry of the organized large retail chains may not have an immediate impact on the trading community. But in the long run, it is clear that small traders and retailers will be affected and the government cannot ignore the issue. While one would ideally like to take the side of the consumers and the farmers on the issue, it is evident that the muscling in of the big retailers may lead to large-scale closures of small trading outlets. And this in turn could affect many families relying on jobs in this sector. At the same time, the investments made by large food retailers in farm production could lead to tremendous savings as huge amounts of fruit and vegetables that cannot be processed are simply thrown away in India.

The government, on its part, insists that small retailers may face competition from the big fish but have definite advantages over them owing to low overheads, local market knowledge and their engaging in services like home delivery and sales on credit. It also points to the fact that wastage estimated in the Indian food chain is around 40 per cent, valued at over Rs. 500 billion ($ 10 billion) annually. A study by the Indian Council for Research on International Economic Relations (ICRIER) has also shown that only about 2 per cent of fruits and vegetables are processed in this country. In this backdrop, it is felt that there is no option but to allow big retail chains to make huge investments needed to create an efficient and modern agro processing industry (Indian Realty News, 2007).

Simplifying India for Global Retailers

Indian merchandise exports grew from US $ 22.2 billion in 1993-94 to US $ 101 billion in 2005-06. They are expected to reach US $ 150 billion in 2008-09. This impressive growth can be attributed to the liberalization of the investment policy, export subsidies and the devaluation of the rupee. Also, global retailers' increased interest in India's unique product mix, available at low costs, fuelled this growth. Sourcing from India is not easy, though. Retailers encounter small factories with limited capacities, and must deal with multiple vendors for different products. Manufacturers' lack of awareness of quality norms and design and trend requirements are other hindrances. Unhealthy working conditions for employees and the language and communication barriers in parts of the country make dealing with Indian manufacturers very difficult. Small Indian manufacturers have their own problems, beginning with a lack of awareness of what is happening around the world. There is little R&D infrastructure in the country to support them.

The absence of any centralized information centre and the lack of information on best manufacturing practices are further handicaps. Small manufacturers are also short on marketing expertise and capital. These roadblocks assume greater significance in view of China's growing strength in areas previously considered India's domain. For example, glass ornaments from Ferozabad are being replaced by plastic ornaments from China. Metal decorative items from Moradabad are being replaced by resin items from China. China has some obvious advantages over India, not the least of which is a head start in manufacturing, high capacity and shorter lead times to markets in the United States and Europe (CII-AT Kearney Report, 2006).

Given these challenges, the emergence of buying houses has been a bonus. Set up mostly by professionals who have worked for the Indian offices of western trading companies, these buying houses are emerging as a link between Indian manufacturers and global retailers. For retailers, these buying houses are business partners who speak the same language, work on transparent terms of payment, and can guarantee that the factories they work with follow environmental and safety norms, and that the goods produced are of acceptable quality. For the manufacturers, buying houses offer guidance on product and process knowledge and can be their advocates with the retailers. Buying houses help vendors develop capacities, research products and pass on the resulting solutions to the manufacturers. They also have more negotiation power with service providers, including logistics players, as they combine volumes from different manufacturers and retailers. With the increase in globalization of retailers both in terms of their points-of-sale, as well as their points-of-supply, the Information Technology (IT) spend in the retail sector has increased considerably and plays an increasingly important role in managing the complexity of retail operations (Syntel, 2008).

Going Global with Pharmaceuticals

At US $ 4.5 billion, the Indian pharmaceutical industry makes up just 1 per cent of the global industry. Yet, there is also the almost US $ 4 billion of rapidly growing exports that include exports to Europe and the United States. The two together add up to a vibrant industry that is coming into its own in a globally resurgent sector. The Indian pharmaceutical industry was born in the 1970s after the government instituted patent laws that encouraged reverse engineering. When government policies became export-oriented in the 1990s, the industry began exporting to developing countries and then later to developed countries. Drug companies went in for backward integration, sourcing building blocks from proliferating small-scale industries. The country's established petrochemical industry pitched in with building blocks of hydrocarbons. A system of science education modeled on the western system, combined with the prevalence of the English language, had already built up an invaluable talent pool.

The presence of multinationals in the country since the 1950s had helped meet international standards in work cultures and fostered a familiarity with regulatory requirements. Over the last seven years, about US $ 1.5 billion have been spent in the country on building up one of the best pharmaceutical manufacturing infrastructures in the world. India has more than 85 plants that are approved by the U.S. FDA—the highest number outside the United States. World-class research institutes are beginning to thrive. The industry has moved from manufacturing bulk drugs to formulations and from generics to the branded sector. Key international players are setting up shop in India either for manufacturing or R&D. The industry is now ready for the next step of getting into the basic research around discovery.

Globally, healthcare cost containment is a priority for the developed world, resulting in legislations promoting generics. In 2006 alone, close to US $ 50 billion worth of patents will expire in the United States. In this scenario, India's huge cost advantage will continue to attract business. Although the cost of manpower is increasing faster than in Europe and the United States, India is still a low cost base for skilled manpower. Every year 10,000 chemists and pharmacists and about 1,500 PhDs in chemistry and pharmacy graduate from good schools in the country. There remain, however, several challenges. For one, India is perceived as inconsistent from a supply chain point of view. Though Indian companies have filed many drug master files, they are yet to deliver sizable quantities of those drugs. Another area of concern is the retention of talent in the current scenario, where different sectors are competing fiercely for the available talent pool. Also, big pharmaceutical companies are more comfortable dealing with European countries than with Asian companies because the perception is that intellectual property may not be so safe with the latter. To continue moving up the value chain, the Indian pharmaceutical industry needs to start thinking like a knowledge base provider rather than just a material base provider. It must invest in people, and buy and build technologies. It also needs to work with the government to push for changes that benefit the industry. The industry should support intellectual property initiatives, push innovation and leverage information technology in pharmaceuticals. It needs to work with academia to align curricula with changing industry needs, and to be open to global talent and practices.

Competitive Intelligence in Pharma Sector

Pharmaceutical companies are globalizing their competitive intelligence groups to match the globalization of brand marketing strategies. A large number of companies examined in Cutting Edge's new report, "Pharmaceutical Competitive Intelligence: Expanding the Role and Reach of CI," (Market Wire, 2008) have globalized competitive intelligence functions, enabling them to deliver most impact at the same place that brand strategies are being set. Globalizing CI groups also eliminates the issue of CI teams being too far removed from upper management's ears to affect strategic choices. Global CI teams' messages have little to no filter before reaching upper management, preventing dilution of messages (http://findarticles.com/p/articles/mi_pwwi/is_200807/ai_n27882276).

"Pharmaceutical Competitive Intelligence: Expanding the Role and Reach of CI," available at www.pharmacompetitiveintelligence.com, examines CI team structures, phase-by-phase spending and staffing, and strategies for improvement. Compiled from surveys and interviews with executives at leading companies, the report enables CI teams to achieve success. "By globally aligning their CI teams, companies are placing a greater emphasis on CI's importance," said David Richardson, lead author of the report. "CI groups are playing ever more important roles in decisions for brands, and sitting where key decisions are made increases CI's level of impact (Reuters Business and Finance, 2008).

Pharmaceutical Competitive Intelligence (PCI): Expanding the Role and Reach of CI focuses on these topics:

— Structuring for Success — provides details on CI structures, including global-level reporting lines and placements; ways in which CI teams trumpet their successes and create CI cultures; and the career paths laid out to make CI teams breeding grounds for future pharma leaders

— Resourcing for Growth — reveals CI department-level budgets and staffing; brand-level phase-by-phase spending and staffing; which groups fund CI; and how companies demonstrate ROI on CI

— Increasing CI's Reach — Examines how companies communicate their strategic value to internal clients and the resources and tools for collecting CI.

The Indian Pharmaceutical Industry: An Overview

The Indian Pharmaceutical Industry today is in the front rank of India's science-based industries with wide ranging capabilities in the complex field of drug manufacture and technology. A highly organized sector, the Indian Pharma Industry is estimated to be worth $ 4.5 billion, growing at about 8 to 9 per cent annually. It ranks very high in the third world, in terms of technology, quality and range of medicines manufactured. From simple headache pills to sophisticated antibiotics and complex cardiac compounds, almost every type of medicine is now made indigenously (http://www.pharmaceutical-drug-manufacturers.com/pharmaceutical-industry/). By playing a key role in promoting and sustaining development in the vital field of medicines, Indian Pharma Industry boasts of quality producers and many units approved by regulatory authorities in USA and UK. International companies associated with this sector have stimulated, assisted and spearheaded this dynamic development in the past 53 years and helped to put India on the pharmaceutical map of the world.

The Indian Pharmaceutical sector is highly fragmented with more than 20,000 registered units. It has expanded drastically in the last two decades. The leading 250 pharmaceutical companies control 70% of the market with market leader holding nearly 7% of the market share. It is an extremely fragmented market with severe price competition and government price control. The pharmaceutical industry in India meets around 70% of the country's demand for bulk drugs, drug intermediates, pharmaceutical formulations, chemicals, tablets, capsules, orals and injectibles. There are about 250 large units and about 8000 Small Scale Units, which form the core of the pharmaceutical industry in India. These units produce the complete range of pharmaceutical formulations, i.e., medicines ready for consumption by patients and about 350 bulk drugs, i.e., chemicals having therapeutic value and used for production of pharmaceutical formulations.

Following the de-licensing of the pharmaceutical industry, industrial licensing for most of the drugs and pharmaceutical products has been done away with.

Manufacturers are free to produce any drug duly approved by the Drug Control Authority. Technologically strong and totally self-reliant, the pharmaceutical industry in India has low costs of production, low R&D costs, innovative scientific manpower, strength of national laboratories and an increasing balance of trade. The Pharmaceutical Industry, with its rich scientific talents and research capabilities, supported by Intellectual Property Protection regime is well set to take on the international market.

ADVANTAGE INDIA

The following aspects underline both comparative as well as competitive advantage for future growth perspective of the Indian Pharma industries:

Competent workforce: India has a pool of personnel with high managerial and technical competence as also skilled workforce. It has an educated work force and English is commonly used. Professional services are easily available.

Cost-effective chemical synthesis: Its track record of development, particularly in the area of improved cost-beneficial chemical synthesis for various drug molecules is excellent. It provides a wide variety of bulk drugs and exports sophisticated bulk drugs.

Legal and Financial Framework: India has a 53-year-old democracy and hence has a solid legal framework and strong financial markets. There is already an established international industry and business community.

Information and Technology: It has a good network of world-class educational institutions and established strengths in Information Technology.

Globalization: The country is committed to a free market economy and globalization. Above all, it has a 70 million middle class market, which is continuously growing.

Consolidation: For the first time in many years, the international pharmaceutical industry is finding great opportunities in India. The process of consolidation, which has become a generalized phenomenon in the world pharmaceutical industry, has started taking place in India.

The Growth Scenario

India's US $ 3.1 billion pharmaceutical industry is growing at the rate of 14 per cent per year. It is one of the largest and most advanced among the developing countries.

Over 20,000 registered pharmaceutical manufacturers exist in the country. The domestic pharmaceuticals industry output is expected to exceed Rs. 260 billion in the financial year 2002, which accounts for merely 1.3% of the global pharmaceutical sector. Of this, bulk drugs will account for Rs. 54 bn (21%) and formulations, the remaining Rs. 210 bn (79%). In financial year 2001, imports were Rs. 20 bn while exports were Rs. 87 bn.

Steps to Strengthen the Pharma Industry

Indian companies need to attain the right product-mix for sustained future growth. Core competencies will play an important role in determining the future of many Indian pharmaceutical companies in the post product-patent regime after 2005. Indian companies, in an effort to consolidate their position, will have to increasingly look at merger and acquisition options of either companies or products. This would help them to offset loss of new product options, improve their R&D efforts and improve distribution to penetrate markets. Research and development has always taken the back seat amongst Indian pharmaceutical companies. In order to stay competitive in the future, Indian companies will have to refocus and invest heavily in R&D.

The Indian pharmaceutical industry also needs to take advantage of the recent advances in biotechnology and information technology. The future of the industry will be determined by how well it markets its products to several regions and distributes risks, its forward and backward integration capabilities, its R&D, its consolidation through mergers and acquisitions, co-marketing and licensing agreements.

Although India currently represents just US $ 6 billion of the $ 550 billion global pharmaceutical industry, its share is increasing at 10% a year. The organized sector of India's pharmaceutical industry consists of 250 to 300 companies, which accounts for 70% of the market, with the top ten companies representing 30%. The Indian pharmaceutical industry has developed wide ranging capabilities in the complex field of drug process development and production technology. It is well ahead of other developing countries in process R&D capabilities and the range of technologically complex medicines manufactured (Kale and Little, 2007). The Indian government adopted a new Patents Act in 1970, which laid the foundations of the modern Indian pharmaceutical industry. It removed product patents for pharmaceuticals, food and agro-chemicals, allowing patents only for production processes. The statutory term for production processes was shortened to five years from grant or seven years from application. The 1970 Patent Act greatly weakened intellectual property protection in India, particularly for pharmaceutical innovations. It started the era of reverse engineering where firms developed new products by changing their production processes. Trained manpower, comparative ease of imitation and a strong chemistry base among Indian research institutes supported manufacturers and gave the Indian pharmaceutical industry its current profile. The industry's exports were worth more than US $ 492.30 in 2005-06 and they have been growing at a compound annual rate of 22.7 per cent over the last few years (National Pharmaceutical Policy, 2005). The value of the Indian pharmaceutical industry's overseas acquisition has grown from just US $ 8 million in 1997 to $ 116 million in 2004 (Bloomberg, 2005). Indian firms have acquired over US $ 1 billion worth of pharmaceutical companies overseas in 2005.

There are 3 developments which are pushing expansion of the Indian pharmaceutical industry into overseas markets:

a. Opportunities opened in the US generic market due to the Hatch-Waxman Act;
b. Increasing outsourcing by MNC pharmaceutical firms; and
c. Strengthening of patent laws in the domestic market.
These three developments are creating new challenges and opportunities for Indian industry and internationalization is one of the routes adopted by Indians to succeed in this new environment.

The generic opportunity is a result of the passing of the Hutch-Waxman Act in the US in 1984. Under this new law, manufacturers of generic drugs no longer had to go through a lengthy period of extensive clinical trials in order to market a generic drug - demonstration of bio-equivalence was sufficient to acquire a patent on a generic drug. Procedures were established for the resolution of disputes between branded drug manufacturers and generic manufacturers. Western markets were a lucrative business opportunity and the low cost advantage enjoyed by Indian firms on account of the cheap availability of scientific labour combined with scale economies inherent in the manufacture of bulk chemicals made for big margins. Between 1999 and 2005 drugs worth $ 64 million went off patent allowing generic companies to take advantage of better business opportunities. In the generics industry prescription drugs worth $ 40 billion in the US and $ 25 billion in Europe are due to lose patent protection by 2007-08. In 2004 the US Senate passed the Greater Access to Affordable Medicine Act diluting some of the renovator provisions of 1984 Hatch-Waxman Act, giving a big boost to the generic business in the US.

Similarly, Europe is emerging as a key market and a potential growth driver. The size of market in 2006 was US $ 14.2 billion with Germany, France, the UK and Italy accounting for more than 50% of market. Governments in Europe are trying to reduce healthcare costs by embracing generic drug companies. Liberalization facilitated the ability of Indian firms to exploit this opportunity to market generics drugs to the US and other Western economies. Indian firms are preparing themselves to take a share of this increasing global market. Indian drug manufacturers currently export their products to more than 65 countries worldwide; the US being the largest customer. However Indian firms face some difficult challenges such as non-tariff barriers, decreasing profits in the generics market, competitive threats from big pharma MNEs and reputation in Western markets. For example, US regulation disqualifies Indian firms from bidding for government contracts and Indian firms have to submit separate applications for each state even when firms have FDA approved products and facilities.

Another challenge is the reduction in profit margin due to intense competition from Chinese and Eastern European manufacturers as well as authorized generics produced by main manufacturer. Currently Indian industry is estimated to account for 22% of generics in the world market. Indian firms are aiming to move up the value chain by developing capabilities to produce 'super generics' rather than 'generics generics' to branded generics. Furthermore, stronger patent protection under the new patent law of 1999 has shut down the avenues for exploitation of generics opportunity in domestic market, but promised large rewards to Indian firms that could leverage their reverse engineering capabilities in advanced markets. The stronger patent law restricts reverse engineering of newly patented molecule, thus affecting an important source of growth for Indian firms. Also multinational pharmaceutical firms have entered India after 2005 and using the same resource base as Indian firms to compete in the Indian domestic market further increasing pressure on profit margins of Indian firms.

The 'Contract research and manufacturing services (CRAM)' market has emerged as huge opportunity for the Indian pharmaceutical industry. The global pharmaceutical industry is at the crossroads. With many of the blockbuster drugs getting off-patented and with increasing R&D costs, it's hard for the companies to maintain their bottom-line and remain unaffected. They have found recourse to outsourcing some of their research and manufacturing activities and saving cost in the process. This has led to the growth of contract research and manufacturing services or CRAMS making the companies in India to rejoice. Business of CRAMS has come as a boon to the mid-cap pharma companies in India, these companies are merrily embracing CRAMS taking full advantage of the features enjoyed by India as a country of diverse origin and strong manufacturing base in pharma for years. India could potentially capture 10% of the global CRAMS market of almost US $ 168 billion by 2009. Overall, the CRAMS segment is expected to have grown at 40-50 per cent in the last few years (http://www.mindbranch.com/listing/product/R3438-14.html).

According to Frost and Sullivan (2005), the global outsourcing market is worth $ 37 billion and growing at almost 11%; 50% of the contract manufacturing market is in North America, 40% in Europe and just 10% in Asia and the rest of the world. Indian firms possess requisite capabilities to cater for the requirements of outsourcing markets, still India accounts for barely 1.5% of the global CRAM industry. Due to untested patent protection law and lack of data protection MNC firms are reluctant to outsource early stage R&D work to Indian firms. Therefore Indian firms are trying to increase their share in the outsourcing market by moving closer to the market. Geographically the overseas acquisition by Indian pharmaceutical firms continues to be directed at developed countries specifically the US and Europe. Out of 32 acquisitions listed in Table 2 only 6 are in developing markets and the remaining rest of 26 are in advanced markets such as the US and Europe. The major acquisitions are in the area of marketing although some companies are investing in building manufacturing and R&D capacities in developed markets. Indian companies have already established manufacturing plants in the US, Europe, Brazil, Russia and China.

Table 2: Recent acquisition by Indian pharmaceutical firms

Company	Focus area	Year	Target	Value US $ Million
Dishman Pharma	Contract manufacturing and research service	2005	Syprotee (UK)	93.5
Dr. Reddy's Laboratories	US generics, speciality products, APIs, formulations, custom synthesis	2004	Trigenesis (US)	11
		n/a	BMS Laboratories and Meridian Health care	16
		2005	Roche's API Business (Mexico)	59
		2006	Betapharm	573
Glenmark Pharma	Drug discovery research formulations	2004	Kinger Lab (Brazil)	5.2
		2005	Uno-Ciclo (Brazil)	4.6
		2005	Servycal SA (Argentina)	n/a
Hikal	API's contract manufacturing	2004	Marsin (Denmark)	6 million for 50% stake
Jubilant Organosys	CRAMS, pharma speciality, chemicals, intermediates formulations, medical chemistry and clinical services	2004	PSI (Belgium)	16
		2005	Trinity Laboratories (along with subsidiary Trigen Laboratories) (US)	20.25 million for 75% stake
		2005	Target Research Associates	33.5
Matrix Labs	CRAMS, generic APIs intermediates and formulations	2005	MICHEM (China) (JV)	n/a
		2005	Docpharma (Belgium)	263
		2005	Explora Laboratories (Switzerland)	n/a
		n/a	Fina Chemicals Corp (South Africa)	n/a
Nicholas Piramal	CRAMS space-contract manufacturing APIs, branded formulations	2004	Doubtrex brand aquisition (US)	
		2004	Rhodia's inhalation business (UK)	14
		2005	Biosyntech (Canada)	6
		2005	Avecia Pharma (UK)	16.9
Strides Lab	Generics, OTC and nutraceuticals	2005	Manufacturing plant (Poland)	8
		2005	Beltapharm (Italy)	EUR 1.6 million (70% stake)
Sun Pharma	Branded formulations US generics, APIs	2005	Two facilities from Valent Pharma (Hungary, US)	10
		1997	Caraco (US)	7.5
		2005	Able Laboratories (US)	23.15

Ranbaxy	US and Europe generic markets	2004	RPG Aventis (France)	84
		n/a	18 generic products from Efarmes S.A. (Spain)	n/a
		2005	Brand – veratide from P&G (Germany)	5
Torrent	Formulations European generic market	2005	Heumann Pharma (Germany)	n/a
Zudus Cadilla	Contract manufacturing and generics	2003	Alpharma (France)	6.6
Wockhardt	Biogenerics, US and Europe generic market	2003	CP Pharma (UK)	20
	Branded generics	2004	Esparma (Germany)	11

Source: KPMG Report, 2006

The major Indian companies such as Ranbaxy, Dr. Reddy's Laboratories, Wockhardt and others have established their own brand image in the international market and are taking steps to consolidate their activities. Indian firms are compensating for the spiraling cost of selling and marketing in advance countries by setting wholly-owned subsidiaries or acquiring local firm thus, reinforcing the argument that Indian firms' internationalization through acquisition is directed towards acquiring new knowledge in different areas such as R&D capabilities, regulatory skills and distribution networks.

Competitiveness of Pharmaceutical Industry in India

The first Indian pharmaceutical company, Bengal Chemicals and Pharmaceutical Works, which still exists today as one of 5 government-owned drug manufacturers, appeared in Calcutta in 1930. For the next 60 years, most of the drugs in India were imported by multinationals either in fully-formulated or bulk form. The government started to encourage the growth of drug manufacturing by Indian companies in the early 1960s, and with the Patents Act in 1970, enabled the industry to become what it is today. This patent act removed composition patents from food and drugs, and though it kept process patents, these were shortened to a period of five to seven years. The lack of patent protection made the Indian market undesirable to the multinational companies that had dominated the market, and while they streamed out, Indian companies started to take their places. They carved a niche in both the Indian and world markets with their expertise in reverse-engineering new processes for manufacturing drugs at low costs. Although some of the larger companies have taken baby steps towards drug innovation, the industry as a whole has been following this business model until the present. In 2002, over 20,000 registered drug manufacturers in India sold $ 9 billion worth of formulations and bulk drugs. 85% of these formulations were sold in India while over 60% of the bulk drugs were exported, mostly to the United States and Russia.

Most of the players in the market are small-to-medium enterprises; 250 of the largest companies control 70% of the Indian market. Thanks to the 1970 Patent Act, multinationals represent only 35% of the market, down from 70% thirty years ago.

Most pharma companies operating in India, even the multinationals, employ Indians almost exclusively from the lowest ranks to high level management. Mirroring the social structure, firms are very hierarchical. Homegrown pharmaceuticals, like many other businesses in India, are often a mix of public and private enterprise. Although many of these companies are publicly owned, leadership passes from father to son and the founding family holds a majority share. In terms of the global market, India currently holds a modest 1-2% share, but it has been growing at approximately 10% per year. India gained its foothold on the global scene with its innovatively-engineered generic drugs and active pharmaceutical ingredients (API), and it is now seeking to become a major player in outsourced clinical research as well as contract manufacturing and research. There are 74 U.S. FDA-approved manufacturing facilities in India, more than in any other country outside the U.S, and in 2005, almost 20% of all 'Abbreviated New Drug Applications' (ANDA) to the FDA are expected to be filed by Indian companies. Growth in other fields notwithstanding, generics is still a large part of the picture. London research company Global Insight estimates that India's share of the global generics market will have risen from 4% to 33% by 2007.

Patents

As it expands its core business, the industry is being forced to adapt its business model to recent changes in the operating environment. The first and most significant change was the January 1, 2005 enactment of an amendment to India's patent law that reinstated product patents for the first time since 1972. The legislation took effect on the deadline set by the WTO's Trade-Related Aspects of Intellectual Property Rights (TRIPS) agreement, which mandated patent protection on both products and processes for a period of 20 years. Under this new law, India will be forced to recognize not only new patents but also any patents filed after January 1, 1995. Indian companies achieved their status in the domestic market by breaking these product patents, and it is estimated that within the next few years, they will lose $ 650 million of the local generics market to rightful patent-holders.

In the domestic market, this new patent legislation has resulted in fairly clear segmentation. The multinationals narrowed their focus onto high-end patients who make up only 12% of the market, taking advantage of their newly-bestowed patent protection. Meanwhile, Indian firms have chosen to take their existing product portfolios and target semi-urban and rural populations. The new patent regime to have taken effect at a time when Indian companies had recently started to aggressively pursue global opportunities, so it is not clear whether the flurry of international activity surrounding the enactment date is a result of the change in legislation. Mergers, acquisitions and alliances have been taking place on an unprecedented scale, most notably with companies in the U.S. and Europe. As stated in 'The Hindu Business Line', "In the last 10-odd months, the Indian pharma industry has possibly seen the single largest number of global transactions in its 50-year history." These transactions provide Indian companies with access to foreign markets and facilitate the process of seeking regulatory approval for new products, which can be quite daunting for a company that only has operations on Indian soil.

Product development

Companies are also starting to adapt their product development processes to the new environment. For years, firms have made their ways into the global market by researching generic competitors to patented drugs and following up with litigation to challenge the patent. This approach remains untouched by the new patent regime and looks to increase in the future. However, those that can afford it have set their sights on an even higher goal: new molecule discovery. Although the initial investment is huge, companies are lured by the promise of hefty profit margins and the recognition as a legitimate competitor in the global industry. Local firms have slowly been investing more money into their R&D programs or have formed alliances to tap into these opportunities.

Small and medium enterprises

As promising as the future is for a whole, the outlook for small and medium enterprises (SME) is not as bright. The excise structure changed so that companies now have to pay a 16% tax on the maximum retail price (MRP) of their products, as opposed to on the ex-factory price. Consequently, larger companies are cutting back on outsourcing and what business is left is shifting to companies with facilities in the four tax-free states - Himachal Pradesh, Jammu and Kashmir, Uttaranchal and Jharkhand.

As SMEs wrestled with the tax structure, they were also scrambling to meet the July 1 deadline for compliance with the revised Schedule M Good Manufacturing Practices (GMP). While this should be beneficial to consumers and the industry at large, SMEs have been finding it difficult to find the funds to upgrade their manufacturing plants, resulting in the closure of many facilities. Others invested the money to bring their facilities to compliance, but these operations were located in non-tax-free states, making it difficult to compete in the wake of the new excise tax.

Challenges

All of these changes are ultimately good for the Indian pharmaceutical industry, which suffered in the past from inadequate regulation and large quantities of spurious drugs. They force the industry to reach a level necessary for global competitiveness. However, they have also exposed some of the inadequacies in the industry today. Its main weakness is an underdeveloped new molecule discovery program. Even after the increased investment, market leaders such as Ranbaxy and Dr. Reddy's Laboratories spent only 5-10% of their revenues on R&D, lagging behind Western pharmaceuticals like Pfizer, whose research budget last year was greater than the combined revenues of the entire Indian pharmaceutical industry. This disparity is too great to be explained by cost differentials, and it comes when advances in genomics have made research equipment more expensive than ever. The drug discovery process is further hindered by a dearth of qualified molecular biologists. Due to the lack of interfacing between curriculum and industry, Pharma sector in India also lack the academic collaboration that is crucial to drug development in the West.

R&D

Both the Indian central and state governments have recognized R&D as an important driver in the growth of their pharma businesses and conferred tax deductions for expenses related to research and development. They have granted other concessions as well, such as reduced interest rates for export financing and a cut in the number of drugs under price control. Government support is not the only thing in Indian pharma's favor, though; companies also have access to a highly-developed IT industry that can partner with them in new molecule discovery.

Labor force

India's greatest strengths lie in its people. India also boasts a cheap, well-educated, English-speaking labor force that is the base of its competitive advantage. Although molecular biologists are in short supply, there are a number of talented chemists who are equally as important in the discovery process. In addition, there has been a reverse brain-drain effect in which scientists are returning from abroad to accept positions at lower salaries at Indian companies. Once there, these foreign-trained scientists can transfer the benefits of their knowledge and experience to all of those who work with them. India's wealth of people extends benefits to another part of the drug commercialization process as well. With one of the largest and most genetically diverse populations in any single country, India can recruit for clinical trials more quickly and perform them more cheaply than countries in the West. Indian firms have just recently started to leverage (http://en.wikipedia.org/wiki/India & http://en.wikipedia.org/wiki/Official_languages_of_India).

Indian Oil and Gas Industry for Energy Security

The Indian Oil and Gas Sector report, developed by specialists after extensive research and due diligence, traces the trends that are most likely to emerge in this industry in the beginning of this new decade. With the Government gradually giving up control on the oil and gas sector in favour of market forces, Indian oil companies—both upstream and downstream players—are getting exposed to international price fluctuations. This is changing the ground realities for this vital sector of the Indian economy (ASSOCHEM, 2007).

The Global Scenario: Globally, the oil and gas sector is dominated by certain large private companies who have a presence in almost all segments of the oil and gas value chain. Historically, oil price has been the single most important challenge facing the global oil industry. The problem is all the more acute as the large private companies account for only a small share of world oil production even as oil prices remain unpredictable and prone to wide fluctuations. Given this backdrop, global oil majors are now increasingly benchmarking their production costs against the oil production costs of the OPEC (Organization of Petroleum Exporting Countries), and increasingly relying on technological innovations and other cost cutting measures to lower their own production costs. The other factors influencing their decisions are the likely fall in oil prices after March 2000, rising demand for gas and lighter petroleum products, and the volatile and unpredictable nature of refining margins.

The Indian Scenario: Unlike their global counterparts, Indian oil and gas companies have so far been operating in specific segments of the value chain. Oil and gas exploration, crude oil refining, distribution and marketing of petroleum products, and natural gas distribution are the key sub-sectors of the Indian oil and gas sector. The total sales turnover of this sector as a whole was around Rs. 1,500 billion as on March 31, 1999. The Indian oil and gas sector has historically been a regulated sector, dominated by Government undertakings. The regulation took the form of the Administered Pricing Mechanism (APM) under which the returns on investment were guaranteed. But now, with the APM being dismantled in phases and private players gaining a presence in the Indian oil and gas sector, the existing public sector oil companies are getting exposed to market forces and competition.

The Indian Upstream Sector: For the upstream players (the crude oil producers), the linkage to international crude oil prices implies volatility in earnings. While a rise in international crude oil prices would translate into a positive contribution to the bottom-line, a decline in the international prices, on the other hand, would exert pressure on the margins of all upstream companies. The national oil companies would, however, is protected from the downside risk by the floor price fixed by the government. But if the floor price is removed and the international oil prices drop to levels lower than the cost of production, even the national oil companies would require government intervention to protect their bottom-line. What aggravates the risk further is the fact that declining oil production and stagnating reserves dictate that the upstream companies venture into exploration areas that have a high-risk-high-return profile (like deep water blocks). And this has implications for future exploration and production (E&P) costs. Given the emerging scenario, expects the strategies of the upstream players to focus on: use of better recovery techniques; employment of cost cutting measures; entry into high-risk-high-return areas (with the assumption that oil prices will not fall below the cost of production); integration into downstream areas; partnering; venturing into other geographical regions; and, undertaking organizational restructuring.

The Indian Downstream Sector: The phased dismantling of the APM has exposed the Indian downstream players (refiners and marketers of petroleum products) to market forces. The refining margins of the Indian refineries are now linked to the international refining margins. A fluctuation in the international prices of crude oil/product translates into a variation in the domestic margins (although they are, to a large extent, protected by the positive net duty protection). In the first 18 months of decontrol the profitability of Indian refineries has increased as their margins have increased following higher duty protection and linkage of crude and product prices with international prices. However, on the flip side, the expected surplus in the domestic market may limit this margin expansion.

The other factors influencing the profitability of Indian refineries in the deregulated scenario would be refinery configuration, operating costs, and refinery location. The ownership of marketing and distribution infrastructure would be of strategic importance and would enhance profitability as the marketing sector is decontrolled. While the profitability of the integrated players would be higher and more resilient to economic troughs, the pure refining companies would find it difficult to sustain profitability in a decontrolled scenario. Accordingly, the pure refining and marketing companies are expected to be merged with the oil majors. A full decontrol of the marketing sector is likely to lead to severe competition among the various players in the industry, and a greater focus on branding and product differentiation. Given the changes taking place, the strategies of downstream players should be focussed on such of those priority areas as: strengthening import infrastructure; enhancing scale of operations; upgrading processing facilities; implementing environmental projects; strengthening marketing and distribution infrastructure and promoting brands; entering into strategic alliances; venturing into other areas of the energy value chain for optimizing the risk-return profile; and restructuring the organization.

The Indian Gas Sub-Sector

The share of natural gas in India's energy mix has increased more than three times since the early 1980s. Energy efficiency, multiplicity of applications, and environment neutrality are the key factors that are likely to propel further rise in demand for gas in India. The increase in demand could come both from the existing uses of natural gas and from newer applications. A rising demand for gas has implications on the supply level. An increased thrust on liquefied natural gas imports would signal positive developments on the supply front. This should accompany the decontrol of the oil sector to enable the existing oil companies to pursue gas exploration and production (E&P) activities more actively. The Gas Authority of India Limited, with a monopoly in natural gas distribution, is likely to benefit from the expected rise in natural gas supplies. Besides, its exposure to price risks would be minimal because of the fixed nature of natural gas transportation tariffs.

Likely Strategic Initiatives: Response to the phased deregulation, the strategic initiatives of the various players in the energy value chain would focus on the following factors.

Product-mix: This will have to be in line with market demand. Technology would play a major role in influencing the product mix. Strategic initiatives (for instance BP-AMOCO's acquisition of ARCO, which has rich gas reserves) would also impact product mix. Cost competitiveness, technological advancements and scale of operations would have an impact on operating costs.

Infrastructure/Logistics: The ownership of infrastructure for sourcing crude oil and the logistics for distributing finished products would have a considerable impact on operating costs. Integration into different elements of the value chain would be imperative for bringing synergetic benefits, reducing volatility in earnings, and enhancing value addition. Brand building, pricing, and packaging would be used as tools to deliver greater value to customers (Global Competitiveness (3)\Indian Oil and Gas Industry - Business Market Reports.htm).

Refinery Capacity and Security

Securing ample supplies of oil and gas represents only part of the equation. We must maintain, expand, and protect the critical infrastructure needed to refine and transport this energy.

- In 1981, the United States had 324 refineries with a total capacity of 18.6 million barrels per day. In 2005, there were just 132 oil refineries with a capacity of 16.8 million barrels per day.
- Growing demand for gasoline has been met by expansion of existing refineries, but expansion has proved difficult under the weight of numerous state, federal, and local regulations and roadblocks.
- Badly needed pipelines, liquefied natural gas ports, and other facilities have been stymied by intense "not-in-my-backyard" opposition.
- Foreign refineries are gaining market share, partially filling the domestic refining gap. Currently, 10% of America's gasoline is refined overseas, but that source of supply is complicated by domestic fuel formulation regulations.

Fewer domestic refineries, along with greater reliance on foreign refineries, carry important national security implications. So, too, does the concentration of a significant share of our oil production, pipeline, and refinery capacity in areas vulnerable to hurricanes.

The Electricity Grid in the Computer Age

Electricity has grown in importance because it powers the information age economy and our abundant way of life. The energy resources, infrastructure, and conveyances needed to produce and deliver electricity to our homes and computers are also overstretched and subject to stringent restrictions. In 1940, 10% of energy consumption in America was used to produce electricity. In 1970, that share was 25%. Today, it is up to 40%. The information economy requires massive amounts of electricity. Electricity consumed by computer servers has doubled in five years and will increase another 75% by 2010. However, while electricity demand increased by about 25% since 1990, construction of transmission facilities decreased about 30%. In fact, annual investment in new transmission facilities has declined over the last 25 years. With anticipated economic growth, use of technology, and the near-term retirement of many aging plants, service quality will degrade and costs will go up unless substantial amounts of capital are invested over the next several decades in new generation, transmission, and distribution facilities. Electricity does not come from turning on a switch. It comes primarily from coal and nuclear fuels that are converted into electricity in the nation's power plants. Continued opposition to expanding these sources and facilities could one day bring our technology-driven economy and lifestyles to a grinding halt.

Indian IT and ITES Sector on the Rise

The information technology and information technology enabled services (IT/ITES) industry has impacted the Indian economy and its social fabric immensely. The irreversible initiatives taken by both government and organizations are a case in point. ITES sector has matured considerably with its expansion into varied verticals, well differentiated service offerings and increasing geographic penetration. India's importance among emerging economies, both as a supply and demand centre is fuelling further growth of the sector. The IT/ITES industry continues to be one of the fastest growing industries in India, while India maintains its position as a strategic off-shoring destination for MNCs worldwide (MeriNews, 2008). The ITES-BPO employee base has grown to 553,000 in FY 07 from 415,000 in FY 06. Over the past decade, the Indian BPO segment has witnessed significant transformation. Starting with basic data entry tasks, the industry graduated to a high proportion of voice-based services and a range of back-office processing activities. The last 3-4 years have seen the scope of services expanding to include increasingly complex processes involving rule-based decision making and even research services requiring informed individual judgment. The rapid expansion in the scope of BPO has been accompanied by an equally rapid adoption across a range of vertical industries. This wide range of services may be summarized into four broad categories comprising customer interaction services (CIS), finance and accounting (F&A), human resource administration and niche business services.

Key highlights of domestic BPO industry

BPO demand in the domestic market has witnessed noticeable growth over the past few years. The annual revenue aggregate of the domestic market for ITES-BPO grew to US $ 1.2 billion in FY 2006-07 from US $ 0.9 billion in FY 2005-06, illustrating a significant increase in demand. While the high growth rate may be attributed to a small-base effect, the rapid adoption of BPO in the domestic market is receiving well-deserved attention. The Indian economy is increasingly being integrated globally, businesses in India are beginning to face increasing levels of global competition and being pushed to deliver world class levels of product and service quality. ITES-BPO has emerged as an effective means of entrusting specialists with the task of consistently delivering the desired high-levels of quality – leaving the client organizations to focus on their core businesses (MeriNews, 2008).

Key growth drivers of Indian ITES-BPO exports

Abundant talent: India's young demographic profile is an inherent advantage complemented by an academic infrastructure that generates a large pool of English-speaking talent. Talent suitability concerns are being addressed through a combination of government, academia and industry-led initiatives. These initiatives include national roll out of skill, setting up finishing schools to supplement graduate education with training in specific technology areas and soft skills and memorandums of understanding (MoUs) with education agencies to facilitate industry inputs on curriculum and teaching and develop faculty development programme.

Sustained cost competitiveness: India has a strong track record of delivering a significant cost advantage, with outsourcing organizations regularly reporting savings of 25-50 per cent over the original cost base. The ability to achieve such high levels of cost advantage by sourcing services from India is driven primarily by the ability to access highly skilled talent at significantly lower wage costs and the resultant productivity gains derived from having a very competent employee base. This is further complemented by relative advantages in other elements of the cost structure (e.g. telecom) that contribute to India's cost competitiveness – even when compared to other low-cost destinations.

Continued focus on quality: Demonstrated process quality and expertise in service delivery has been a key factor driving India's sustained leadership in global service delivery. Since the inception of the industry in India, players within the country have been focusing on quality initiatives, to align themselves with international standards. Over the years, the industry has built robust processes and procedures to offer world class IT software and technology related services.

World class information security environment: Stakeholders of the Indian BPO companies recognizes security as an indispensable element of global service delivery. Individual firm level efforts are complemented by a comprehensive policy framework established by the Indian authorities, which has built a strong foundation for an 'info-secure' environment in the country.

Business infrastructure: Rapid growth in key business infrastructure has ensured unhindered growth and expansion of this sector. The BPO sector has been a key beneficiary with the cost of international connectivity declining rapidly and service level improving significantly. The growth is taking place not only in existing urban centres but increasingly in satellite towns and smaller cities as well. Critical business infrastructure such as telecom and commercial real estate is well in place, improving other supporting infrastructure a key priority for the government. STPI (software technology parks of India) infrastructure available across the country and magnitude of investments shows government support to the industry.

Enabling Business policy and Regulatory environment: The enabling policy environment in India was instrumental in catalyzing the early phases of growth in this sector. Policy makers in India have laid special emphasis on encouraging foreign participation in most sectors of the economy, recognizing its importance not only as a source of financial capital but also as a facilitator of knowledge and technology transfer.

The Indian ITES-BPO sector has benefited from this approach, with participating firms enjoying minimal regulatory and policy restrictions along with a broad range of fiscal and procedural incentives. Outsourcing brings substantial benefits to the global economy, and the lion's share will likely go to the US economy. Businesses can dramatically reduce costs and improve their competitive position and the economy can generate more output.

For India to fully capitalize on the opportunity and sustain a disproportionate lead in the global IT-ITES space, we need to focus on five key areas:

- Enhancing the talent pool advantage — focus on skill development to better leverage the world's largest working population.
- Strengthening urban infrastructure in existing (tier I) and emerging (tier II and tier III) cities and continued emphasis on proactive regulatory reform to facilitate greater ease of doing business.
- Driving a philosophy of operational excellence amongst industry players (across the board) to ensure that India-based delivery sustains world-leading benchmarks in performance.
- Catalyzing domestic market development.
- Actively promoting an uncompromised agenda towards global free trade.

India will be uniquely positioned to sustain its global leadership position, grow its offshore IT-ITES industries at an annual rate of 24% to 25%, sustain nearly 10 m jobs, and generate export revenues of more than US \$ 86 bn by FY12 (as per NASSCOM estimates). Additionally, industry participants can further accelerate this export growth through deep and stable innovation. Such extensive innovation could generate an additional US \$ 15 to US \$ 20 bn in export revenue over the next five to ten years. Further, establishing India's leadership in the global IT-ITES sector will mean more than achieving a targeted growth in exports. Achieving these growth targets will entail a significant demand for incremental human and financial capital in the country. US \$ 86 bn in IT-

ITES exports by FY12 translates to incremental direct employment of about 2.5 m people and capital investment of approximately US $ 20 bn (Table 3). This is based on industry average capital to revenue ratio of 1 : 5 and lead-time of 3 years in the investment cycle (equitymaster.com: http://www.equitymaster.com/detail.asp?date=6/4/2007&story=3)

Table 3: IT-ITES export from India

IT-ITES exports (US $ bn)			
FY06	23.6	FY14E	124.9
FY07	29.8	FY15E	150.0
FY08E	37.6	FY16E	175.5
FY09E	47.5	FY17E	205.3
FY10E	60.0	FY18E	240.2
FY11E	72.1	FY19E	281.1
FY12E	86.6	FY20E	328.9
FY13E	104.0	CAGR	20.7%

Source: NASSCOM, McKinsey Research

India holds a dominant share of the global offshore IT-ITES sector (65% of the global market in offshore IT and 46% of the ITES market). Yet, at US $ 31.3 bn in FY07, Indian IT-ITES exports accounted for less than 3% of the global spend on IT-ITES (Table 4). This clearly indicates significant headroom for growth. If India maintains its current share of the global offshore IT-ITES market, IT-ITES exports from India will exceed US $ 60 bn by FY10 and US $ 86 bn by FY12. Further, growing at current trends, Indian IT-ITES exports are projected to reach nearly US $ 330 bn by FY20 (nearly 14% of the projected worldwide spend). But the Indian IT companies will have to move up in the value chain and concentrate more on high value added services.

Table 4: IT exports from India during 2005-07

	IT Exports in US $ bn			% of market		
	FY05	**FY06**	**FY07**	**FY05**	**FY06**	**FY07**
IT consulting	0.3	0.3	0.5	1.1	1.4	1.8
System integration	0.2	0.4	0.5	0.3	0.5	0.6
Network consulting and integration	0.2	0.2	0.2	0.6	0.6	0.7
Custom application development	5.0	6.5	8.9	22.5	27.8	36.4
Application management	2.7	1.6	2.2	14.8	7.8	9.6
IS outsourcing	0.6	0.8	1.1	0.7	1.0	1.2
Support and training	1.1	1.2	1.7	0.9	0.9	1.2
Others	—	2.3	3.0	—	—	—
	10.1	13.3	18.1	40.9	40.0	51.5

Source: NASSCOM, McKinsey Research

Infrastructure management services (included in IT outsourcing) and system integration services are forecasted to be high growth areas in offshore IT services sourced from India. In case of offshore BPO, relatively lower penetration levels and significant untapped potential is expected to lead significant growth (CAGR 33% to 45%), across vertical markets, over the next five years. But to achieve these targets, there lies some big roadblocks in between them. They are:

Shortage in supply of suitable talent: While India's young profile has the country favourably placed in terms of its quantitative manpower requirements, gaps in suitability and access to the entire available pool are beginning to reflect in talent supply shortages which are indicated by continued above average wage inflation and high attrition levels in the sector. To achieve US $ 86 bn in export revenues and to continue to grow the domestic IT industry, the IT and ITES industries will need to employ nearly 2.5 m professionals. Further, the number of Indian students going abroad annually is currently over 100,000 and is projected to cross 200,000 by the end of FY10. In comparison, the number of foreign national students coming to pursue studies in India is estimated at less than 10,000 each year. As a result, the net annual outflow on account of education, currently estimated to be in excess of Rs. 150 bn (US $ 3.5 b), is likely to continue to rise rapidly.

Lack of adequate infrastructure: The demand for infrastructure and indirect resources poses a key challenge for the IT-ITES sector. The incremental infrastructure required to support the projected growth is unlikely to be absorbed into the existing city centres in Tier I and Tier II cities, which are already witnessing signs of strain. With Tier III and Tier IV cities lacking important elements of business and social infrastructure, decentralized growth of the IT-ITES sector will require a coordinated, large-scale urban planning exercise. The IT-ITES sectors will likely employ an additional 2.5 m professionals (export sectors alone) by FY12. In addition to basic utilities and physical infrastructure, growth in the sector will also generate significant demand for world-class business and social infrastructure. Existing Tier I and Tier II cities are already overcrowded, choked, and struggling to provide basic urban services. Upgrading these existing centres is necessary, but can only reduce rather than solve the problem. Further, decentralizing the industry beyond existing hubs is essential to allow wider distribution of the development benefits driven by the growth of the sector. Therefore, this demand will need to be met by developing new townships to house the young population.

Sustaining cost competitiveness: Cost savings remain the primary driver for offshore sourcing of IT-ITES. In addition to the potential loss of absolute cost arbitrage due to wage inflation, firms are becoming increasingly concerned about increasing cost of doing business in India due to infrastructure constraints. The recently introduced SEZ policy is a positive measure, however, it does not adequately accommodate the requirements of this sector and is likely to have unfavourable implications for SMEs and smaller cities. Further, India still ranks poorly on other aspects of 'ease of doing business' when compared to other emerging competitor locations which also impacts the cost of doing business in India. India currently ranks 116th out of 155 countries. (Source: www.doingbusiness.org)

Conclusion

The IT and ITES have been the largest industry segments responsible for contributing to the growth of the Indian economy in the past few years. A gradual shift has been seen, in terms of the choice of one's profession, with an increasing number of people from diverse backgrounds opting for a career in IT and ITES. In the past few years, a large number of graduates, from a diverse range of backgrounds, have been leaving their chosen disciplines and joining the IT sector. Shortage of graduates in basic science and engineering streams may result in the near future. This is likely to have an impact on research and innovation and also on other primary and secondary sector of economy. Further, as the ITES-BPO industry shifts to Tier II cities, there will be an increase in the infrastructure requirements in those semi-urban areas also. In addition to this, there are challenges arising out of social and cultural changes that are being brought out by the IT-ITES Industry growth, since the professionals are employed in the virtual environment of the target industry. There is a need to continuously study the changes that are taking place in economic as well as cultural domain of various sectors also as a result of IT-ITES growth.

Foreign Direct Investment Policy and Business Opportunity in India

India is the second most populous country and the largest democracy in the world. The far reaching and sweeping economic reform undertaken since 1991 have unleashed the enormous growth potential of the economy. There has been a rapid, yet calibrated, move towards deregulation and liberalization, which has resulted in India becoming a favourite destination for foreign investment. The mood is upbeat and the signals strong. Undoubtedly India has emerged as one of the most vibrant and dynamic of the developing economics (Indian Investment Centre: http://www.iic.nic.in/iic3_a.htm).

On the question of India offering FDI opportunities for domestic investment the following is the rationale and key potential strengths as a Nation to create new business opportunities for India in order to achieve global competitiveness:

- One of the largest economies of the world, fourth largest economy in terms of purchasing power parity.
- Large and rapidly growing consumer market-up to 300 million people constitute the market for branded consumer products.
- Easy access to markets of the other nations belonging to the South Asian Association for Regional Cooperation (Bangladesh, Bhutan, Maldives, Nepal, Pakistan and Sri Lanka).

- Large and diversified infrastructure spread across the country.
- Promising future in the Information technology industry.
- Large manufacturing capability, spanning almost all areas of manufacturing activities.
- Well-developed research and development (R&D) infrastructure and technical and marketing services.
- Well established knowledge industry.
- Abundance of natural resources (has a rich mineral base), and agricultural self-sufficiency.
- Developed banking system-commercial banking network of over 63,000 branches supported by a number of National and State level financial institutions.
- Vibrant capital market consisting of 22 stock exchanges with over 9,000 listed companies.
- Skilled manpower and professional management including engineers, managerial personnel, accountants, and lawyers, available at competitive costs.
- Conducive foreign investment environment that provides freedom of entry, investment, location, choice of technology, import and export.
- The policy environment provides clear guidelines for entry, freedom of location, choice of technology, production, repatriation of capital, dividends, etc., which is specifically aimed of enhancing the flow of FDI.
- Well-balanced package of fiscal incentives.
- Stable democratic environment fostered by over 53 years of Independence.
- Established, Independent judiciary.
- English the preferred business language.

Foreign Direct Investment: Framework of Policy and Procedures

As part of the economic reforms programme, policy and procedures governing foreign investment and technology transfer have been significantly simplified and streamlined (http://www.iic.nic.in/iic3_a.htm).

Automatic Route

Today, foreign investment is freely allowed in all sectors including the services, sector except in cases where there are sectoral ceilings.

All items/activities except the following are under the automatic route for foreign direct investment (FDI):

i. All proposals that require an industrial Licence. An industrial Licence is mandatory if:
   a. the item involved requires on industrial licence under the Industries (Development and Regulation) Act, 1951 or

  b. the foreign equity portion is more than 24% of the equity capital of units manufacturing items reserved for small scale industries; or
  c. the item concerned requires an industrial Licence in terms of the locational policy

ii. All proposals in which the foreign collaborator has a previous venture or tie-up in India (Excluding IT sector).

iii. All proposals relating to the acquisition of shares in an existing Indian company in favour of a foreign investor.

iv. All proposals outside the notified sectoral policy/caps, or under sectors in which FDI is not permitted

Investment in public sector units as also in Export Oriented Units (EOUs), and units in Export Processing Zones (EPZs), Special Economic Zones (SEZs), Software Technology Parks (STPs) and Electronics Hardware Technology Parks (EHTPs) also quality for the Automatic Route.

FDI in the Sector upto 26% is allowed under the automatic route subject to licence from the insurance regulatory and development Authority for undertaking insurance activities.

In addition to Automatic Approval for new companies, such approval can also be granted for existing companies proposing to induct foreign equity, for existing companies with an expansion programme, the additional requirements are that:

i. the increase in equity level must result from the expansion of the equity base of the existing company

ii. the money to be remitted should be in foreign currency, and

iii. the proposed expansion programme should be predominantly in the sector(s) under automatic route.

For existing companies without an expansion programme, the additional requirements for eligibility for automatic approval are:

i. They should be engaged predominantly in industries under the automatic route

ii. The increase in equity level must be from expansion of the equity base; and

iii. The foreign equity must come in foreign currency.

Otherwise, the proposal would need Government approval through the Foreign Investment Promotion Board (FIPB).

Investors coming through the Automatic Route are required to file relevant documents with the Reserve Bank of India within 30 days after the issue of shares to foreign investors. Proposals which do not fulfill the conditions for automatic approval will require the approval of the Government. The investors have to make an application to the Foreign Investment Promotion Board, Ministry of Commerce and Industry, New Delhi, for obtaining such approval.

Prime Sectoral Business Opportunities

The reform process has deregulated the economy and stimulated domestic and foreign investments, taking India firmly into the forefront of investment destinations. The Government, keen to promote investment in the country has radically simplified and rationalized polices, procedures and regulatory aspects, Foreign investment is welcome in almost all sectors, except those of strategic concern (viz. defence and atomic energy). A series of incentives has been announced to promote investments. These include import of capital goods at concessional customs duty (subject to fulfillment of certain export obligations), liberalization of external commercial borrowing norms, tax holiday, and concessional tax treatment for certain sector. In addition, several State Government offer incentives, such as subsidy on fixed capital, loans at concessional rates of interest, and attractive power rates, while several incentives are project specific, a number of firms have been successful in negotiating favourable investment terms with the State Government concerned. Since the initiation of the economic liberalization process in 1991, sectors such as automobiles, chemicals, food processing, oil and natural gas, petrochemicals, power, services, and telecommunications have attracted considerable investments. Today, in the changes investment climate, India offers exciting business opportunities in virtually every sector of the economy.

Energy

Power

Investment Policy

The 1991 Power Policy seeks to attract significant private sector investment in the Indian power sector. The key initiatives include:

- Private sector permitted to set up cool, gas or liquid based thermal project, hydel projects and wind or solar projects of any size.
- Foreign equity participation brought under automatic approval of generation, transmission and distribution of power generated in hydro-electric, oil-based and coal/lignite-based power projects.
- Role of the Central Government curtailed and the State Governments and State Electricity Boards (SEBs) empowered to negotiate directly with developers, facilitating speedy clearances for the investor.
- Ancillary sector such as cool significantly deregulated.
- 100% foreign equity permitted.

Opportunities

Demand is expected to grow to 570 billion KWh by 2001-02 and to 782 billion KWh by 2006-07. Over the 10 year period from 1997-2007, a total capacity addition of 98,000 MW is envisaged, entailing an investment of Rs. 5,750 billion in power generation, transmission and distribution.

The specific project opportunities expected in the near future include:

Liquid Fuel Based Projects using low sulphur heavy stock (LSHS), furnace oil (FO), heavy petroleum stock (HPS), Naphtha, Vacuum Residue, Condensate and Orimulsion are permitted by the Government. Import of liquefied natural gas (LNG) is also being considered for setting up large capacity combined cycle power plants, Transmission projects for power transfer are available for competitive bidding by the Central Transmission Utility (Power Grid) and State Transmission Utilities (SEBs)/Grid Corporations). The transmission system projects are being identified for competitive bidding by the Central and State Transmission Utilities. Attractive investment opportunities are likely to develop in distribution of power as several State governments have agreed to allow the gradual entry of the private sector in distribution.

Non-Conventional Energy Sources

Investment Policy

Foreign Investors can enter into a joint venture with an Indian partner for financial and/or technical collaboration and also for setting up of renewable energy based power generation projects. The liberalized foreign investment approval regime is aimed at facilitating foreign investment and transfer of technology through joint ventures.

100% foreign investment as equity is permissible.

Government of India encouraging foreign investors to set up renewable energy based power generation project on Build-Own-Operate basis.

Opportunities

In India, investment opportunities are available for the following types of investors and users:

Investment by foreign investors in renewable energy

Wind, Solar Photo-voltaic, Solar Thermal, Small Hydro, Biomass, Co-generation, Geothermal, Tidal and Urban and Industrial Wastes based power projects.

Investment by foreign investors for manufacturing of renewable energy systems and devices based on: Wind, Solar Photo-voltaic, Solar Thermal, Small Hydro, Biomass, Co-generation, Geothermal, Tidal and Urban and Industrial Wastes for their utilization in India and also for exports to developing and Third World countries.

FDI Policy in Oil and Natural Gas Sector

The Government has announced significant new policy initiatives to attract foreign investment:

In exploration and production, oil and gas fields are open to the private sector as well as for foreign participation under production sharing contracts. Foreign investment it to be permitted up to:

- 100% in small-sized oil fields
- 60% for unincorporated joint ventures and 51% for incorporated joint ventures
- 100% for exploration and production of blocks identified under the new Exploration Licensing Policy
- In the case of private Indian companies, FDI in refining is permitted up to 49%. The level of FDI in the oil refining sector under automatic approval has been raised from 49% to 100% EOU refineries, 100% FDI is permitted.
- For gas fields developed in the private sector, promoters are free to market the gas at market related prices.
- For the petroleum products and pipeline sector, FDI is permitted up to 51%
- FDI is permitted up to 74% in infrastructure related to marketing and marketing of petroleum products.
- 100% wholly-owned subsidiary (WOS) is permitted for purpose of market study and formulation.
- 100% wholly-owned subsidiary is permitted for investment/financing.
- For actual trading and marketing, minimum 26% Indian equity is required over 5 years.

Opportunities

Total sedimentary basins, including deep waters; 3.14 million sq. kms (41% of this still unexplored). There is a large demand for natural gas, as may be seen from the following table 5:

Table 5:

Year	Demand (MMSCMD)*
1999	110
2002	151
2007	231
2012	313
2025	391

* *MMSCMD: Million Standard Cubic Metres per Day*

The present domestic gas supply is only 65 MMSCMD. The increasing demand-supply gap is expected to be met by imports. The divergent source of Infrastructure required for Natural Gas is quite enormous, going by long-term projection, as may be seen from the following table 6.

Table 6: Development of infrastructure

	1998-99	2024-25
Product Pipeline Capacity (MMT pa)	22.85	166
Port Capacity (MMT)	111.00	361

Coal

Investment Policy

Private Indian companies setting up or operating power projects as well as cool or lignite mines for captive consumption are allowed FDI up to 100%.

100% FDI is allowed for setting up coal processing plants subject to the condition that the company shall not do coal mining and shall not sell washed coal or sized coal from its coal processing plants in the open market and shall supply the washed or sized coal to those parties who are supplying raw coal to coal processing plants for washing or sizing.

FDI up to 74% is allowed for exploration or mining of coal or lignite for captive consumption. In all the above cases, FDI is allowed up to 50% under the 'Automatic Route' subject to the condition that such investment shall not exceed 49% of the equity of a PSU (Public Sector Undertaking).

COMMUNICATION AND INFORMATION TECHNOLOGY

Telecommunication

FDI is limited to 49% subject to grant of licence from the Department of Telecommunications and adherence by the companies (who are investing and the companies in which investment is being made) to the licence condition for foreign equity cap and lock-in-period for transfer and addition of equity and other licence provisions.

FDI up to 100% is allowed for the following activities in the telecom sector.

a. ISPs not providing gateways (both for satellite and submarine cables);
b. Infrastructure Providers providing dark fibre (IP category);
c. Electronic Mail; and
d. Voice Mail.

Up to 100% FDI in telecom manufacturing activities on automatic approval basis.

Opportunities

There exists an enormous demand-supply gap for basic services, with the average waiting period for telephone connections exceeding one year, as may be seem from the following table 7.

Table 7:

Sector	Current Size	Projections
Basic Service	19 million lines	Additional 64 million lines required over the next 9 years to meet the demand for basic services; 20.4 million lines expected to be provided by the private sector.
Cellular Services	0.9 million subscribers	Cellular subscribers expected to cross 1.6 million by March, 2000.
Radio Paging	0.8 million subscribers	1.5 million subscribers expected by the end of financial year 2000.
Very Small Apertue Terminal (VSAT)	6,000	VSAT demand estimated at 11,000 shared hubs and dedicated hub. terminals by 2000.
Internet	150,000	2 million Internet subscribers expected by the year 2000.

Internet Services

There in no restriction on the number of Internet Service Providers (ISPs). No licence fee is payable up to October 31, 2003; thereafter a token licence fee of Re 1 per annum is payable, ISP are free to fix their own tariff; ISPs have been permitted to establish their own international gateways for carrying internet traffic. They can obtain transmission link on lease from DTS, licensed basic service providers, railways, SEBs, Power Grid Corporation or any other operator specially authorized to lease such lines, ISPs can also establish their own transmission link within their service area if such links are not available from any of the authorized agencies.

Basic Telephone Services

Basic service providers are permitted to establish last mile linkages and carry their own long distance traffic within their service area. They are to be permitted direct interconnectivity and sharing of infrastructure with other basic service providers or any other type of service providers in their area of operation.

Cellular Mobile Services

Cellular service providers are permitted to carry their own long distance traffic within their service area. They are to be permitted direct interconnectivity and sharing of infrastructure with other cellular service providers or any other type of service providers in their area in their area of operation.

National Long Distance Services

As per the National Telecom policy '99, National Long Distance Services (NLD) beyond the service area shall be opened for competition. With a view to providing choice to consumers and promoting competition, all access provides would be mandatorily required to provide interconnection to all NLD providers.

Global Mobile Personal Communication by Satellite (GMPCS)

There is no restriction on the number of GMPCS licences and licences are issued on first-come-first-served basis. Gateways for GMPCS are to be located in India and operation and maintenance of the same are to be with an organization designated by the Government. A two-tier licence fee is payable-a fixed component plus a variable component as percentage of revenues.

Other Value Added Services

As the telecommunications and Information Technology (IT) infrastructure in the country is expanding, there is a surge in demand for a range of value added services. The scheme for value added services has been considerably liberalized. These services include radio paging, public mobile radio trunking, and domestic data using VASTs, Evolving of new services—Tele-education, Tele-medicine, Tele-banking, Call Centre—is catching up with the Indian Industry and has recently witnessed significant investments from domestic and foreign investors.

Information Technology

Investment Policy

Automatic approval for foreign equity in software and almost all areas of electronics Automatic approval accorded for foreign technology agreements in all areas of electronics except aero-space and defence, subject to specified conditions.

100% foreign investment permitted in units set up exclusively for exports. Such units can be set up under any one of the following schemes; EHTPs, STPs, Free Trade Zones/EPZs, and 100% EOUs.

Opportunities

According to a recent World Bank study, India is the preferred location for software vendors for its quality and cost. India has strong UNIX base which provides opportunity for the development of products for internet based applications. Further, India has global connectivity with international dialing facility from over 13220 locations, Leased/switched high-speed data links from major centres through STPs and VSNL for point-to-point communication are also available. Internet connectivity is provided through several networks. Abundant investment opportunities exist in the following thrust areas in India:

- Communication Infrastructure
- Optic Fibre Cable
- Gateways
- Satellite-based Communication Wireless
- Software Development
- IT-enables Services
- IT Education (100,000 post graduate professionals in IT required annually by 2004)
- IT-enabled education
- Data Centres and Server Farms

E-commerce

Investment Policy

Up to 100% FDI is permitted for e-commerce, subject to the condition that the companies concerned would divest 26% of their equity in favour of the Indian public in five years, if the companies are listed in other parts of the world.

Opportunity

According to a study by ICRA Ltd., the volume of e-business in India is likely to increase from the level of Rs. 4.7 billion in 1999-00 to a level above Rs. 250 billion in the next three to four years; the figure makes a clear case for large scale investments in the Indian e-commerce sector.

Knowledge-Based Industries

Pharmaceuticals

Investment Policy

Automatic approval for up to 74% foreign equity in the case of bulk drugs, their intermediates and formulations (except those produced by the use of recombinant DNA technology).

Opportunities

India pharmaceutical industry has shown tremendous progress in terms of infrastructure development, technology base and range of production, India derives its technological strengths in pharmaceuticals on the following bases:

Self-reliance displayed by the production of 70% of bulk drugs and almost the entire requirement of formulations within the country.

Low cost of production

Low R&D costs
Innovative scientific manpower
Strength National Laboratories
Increasing balance of trade in Pharma sector

Chemicals and biotechnology

Opportunities

Chemicals

The chemical industry in India is well established and has recorded a steady growth in the overall Indian industrial scenario. The chemical and allied industries have been amongst the faster growing segments of the Indian industry. The Indian chemical industry had a turnover of around Rs. 900 billion in 1996-97. The chemicals industry also accounted for over 10% of total Indian exports during 1997-98. The chemical industry is highly heterogeneous encompassing many sector like organic and inorganic chemicals, dyestuffs, paints, pesticides, and specialty chemicals, Some of the prominent individual chemical industries are caustic soda, soda ash, carbon black, phenol, acetic acid, methanol and azo dyes. Currently, there is tremendous scope for growth in chemical sector. The per capita consumption of chemicals in India is well below the prevailing world level. For instance, in sulphuric acid, which is considered the barometer of growth in the chemical industry, the per capita consumption is only about 5 kg per annum in India as compared to 40 kg in industrially developed countries.

Biotechnology

The setting up of a separate Department of Biotechnology (DBT) under the Ministry of Science and Technology in 1986 gave a new impetus to the development of modern biology and biotechnology in India. In more than a decade of its existence, the department has promoted and accelerated the pace of development of biotechnology in the country. In India, concerted efforts for over a decade in R&D in the identified areas of modern biology and biotechnology have paid rich dividends. The proven technologies at the laboratory level have been scaled up and demonstrated in field. Patenting of innovations, technology transfer to industries and close interaction with them have given a new direction to biotechnology research. Necessary guidelines for transgenic plants, recombinant vaccines and drugs have also been evolved. A strong base of indigenous capabilities has been created.

Opportunities

Biotechnology industry serves as a research arm to Agritech and Pharma industry with increased potential for strategic alliances. Global trends show that all large pharmaceutical players are putting their money in healthcare for long term benefits. It is expected that nearly half the drugs in the next decade would be biotech Products. These also exists tremendous potential in agri-business that the, transgenic seeds, bio-fertilizers etc. especially considering the fact number of small firms is high, knowledge-based, research-intensive industry with low capital requirements. This suits agro-based economy of India (Table 8).

Table 8: Status and Scope of agro-based and Allied Industries

	Sector Estimated Turnover	Turnover (1997) for 2000 (million US $)	Estimated Turnover for 2005 (million)
Healthcare Products	650	800	1,300
Agriculture	480	650	1,110
Industrial Products	556	67	830
Total (including other)	1,790	2,100	3,240

The field of biotechnology both for new innovations and application would form a major research and commercial endeavour for socio economic development in this decade.

Infrastructure Sector

Roads

Investment Policy

FDI up to 100% under automatic route is permitted in projects for construction and maintenance of roads, highways, vehicular bridges, toll roads, vehicular tunnels, ports and harbours.

Opportunities

Investment worth an estimated US $ 34 billion needed, till 2005-06, for the development of National and Stte Highways. Of this figure, the requirement of private sector investment is US $ 8.3 billion.

Opportunities exist in:

Highway construction
Four-Lining of over 35,000 km of National Highways
Highway related en route activities like restaurants, motels, and rest/parking areas as may be decided by the implementing agency.

Select project opportunities include:

Chennai-Nellor (US $ 350 million)
Bangalore-Chennai (US $ 305 million)
Surat-Manor (US $ 180 million)
Jaipur-Ajmer (US $ 147 million)

Ports

Investment Policy

The principal legislations governing Indian ports are The Indian Ports Act, 1908, and the Major Ports Trust Act, 1963, the Indian Government recently announced a series of measures to promote foreign investment in the port sector as listed below:

- No approval required for foreign equity up to 51% in projects providing supporting services to water transport, such as operation and maintenance of piers, loading and discharging of vehicles.
- Automatic approval for foreign equity up to 100% in construction and maintenance of ports and harbours, However, if the total foreign equity investment exceeds Rs. 15 billion, the proposal will be referred to the FIPB.
- Open tenders are to be invited for private sector participation on a Build-Operate-Transfer (BOT) basis. Evaluation of bids will be based on the maximum licence period will not exceed 30 years and at the end of the BOT period all assets will revert to the port in accordance with the conditions of the agreement.

The Government has announced guidelines for private/foreign participation that permit formation of joint venture between major ports and foreign ports, between major ports and minor ports, and between major ports and companies. The measures are aimed at attracting new technology, fostering strategic alliances with minor ports to create on optimal port infrastructure and enhancing private sector confidence in the funding of ports.

The guidelines permit the formation of a joint venture between:

- A major port and foreign ports for the purposes of constructing new port facilities within existing ports, improving productivity of existing ports, and development of new port;
- A major port trust and a company or a consortium of companies where;
- A company or a consortium of companies, selected through BOT (Build, Operate and Transfer) bidding under the guidelines of private sector participation alliances with a major port trust for improving the viability of the scheme and/or to enhance the confidence of the private sector.
- A company or a consortium of companies is selected under the scheme of innovative/unsolicited proposals

- Oil PSUs/a joint venture company of oil PSUs are/is selected for oil related port facility as a port-based industry.

Opportunities

The areas identified for privatization or investment by the private sector include:

- Leasing out of existing port assets
- Creating of additional assets
- Construction or operation of container terminals
- Construction or operation of break-bulk, multipurpose and specialized cargo berths
- Warehousing, container freight stations, storage facilities and tank farms
- Cranage and handling equipment
- Setting up captive power plants,
- Dry docking and ship repair facilities
- Leasing of equipment and floating craft from the private sector
- Pilotages
- Captive facilities for port-based industries.

Civil Aviation

Investment Policy

The monopoly of public sector air carriers ended with the introduction of Air Corporation Act, 1953 on March 1, 1994.

Automatic approval for foreign equity participation in Airport infrastructure upto 100 per cent; Foreign equity upto 40 per cent; investment by Non-Resident Indians upto 100 per cent permitted in domestic air-transport services.

Equity from foreign airlines not allowed in domestic air-transport services either or indirectly.

Foreign Financial Institutions allowed to hold equity in the domestic air-transport sector provided they do not have foreign airlines as their shareholders.

Foreign investors allowed having representation (upto 33 per cent of total) on Board of Directors of the domestic airline company.

Government considers private sector participation in construction and operation of new airports on a BOT basis.

Minimum fleet size for a scheduled operator raised from the existing 3 aircraft to 5. Management contract with a foreign airline is not permitted.

Opportunities

Construction of world class international airports in five cities, permitting upto 100% foreign equity investment announced. Important private sector-aided projects: New airport near Kochi (US $ 85.7 million). Projects for development of new airports at Bangalore and Mumbai with private sector participation are under consideration.

Other private sector-aided airports planned: Ahmedabad airport, Amritsar airport upgradation, Chennai cargo complex, new international terminal and a second runway for Delhi airport, runway extension and international block for Jaipur airport, Hyderabad and Bangalore airports.

FDI in Indian Infrastructure

Infrastructure in India include transportation, agriculture, water management, telecommunications, industrial and commercial development, power, petroleum and natural gas, housing and other segments such as mining, disaster management services, technology-related infrastructure (Asia TradeHub.com: http://www.asiatradehub.com/India/intro.asp).

Important sectors in Infrastructure in India

Within the Infrastructure of India, the transportation sector is the most important, including the aviation, ports, roads, rail system and logistics. The agriculture sector comprises infrastructure-related storage facilities, construction relating to agro-processing projects and reservation and storage of perishable goods. Among others essential sectors, real-estate development, including industrial parks, special economic zones, tourism and entertainment centers, educational institutions and hospitals and solid waste management systems, also play significant role in Indian economy. India initiated an ambitious reform programme, involving a shift from a controlled to an open market economy showing signs of overheating because of basic infrastructure constraints, both physical and human. So far, the bulk of infrastructure was in the public sector. Public sector in India operating in a protected set up has been largely subsidized by the Government. Since the launching of reform, Government is trying to reduce its borrowing which means that further subsidization will not be possible. There is one area where there is a need for private sector and foreign investment to come in. Because of the long gestation period, and many social implications, the infrastructure sector compares unfavorably with manufacturing and many other sectors. For this, specific policies in this area are needed to make infrastructure attractive. Clearly, there is a wide gap between the potential demand for infrastructure for high growth and the available supply. This is the challenge placed before the economy, i.e. before the public and private sector and foreign investors. This can also be seen as an opportunity for a widening market and enhanced production.

Capital Needs for Investment

According to the India infrastructure Report (IIR, 2006- http://www.iitk.ac.in/3inetwork/html/reports/IIR2006/iir2006.html), currently 5.5 per cent of the GDP is invested in the infrastructure sector. This needs to be increased to 7 per cent within the next three years and 8 per cent by 2005-06, by which time the annual level of investment in infrastructural facilities is projected to treble or rise even more, from the current level of Rs. 6000 billion (US $ 52 billion) by 2005-2006. The total infrastructure investment requirements for the next five years again have been estimated in the report at about Rs. 4000-4500 billion (US $ 115-130 billion). The task of finding such large amounts and thereafter deploying them productively calls for a close partnership between the public and private sectors, with a vital role reserved for foreign capital. To finance this large short fall, the domestic saving rate needs to be increased by a minimum of 26.7%. Besides, this has to be supplemented at the margin by FDI. However, this margin is indeed very important since the role of foreign investment has to be read not only as a gap filler between saving and investment but also as a means for bringing better technology and management.

India Infrastructure Finance Company

The Finance Minister announced a special purpose vehicle (SPV) to fund infrastructure projects in his 2005 budget speech. The SPV, India Infrastructure Finance Company (IIFC) is proposed to be a wholly owned government entity under the Companies Act. The authorized capital of the company is fixed at Rs. 1000 crore and the borrowing limit for the current fiscal has been pegged at Rs. 10,000 crore. The company will fund projects in urban infrastructure, roads, power, railways, ports, airports, and tourism. The projects could be publicly or privately owned or could be schemes involving public–private partnerships. In case of projects authorities when due, and obtain reimbursement from the empowered institution (GOI, 2005).

The scheme covers roads, railways, seaports, airports, inland waterways, power, infrastructure projects in SEZs, international convention centres and other tourism infrastructure projects, urban transport, water supply, sewerage, solid waste management and other physical infrastructure projects in urban areas. Salient provisions under the scheme are:

- infrastructure asset indirectly owned by the government;
- project built and maintained by a private sector entity;
- project designed and an estimate of viability gap given by a government entity;
- viability gap fund—one time or deferred grant—provided by the government;
- viability gap fund not to exceed 20 per cent of the total project cost; but the entity that owns the project may provide additional grants up to another 20 per cent of the project cost from its own budget;
- a pre-determined tariff or user charge to be collected from users.

A revolving fund of Rs. 200 crore shall be provided by the Ministry of Finance to the empowered institution, which will disburse funds to the lead financial institution and claim reimbursement from the Ministry of Finance. The government is yet to nominate the empowered institution to implement the scheme (GOI, 2005). The new institutional mechanisms proposed by the government to build infrastructure are yet to bear fruit. Pace of development of different infrastructure sub-sectors has been quite uneven in the last two years. We capture essence of new developments in telecom, power, transport, and urban infrastructure and analyze reasons underlying the irregular pace of development and issues that have either helped in accelerating or impeding growth as the case may be.

Importance of Port Infrastructure

The port sector has been identified as the prime catalyst to accelerate the process of industrialization, international trade and economic progress. Port development and economic development are mutually related. On one hand economic development necessitates port development as a part of infrastructure development and on other hand, port development itself facilitates import-export and attracts industries to its hinterland, which in turn create forward and backward linkage with the rest of the economy. The development of port sector as associated with maritime trade is an axiom that no maritime nation can afford to ignore in today's global world. With the thrust towards economic reforms in India and the capacity limitations of major ports, the state governments have to pay attention to the development of their minor ports often combining industrial sites development projects with port development. India, with the port reforms has to prove that any globalization that is to take place has to take place through the ports of international class only.

Airport infrastructure

In India, airports were totally owned and managed by central government or the armed forces. The Airport Authority of India (AAI), a body functioning under the Ministry of Civil Aviation was responsible for managing the airports in India. It owns 122 airports, 61 of which are operational. The breakdown is as follows:

- 11 international
- 94 civil and
- 27 civil enclaves at defence airfields.

The AAI operate most aspects of the airport (including air traffic control) and procure most of their equipment directly (via global/local tenders). India's airports handle 42 million passengers, of which the four Metro gateway airports (Delhi, Mumbai, Kolkata and Chennai) account for 47% of revenue and 66% of the passengers. Until 2000, there were five major international airports—Mumbai, Kolkata, Delhi, Chennai and Trivandrum. But the GoI announced a further six airports including Amritsar, Bangalore, Hyderabad, Cochin during the course of 2002. According to projections, Indian air passenger traffic was estimated to grow to 100 million passengers by 2012 from 36.98 million in 1998-99. Growth projections in the cargo front were also promising. Airport infrastructure is linked to development of India's international competitiveness and her ability to attract foreign investments. The policy opened the doors of private investment in this sector, including investments from foreign airport authorities (Global Competitiveness (3)\Study of the Indian Aviation Industry.htm).

The Indian civil aviation sector is showing an extraordinary growth rate in the last few years. In 2005-06, the passenger traffic rose by 25-30% and is expected to grow by 25% year-on-year over the next five years. However, such a pace of growth in air traffic has also resulted in a strain on the aviation infrastructure, which is already stretched – resulting in traffic congestions and delays at majority of the airports. At Delhi airport, approximately 327 domestic aircrafts land and take-off everyday. This means that about 10.04 million passengers are ferried by the domestic airlines alone every year, while the terminal can handle only a meager 7.15 million. Hence, if a high growth in civil aviation sector is to be sustained, it would call for improvement of infrastructure facilities on several fronts.

As per certain projections, by 2020, Indian airports are estimated to handle:

- 100 million passengers
- Including 60 million domestic passengers
- Cargo in the range of 3.4 million tonnes per annum

The Government has taken a number of measures to step up the airport infrastructure for the country. It has envisaged a modernization plan with a view to modernize 37 non-metro airports. On the lines of the successful model of the Central Road fund, the government is considering setting up the Essential Air Service Fund to support the country's airport infrastructure (CII, 2008). Keeping in mind the huge requirement of funds for the development of airport infrastructure and the financial constraints coupled with other conflicting budgetary priorities of the government, the government has invited private participation in the modernization program of the major airports. Delhi and Mumbai airport development projects are being undertaken through public-private Partnership ventures.

There needs to be an effort towards optimum utilization of the existing airports by addressing the problems of outdated infrastructure, inadequate ground handling systems and night landing facilities, and poor passenger amenities. At the same time it will also be required to create new airports at several places where there is a scope. There needs to be improvement in the airside infrastructure and terminal infrastructure at India's airports.

Indian Aviation Industry to Match Global Standards

The Aviation industry has contributed enormously in the recent past to the current growth scenario. An upsurge in terms of passenger traffic and growth rate, particularly in the domestic sector has far outstripped the growth of the industry even in the Asia Pacific region. Nearly a quarter of the total sales for corporations' world over are dependent on a good air transport links. The Government also has definitive plans to develop 35 non-metro airports under public private partnership model and 10 airports would be announced in the next two months. There has been a tremendous growth in this sector in the last decade but the hiccups of abysmal maintenance and hospitality conditions at airports have been constantly begging for explanations. The Budget off late has brought good news for infrastructure related concerns as the booming Aviation industry has aggressively demanded an optimum allocation in this sphere. Apart from low infrastructural facilities, Aircraft safety requires contemplation.

While the sector is making positive strides the above mentioned fissures need to be filled before they become gaping holes. India's booming aviation business needs more airports, pilots, flight crew and less-stressed air traffic controllers. The government needs to be mindful of these and address them immediately. Apart from the visible infrastructure level improvements, modernization, HR issues, aviation methodology, technological growth and controlling traffic congestion are some of the other issues that demand careful and timely attention. There is also a need to accelerate the decision making in terms of policy parameters. The policy has to be such which encourages increased private sector participation because the government is not well poised to solely fund infrastructure, it needs the services of the private sector in terms of expertise, skills, human resource etc to make this industry one of its kind. The growth numbers though sound good, they still weigh less than our competitors in China and US, the prime reason being growth constraints as a result of poor infrastructure. Infrastructure is the key to all aviation related problems and the government should take steps to address them effectively and efficiently. Indian carriers can compete with the best in the world and can contribute significantly to the promotion of tourism in India supported by the right policies, good infrastructure and correct operating environment. The aviation industry is a success story till now, however if infrastructural aspects are neglected anymore it will soon become a nightmare.

Indian Scenario of Aviation Industry

India is a country with tremendous growth opportunities given its position in the world today. Vast distances between cities and towns and poor surface transport are in the West however, Governments have no participation given the capital intensive and long gestation periods involved. Market forces have tended to dominate in the past decade and have forced restructuring of organizations and governments have privatized a number of companies that were once state owned. At present, we are witnessing a consolidation phase m the industry. Governments also represent companies in trade talks, negotiate bilateral arrangements for landing slots at airports, represent the industry's interests at GATT/WTO, and have been known to link development aid to purchase of aviation products manufactured in the donor country. Certification enables aircraft and aircraft components manufactured in one country to be certified in another automatically. Potential for air traffic important reasons to believe that such a potential exists. Growth is expected from tourism domestic and international travel for business and pleasure (Dhawan *et al.*, 2007).

About 12 million passengers used domestic airlines in 1995 and about 2 million tourists arrived in the country in the same year. A Ministry of Civil Aviation estimate projects about 22 million. In comparison to other countries, this figure is still considerably small. Air traffic growth is closely linked to economic activity. Econometric models developed in the country to predict traffic growth considered economic indicators like GDP, industrial production (IIP), foreign tourist arrivals (FTA) as main parameters. There is a view that growth may not he sensitive to yields unlike other countries. There are primarily two factors for this view: lack of adequate competition and the nature of the travelers, the majority of who travel on business (Dhawan *et al.*, 2008).

Air Routes

Air fares have risen about 2.3 times from December 1990. This is due to fuel costs and capital costs in purchase and leasing. This is in sharp contrast to the constant decline in yields around the world allowing vast majority of people to travel and is primarily responsible for the growth in air traffic since 1960. Yet in dollar terms, air travel is cheaper in India. Air travel in India is cheaper than Indonesia or Pakistan and presently works out to be about 9 cents per kilometer against 17 cents in Pakistan. However, when we consider the average Indian's purchasing power, it is beyond his reach. In a population close to a billion, only 12 million trips were made showing 0.013 trips per capita. It is possible that among the 12 million, a number of persons made more than a single trip. India will require about 100 million passengers and over 500 aircraft compared to the 70 aircraft operating on trunk routes today. An average growth of about 12% in travel would lead to 100 million passengers only by 2015. A target of about 100 million passengers and about 500 aircraft would lead to a healthy domestic industry. The trunk routes may only contribute to sedate growth in air traffic as there is congestion already in these routes and development of new airports and runways is not easy in the metropolitan cities. As the economy grows ploy skilled labour ranks next only to the automobile industry. Development of aircraft production facilities, runways and airports present enormous potential in the aerospace production (Dhawan *et al.*, 2008).

Appropriate technology

India presents the need for the most advanced technology for trunk routes and international travel. The real addition will come from feeder routes, feeder to hubs and new city pairs which have potential to provide traffic because of economic activity or tourism. This will require considerable investment in appropriate commuter and regional aircraft and airport infrastructure at district headquarters, tourist spots and locations where industrial activity can be identified. States like Maharashtra, Karnataka, Gujarat, UP and have considered investment and incentives for this sector. NAL's (National Aeronautical Limited) market research shows that there exists demand in the corporate sector from the further; many new organizations will be interested in acquiring corporate aircraft. It is expected that charter for aircraft of corporate travel will grow considerably. NAL for example, recently announced a scheme to hire its rugged aircraft to corporate traveling into remote parts of the country where aircraft have to use semi-prepared runways.

Investment into Airport Infrastructure

With the increase in traffic for both passenger and cargo aviation services in India, the government has put in place a program for directing investments in the Airport infrastructure – through both internal resource mobilization, as well as through private sector participation in modernizing specific airports. The Committee on Infrastructure has initiated several policy measures that would build world-class airport infrastructure in India (CII, 2008). A Model Concession Agreement is also being developed for standardizing and simplifying the PPP transactions for airports. In any future projects for development of existing airports, it has been decided that the length of the runway would be at least 7,500 feet (which is needed for the A 320 and A 380 or similar aircrafts).

Hotel Industry in India

Hotel Industry in India has witnessed tremendous boom in recent years. Hotel Industry is inextricably linked to the tourism industry and the growth in the Indian tourism industry has fuelled the growth of Indian hotel industry. The thriving economy and increased business opportunities in India have acted as a boon for Indian hotel industry. The arrival of low-cost airlines and the associated price wars have given domestic tourists a host of options. In recent years, government has taken several steps to boost travel and tourism which have benefited hotel industry in India. These include the abolishment of the inland air travel tax of 15%; reduction in excise duty on aviation turbine fuel to 8%;

and removal of a number of restrictions on outbound chartered flights, including those relating to frequency and size of aircraft. The government's recent decision to treat convention centres as part of core infrastructure, allowing the government to provide critical funding for the large capital investment that may be required has also fuelled the demand for hotel rooms.

The opening up of the aviation industry in India has exciting opportunities for hotel industry as it relies on airlines to transport 80% of international arrivals. The government's decision to substantially upgrade 28 regional airports in smaller towns and privatization and expansion of Delhi, Mumbai, Hyderabad, Bangalore airports will improve the business prospects of hotel industry in India. Substantial investments in tourism infrastructure are essential for Indian hotel industry to achieve its potential. The upgrading of national highways connecting various parts of India has opened new avenues for the development of budget hotels in India. Taking advantage of this opportunity Tata group and another hotel chain called 'Homotel' have entered this business segment.

According to a report, Hotel Industry in India currently has supply of 110,000 rooms and there is a shortage of 150,000 rooms fueling hotel room rates across India. According to estimates demand is going to exceed supply by at least 100% over the next 2 years. Five-star hotels in metro cities allot same room, more than once a day to different guests, receiving almost 24-hour rates from both guests against 6-8 hours usage. With demand-supply disparity, hotel rates in India are likely to rise by 25% annually and occupancy by 80%, over the next two years. This will affect the competitiveness of India as a cost-effective tourist destination.

To overcome, this shortage Indian hotel industry is adding about 60,000 quality rooms, currently in different stages of planning and development, which should be ready by 2012. Hotel Industry in India is also set to get a fillip with Delhi hosting 2010 Commonwealth Games. Government has approved 300 hotel projects, nearly half of which are in the luxury range. The future scenario of Indian hotel industry looks extremely rosy. It is expected that the budget and mid-market hotel segment will witness huge growth and expansion while the luxury segment will continue to perform extremely well over the next few years. With the US $ 23 billion software services sector pushing the Indian economy skywards, more and more IT professionals are flocking to Indian metro cities. 'Hotel Industry in India' is set to grow at 15% a year. This figure will skyrocket in 2010, when Delhi hosts the Commonwealth Games. Already, more than 50 international budget hotel chains are moving into India to stake their turf. Therefore, with opportunities galore the future 'Scenario of Indian Hotel Industry' looks rosy (Indian Business Directory, 2008).

Indian Tourism Industry Analysis

Indian Tourism Industry Analysis provides an insight into the Indian tourism market (http://www.marketresearch.com/product/display.asp?productid=

1807636&g=1). It evaluates the past, present and future scenario of the Indian tourism market and discusses the key factors which are making India a potential tourism destination. With focuses on different parameters of tourism industry, including inbound tourism, outbound tourism, expenditure by inbound tourists, medical tourism, and hotel industry, the report gives a thorough analysis on the tourism industry in India. According to the report, India represents one of the most potential tourism markets in the world. It has expanded rapidly over the past few years and underpinned by the government support, rising income level and various international sports events, the Indian tourism industry will continue to grow at the fastest pace in the coming years. However, the industry may have to cope up with several challenges which will limit its growth (Market Research.com, 2008).

Key Findings

India is expected to see an influx of 10 million international tourists by 2010, up from just 5 million in 2007. Andhra Pradesh, Uttar Pradesh, Tamil Nadu, Karnataka and Rajasthan are the leading tourism destinations in India in terms of total tourist arrivals. India has been promoting its healthcare tourism by providing the visitors with private healthcare facilities. It is expected that the total market for medical tourism will reach US $ 2 billion by 2012, representing a CAGR of 60.69%. Personal disposable income during 2002-2007 grew at a CAGR of 14.16%, thereby driving domestic as well as outbound tourism. Indian outbound tourist flow is expected to increase at a CAGR of 13.30% over the five-year period spanning from 2008 to 2012. India's share in the global tourism is expected to reach 1.5% by 2010. The growth in India's tourism market is expected to serve as a boon, driving the growth of several associated industries, including hotel industry, medical tourism industry and aviation industry (www.companiesandmarkets.com).

India's tourism sector has the potential to generate significant additional income and employment. In 2005, international tourist arrivals were just under 4 million, though the average stay per visitor was over 20 days. India's domestic tourism increased from 67 million in 1991 to 366 million in 2004, and is also growing rapidly. However, in 2004, India had only 1892 approved hotels, with slightly less than 100,000 rooms (as compared to 1.2 million in China, and 4.4 million rooms in the U.S). The demand-supply gap is expected to narrow, and market forces are likely to bring about lower hotel room rates in the next few years. India's tourism sector thus provides substantial business opportunities for Asian and other businesses. India also hopes to expand its medical tourism industry. In 2005, India provided medical services to 200,000 patients from abroad. India is also executing medical services outsourced by the National Health Service (NHS) of UK.

A recent study by India's Confederation of Indian Industry (CII) and McKinsey has projected that India could earn around US $ 2 billion through medical tourism by 2012 (www.medical-tourism-india.com). While there is some competition among India and some of the other Asian countries in this area, as in the IT and ITES sector, there are also likely to be complementarities. Moreover, India's rising medical needs will provide substantial opportunities for Asian countries to operate in India. Similarly, the healthcare industry of India also has plans to expand abroad. India's performance in providing affordable health services to its population is however quite modest.

The 'Indian Tourism Industry Forecast (2007-2011)' Report provides an objective analysis of the present scenario and future prospects of the Indian tourism industry. This report focuses on different parameters of tourism industry including: inbound tourism, outbound tourism, expenditure by inbound tourists, and medical tourism in India. It also helps clients to analyze the opportunities and factors critical to the success of tourism industry in India (Research and Markets, 2007).

Key Findings

- In India, inbound tourist expenditure per head is third highest in the world and even more than global average tourist spending.
- India has been promoting its healthcare tourism by providing the visitors with private healthcare facilities. It is expected that the number of tourists visiting India for the purpose of medical treatment will reach one million by 2012, representing a CAGR of 28.09% from 2007.
- Disposable income in past (during 2001-2006) grew at a CAGR of 10.11%, thereby driving domestic as well as outbound tourism.
- Room rent accounts for more than 50% of revenue earned by Indian hotel industry.
- Indian outbound tourist flow is expected to increase at a CAGR of 12.79% over the five-year period spanning 2007-2011.
- Tourist influx to India is expected to increase at a CAGR of 22.65% between 2007 and 2011.
- India's share in global tourism is expected to reach 1.5% by 2010.

Medical Tourism – Healthcare in the Competitive Global Marketplace

Medical tourism is a marketplace phenomenon that works outside the organized medical community and usual medical referral systems. Patients pursue offshore healthcare options because this enables them to maximize value. Medical tourism is a clear signal that patients greatly value the opportunity to receive the care they need promptly while conserving personal resources and avoiding financial distress (Changemakers.net: http://www.changemakers.net/node/1086). Accordingly, medical tourism has substantial potential to transform healthcare in several ways:

- Patients unable to get care within their own country are able to successfully participate in a global marketplace. Patients who feel disenfranchised are able to identify, investigate and arrange care around the world utilizing their home computer either independently or with the assistance and advice of a medical tourism agency. Thus, patients become empowered in the global marketplace.
- The insurance industry has become very interested in medical tourism. Several major insurance companies, including Blue Cross and Blue Shield, have expanded their provider networks to include medical tourism destinations. Furthermore, several Fortune 500 Corporations are exploring the option of utilizing offshore medical centers to reduce the cost of employee healthcare (Appleby and Schmidt, 2006).
- Overburdened domestic healthcare facilities and philanthropic organizations may be able to better utilize their limited resourced by directing unfunded low income patients to low cost offshore medical destinations for expensive surgical procedures.
- The financial and symbolic implications of medical tourism will stimulate desirable changes within the American healthcare system. Providers will be forced to deliver greater value to patients and third-party payors to successfully compete in the global healthcare arena. Some domestic healthcare providers are now offering steeply discounted surgical procedures for American patients referred by medical tourism agencies (Van Dusen, 2007).

Context for Disruption: Medical tourism is a rapidly growing phenomenon wherein people from industrialized nations bypass physicians and hospitals in their own community to travel to faraway healthcare destinations in a variety of developing countries for medical, surgical and dental care. Approximately 750,000 Americans will travel to offshore medical facilities in 2007, and the number is projected to increase to 6 million in 2010 (Baliga, 2006). It is estimated that the worldwide medical tourism business generates annual revenue of $ 60 billion (MacReady, 2007).

The primary reason that patients from the United States travel abroad for healthcare is affordability. These patients are willing to bear the inconvenience and uncertainties of offshore healthcare to obtain service that they can comfortably afford. In an article in the New England Journal of Medicine, October 16, 2006, Milstein and Smith describe these patients as "middle-income Americans evading impoverishment by expensive, medically necessary operations". In addition, American patients travel to medical tourism destinations for cosmetic surgery, dental care, fertility therapy and other procedures not covered by health insurance. The cost of care in India and Thailand is 10-20% of the cost in the United States.

Patients from nations where governmental health systems control access to services pursue medical tourism to circumvent the delays in treatment associated with waiting lists. Another reason patients travel to offshore destinations for healthcare is to have certain procedures not available in their own country. These patients are unable to access the care they need or want within their own community because of barriers related to affordability, timeliness or availability. However, in the global marketplace, these patients are desirable customers. For American patients, the financial resources that are inadequate at home are ample for them to purchase care in developing economies.

Delivery Model: Medical Tourism will likely be very disruptive to the American healthcare system. The disruptive potential of this phenomenon has been substantially increased by the participation of insurance companies and corporate health benefit plans. Medical tourism destinations seek to benefit from this potentially lucrative business. On the other hand, the loss of well funded patients may have serious adverse consequences for some domestic providers and facilities. Many parties will likely be impacted by medical tourism. As this phenomenon rapidly evolves, numerous stakeholders in the global healthcare marketplace will have a great need for credible information, thoughtful analysis, insightful forecasting and reliable advice. Medical Insights International's goal is to become a leader in providing valuable objective information and advice to parties involved or interested in the medical tourism industry. Medical Insights International will serve clients utilizing a portfolio of services that will be progressively expanded over time.

These services include:

- Consulting engagements
- Research projects
- Presentations, symposia and seminars
- Newsletters
- Monographs and white papers

Key Operational Partnerships: Medical Insights International has existing relationships with a number of parties involved in medical tourism. Medical Insights International will continue to develop partnerships with individuals and organizations from many disciplines and spheres including medicine, public health, health policy, medical ethics, economics, finance, insurance, international relations, government, philanthropy, and the travel and hospitality industry. Medical Insights International will develop additional relationships with current participants in the medical tourism industry, including medical tourism agencies and healthcare providers and facilities in destination countries. Finally, Medical Insights International will seek partnerships with knowledgeable, insightful and innovative people and entities that we believe can make meaningful future contributions, even though they may have no previous involvement with medical tourism.

Financial Model: Medical Insights International is a start-up business in the demonstration stages of its development. The firm expects to begin earning revenue from services provided to clients in early 2008. These services will initially consist of consulting engagements and research projects for clients.

Additional sources of revenue will be developed over the next year including fees from presentations, symposia and seminars. In addition, under the Financial Model, revenues will be generated from newsletter subscriptions and other publications. Medical Insights International will use any funds derived from this competition awards to implement a greater range of client services and products on an accelerated schedule. Capital received from investors would similarly facilitate development of a full portfolio of services at an earlier time.

Effectiveness: Medical Insights International has met its initial start-up goals. A library of materials about medical tourism has been assembled and information has been studied and analyzed. Relationships have been established with a number of parties in medical tourism. Medical Insights International has been very effective in the early goal of preparing informative manuscripts for publication. In light of the anticipated magnitude of medical tourism, Medical Insights International forecasts that there will be a substantial demand for accurate information and thoughtful analysis regarding this burgeoning world-wide business. Medical Insights International expects to have abundant opportunities to provide services to the many companies and organizations involved, or potentially involved, in the medical tourism industry.

Scaling-up Strategy: Medical Insights International has met its initial start-up goals, as described above. The firm will begin providing consulting services and conducting research projects for clients in early 2008.

The rapidity with which Medical Insights International will be able to institute all planned portfolio services will be adjusted based on the demand for its services as well as circumstances in the medical tourism industry. The modus operandi of Medical Insights International is as follows:

- Stage of the initiative: Start-up
- Expansion plan: To provide a robust portfolio of services for a growing number of clients, Medical Insights International must recruit additional employees to undertake consulting engagements, perform research, manage a data base, draft reports and manuscripts, and develop and maintain a web site. In addition, employees and facilities will be required for administrative and support functions. Medical Insights International's timely expansion will require appropriate funding within the 18-month period ending December 2008. Alternatively, Medical Insights International would be able to expand services by synergistic strategic alliances or merger with a suitable existing firm. Similarly, Medical Insights International would be able to expand its services and client base through acquisition by an appropriate entity.

Meeting the Challenge of Medical Tourism with Healthcare Business Intelligence

As the name implies, medical tourism means traveling to another country (or to a lesser degree, another state) for medical care. The target for most medical tourists is surgery, especially expensive surgeries (both medically necessary as well as elective), and the reason is price. One popular story circulating around the Web news is of a man who had heart bypass surgery in India at a cost of $ 15,000. The same surgery in the United States would have cost him $ 150,000. A number of stories such as this are touting trips to developing nations for medical procedures with prices that run 10-30% of the comparative prices at home. In terms of the healthcare industry as a whole, medical tourism is currently an extremely small slice of the pie. For a $ 2 trillion industry, a paltry $ 5-6 billion (about three-tenths of one per cent) going overseas does not seem significant or worrisome. However, the following three important factors are crucial determinants of success in the Medical Tourism venture (http://www.b-eye-network.com/view/4324):

- *Impact is multiplied:* The figures for the size of the medical segment of the tourism industry represent dollars that are received by the competition. Every medical tourist dollar could mean as much as ten dollars of revenue loss to the customer.
- *Trends Start Small:* Forty years ago, the bulk of the manufacturing sector could say the same thing about foreign competition – that it is not something to lose sleep over. Twenty years ago, information technology workers could say the same thing about off-shoring programmers. Perhaps now is the time for the healthcare industry to be one step ahead of the rest of the country.
- *Impact is not evenly spread:* At any rate, for the three-fourths of the healthcare industry who are part of organizations of less than 20 and who are highly specialized, a few well placed revenue losses can put you out of business. Plus, these types of trends tend to be viral (no pun intended), as word of mouth alerts more of your local customers to the idea of taking your revenue elsewhere.

The Value Proposition of Medical Tourism

Before going into a description of the effective responses to medical tourism and how business intelligence can help make this trend an opportunity, it is necessary to describe a few of the basics of the value proposition of this practice.

Cost: The obvious draw is reduced cost (actually price) for the purchaser of the healthcare services. As mentioned earlier, certain services in Asian, Eastern European, Middle Eastern or Latin American countries can be priced at 10-20% of the comparative prices here in the U.S. For patients in other developed nations such as Canada and Western Europe, the draw is availability of services since it can take a year or more to schedule some surgeries in those nations.

Quality: Individual facilities in the destination countries are responding very well to the call for quality by payers, purchasers, patients, politicians and governmental agencies here in the United States. Many Indian and Thai hospitals, for instance, are applying for and receiving accreditation from the Joint Commission. In addition, other hospitals (e.g., Singapore) are developing impressive research and ancillary service infrastructures to support the importation of patients to their facilities.

Luxury: In many ways, the medical tourism industry is mimicking the cruise ship tour industry in terms of developing a luxury experience for patients. Because a person is traveling from a developed nation to a developing nation, it is often necessary to shield that person from some of the realities of the destination country. The challenge, for instance, is how to get a patient from the air-conditioned airport to the air-conditioned hospital without getting them stuck in a four-hour traffic jam in a hot, sticky taxi, or having them pass groups of children digging through dumpsters for food. Neither situation instills much confidence in the patient as to the quality of the medical site. To combat these challenges, many of the medical tourism companies and hospitals are developing something of a tourist oasis near the point of patient arrival. Make no mistake about it, as a healthcare provider; the Medico-Tourism Industry will have formidable opponents in the race for medical revenue by integrating these multipronged strategies:

- *Foreign Healthcare Facilities:* The motivation is obvious for this group – revenue.
- *Travel Industry:* Once again, the primary motivation is revenue. In this case, the revenue potential is growing at an estimated 20-30% per year, compared to 4-5% for other types of travel.
- *Local Governments:* Governments like revenue too. Plus, they like higher employment rates in more highly skilled jobs.
- *Purchasers:* One person's revenue is another person's cost. The potential 80-90% savings for medical services is very attractive. In fact, some employers are offering their employees incentives to take this route and save them some money.
- *Payers:* Several health plans are offering a medical tourism option as a way to improve their value to their customers.

Four Types of Healthcare Services

Healthcare services come in four varieties. The classification of a specific service into one of these four varieties is essential to understanding and selecting the most appropriate response to the challenge medical tourism poses.

- *Big Healthcare Events:* This is the primary target for medical tourism – inpatient surgeries, for the most part. For the patient, these are both clinically and financially big events, such as heart surgeries, hip replacements, neurosurgery, cancer surgeries, etc. Some of the surgeries are actually outpatient (e.g., major dental surgery, etc.). It is somewhat ironic that in other industries, it was the smaller, commodity goods and services that were the first targets for off-shoring; but in healthcare, it is the big, expensive, complex events that are the first targets.

- *Small Healthcare Events:* Today, outpatient surgeries are not the primary target for medical tours. For instance, one of my sons broke his arm skiing a couple of weeks ago. We were not going to get on a plane to have it set and cast. Other "small" healthcare events include immunizations, many dental procedures, etc. The return on investment, as well as the risk and time away, just do not justify all of the overhead associated with the treatment event.
- *Big Healthcare Relationships:* Think chronic disease management, which sadly involves what are often long, protracted, expensive relationships with one's healthcare providers. While there is a seminal event (e.g., initial diagnosis), the time, clinical intervention and the cost do not come in one or a few discrete chunks. These are currently not a major target for medical tourism.
- *Small Healthcare Relationships:* Most people have a very good relationship with their primary care physician as well as with the professional staff (PAs, NPs, RNs, etc.) that they see frequently. This is due to many small contact points between patient and provider. Checkups, immunizations, routine and some focused visits make up a significant portion of healthcare providers' revenue streams and form the basis of a relationship with the person and the community. Obviously, these are not even on the radar screen for medical tourism firms.

Future Perspective

Medical tourism today is a relatively small segment of the enormous healthcare industry. This segment is, however, receiving a lot of press and is rapidly becoming one of the darlings of the industry in the eyes of purchasers, payers, travel agencies and political interests on both sides of the ocean. The potential revenue impact cannot be ignored. There are positive business responses to meeting this challenge. Like many challenges faced by healthcare organizations, or any type of organization, it comes with the gift of making those organizations stronger through greater self-awareness of the strengths they possess.

Indian Entertainment and Media (E&M) Industries

The Indian entertainment and media (E&M) industry has out-performed the Indian economy and is one of the fastest growing sectors in India. The E&M industry generally tends to grow faster when the economy is expanding. The Indian economy has been growing at a fast clip over the last few years, and the income levels too have been experiencing a high growth rate. Above that, consumer spending is also on the rise, due to a sustained increase in disposable incomes, brought about by reduction in personal income tax over the last decade. All these factors have given an impetus to the E&M industry and are likely to contribute to the growth of this industry in the future. Besides these economic and personal income-linked factors, there are a host of other factors that are contributing to this high growth rate (PWC, 2006).

The Indian economy continues to perform strongly and one of the key sectors that benefits from this fast economic growth is the E&M industry. This is because the E&M industry is a cyclical industry that grows faster when the economy is expanding. It also grows faster than the nominal GDP during all phases of economic activity due to its income elasticity wherein when incomes rise, more resources get spent on leisure and entertainment and less on necessities. Further, consumption spending itself is increasing due to rising disposable incomes on account of sustained growth in income levels, and this also builds the case for a strong bullish growth in the sector.

The size of E&M in India is currently estimated at INR 353 billion and is expected to grow at a compounded annual growth rate of 19 per cent over the next five years. The television industry continues to dominate the E&M industry by garnering a share of over 42 per cent, which is expected to increase by a further 9 per cent to reach about 51 per cent. The share of the film industry, which currently stands at 19 per cent, is not expected to change materially over the next five years. Print media, which stands at over 31 per cent, is projected to lose some of its share in favour of the emerging segments.

Today, India has probably one of the most liberal investment regimes amongst the emerging economies with a conducive foreign direct investment (FDI) environment. The E&M industry has significantly benefited from this liberal regime and most segments of the E&M industry today allow foreign investment. Recently FDI was permitted in the two important sectors – print media and radio. Films, television and other segments are already open to foreign investment.

In the print media segment, 100 per cent FDI is now allowed for non-news publications and 26 per cent FDI is allowed for news publications. Printing of facsimile editions of foreign journals is now also allowed in India. This policy is helping foreign journals save on the cost of distribution while servicing the Indian market audiences more effectively. Thc FM radio sector too was opened for foreign investment recently with 20 per cent FDI being allowed. The FM radio sector itself has expanded by opening 338 licenses for private investment, which currently is underway. As a result, the radio sector is expanding rapidly with forecasted growth rates of 32 per cent per annum.

Entry of new players

The year 2005 saw the entry of new players across all segments of the E&M industry. The most prominent entry was that of the Reliance Group in the filmed entertainment and radio segment. During 2005, Reliance Capital bought a majority stake in Adlabs which enabled it to have a presence across the entire value chain of the filmed entertainment segment ranging from film production, exhibition and distribution. Through Adlabs, Reliance also made its entry into the radio segment by bidding for over 50 FM radio stations across the country with aggregate bids of over INR 1.5 billion. The other significant entry into the entertainment and media segment was that of the Tata group, through its subsidiary Videsh Sanchar Nigam Limited (VSNL). VSNL tied up with the Paris-based Thomson Group in 2005 with the objective of identifying opportunities in managing and delivering content for third parties, including broadcasters and content providers. Thomson Group also recently announced its partnership with Tata Sky Limited for manufacturing set-top-boxes and providing sales service and support network for their DTH customers (PWC, 2006).

Foreign investment

Owing to the strong impetus for growth from the economic and demographic factors coupled with some regulatory corrections, the sector also recently witnessed increasing foreign investment inflows in most segments of the E&M industry, especially the print media. Recent examples include foreign investment in English dailies such as Hindustan Times and Business Standard by Henderson Global and Financial Times respectively. Vernacular media too saw its share of foreign investment with a strategic equity investment by Independent News and Media in Dainik Jagran, a leading Hindi Daily. In the broadcasting space, most channels beaming into India (such as Walt Disney, ESPN-Star Sports, Star, Discovery, BBC etc.) have established foreign investment subsidiary companies for content development and advertisement airtime sales. In the television distribution space arena, foreign investment is being drawn by the larger cable operators referred to as 'multi-system operators (MSO)' such as Hathway and Hindujas. In the television content space, the recent investment in Nimbus Communications by a foreign private equity player is seen as the start of a significant trend of foreign investment inflows (PWC, 2006).

Management Education in India

Management education in India is a fairly recent happening in India; it has taken its practical shape during early sixties with establishment of Indian Institute of Management to train the people with management concepts. After that many institutions, universities have also come forward to provide management education to cater the increasing demand of good managers. The concept of global village and the revolution in the area of information technology is increasing integration of economies around the globe and attainment of global competitiveness has become a necessity for the survival and growth. The liberalization of Indian economy has resulted in a highly competitive environment, with much greater emphasis on technology, quality, and concern for society as well as the environmental issues and what is most sticking is the unprecedented development and use of information technology.

The process of liberalization and globalization has created enormous opportunities and challenges and in the era of global competitiveness we need to enhance our core competencies and other managerial capabilities to compete internationally. In the era of fast emerging changes, there is a need for future global managers with qualities and competencies in global perspective. Quality is the only attribute, which is accepted universally. In management education, quality has become a necessity and circumstances require total quality management. The make India an intellectual capital of the world we have to rethink about the management education and concerted efforts should be made to create a dynamic environment, which can render quality management education (Priya, 2008).

The management education in India has come a long way. The first Business School in India was Indian Institute of Social Welfare and Business Management, Calcutta, which was established in 1953. The next one was established as the Indian Institute of Management, Calcutta in 1961. Starting of with the establishment of 4 Indian Institutes of Management, Calcutta (1961), Ahmedabad (1962), Banglore (1973), Lucknow (1984), the setting up of XLRI, Jamshedpur and the offering of full time/part time MBA programmes by some leading universities in the country, much strides have been made to expand the horizon of Management Education in India.

The early 90's saw the boom of founding new management schools, most of them in private sector. In the last three years alone 400 Business Schools came into being. Few Business Schools have also established collaboration with some western Universities. India management institutions produce over 30,000 full-time MBAs and 10,000 part-time MBAs every year. There is also something called as MBA-Equivalent graduation programs that come out of Distance Education Programs of IGNOU, AIMA, AOU and so on. Even some of the leading business houses are establishing their own business schools. The latest one to enter the field is Kirloskar with a Business School in Karnataka, Reliance, IRMA etc. Today there are over 750 management institutions in the country.

Recently, and more particularly during the last one decade, the country has witnessed a tremendous growth in the founding of management institutions most of them in private sector offering management programs in different functional areas of management. Concurrently, there is a mushrooming of B-schools in the country: over 1,700 institutes, of which about 900 are certified by the All India Council for Technical Education (AICTE). In India, All India Council of Technical Education (AICTE) is entrusted with the responsibility of regulating, controlling and ensuring the quality of management education in the country. The formation of National Board of Accreditation (NBA) and the workshops that it had organized have contributed substantially to widespread awareness and concern for the quality of management education, but can the AICTE, in all honesty, claim that their approvals would result in quality management education of global standard.

In the context of the imperative needs of the emerging Indian economy and the preconditions of multilateral corporation among wealth-creating national entities, the following broad themes and dimensions of management teaching and research seem to be emerging (Priya, 2008):

- Requirement of well coordinated and flexible orchestration of the government's industrial technology, trade, education, labor, rural development, infrastructure and economic policies directed toward expansion and technological up gradation of all national economy in an ongoing manner.
- Management of technology and innovation towards continual strengthening of the country's and the companies technological capabilities through innovation; technology acquisition, assimilation and development, skill formation and both short and long-term collaborative development of nationally relevant core technologies.
- Identification and creation of an easily accessible bank of best industry practices across the world in all areas ranging from production and marketing to finance, logistics and R&D.
- Enhancement of the nation-wide development and use of information technology for development and use of information technology for accelerating towards break through improvements in cost-reduction, speed, output, quality and performance.
- Extensive use of business process reengineering and Total Quality Management in and by Indian enterprise towards raising their productivity and quality to world class levels.

Internationalise Management Education

As the business is getting global, day-by-day, there is an increasing need for the colleges to produce global managers. Therefore, it has become necessary that Indian Management education should also become more global. The message is quite clear: the response to the globalization of business is the globalization of management education. The following are the directions in which the Business Schools can focus to make management education global (http://www.123eng.com/forum/viewtopic.php?t=12646):

i. The business schools must admit international students to the program. The Indian management institutes are the only ones with no international participation.

ii. The business schools should induct a few international faculties and provide an opportunity to the students to listen about other country's business culture and systems.

iii. They should provide an active program of students and faculty exchange with advanced countries.

iv. To ensure that at least 25% of the curriculum deals with international subjects like international economics, international marketing, international financial management, etc.

v. They should collaborate with some well known foreign Business Schools by which Indian students can do part of their education in those institutes.
vi. Lastly, the Business Schools also collaborate with some foreign placement consultancies to make sure at least some students can attain jobs abroad.

Banking and Insurance Sector: An Overview

The economic reforms undertaken in the last 15 years have brought about a considerable improvement in the health of banks and financial institutions in India. The banking sector is a very important sector of the Indian economy. The sector has made a marked improvement in the liberalization period. There has been extraordinary progress in the financial health of the commercial banks with respect to capital adequacy, profitability, and asset quality and risk management. Deregulation has opened new doors for banks to increase revenues by entering into investment banking, insurance, credit cards, depository services, mortgage, securitization, etc.

The limit for foreign direct investment in private banks has been increased from 49% to 74%. In addition, the limit for foreign institutional investment in private banks is 49%. Liberalization and globalization have created a more challenging environment in the banking sector as well as in the other segments of the financial sector such as mutual funds, Non-Banking Finance Companies, post offices, capital markets, venture capitalists, etc. Now the challenges faced by the sector would be gaining profitability, reinforcing technology, maintaining global standards, corporate governance, sharpening skills, risk management and, the most important of all, to establish 'Customer Intimacy'.

The insurance business is one of the most rapidly growing areas in the financial sector. As an economy grows over the years, insurance sector intensifies and broadens its reach. Every practical and futuristic individual would want himself, his family and his assets to be insured. Insurance deals mainly with life and general insurance. India has a large insurance market commensurate with its population. The IRDA Act 1999 (Insurance Regulatory and Development Authority of India Act) has given new opportunities to private players to enter into the market on the fulfillment of certain prerequisites. The IRDA is the licensing authority in the sector; the current FDI cap/equity in the sector stands at 26 per cent.

There is no doubt the challenges ahead will become tougher with more companies competing both in general and life insurance. Also mortgage insurance will soon be coming into the industry. New players have contributed to the launch of innovative products, services and value-added benefits. Major foreign players have entered the country and announced their participation in joint ventures - both in life and non-life areas. These include New York Life, Aviva, Tokio Marine, Allianz, Standard Life, Lombard General, AIG, AMP and Sun Life among others. Commercial banks are coming up with more and more vacancies, and the banking sector now has more new jobs than any other sector. Right from the branch level to the highest level, there is tremendous range of opportunities available in the sector. Jobs in this sector can be both rewarding and enjoyable, as you get opportunities to learn about business, interact with people and build up clientele. The same is the case with insurance, as it is the fastest growing industry under the financial sector. Both government and private players are currently offering a plenty of jobs in this sector.

Future Growth Prospects of the Banking and Insurance Industry

Certain critical areas which have a key bearing on the ability of Indian banks to remain globally competitive and be able to enhance soundness in business operations include the following (Reddy, 2004):

Cost management: Cost containment is a key to sustainability of bank profits and their long-term viability as well. To highlight this point, let me, take recourse to some figures. In 2003, operating costs of banks as per cent of total average asset (i.e., total asset at the beginning of the year plus total asset at the beginning of the subsequent year) in UK were 2.12, for those in Switzerland they were 2.03 per cent, and less than 2 per cent in major European economies like Sweden, Austria, Germany and France. In India, in 2003, operating costs as per cent of total asset of scheduled commercial banks were 2.24 per cent. The tasks ahead are thus clear and within reach.

Recovery management: This is a key to the stability of the banking sector. There should be no hesitation in stating that Indian banks have done a remarkable job in containment of non-performing loans (NPL) considering the overhang issues and overall difficult environment. The process would, however, need to be pursued in right earnest, while persisting with changes in legal, institutional and procedural aspects to bring about a conducive environment for banks' operations. In 2003, non-performing loans to total loans of banks were 1.2 per cent in US, 1.4 per cent in Canada and in the range of 2-5 per cent in major European economies; France was an exception at 4.9 per cent. In contrast, the same for Indian banks was 8.8 per cent and that for Chinese state-owned banks was 22.0 per cent. Let me add that the 2004 gross NPL ratio for Indian scheduled commercial banks at 7.3 per cent is ample testimony to the impressive efforts being made by our banking system. In fact, recovery management is also linked to banks' interest margins. Net interest margins of scheduled commercial banks in India was 2.8 per cent in 2003, whereas it stood far lower in the range of 0.6-2.4 per cent at major European and Japanese banks. Clearly, cost and recovery management supported by enabling legal framework holds the key to future competitiveness of Indian banks.

Technological intensity of banking: This is one area where perhaps India needs to do significant 'catching up', notwithstanding the rapid strides made over the last few years, though data on this score are difficult to come by. Some available figures indicate that in late 1999, the percentage of customers using online banking was less than 1 per cent in India, compared with anywhere between 6-30 per cent in developed economies like US, UK, Germany, Finland and Sweden. Even in Latin America, these figures are much higher than India's. While admittedly the numbers for India are likely to be much higher at present than these figures suggest, so would be the case for these other economies as well. The issue, therefore, remains what has been the extent of 'catching up' by India on this score? In fact, this seems somewhat intriguing: India happens to be a world leader in information technology, but its usage by our banking system is somewhat muted. It is wise for Indian banks to exploit this globally state-of-art expertise domestically available to their fullest advantage.

Risk management: Banking in modern economies is all about risk management. The successful negotiation and implementation of Basel II is likely to lead to an even closer focus on risk measurement and risk management at the institutional level. Thankfully, Basel II has, through their various publications, provided useful guidelines on managing the various facets of risk. The institution of sound risk management practices would be an important pillar for remaining ahead of the increasing competition. Banks can, on their part, formulate 'early warning indicators' suited to their own requirements, business profile and risk appetite in order to better monitor and manage risks.

Corporate governance: The recent irregularities involving accounting firms in the US have amply demonstrated the importance of good corporate governance practices. The quality of corporate governance in the banks becomes critical as competition intensifies, banks strive to retain their client base, and regulators move out of controls and micro-regulation. No doubt, there is nothing like an 'optimal' level of governance for one to be satisfied with. The objective should be to continuously strive for excellence. The RBI has, on its part, made significant efforts to improve governance practices in banks, drawing upon international best practices. It is heartening to note that corporate governance presently finds explicit mention in the annual reports of several banks. The improved corporate governance practice would also provide an opportunity to accord greater freedom to banks' boards and move away from micro regulation to macro management.

Insurance Sector Poised for 200% Growth

Indian insurance sector is likely to register unprecedented growth of 200% and attain a size of Rs. 2000 billion by 2009-10, in which a private sector insurance business will achieve a growth rate of 140% as a result of aggressive marketing technique being adopted by them against 35-40% growth rate of state owned insurance companies.

The aforesaid findings are made by The Associated Chambers of Commerce and Industry of India (ASSOCHAM) on 'Insurance in Next 2 Years', saying that in the last couple of years, the insurance sector has grown by CAGR of around 175% and the trend will emerge still better because of potential factor. Currently, the insurance sector size is estimated at Rs.500 billion. On account of intense marketing strategies adopted by private insurance players, the market share of state-owned insurance companies like GIC, LIC and others have come down to 70% in last 4-5 years from over 97%.

The private insurance players despite the sector is still regulated has been offering rate of return (RoR) to its policy holders which is estimated at about 35% as against 20% of domestic insurance companies. This factor is mainly responsible for hike in private insurance market share which will grow further which is why the ASSOCHAM estimates that its growth rate could even exceed 140%.

Secondly, the state-owned insurance companies such as LIC and GIC have limited number of policies to offer to their subscribers while in case of private insurance companies, their policy numbers are many more and the premium amount as well as the maturity period is much competitive as against those of government insurance companies.

The Chamber (ASSOCHAM) has projected that in rural markets, the share of private insurance players would increase substantially as these have been able to generate a faith among their rural consumers. Estimating the potential of the Indian insurance market from the perspective of macro-economic variables such as the ratio of premium to GDP, ASSOCHAM reveals that India's life insurance premium, as a percentage of GDP is 1.8% against 5.2% in the US, 6.5% in the UK or 8% in South Korea.

ASSOCHAM's findings further reveal that in the coming years, the corporate segment, as a whole will not be a big growth area for insurance companies. This is because penetration is already good and companies receive good services. In both volumes and profitability therefore, the scope for expansion is modest. The Chamber has suggested that insurer's strategy should be to stimulate demand in areas that are currently not served at all. Insurance companies mostly focus on manufacturing sector; however, the services sector is taking a large and growing share of India's GDP. This offers immense opportunities for expansion opportunities.

To understand the prospects for insurance companies in rural India, it is very important to understand the requirements of India's villagers, their daily lives, their peculiar needs and their occupational structures. There are farmers, craftsmen, milkmen, weavers, casual labourers, construction workers and shopkeepers and so on. More often than not, they are into more than one profession.

The rural market offers tremendous growth opportunities for insurance companies and insurers should develop viable and cost-effective distribution channels; build consumer awareness and confidence. The ASSOCHAM found that there are a total 124 million rural households. Nearly 20% of all farmers in rural India own Kissan (Farmers) Credit cards. The 25 million credit cards used till date offer a huge data base and opportunity for insurance companies. An extensive rural agent network for sale of insurance products could be established. The agent can play a major role in creating awareness, motivating purchase and rendering insurance services.

There should be nothing to stop insurance companies from trying to pursue their own unique policies and target whatever needs that they want to target in rural India. ASSOCHAM suggests that insurance needs to be packaged in such a form that it appears as an acceptable investment to the rural people. Insurance sector in India is poised for tremendous expansion said Shri Pawan Kumar Bansal, the Minister of State for Finance while addressing a meeting of Insurance Australia Group on 21st September 2007 in Sydney. Shri Bansal said the banks also have entered the insurance sector in the form of corporate agencies or under referral arrangements to utilize the extensive and broad reach for marketing of insurance products (banknet.india, 2008).

IRDA has also notified Micro Insurance regulations facilitating insurers to tap the potential of rural markets. As per these regulations like Non-Government Organizations (NGO), Micro Finance Institutions (MFI) and Self Help Groups (SHG) have been recognized as micro insurance agents. It is envisaged that micro insurance would facilitate penetration of insurance to rural and remote areas. He said that micro insurance being an integral part of overall insurance system, attempts to offer the target specific insurance products at a relatively lower cost, for a lower coverage of amount.

Foreign equity upto 26% is allowed in the insurance sector. The entry of foreign partners has resulted in the sector attracting FDI of US 543 million as on 31 st March, 2007. The private companies have created a niche for themselves. They have been able to increase their share in the insurance market in competition with their counterparts in the public sector. As a part of the reform process, premium rates for non-life insurance products have been de-tariffed w.e.f. 1.1.2007. In insurance sector though the growth in recent years has been significant, India is far behind the world averages and ranks 78th in terms of insurance density and 54th in terms of insurance penetration. The world averages are US $ 469.6 in terms of insurance density and 8.06% in terms of insurance penetration. Against this, insurance density was US $ 19.70 and insurance penetration was 3.17% in India for the year 2003. However, these two indices have increased following the opening of this sector (http://www.banknetindia.com/finance/ins_bansal.htm). Insurance Regulatory and Development Authority has granted registration to 37 insurance companies, which include 17 life insurance (including one PSU), 19 non-life insurance (including four PSU, one AICL and one ECGC) companies and one re-insurance company. At present, seventeen insurance companies are operating in the general insurance side and seventeen insurance companies on the life side.

A.T. Kearney in 'The FDI Confidence Index 2005'(Global Business Policy Council, 2005) has ranked India as the 2nd most attractive investment destination just behind China whereas 'World Investment Report, 2005' ranked India as the 2nd most attractive investment destination among Transnational Corporations.

FDI is now permitted in 21 activities through the auto-route. These include FDI in development of township, housing, built-up infrastructure and construction development projects, exploration and mining of diamonds and precious stones and insurance.

Insurance companies should offer innovative products to tap huge amount of resources for the developmental activities. Focus of insurance industry is changing towards providing a mix of protection/risk cover and long-term investment opportunities. In India, only 10% of the market share has been tapped by LIC and GIC and the balance 90% of the market still remains untapped. This vast potential can be tapped only by a large number of insurance. To serve the population of more than 100 crore Indians, Indian insurance market offers tremendous opportunities to private insurers. With the increase in the life expectancy of individuals and disintegration of joint family system, each individual now has arranged cover for himself and for his family. Therefore, coverage of insurers has to grow very fast. The needs of the nation and its people have finally prevailed and privatization of insurance is now a reality towards further liberalization of the Indian economy. With the opening up of the industry after reforms, private sector operators in collaboration with their overseas partners are likely to bring in a more professional and focused approach. Hence, in this millennium, insurance industry is likely to play an important role in changing the economic landscape of the country. However the success of the insurance industry will primarily depend upon meeting the rising expectations of the consumers who will be the real king in the liberalized insurance market in future (Vijaykumar, 2007).

Winning the Global Competitive Race: Areas Needing Attention for India

Over the next fifty years Brazil, Russia, India and China—the BRICs economies—could become a much larger force in the economy. We map out GDP growth, income per capita and currency movements in the BRICs economies until 2050 (Bhandari, 2008). The results are startling .If things go right, in less than 40 years; the BRICs economies together could be larger than the G6 in US dollar terms. By 2025 they could account for over half the size of the G6. Of the current G6, only the Japan and US may be among the six largest economies in US dollar terms in 2050.

The 2003 Goldman Sachs - BRIC Report projected China's GDP in 2050 at $ 44.45 trillion while India's GDP was projected at $ 27.8 trillion and that of US was projected at $ 35.17 trillion. BRIC II (a sectoral analysis in 2004) underscored Chinidia's importance. The latest Goldman Sachs Report (January 22, 2007 - Global Economics Paper No. 152) says India's GDP will surpass that of the USA before 2050. In the coming years the world economic scenario is going to change dramatically. The advantage as predicted by the report shall shift in favour of four countries–India being one of the forerunners in leading the world towards a new economic order. India today is poised for change on a scale that is unimaginable. India is catapult into a completely new era—ready to take over its competitors and win the global competitive race. In its stride to win the global competitive race India is well supported by three powers namely; power of youth, power of knowledge and the power of enterprise.

- ***Power of Youth***

"The dynamic emerging economies - led by the two main BRIC countries—mainland China and India—will grow strongly," says a 2007 report by international accounting and consulting firm Grant Thornton. "However mainland China may face potential problems with its aging population and rising age old dependency ratio." Young India is waiting to take up the slack. India is a vibrant country, full of enthusiasm and youth. Some 65 per cent of India is below 35 and 50 per cent below 25. One of the oldest civilizations in the world is one of the youngest in the century. In 2025, the median age for India will be 31, against 39 for the US and China and 44 for Russia and the UK. As societies around the world are growing grey India will be the source of tomorrow's manpower requirements. The share of those aged 65 and above in the total population is less than 5 per cent in India, compared to 19 per cent in Japan, 18 per cent in Germany, 12 per cent in the US and close to 8 per cent in China. The young population of the country will make the country a powerhouse supplier for skilled manpower and will also raise the saving rates in the country allowing a substantial rise in country's investment rates.

- ***Power of Knowledge***

Indians have become the "brains of the world", backed by the excellent English and communication skills. The horde of world class engineers and professionals produced by the country's IITs, IIMs and other institutions have already started making their mark as workers to the world. First came Information Technology (IT) services then came the Business Process Outsourcing (BPO) and now it is the time for Knowledge Process Outsourcing (KPO). Indians are going offshore like never before. Some are being captured on campuses for bulge bracket jobs in London and New York. And they are wanted everywhere. In recent years a number of multinationals Nokia, Samsung, Ericsson, Vestas, POSCO and many more have set up their shops and back offices in the country, encouraged by the availability of educated and experienced manpower.

- ***Power of Enterprise***

Enterprise has always existed in India and today it is even more visible. At IIMs, the students are turning down Rs. 1 crore plus salary to start ventures of their own. The fear of failure has almost vanished from the minds of the budding entrepreneurs. India's roaring entrepreneurial culture has also outbid Chinese in serious business overseas. A recent study by the Duke University's School of Engineering and University of California's Berkley School of Information reveals that between 1996 and 2006, Indian immigrants founded more engineering and technology companies in the US than Chinese and Taiwanese and British immigrants put together. In fact, one in every four technology companies set up by immigrants had an Indian founder.

Areas needing attention

The indications from the Goldman Sachs Report has nominated India for the Global Competitiveness Race ahead. The race will have traditional co-participants —US, Japan and other developed countries and new emerging co-participants like Brazil, Russia and China, which will give strong competition to India.

India ranked 43rd overall in the Global Competitiveness Report 2006-2007 (http://en.wikipedia.org/wiki/Global_Competitiveness_Report), with excellent scores in capacity for innovation and sophistication of firm operations. Firm use of technology and rates of technology transfer are high, although penetration rates of the latest technologies are still quite low by international standards, reflecting India's low levels of per capita income and high incidence of poverty. Despite these encouraging results, insufficient health services and education as well as a poorly developed infrastructure are limiting a more equitable distribution of the benefits of India's high growth rates. Moreover, successive Indian governments have proven remarkably ineffective in reducing the public sector deficit, one of the highest in the world. To win the global competitive race, India has to keep its house in order and pay special attention to various areas. This paper identifies three such areas namely—Education, Health and Infrastructure. Reforms and up gradation are required in these areas which are possible by the combined efforts of government, policy makers and public private partnerships.

• ***Education***

Literacy and general education form the base of knowledge pyramid that is essential for rapid and sustainable development. Though projected as centres of learning most of the colleges and schools are actually institutions of teaching. Nearly the entire current educational system has been designed according to the convenience of teaching and not learning. In Indian thought, knowledge is seen as something which liberates. Time has now come to liberate learning from the institutionalized learning.

The present times call for a revamp of curricula to train people for jobs that are being created, rather than providing them with meaningless degrees, which provide them no useful skills. India is rightly proud of her seven IITs and six IIMs, which are tiny hubs of educational excellence. A handful of such institutions is not enough. The country needs many of such institutions to meet the forthcoming needs. These Ivey League Institutions are just ensuring excellence despite dwindling faculty and disappearing funds. Though each of them boasts of state-of-the-art library and adequate journals, much needs to be done in terms of research and development. India needs large number of talented youth with higher education for the task of knowledge acquisition, knowledge imparting, knowledge creation and knowledge sharing. This is an important task in which all universities, academic specialists, colleges, vocational training institutions, certification agencies, banking systems and industrial enterprises can contribute in terms of assessing correct numbers, designing courses related to nation building tasks, assessing and providing infrastructural requirement, improving the quality of teachers, ensuring teachers-students ratio, complimenting the class room education with virtual class rooms through tele-education and above all ensuring that the students are able to face international competition in employable skills. Systems must be designed in such a way that no aspiring competent student should be denied quality education Physical infrastructure should be complimented with the interdisciplinary teams working together on common problems with team members not necessarily required to be in the same location. The system of education must be able to maintain the required output quality to meet global competitive standards.

• ***Infrastructure***

Development involves a continuous increase in the number of physical transactions and the speed with which they occur, both of which are highly dependent on the nation's infrastructure. India is adding more phones per month than in first 45 years since independence. It is happening because it is making commercial sense. India has suddenly become a small country; connectivity has compressed the large geographic dimensions of the country. It is also a smaller place because of the boom in civil aviation and the rapid growth of low-cost carriers. But that is a story at the starter's gate; much still needs to be done. Traditionally, India has spent a 4 per cent of its GDP on infrastructure as compared to China's 9 per cent. Looking at the length and the breadth of the country and the ever-increasing requirements of the growing economy, this investment is inadequate.

The country's poor infrastructure is already struggling to keep pace with growth, power cuts are common as there isn't enough electricity to meet current demand, and ports are overflowing, many roads and highways pot-holed and crumbling. The inadequate stretch of the roadways and highways act as an impediment to transport of goods to their destination points. The power-cuts hamper industrial production, reduce the production capacity of the industrial units and also affect the quality of production. These gross inadequacies of infrastructure demand for corrective action. The corrective action requires a strategy for developing capabilities within the urban and rural local bodies to cope with the deficiencies, with genuine decentralization of financial and administrative powers and restructuring of the entities on the basis of sound management practices.

Attracting infrastructure investment has the double benefit of inducing growth as well as kick starting a virtuous cycle of investment in all other sectors of the economy. In particular, we stand no chance of becoming a manufacturing power without the bedrock foundation of efficient infrastructure. In order to make headway here, we need to speedily put together templates for various infrastructure projects. Total investment needed for creation, upgradation and maintenance of the total infrastructural setup requires an increase to levels three to four times higher than the present investment. While government will be the major source of funds for infrastructure, internal generation of resources by the transport services will have to increase, supported by the more realistic pricing of services, reduction in the operating costs and active involvement of the private sector in the development and maintenance of the infrastructure.

To meet the power crisis in the country, a concerted effort is required for alternative energy generation in the form of wind power, solar photovoltaic, solar thermal, small hydro, and biomass power and bio fuel. Enhanced adoption by the public and private sector of best practices and environment–friendly technologies, more efficient use of energy, promoting private sector investment, and greater efforts to protect the environment will be required to cope effectively with the nation's growing energy requirements. Building up appropriate and adequate infrastructure will have the double benefit of inducing growth as well as kick starting a virtuous circle of investment and employment in all other sectors of economy.

• ***Health***

The health of a nation is a product of many factors and forces that combine and interact. Economic growth, per capita income, employment, literacy, education, age at marriage, birth rates, availability of information regarding health care and nutrition, access to safe drinking water, public and private health care infrastructure, access to preventive health, health and medical care, and health insurance are among the contributing factors. While the economic development in India has been gaining momentum over the last decade, our health system is at crossroads today. Even though Government initiatives in public health have recorded some noteworthy successes over time, the Indian health system is ranked 118 among 191 WHO member countries on overall health performance (Ramani, 2007).

Medical tourists are flocking to India and the country is fast becoming the pharmacy of the world.

But still basic health services are unavailable to millions of Indians, especially in the rural areas.

Communicable diseases remain the major cause of illness even today. The infant and maternal mortality rates are high. India needs a strong dose of reforms to boost this sector. Upgradation of health infrastructure is urgently required. The health infrastructure should include homeopathy, *ayurveda* and *unani* systems of medicine besides the allopathic system of medicine. This infrastructure should be aptly manned, equipped and financed to cope with the challenge of eradicating the major threats to human life. This infrastructure should be strengthened at the rural level and should involve the active participation of volunteers and self help groups. The infrastructure and the health system should be able to provide quality services for maternal and child health, contraceptive care and prevention and treatment of communicable diseases effectively and efficiently. The development plans for India's health care systems need to place greater emphasis on public health education and prevention of communicable diseases. Along with the traditional channels used for dissemination of health and nutrition related information, the modern channels of television, radio, prints and electronic media should also be used. The infrastructure thus created should be able to meet the requirements of the masses especially in the rural areas. A healthy and fit nation will help the country to win the race.

Conclusion

The Goldman Sachs report has just nominated the India for the global competitive race. To win this race India is backed strongly by the powers of youth, knowledge and enterprise. But this does not make India the winner of the race. To win the global competitive race the country needs to be strong on the other three pillars of education, health and infrastructure. The strengthening of these pillars will make the country's people better fed, dressed and housed, healthier, more educated and longer living than any generation in the country's history. Rising levels of education, health, employment and incomes will help stabilize India's social environment and integrate the country with the global economy. The maintenance and upgradation of these pillars will help the country to build up its social, physical and economic infrastructure. All these will help India to win the global competitive race. The sentiments of the President and Prime Minister of India with regards to India's position in the global context also reflects the vision of India as a winner of the race taking into consideration the interests of all the groups concerned.

"Through responsive and innovative venture systems and entrepreneurial training both in schools and colleges; we will have more enterprises leading to large number of employment generators rather than employment seekers. A pro-active healthcare system delivered through innovative schemes will provide quality healthcare access at an affordable cost to all the people of the country including those living in remote areas. Everyone will have an opportunity to take up and complete courses of choice in higher education. I am sure you will all see prosperity in the country, which will replace scarcity and control. In addition to the above economic, social and human development, India will also have a visible global presence in strategic sectors and will contribute to world peace. All our technological and economical advances while enhancing our prosperity would embed our value system derived from our civilization heritage. This unique combination will make our growth robust and sustainable and will lead to a peaceful, secure, happy and prosperous society." (Kalam, 2007)

"Every generation would like to believe that it is entering a brave new world. That spirit is natural and welcomed. It inspires each generation to seek new horizons and find answers to problems old and new. Many, however, will rest content reinventing the wheel and pouring old wine in new bottles. But some will strike out and truly find new paths. A society that encourages creativity, enterprise, innovation and risk taking will be a vibrant society and the future belong to such a society, which will be capable of dealing with the challenges of the brave new world. I believe we must do all that is possible allow the full expression of such human creativity and ingenuity to flourish in our country. This we can do best within the framework of an open society. But such a society will have to be a literate and educated one. It will have to be healthy and caring. It will have to be knowledge–empowered society. A free and egalitarian society functioning within the parameters of the rule of law and civilized conducts and discourses. Above all it will have to be an inclusive society." (Kalam, 2007)

Branding India for Global Competitiveness

Brand India is a phrase used to describe the campaign India is using to attract business. Basically the campaign is to project the attractiveness of India as an emerging destination for business in the fields of service sector, manufacturing, information technology, infrastructure, information technology enabled services, etc. The campaign uses both India as huge market for products and services as well as a lucrative destination for investment. The federal government is spearheading the campaign with considerable cooperation from the domestic business body Confederation of Indian Industry (CII) and the more informal India Inc abroad.

Amongst the leading organizations working on building Brand India is India Brand Equity Foundation (IBEF), a public-private partnership between the Ministry of Commerce and Industry, Government of India, and the Confederation of Indian Industry. It aims to effectively present the India business perspective and leverage business partnerships in a globalizing market-place. Its website (ibef.org) is a resource centre for global investors, international policy-makers and world media seeking updated, accurate and comprehensive information on the Indian economy, states and sectors. IBEF regularly tracks government announcements in policy, foreign investment, macroeconomic indicators and business trends (http://en.wikipedia.org/wiki/Brand_India).

There has been a lot of talk and activity, at the highest levels of the Government and corporate India, regarding 'Brand India.' The popular view seems to be that a concerted attempt must be made to present 'Brand India' to the world. A corpus fund has, in fact, been created to promote the brand with the tagline, 'Incredible India.' There has been a lot of debate in the press lately on the idea of Brand India. Fundamentally, three broad questions have emerged (Khanna, 2006):

- First, should we brand India?
- Second, is this the right time to brand India?
- Third, how should we go about the task?

Let us begin by addressing the first, and the easiest.

The idea of whether or not India should be branded induces reactions that range from mild discontent to violent disagreement. "Selling India is a pointless business"; "No amount of hard-sell can convince buyers to take a 'Made in India' label at face value..."; "...any marketing exercise [to brand India] is a waste of time and effort"; "Efficiency and quality don't require any hard sell", etc. These are just some of the refrains heard in recent months. Such rhetoric is far too exaggerated. And going by the rapid progress of "Made in India", this opinion is a little misplaced. Let us put the situation in the proper perspective.

Gap, Tommy Hilfiger, Espirit, Wal-Mart, Polo all buy clothes from India. Garment exports at US $ 6 billion, and are expected to increase 8-10 times by 2010. In the first six months of 03-04, India exported over 220,000 cars and bikes worldwide. Auto giants – Daimler Chrysler, Volvo, and Benz – source parts worth US $ 1.5 bn from India. Data aside, in an increasingly competitive world, the global consumer is faced with a sea of choices. Whether the decision is to set up a manufacturing facility, or to decide on a holiday destination, consumers have several options. They expect to be wooed and convinced through creative and insightful communication, besides of course, being made a competitive offer.

Nation-states are competing aggressively with each other to position themselves as competitive destinations for investments and tourism. In a rapidly evolving global village, it is the intangible "feeling" behind the data and numbers that really drives decisions in favour, or against nations. The last 50 years have seen this brand get increasingly distorted in the absence of a coherent effort to manage and develop its associations, with the result that Brand India today, stands for Snake Charmers, Elephants and Rope Tricks.

It is in this context that Branding, or rather re-Branding India, is not a choice but an obvious necessity. If we won't do it, other nations are doing so any way! And position India the way it fits their competitive global strategy. Let us now try and address the second and more important issue whether this is the right time to launch a concerted branding campaign for India. India's economic indicators are encouraging. Reforms are moving ahead, yet investors are looking for further signs of the Government's commitment.

In today's global marketplace, MNCs need to set up effective branding strategies in order to be competitive. Depending on the structure of the company and the products offered, MNCs can use different strategies. There are certain characteristics that will affect the type of strategy chosen. In order to reach economies of scale and scope, many MNCs standardize their branding and marketing activities. However, MNCs are often required to adapt to local preferences and cultures (http://epubl.luth.se/1402-1552/2008/005/index.html).

Some Perspectives for India

- 15 of the world's major automobile makers are obtaining components from Indian companies. This business fetched India in 2003 US $ 1.5 billion.
- At US $ 6.5 billion and growing at 8-10 per cent annually, India's pharmaceutical industry is 4th largest in the world.
- As for technology, India is among the three countries that have built super computers on their own.
- Indian exports were up by 19 per cent in 2003, and the country's foreign exchange reserves are in excess of US $ 100 billion. India is dishing out aid to 11 countries, prepaying its debt and loaned IMF US $ 300 million!
- A cataract operation costs US $ 1500 in the US. In India, US $ 12. A Heart-bypass surgery in the US anywhere up to US $ 13000. In India, it is US $ 900. Over 70 MNCs have set up R&D facilities in India in the past five years.
- With better systems comes efficiency. The turnaround time in Indian ports is down to 4 days from 10 and its telecom infrastructure in 1999 provided a bandwidth of 155 Mbps. Today, it is 75,000 times more and with fibre-optic networks in 300 cities, it will change the face of business.

Clearly, Brand India's success lies in managing and leveraging this opportunity. The India Brand Equity Foundation (IBEF—earlier India Brand Equity Fund) was founded under the aegis of the Ministry of Commerce of the Government of India with the explicit purpose of developing a strong global identity for India, by leveraging these emergent opportunities. The IBEF aims to do this through a proactive effort to create a strong Nation Brand for the country based on positive and relevant associations. The entire effort is directed towards taking India beyond name recognition, by firmly establishing a relevant position for the country on the world map. The immediate goal: build positive economic perceptions of India in key global markets.

The IBEF moved to the CII to manage, in October 2002. It was decided that a broad-based branding exercise would best be facilitated through a strong partnership between the government and industry. It is in this context that the CII provides for the executive management and the operational day-to-day functioning of the Foundation, under the Chairmanship of the Commerce Secretary.

Indian Industry is becoming globally competitive in many sectors such as Pharmaceuticals, Auto Components, IT, Biotech, R&D and ITES. Second, the abundant intellectual capital available in the country continues to provide further impetus to an emergent world-scale economy that is slated to be the 3rd largest by 2050. Third, the achievements of global Indians, and the contributions of the Indian Diaspora abroad, are a tremendous source of pride, and strongly reinforce the competitiveness of Indians across sectors.

It is in this context, that we are undertaking the task of Nation Brand Building, which is firmly rooted in the positive, changing reality of the 21st century India. IBEF plans to include a series of coordinated marketing initiatives that will use conventional methods like advertising and developing a brand ambassador's network to make an impact in the short term. Innovative and proactive measures like bringing select groups from media houses and educational institutions for structured India Tours are also planned to support the development of the brand over the long term.

On the domestic front, IBEF drives alignment across stakeholders to ensure that messages emanating from the country are coherent and consistent. With this view, the IBEF is developing a strong partner network that includes select Ministries, Sectoral Associations and Community Institutions to drive alignment and coherence in brand communication efforts. As a facilitator, IBEF services this network through workshops, a brand communication toolkit, and research reports that help track perceptions of brand India.

Building the India Brand in Software

NASSCOM promotes, develops and protects the interests of the IT software and service industry both within India and overseas. This is done by encouraging and fostering activities within the industry, between NASSCOM members and other relevant associations and government bodies.

To facilitate international trade for its members, NASSCOM has set for itself the objective of participating actively in international events which include trade missions, conferences and trade fairs. NASSCOM also ensures that international enquiries for trade opportunities are channelled through to members (http://www.nasscom.in/Nasscom/templates/NormalPage.aspx?id=5355).

NASSCOM also plays an active role in the international software community. The apex software industry association is a member of the Asian Oceanian Computing Industry Organization (ASOCIO). ASOCIO is a group of computing industry associations from the Asian Oceanian Region and comprises representative from 16 countries. NASSCOM is also a founder member of the World Information Technology and Services Alliances (WITSA). This forum is constituted by member associations from 32 leading countries of the world.

Index